AF505688

JORDAN KANTOR

SELECTED EXHIBITIONS 2006–2016

Jordan Kantor : Selected Exhibitions 2006–2016
Published in 2016 by no place press, San Francisco, California.

Edited by Rachel Churner
Designed by Geoff Kaplan/General Working Group and Jordan Kantor
Contribution by Yve-Alain Bois

© 2016 Jordan Kantor

Jordan Kantor ; edited by Rachel Churner with a contribution by Yve-Alain Bois.
Kantor, Jordan, 1972–[author]
San Francisco : no place press, 2016. Distributed in the United States and Canada by D.A.P./
Distributed Art Publishers, c. 2016–2017.
240 pages : illustrations (color) ; 24 cm

ISBN-13: 978-0-9898320-5-2 (cloth)

English

First edition of 500

Printed in Shenzhen, China
by Artron Art Printing Limited
Brokered by InnerWorkings, Inc., San Francisco

Specifications:
Book: 24 x 17 cm
Press: LITHRONE S40SP printing press
(72 x 103 cm; 32 pages per sheet)
Cover: cloth, foil stamped, over 3 mm board
Paper: 157 gsm Chinese OJI matte art paper
End papers: 200 gsm Da Song woodfree
Text: Berthold Akzidenz Grotesk, drawn by H. Berthold and Günther Gerhard Lange

no place press
San Francisco
noplacepress.com 

Distributed by D.A.P./ Distributed Art Publishers
155 Sixth Avenue, 2nd Floor, New York, NY 10013
Tel: 212.627.1999 Fax: 212.627.9484

TABLE OF CONTENTS

SELECTED EXHIBITIONS

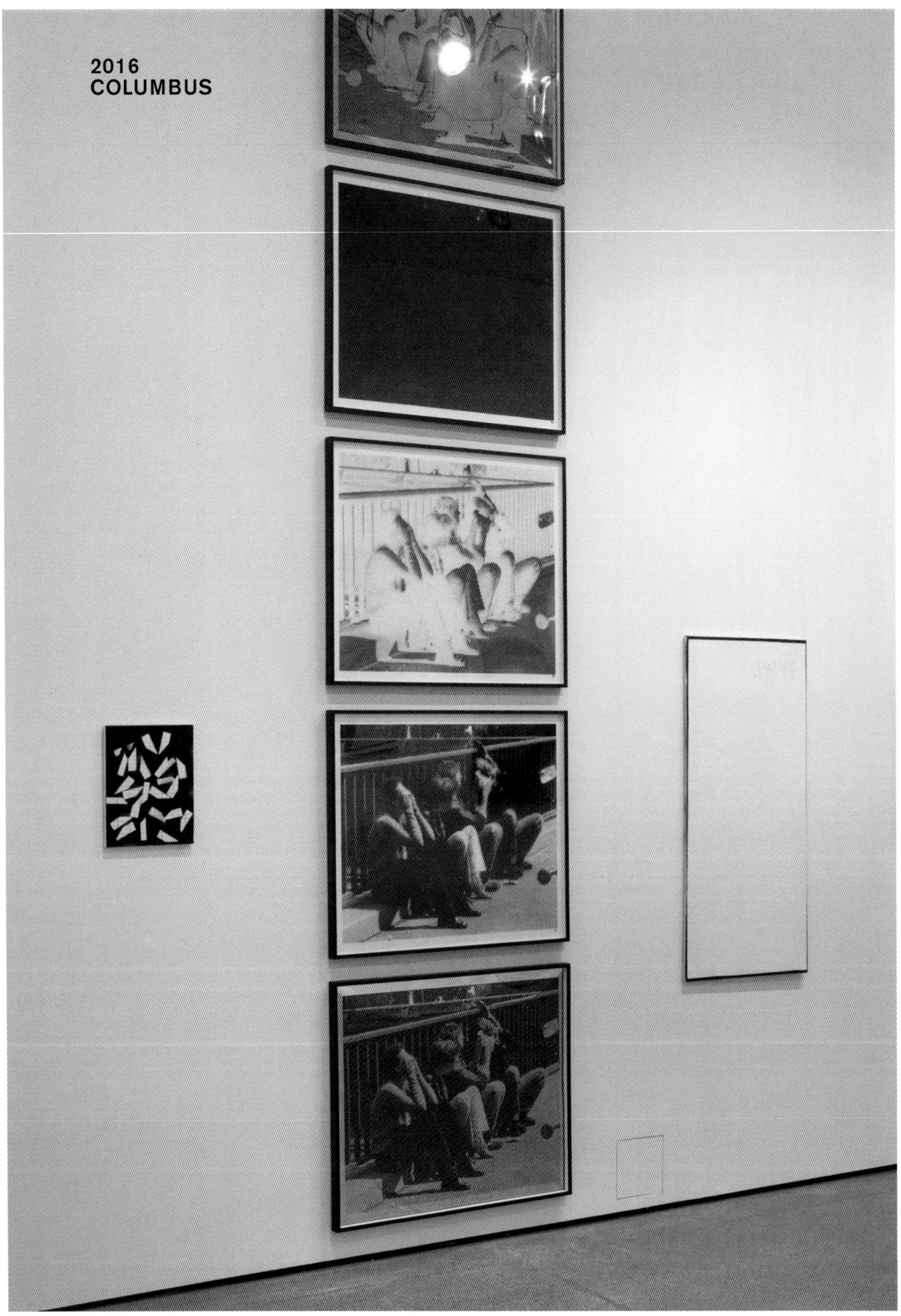

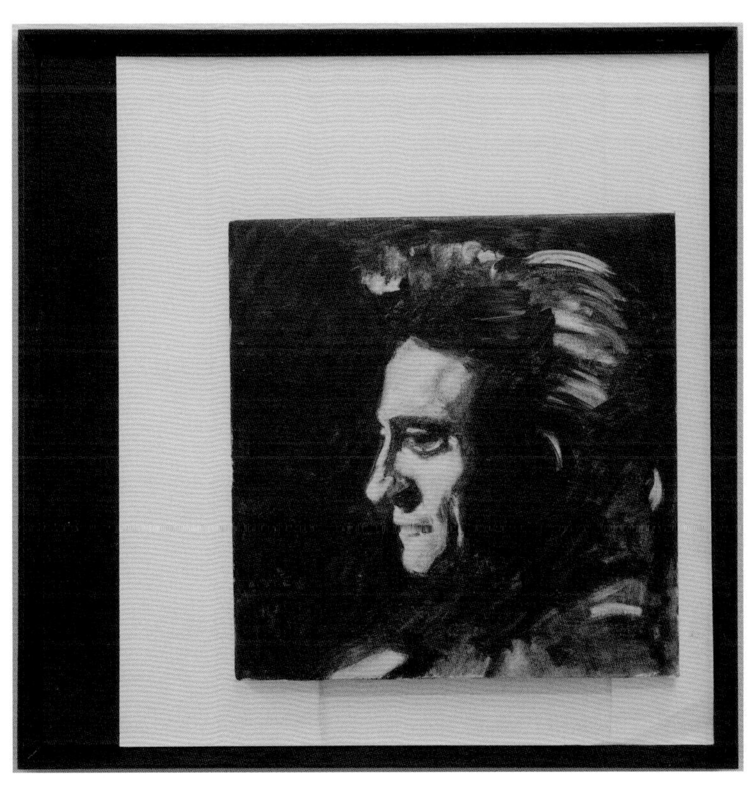

UNTITLED (JC/VM PHOTO), 2016

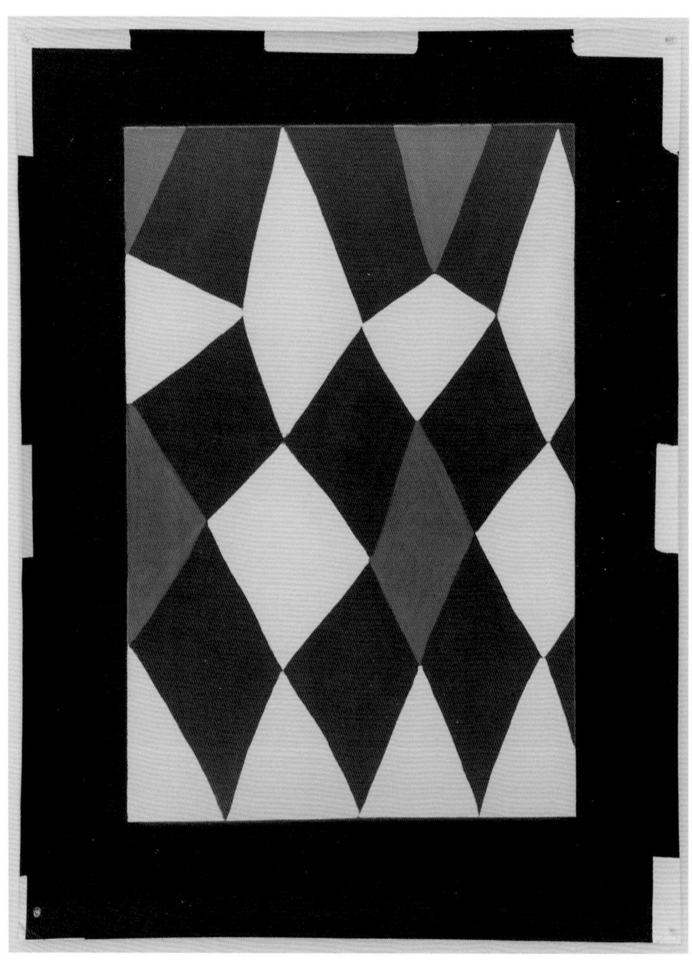

UNTITLED (HARLEQUIN), 2015

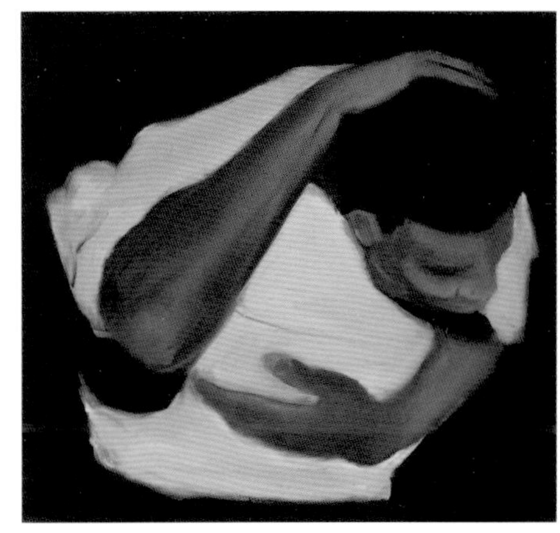

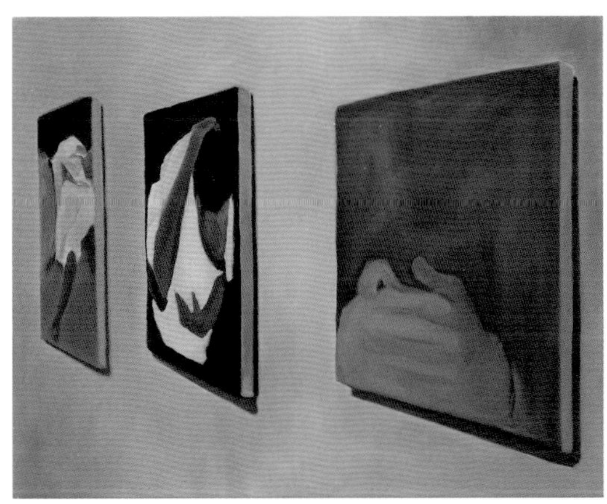

UNTITLED, 2004
UNTITLED (THREE PAINTINGS), 2005

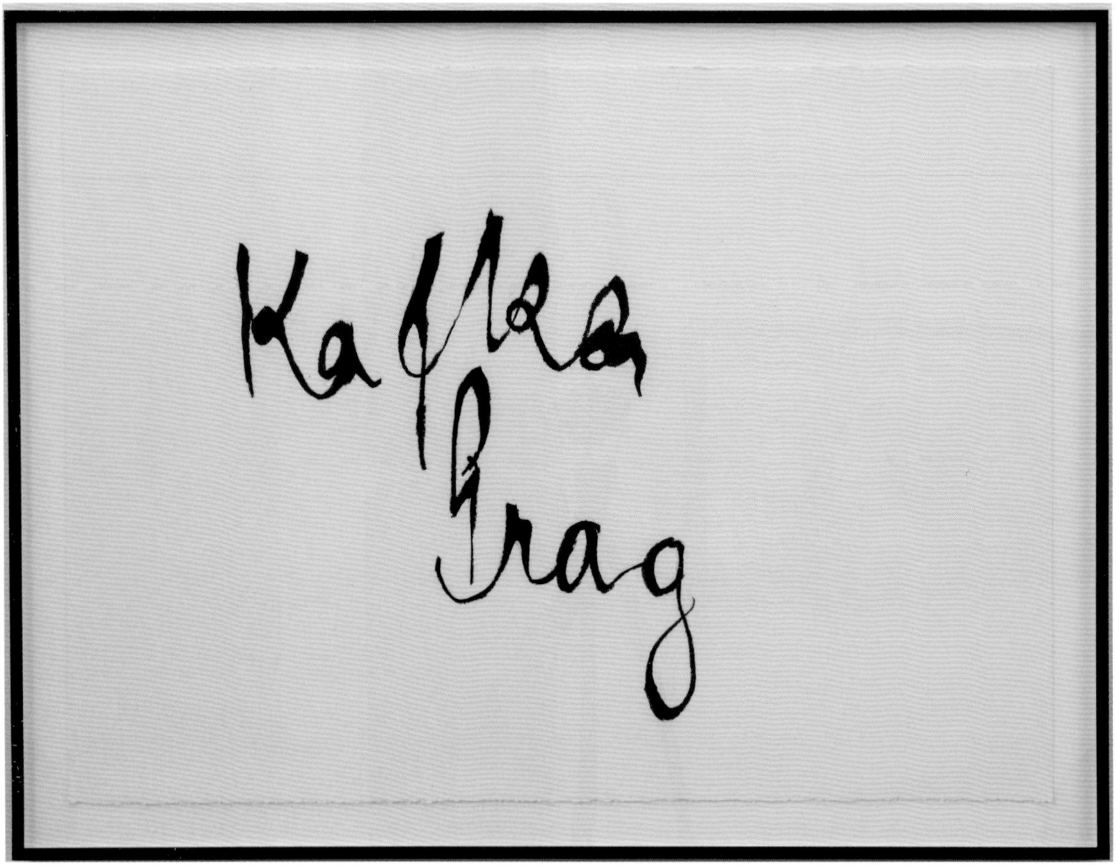

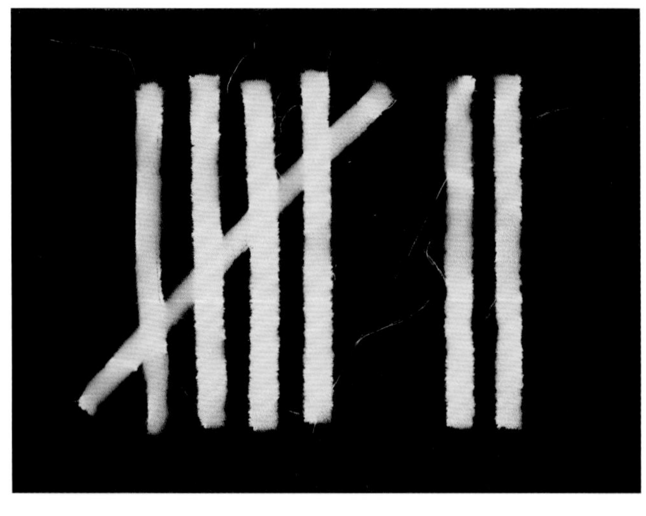

KAFKA PRAG, 2004
UNTITLED (COUNTDOWN 7), 2009

UNTITLED (T-SQUARE), 2016

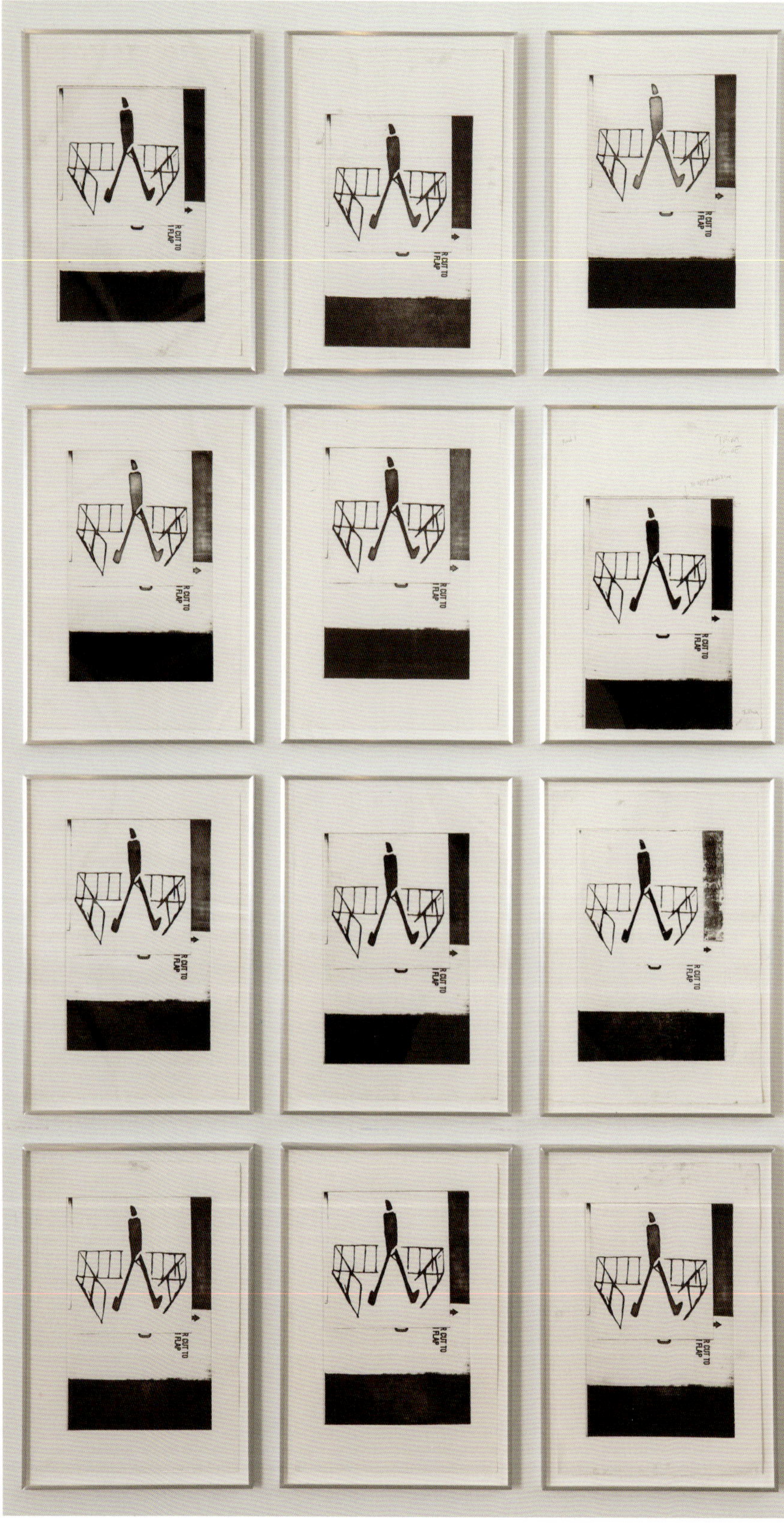

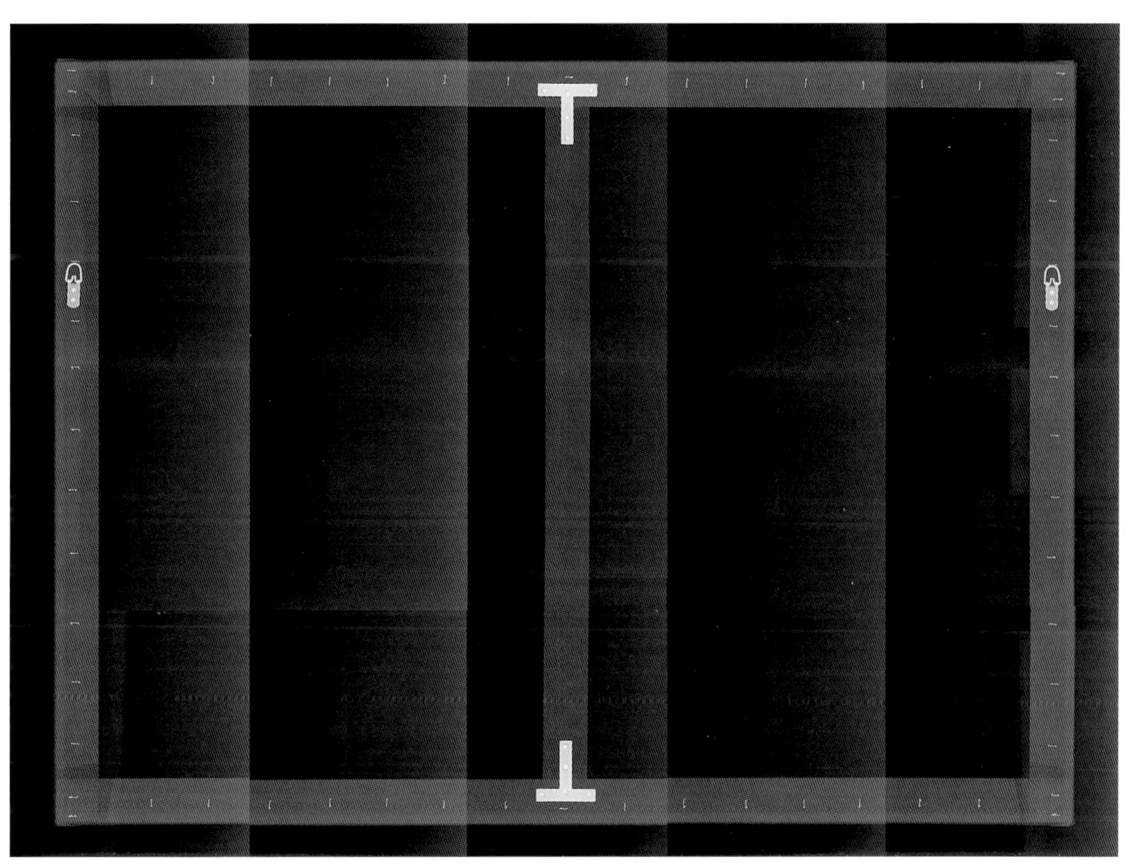

UNTITLED (WORKING SPACE), 2006   *UNTITLED (X-RAY PHOTOGRAPH)*, 2009

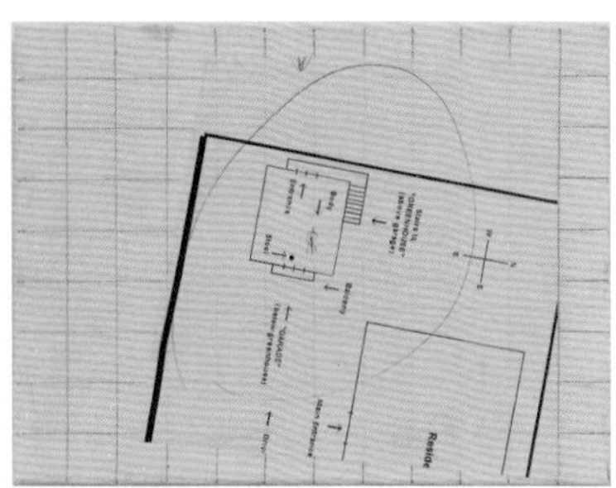

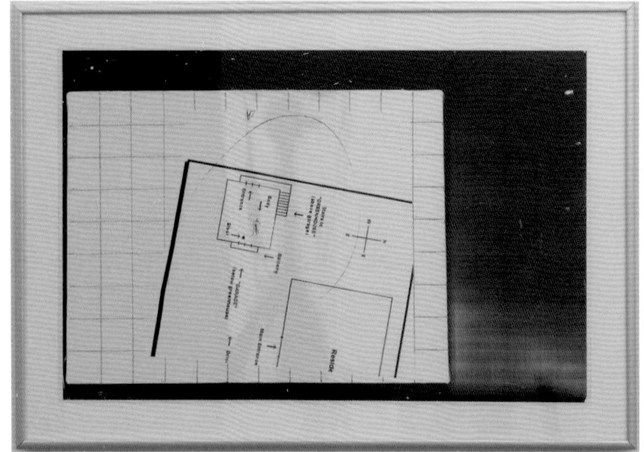

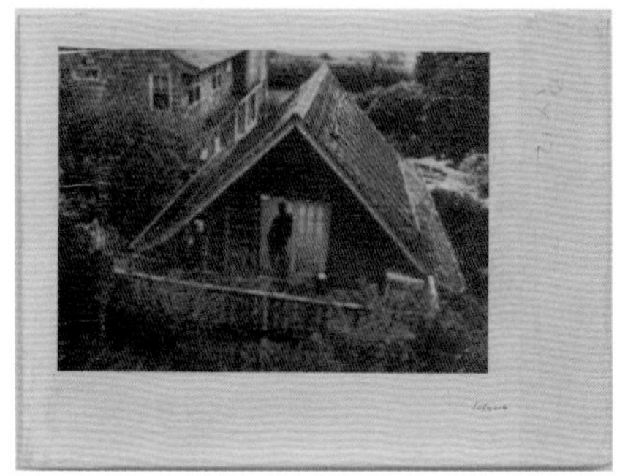

UNTITLED (GREENHOUSE DIAGRAM), 2007
UNTITLED (GREENHOUSE DIAGRAM CLEAR PHOTOCOPY), 2006
UNTITLED (GREENHOUSE), 2006

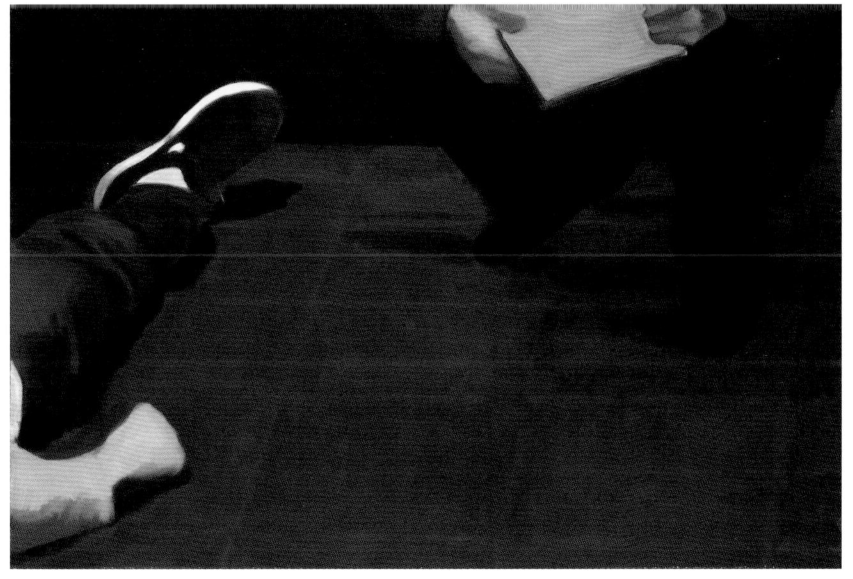

UNTITLED (FORENSIC SCENE), 2004

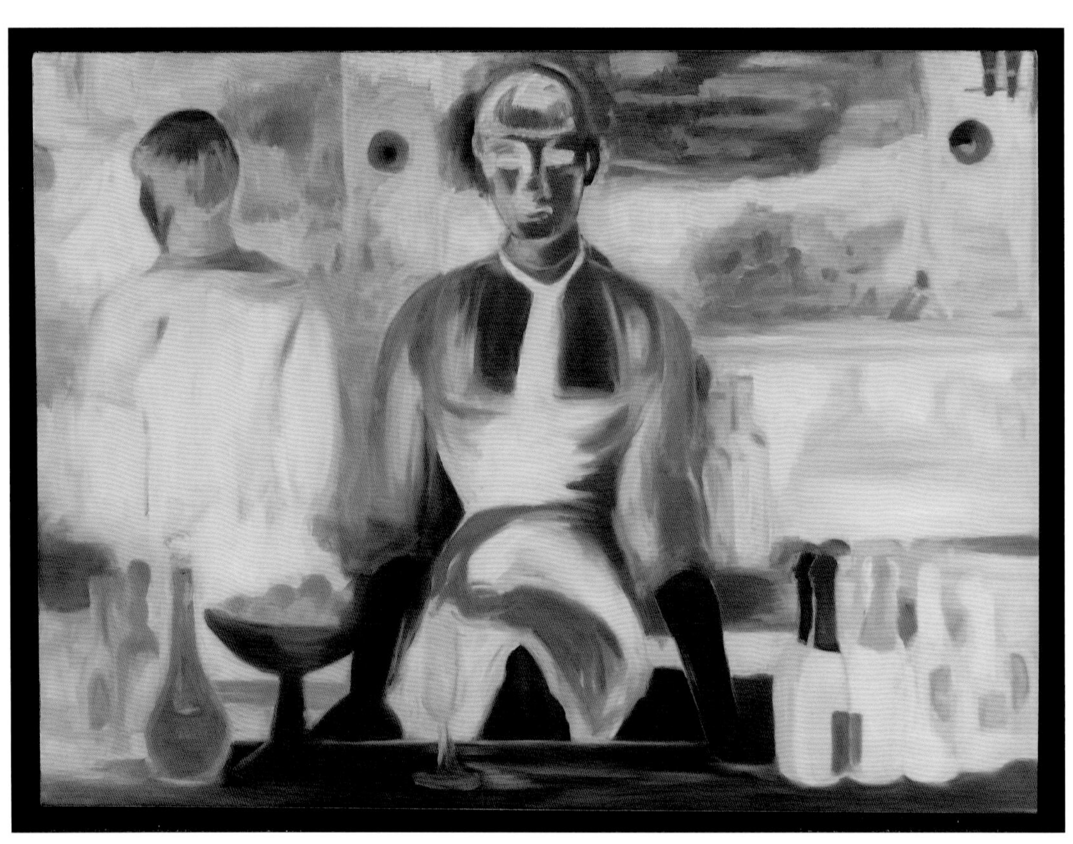

UNTITLED (THE BAR), 2009

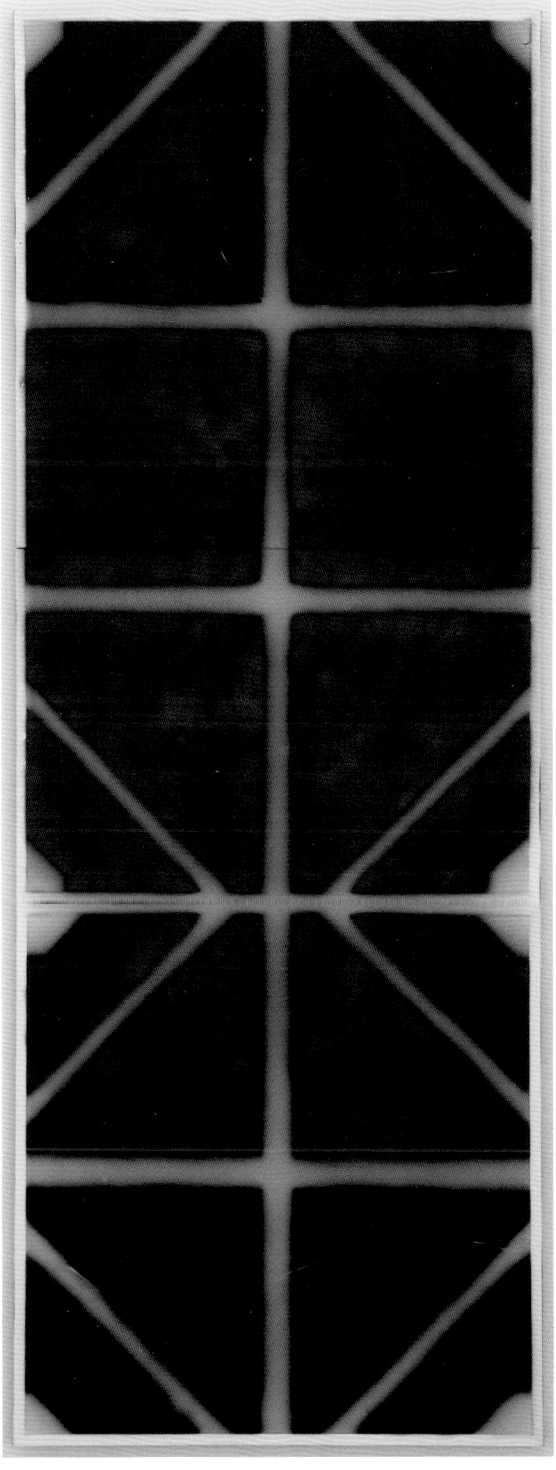

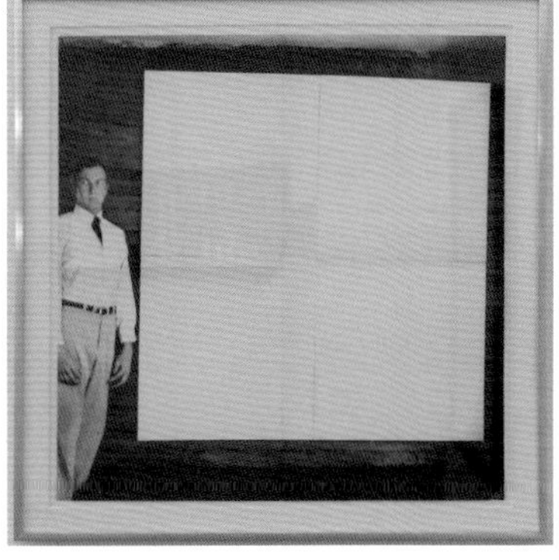

UNTITLED (NUMBER 1), 2015
UNTITLED (RAUSCHENBERG POSTER), 1968/2015

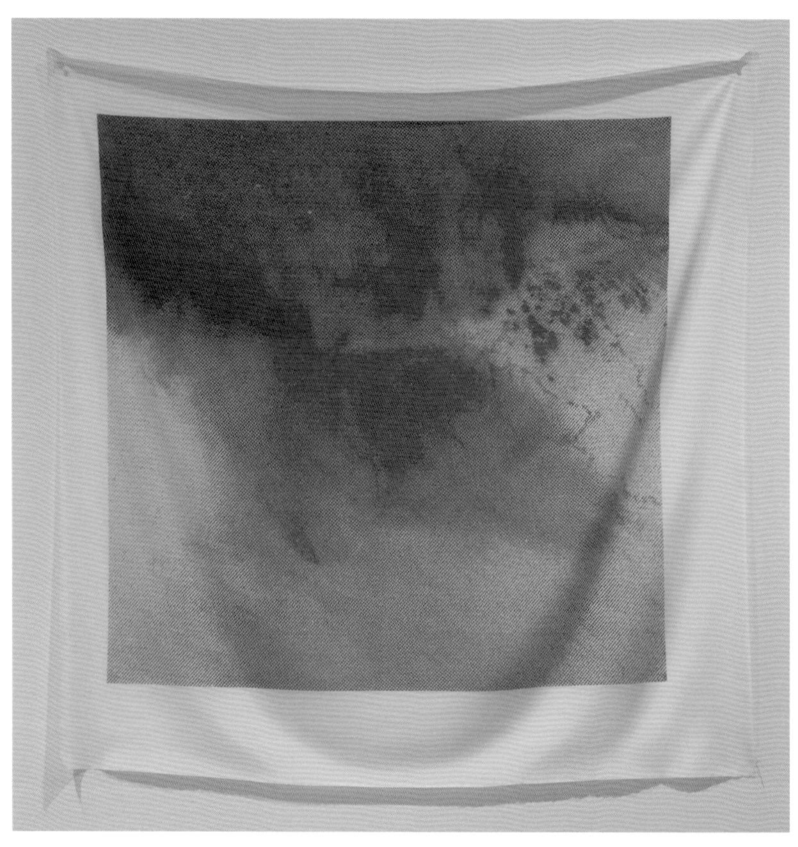

UNTITLED (HANDS AND GLASSES), 2004
UNTITLED, 2015
UNTITLED (MANIFESTO), 2006

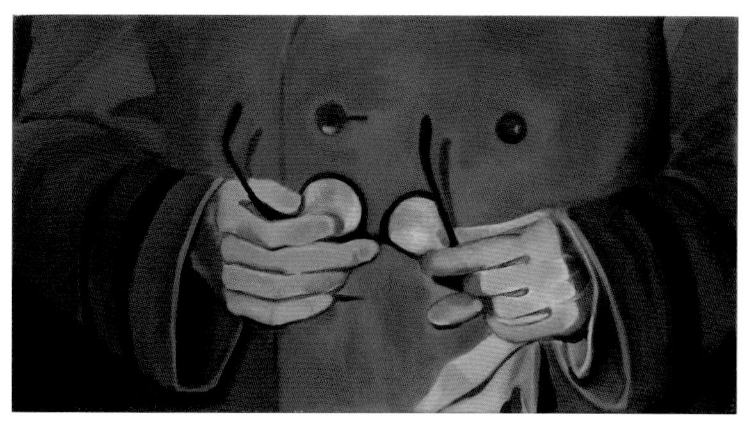

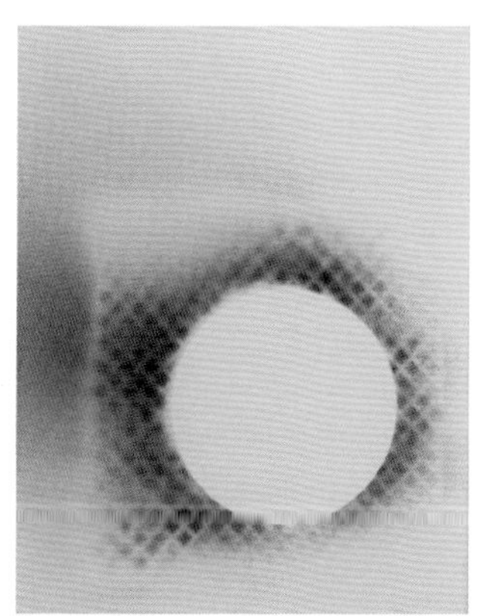

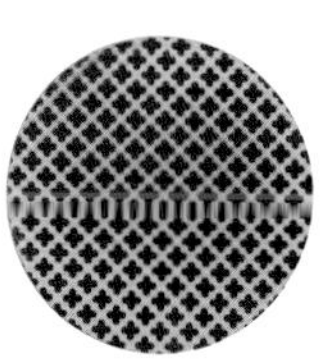

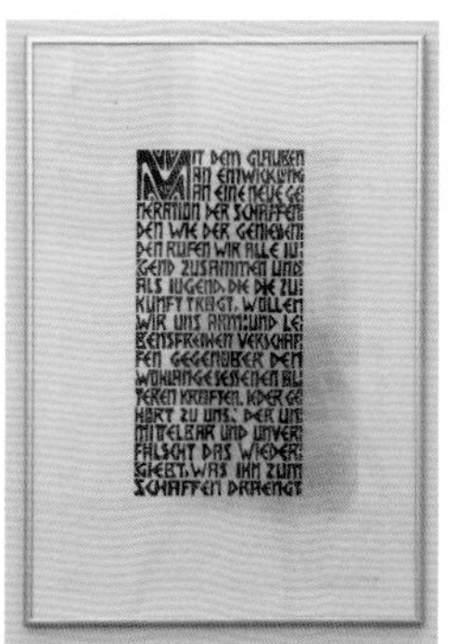

MIT DEM GLAUBEN AN ENTWICKLUNG AN EINE NEUE GENERATION DER SCHAFFENDEN WIE DER GENIESSENDEN RUFEN WIR ALLE JUGEND ZUSAMMEN UND ALS JUGEND, DIE DIE ZUKUNFT TRÄGT, WOLLEN WIR UNS ARM UND LEBENSFREIEN VERSCHAFFEN GEGENÜBER DEN WOHLANGESESSENEN ÄLTEREN KRÄFTEN. WER GEHÖRT ZU UNS? WER UNMITTELBAR UND UNVERFÄLSCHT DAS WIEDERGIEBT, WAS IHN ZUM SCHAFFEN DRÄNGT

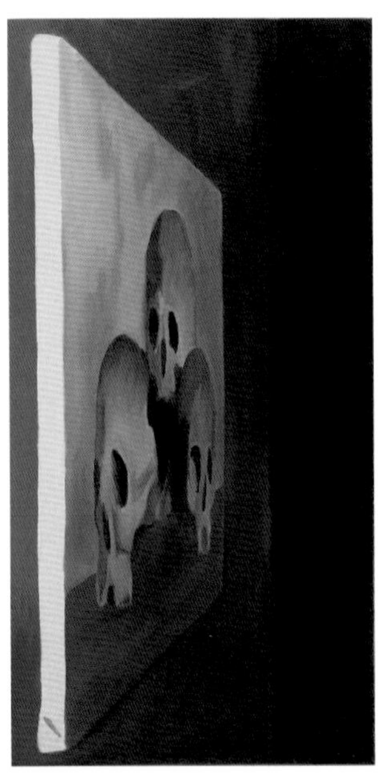

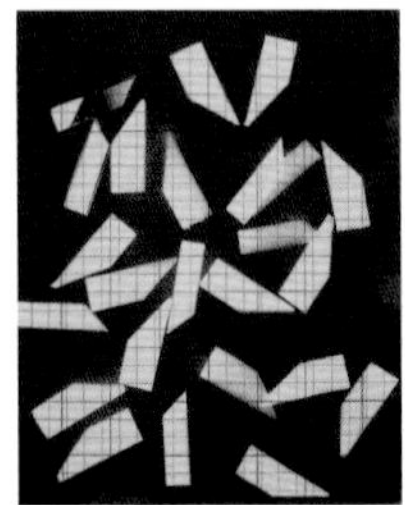

UNTITLED (PERSPECTIVE SKULLS), 2005
UNTITLED (GRID AND KEYS), 2007

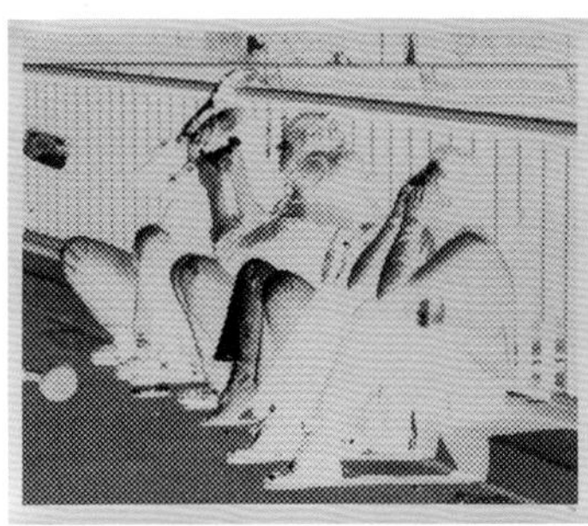

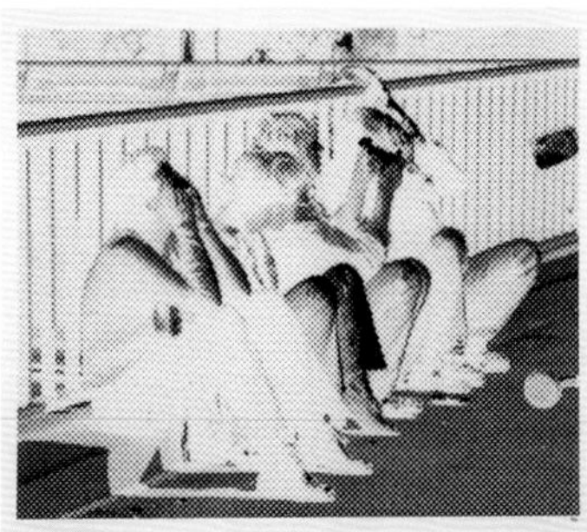

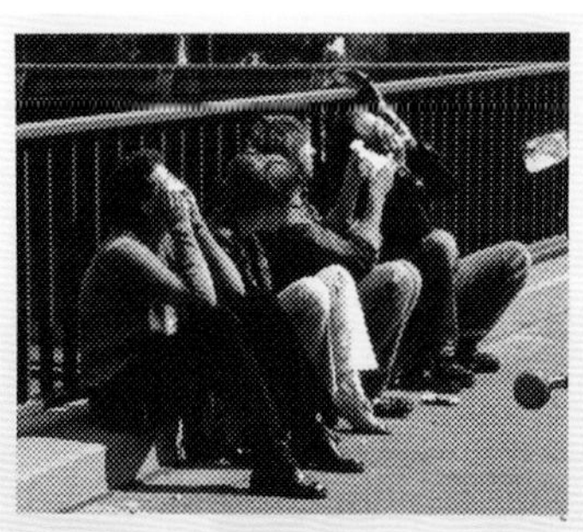

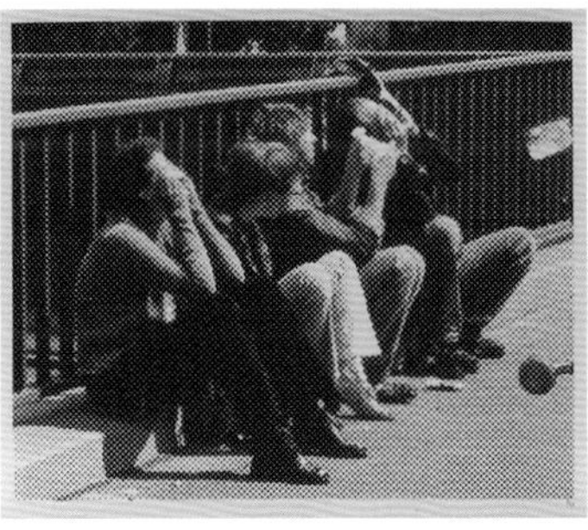

ECLIPSE, 2009
UNTITLED (CORRECTION PAINTING), 2007

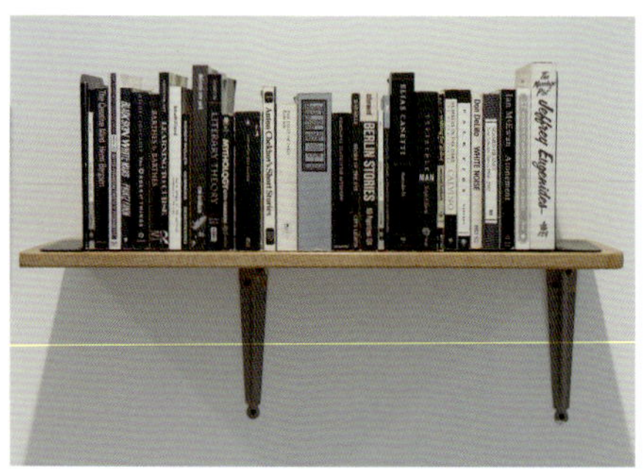

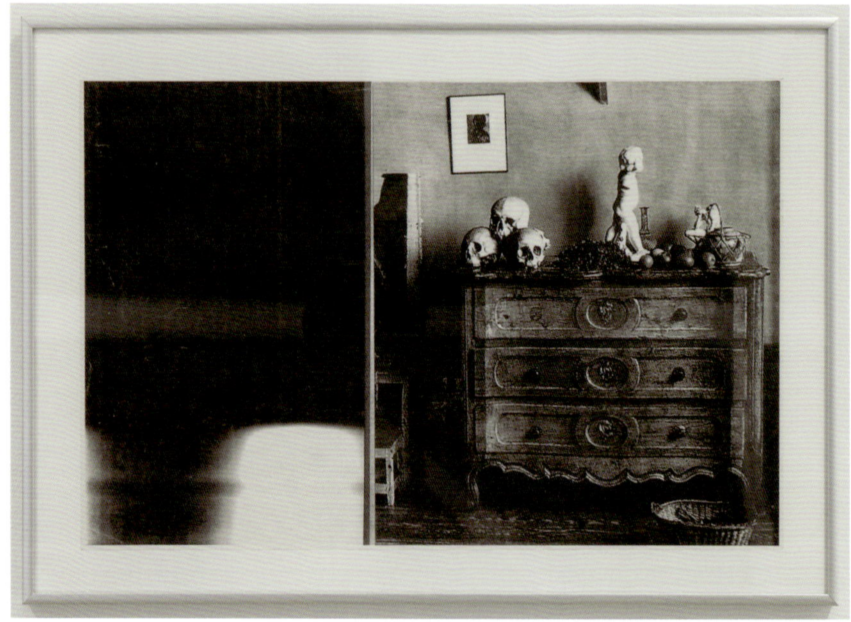

UNTITLED (B/W SHELF PIECE), 2015,
at reduced relative scale
UNTITLED (CEZANNE'S STUDIO), 2005

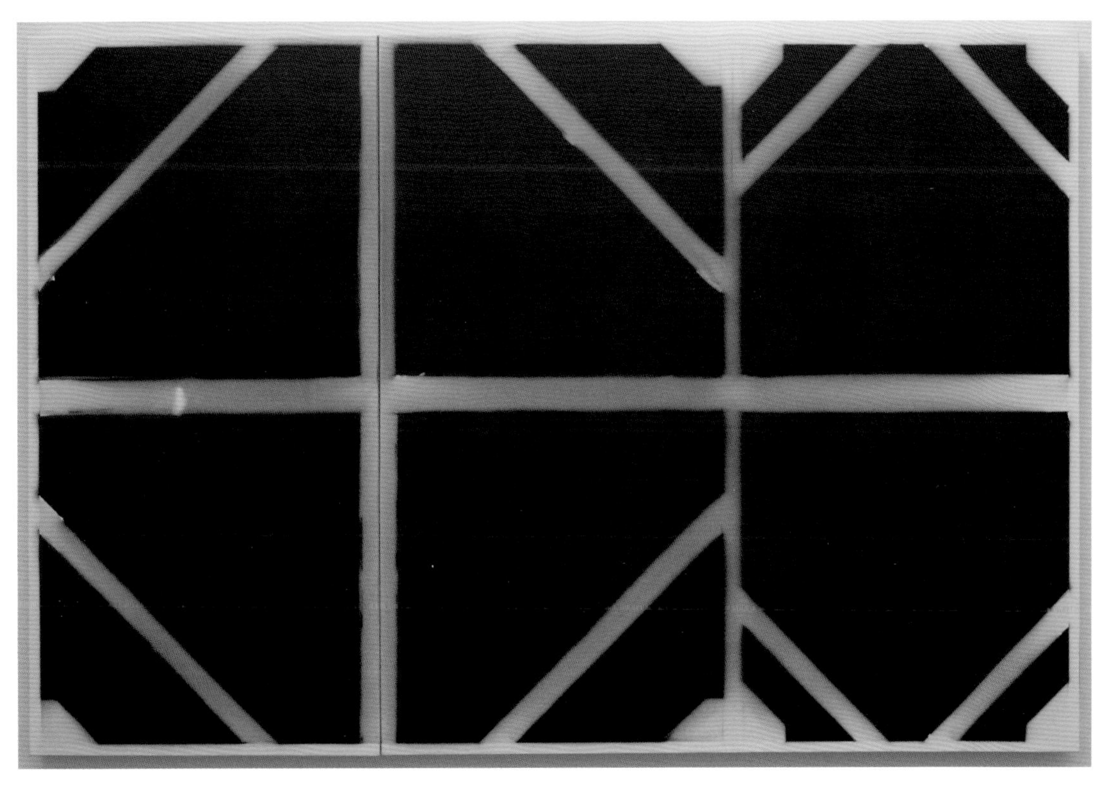

UNTITLED (NUMBER 2), 2015

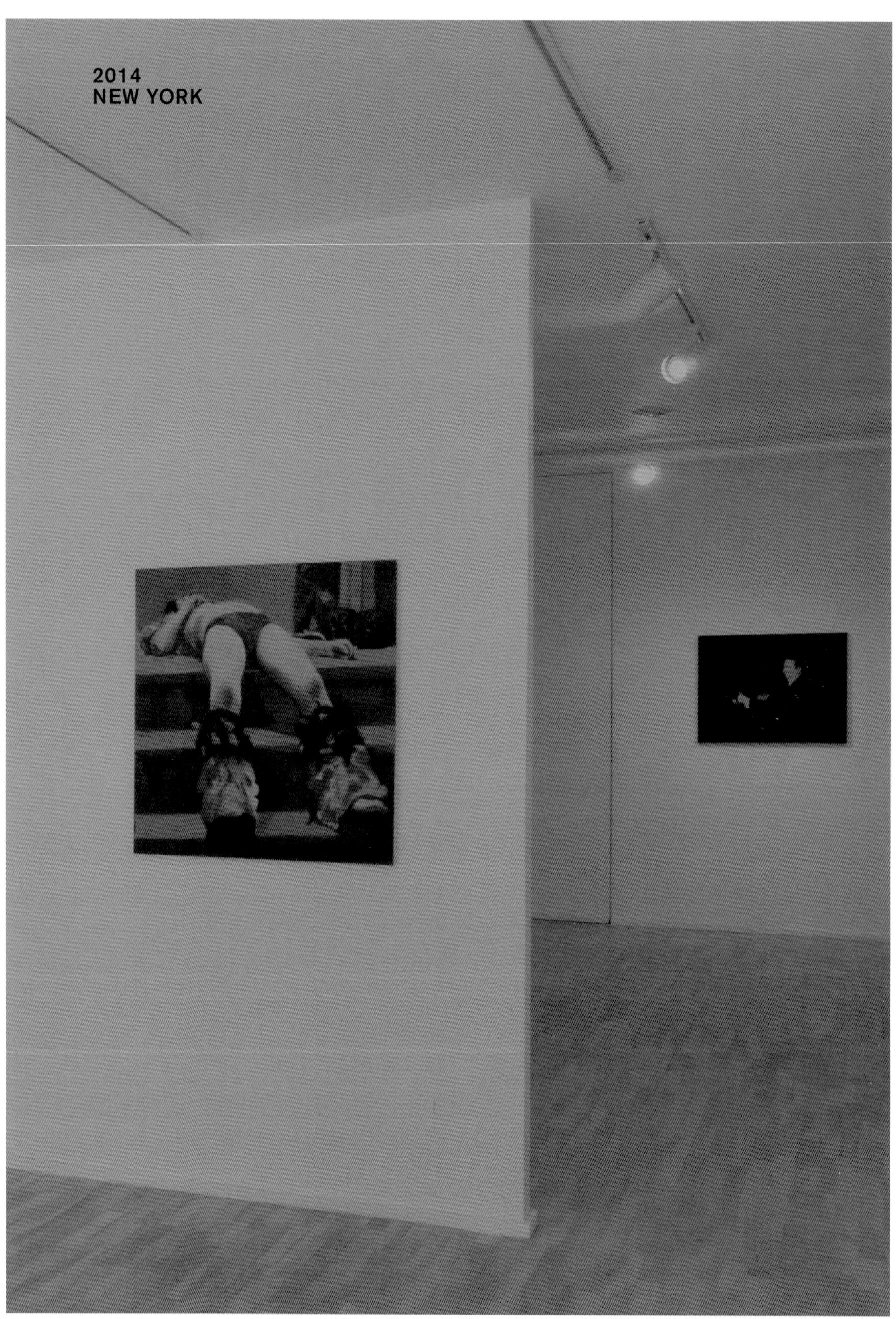

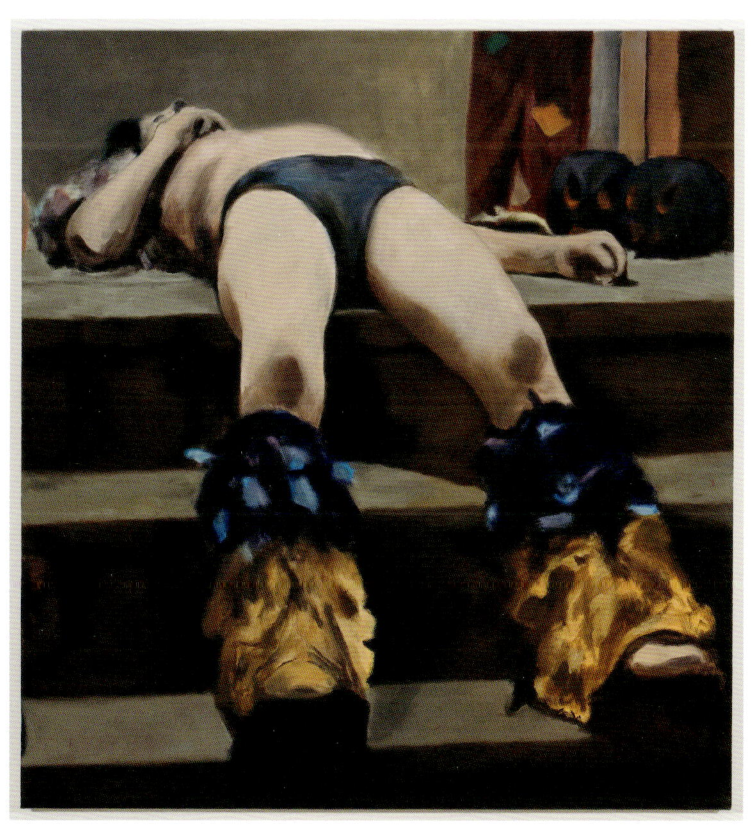

UNTITLED (NEIGHBOR), 2013–14

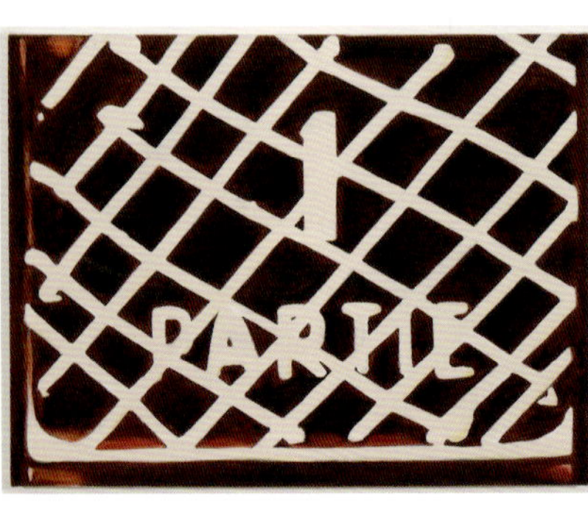

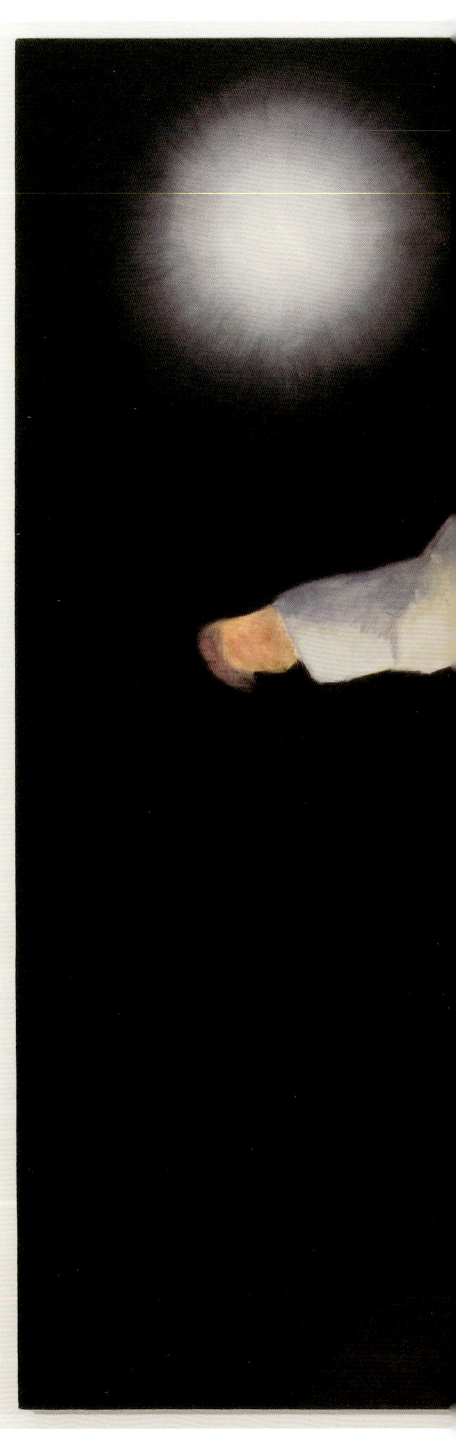

UNTITLED (FILM LEADER, PARTIE), 2010

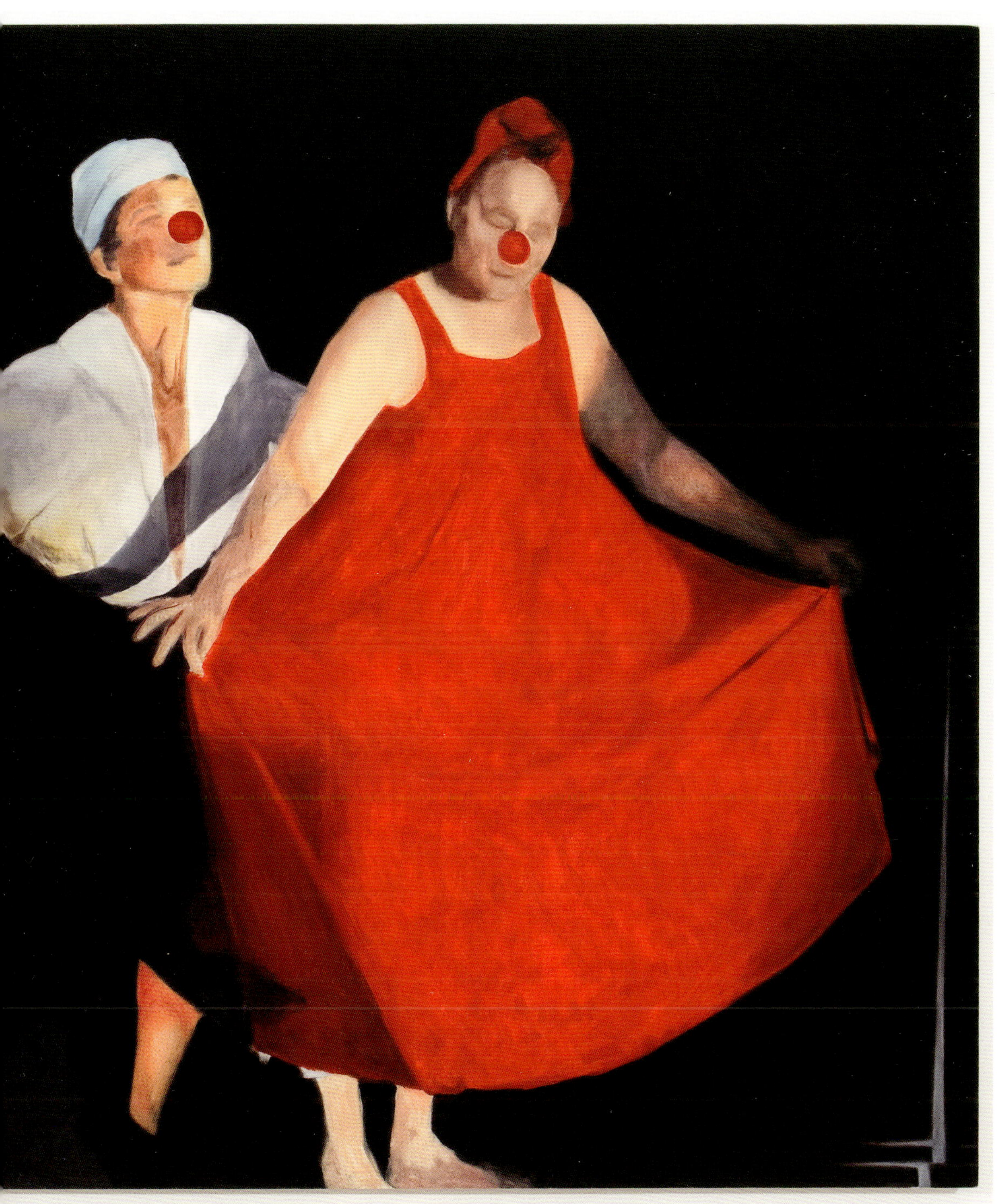

UNTITLED (CLOWN DANCE), 2012–13

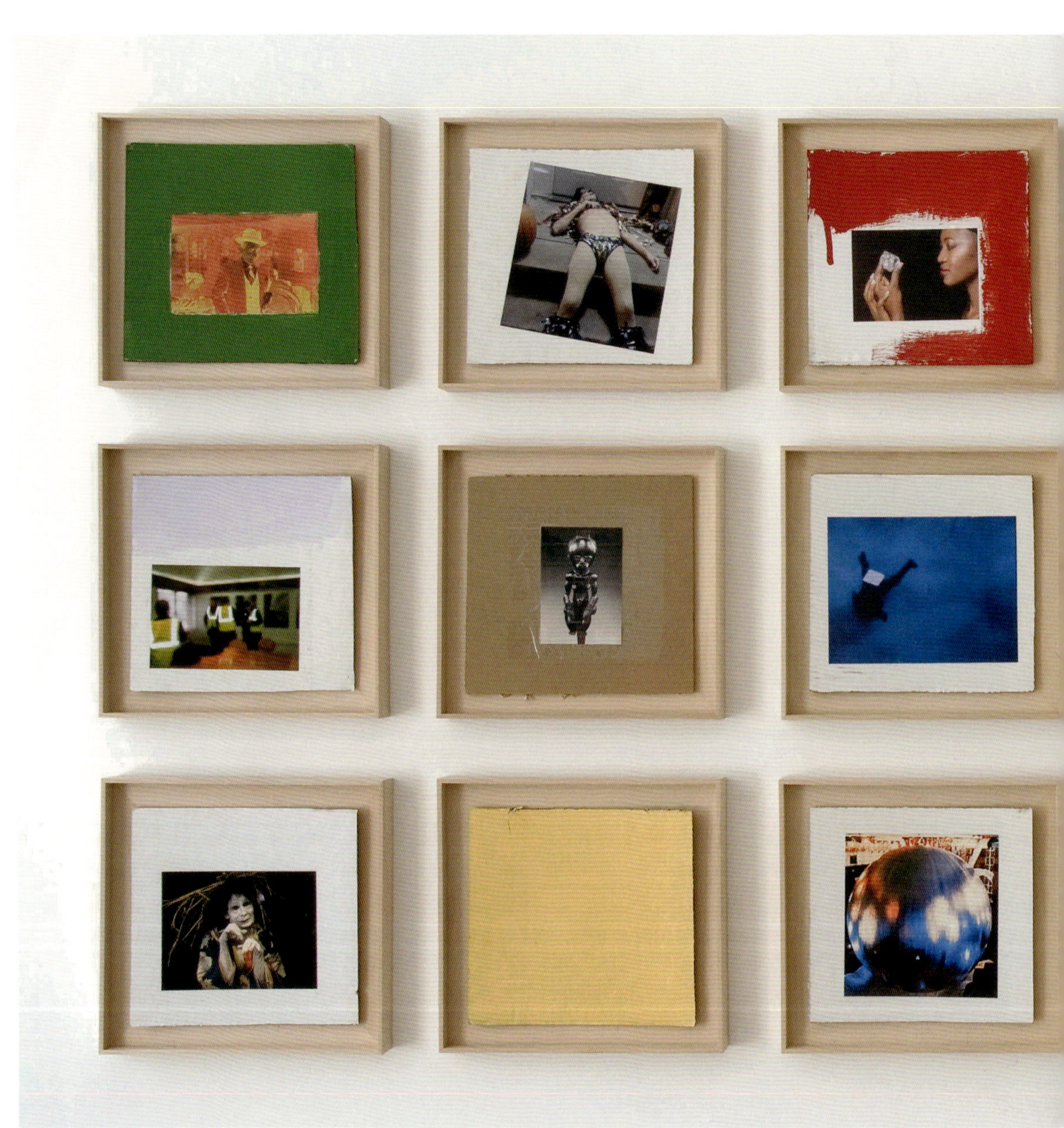

UNTITLED (COLLAGE WALL), 2011

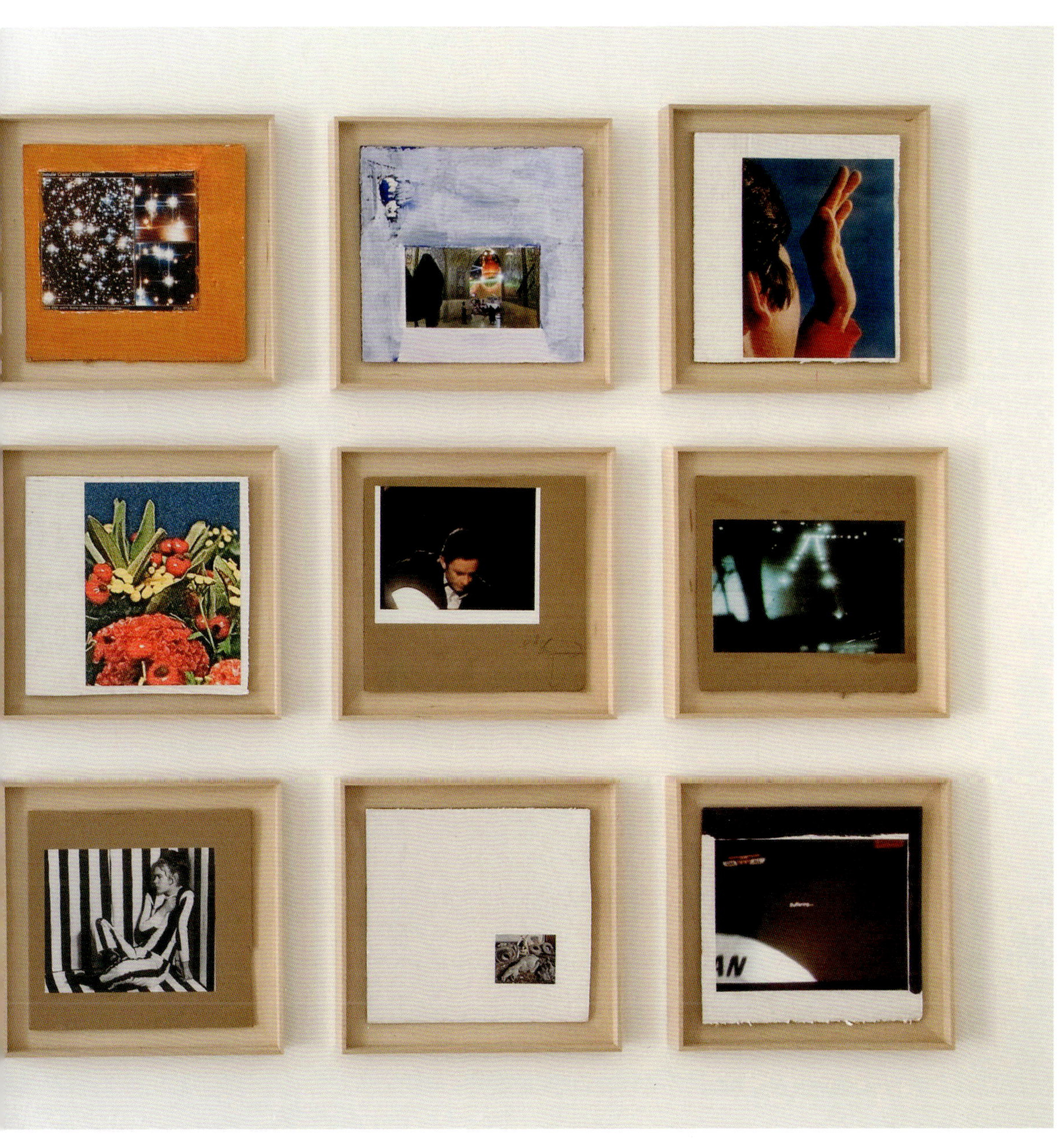

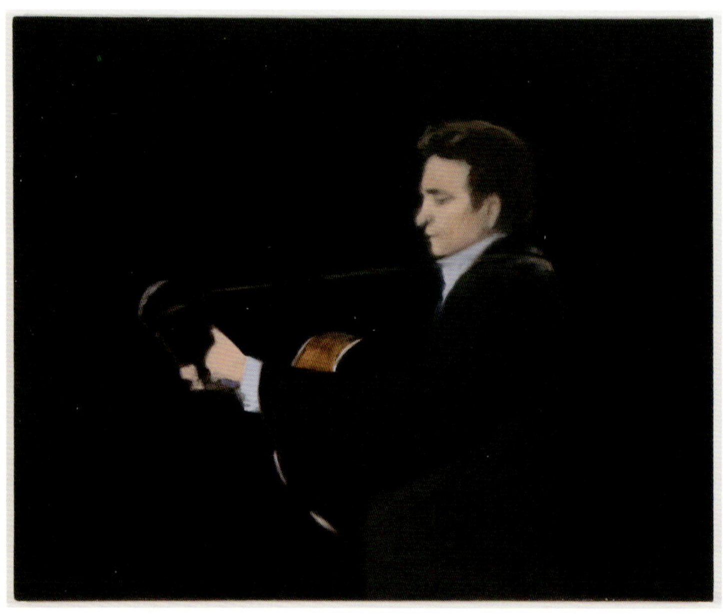

UNTITLED (THE GUITAR PLAYER), 2012–13

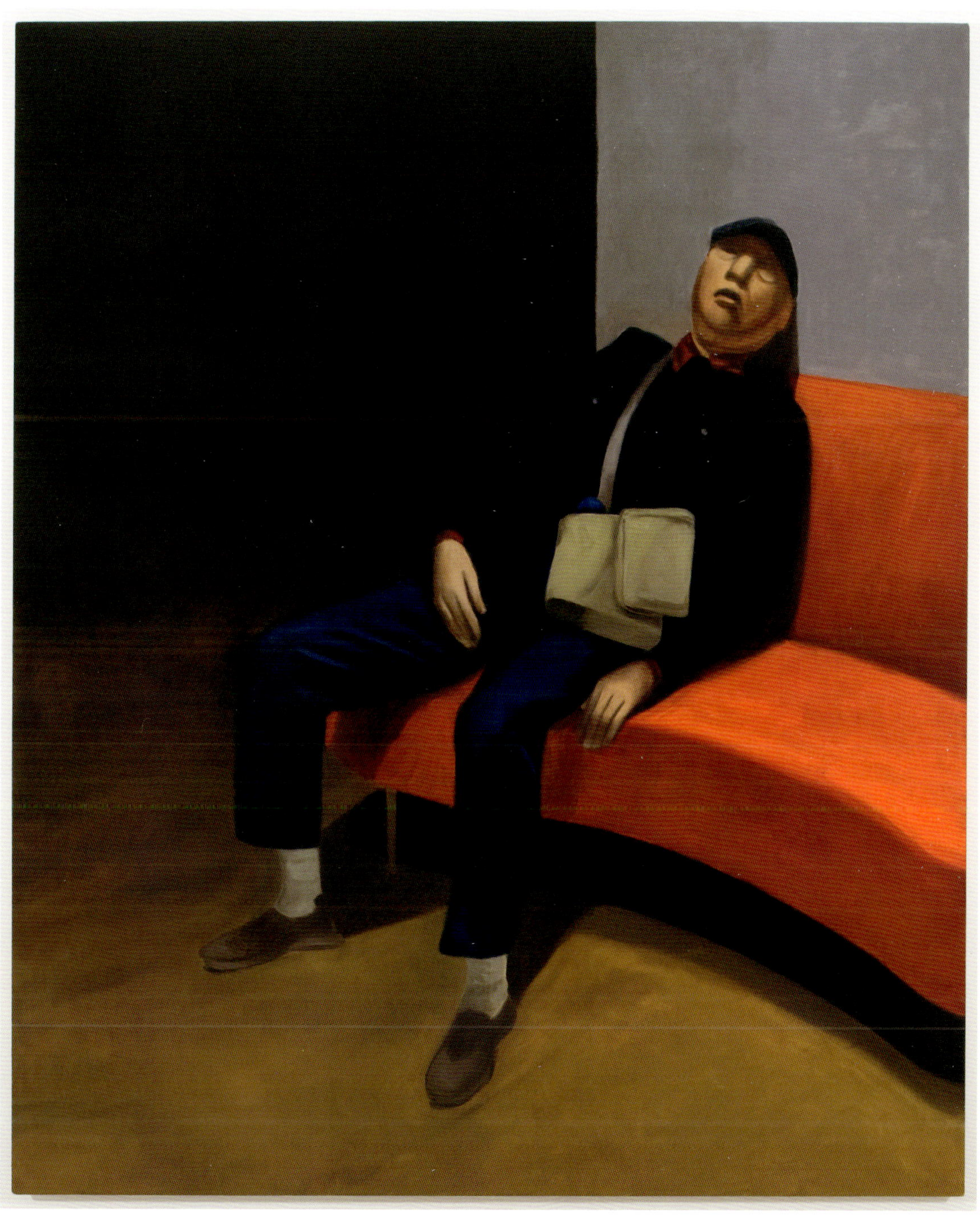

UNTITLED (PARIS, ASLEEP), 2014

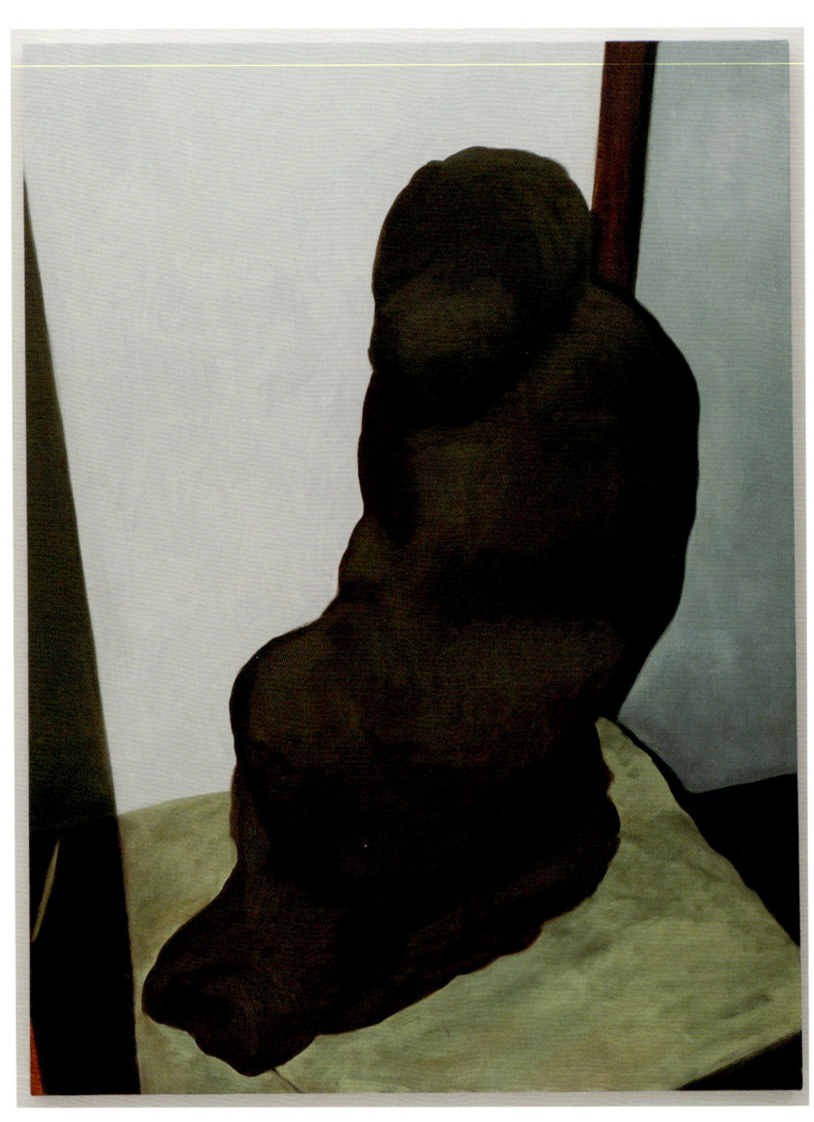

UNTITLED (BABOON MUMMY 2), 2013

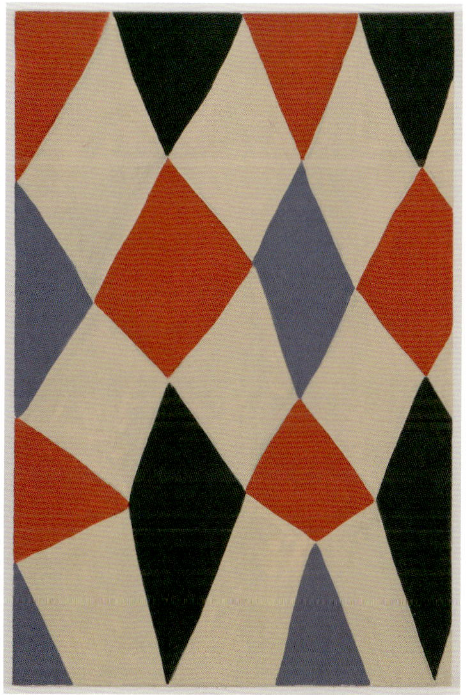

UNTITLED (HARLEQUIN ABSTRACTION), 2007

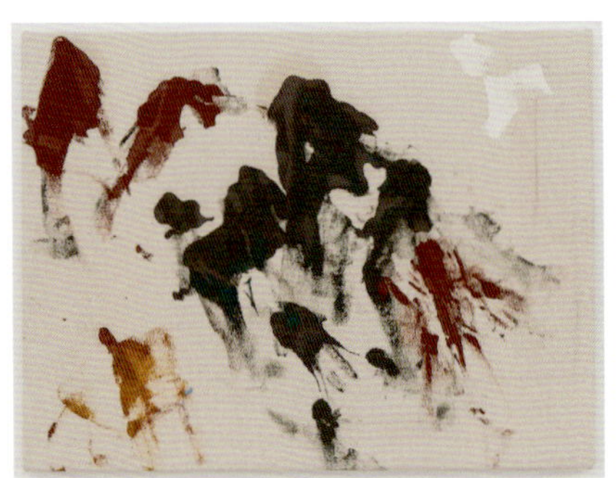

UNTITLED (BURGUNDY, GREEN, RUST AND WHITE), 2012

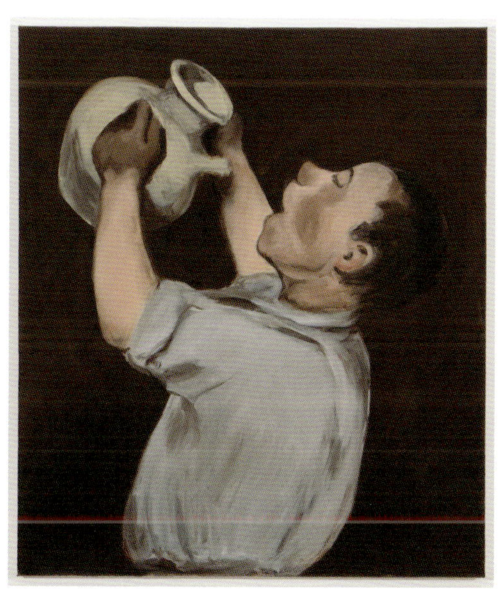

UNTITLED (BOY WITH PITCHER, AFTER MANET), 2008/2013–14

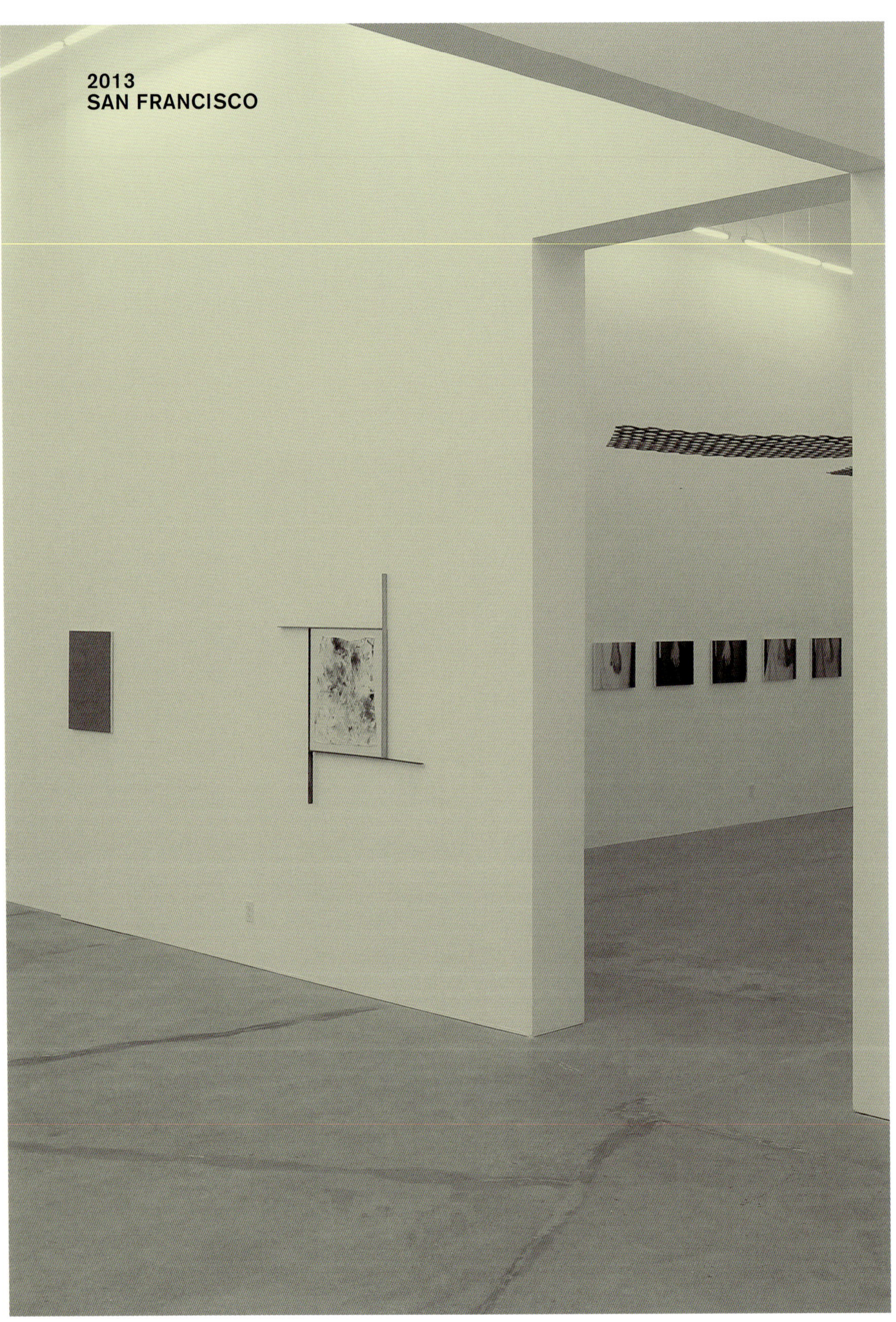

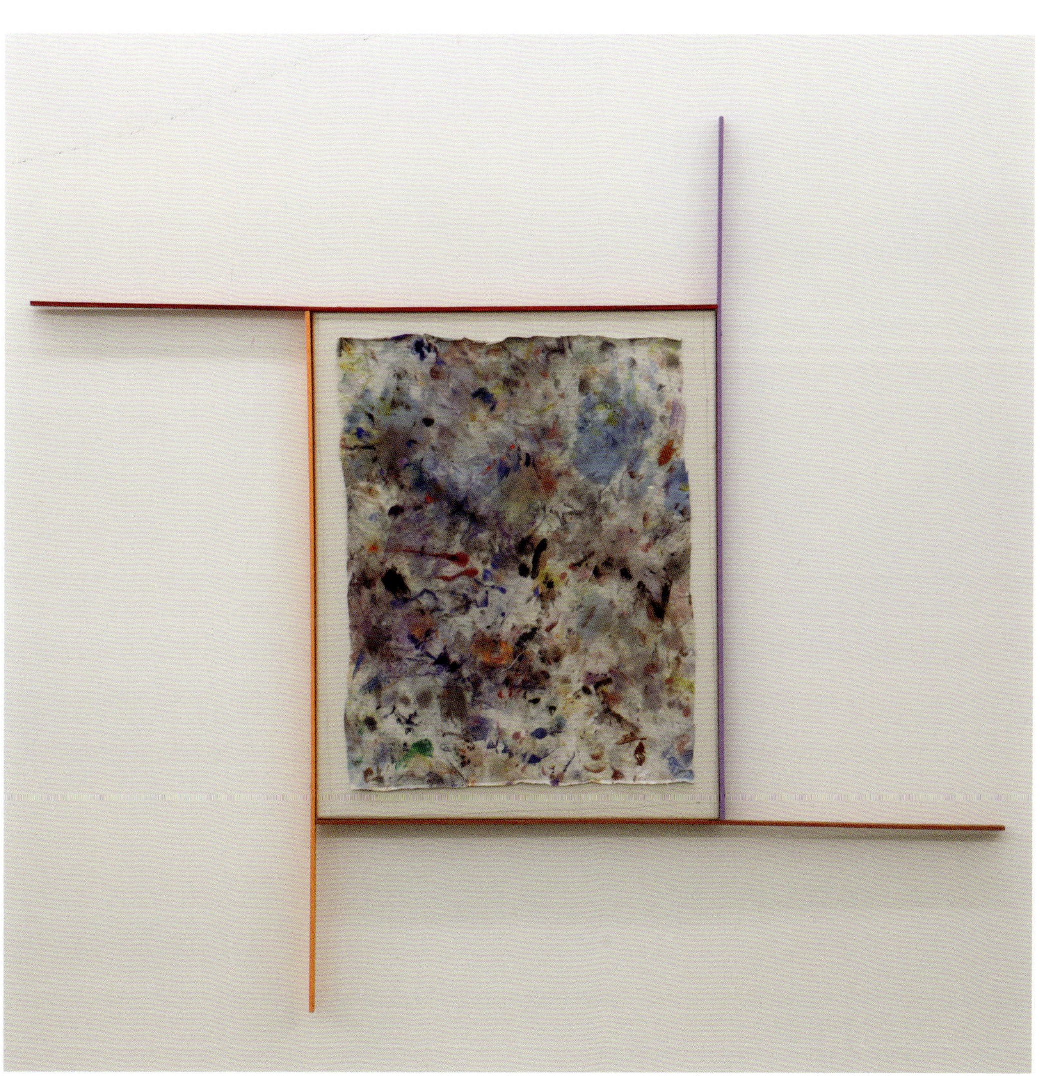

UNTITLED (13A), 2012

UNTITLED (12B), 2012

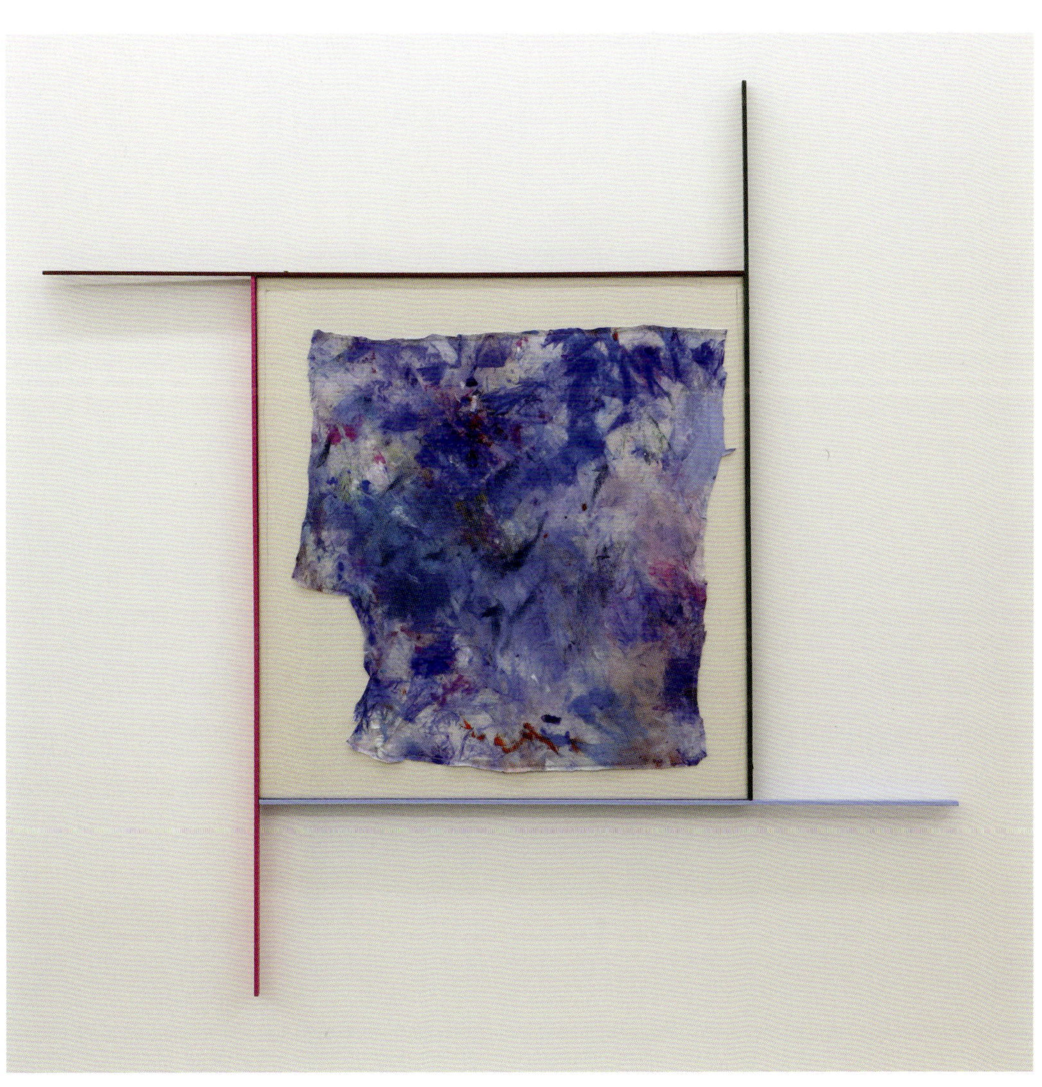

UNTITLED (8A), 2012

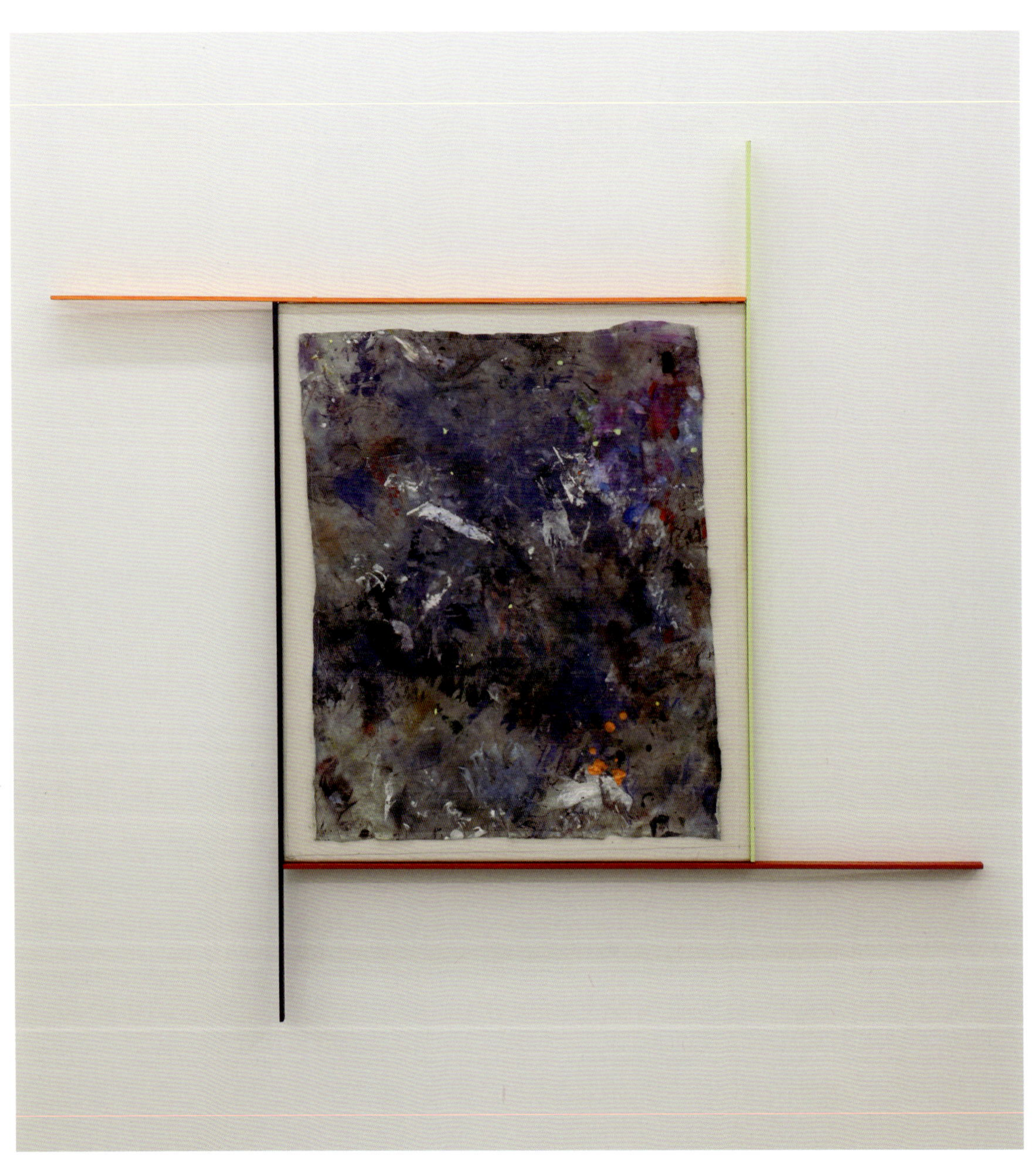

UNTITLED (14A), 2012

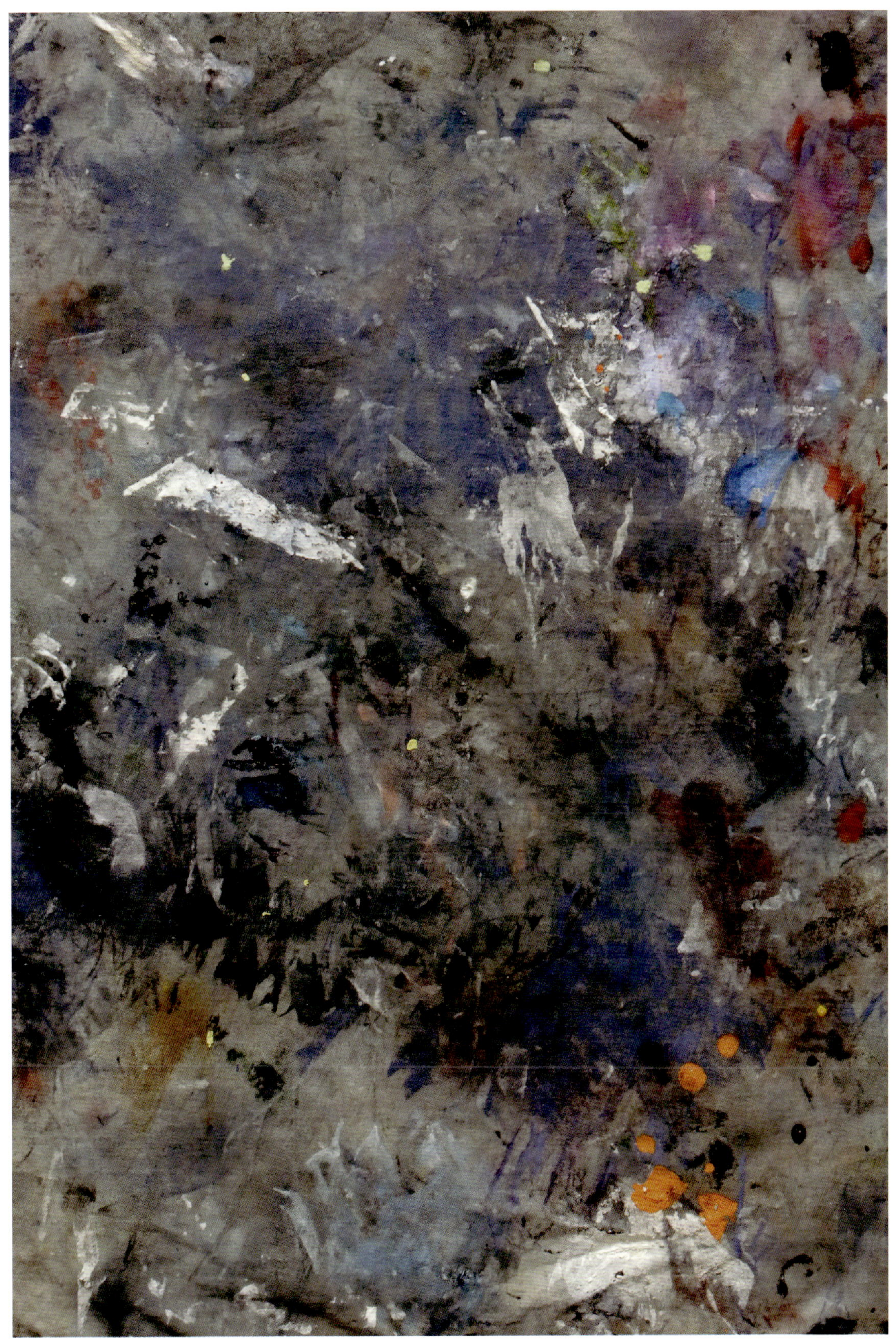

UNTITLED (14A), 2012 (detail)

UNTITLED (5B), 2012

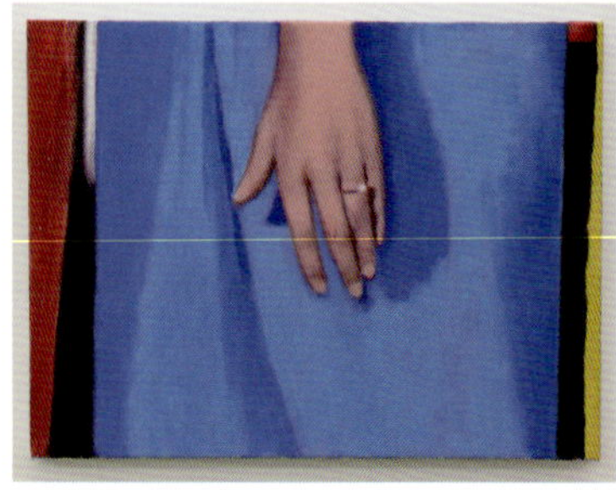
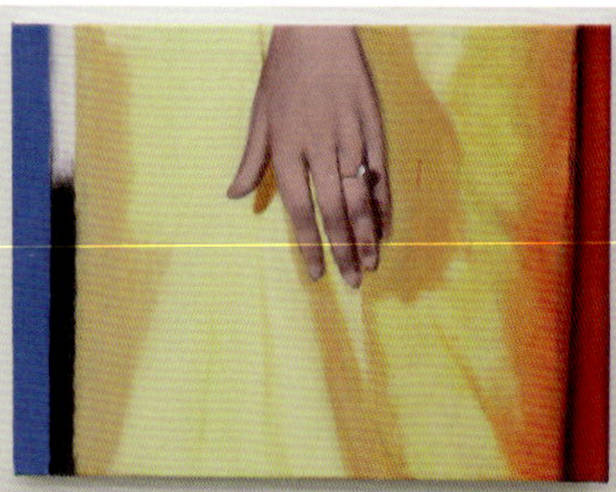
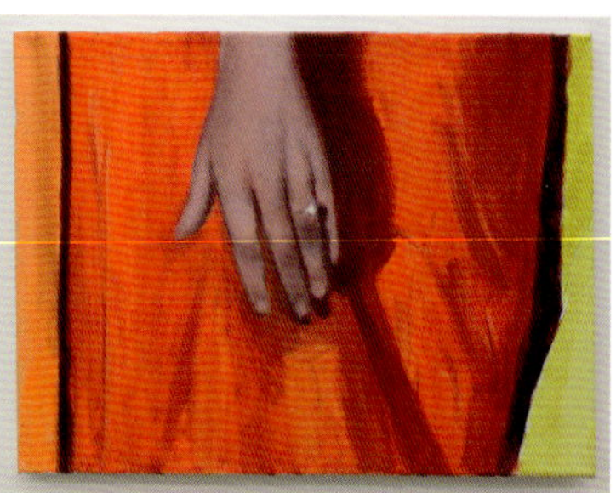
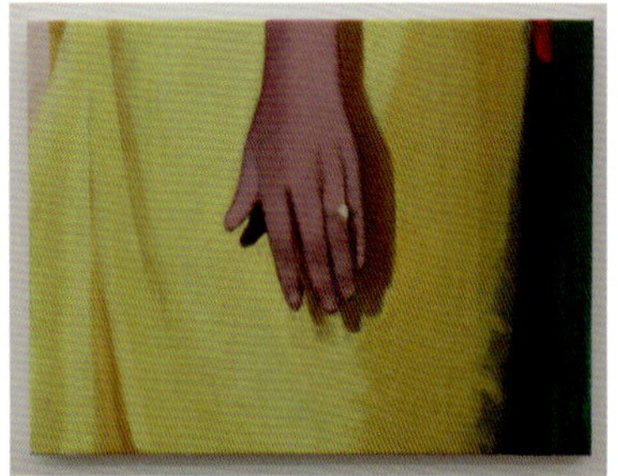
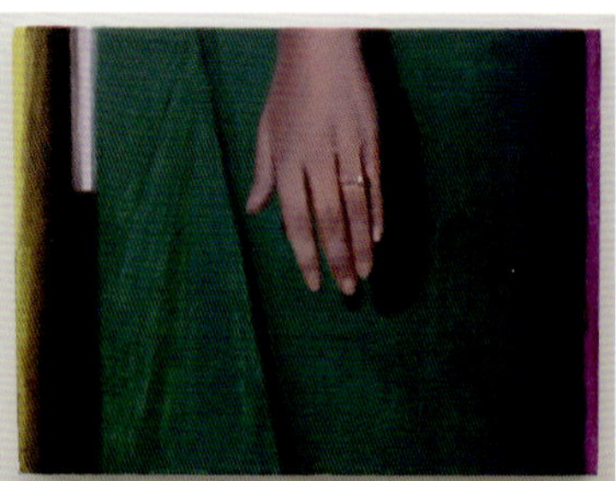
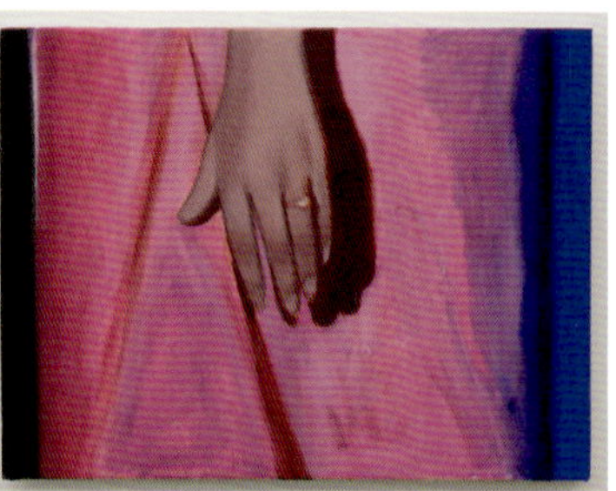
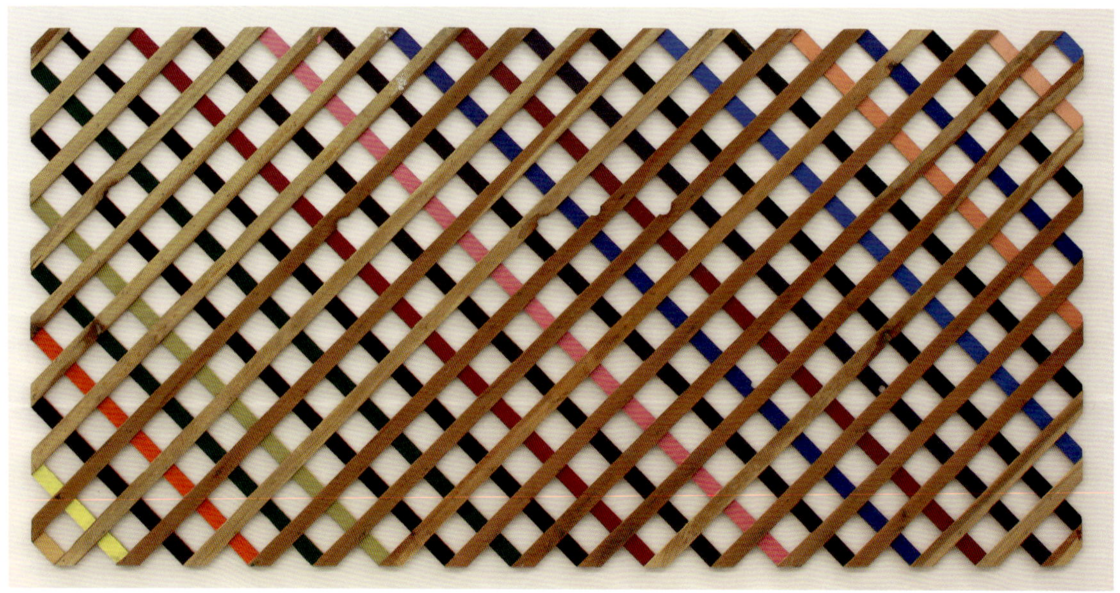

UNTITLED (COLOR TEST HANDS #1–10), 2008–2012
UNTITLED (LATTICE 1), 2012

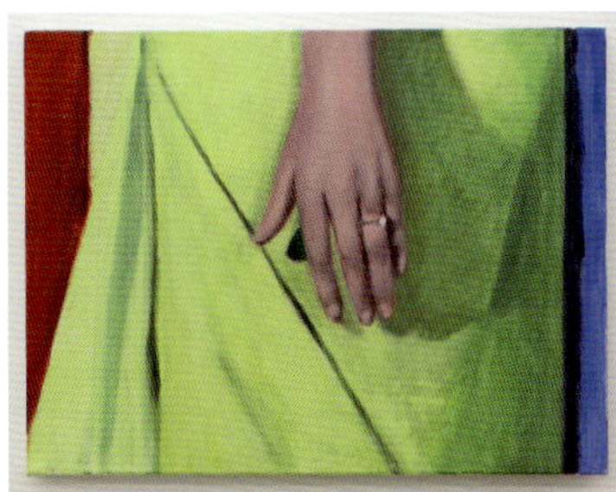
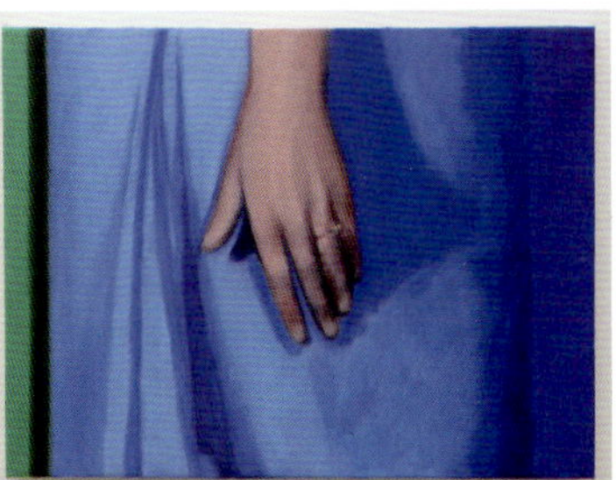
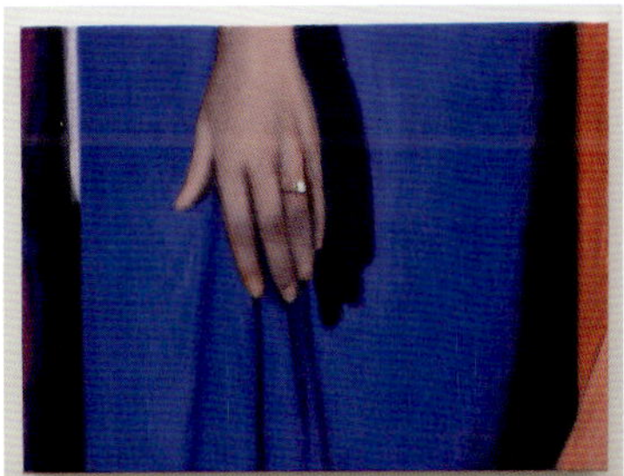
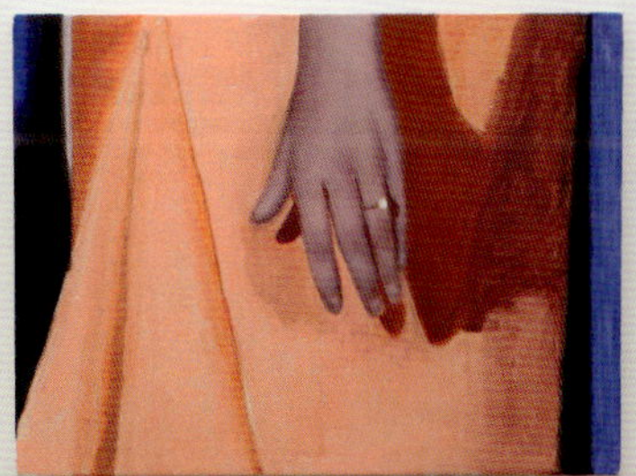
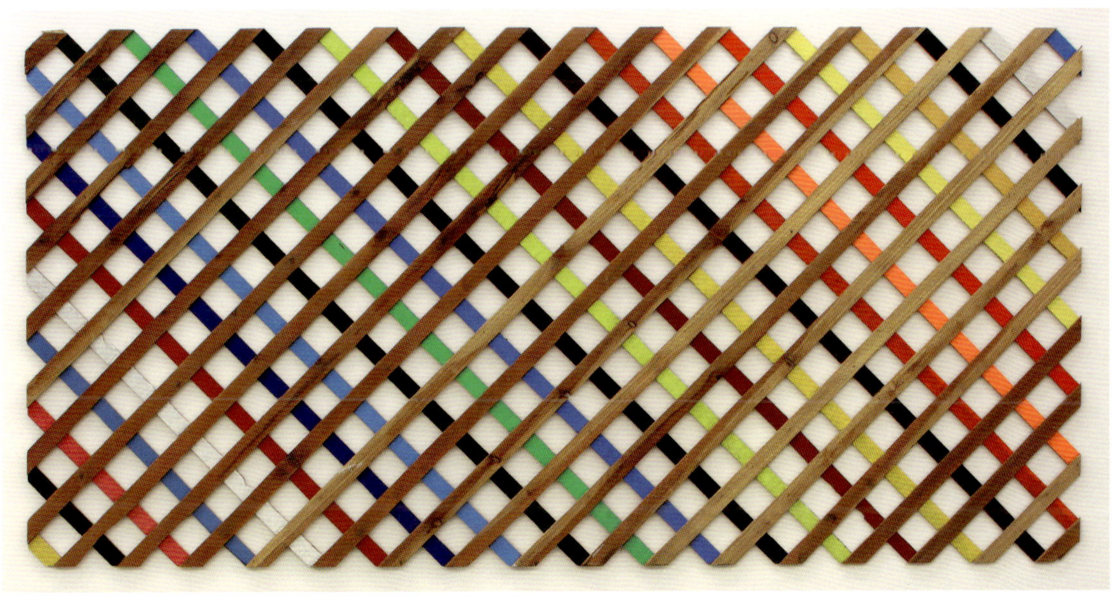

UNTITLED (LATTICE 2), 2012

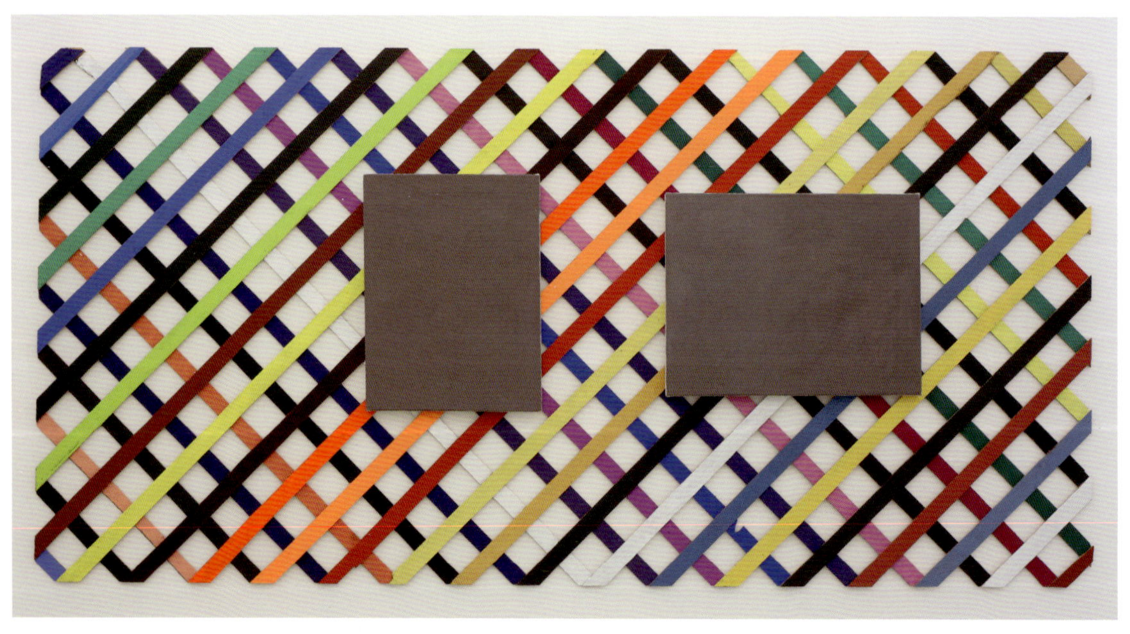

UNTITLED (LATTICE 3), 2012
UNTITLED (10B), 2012
UNTITLED (23B), 2012

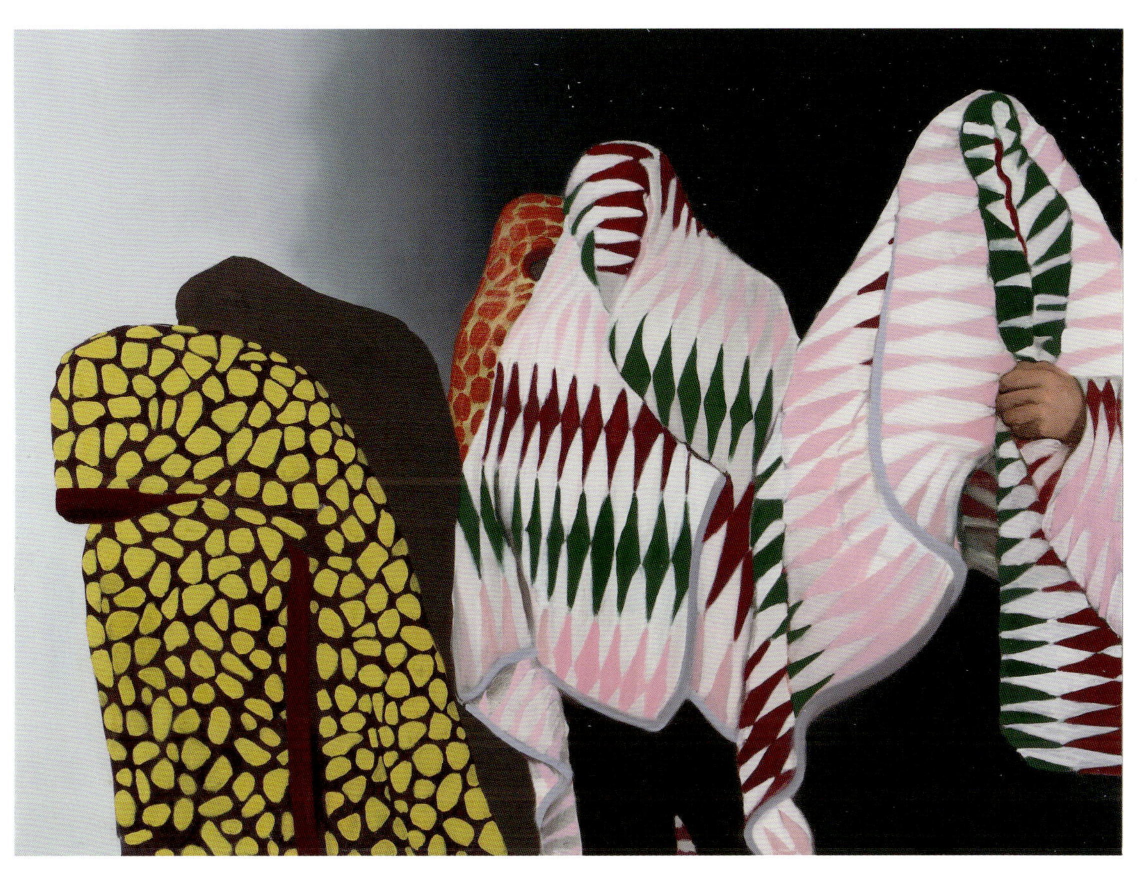

UNTITLED (INFORMERS), 2006

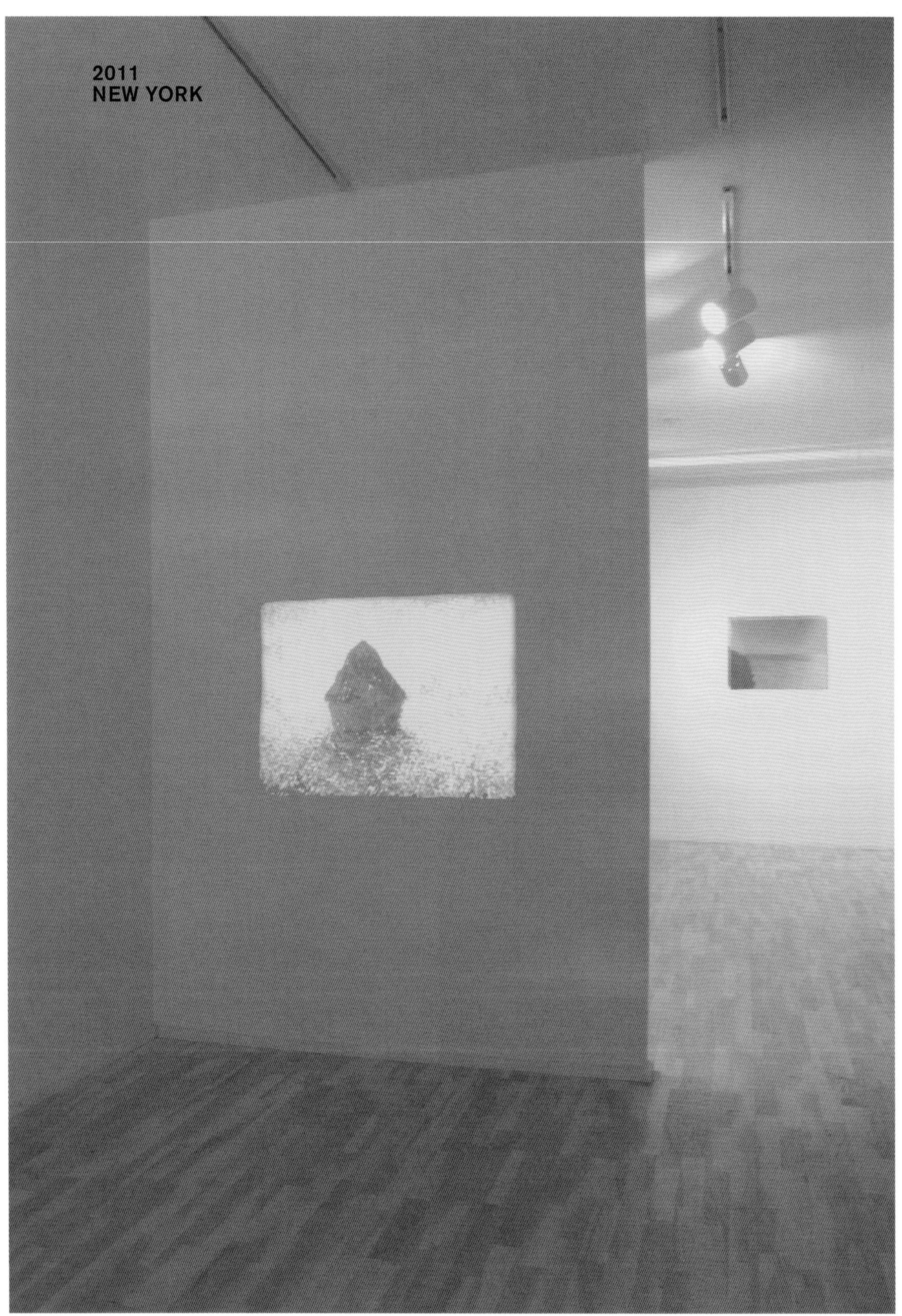
2011
NEW YORK

UNTITLED (113590 REV 2), 2011

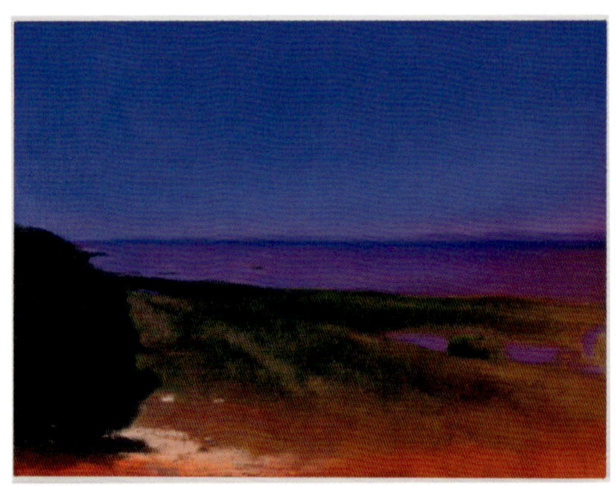

UNTITLED (113557), 2011

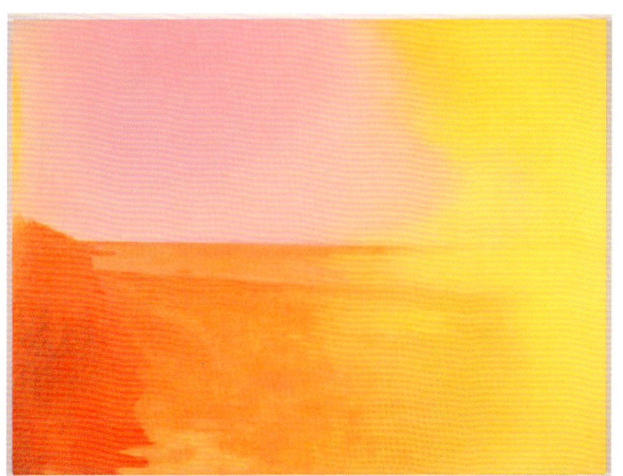

UNTITLED (113577), 2011
UNTITLED (113606), 2011

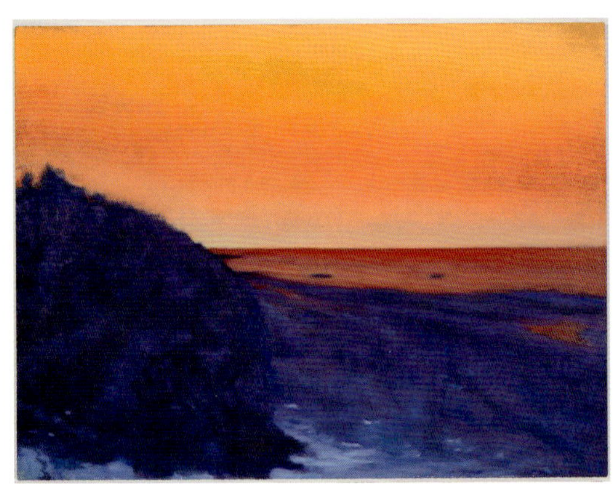

UNTITLED (113590 REV 1), 2011

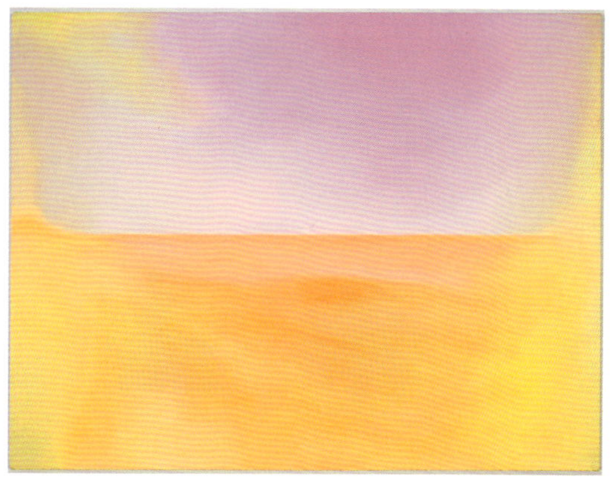

UNTITLED (BASEL LENS FLARE 8017), 2011

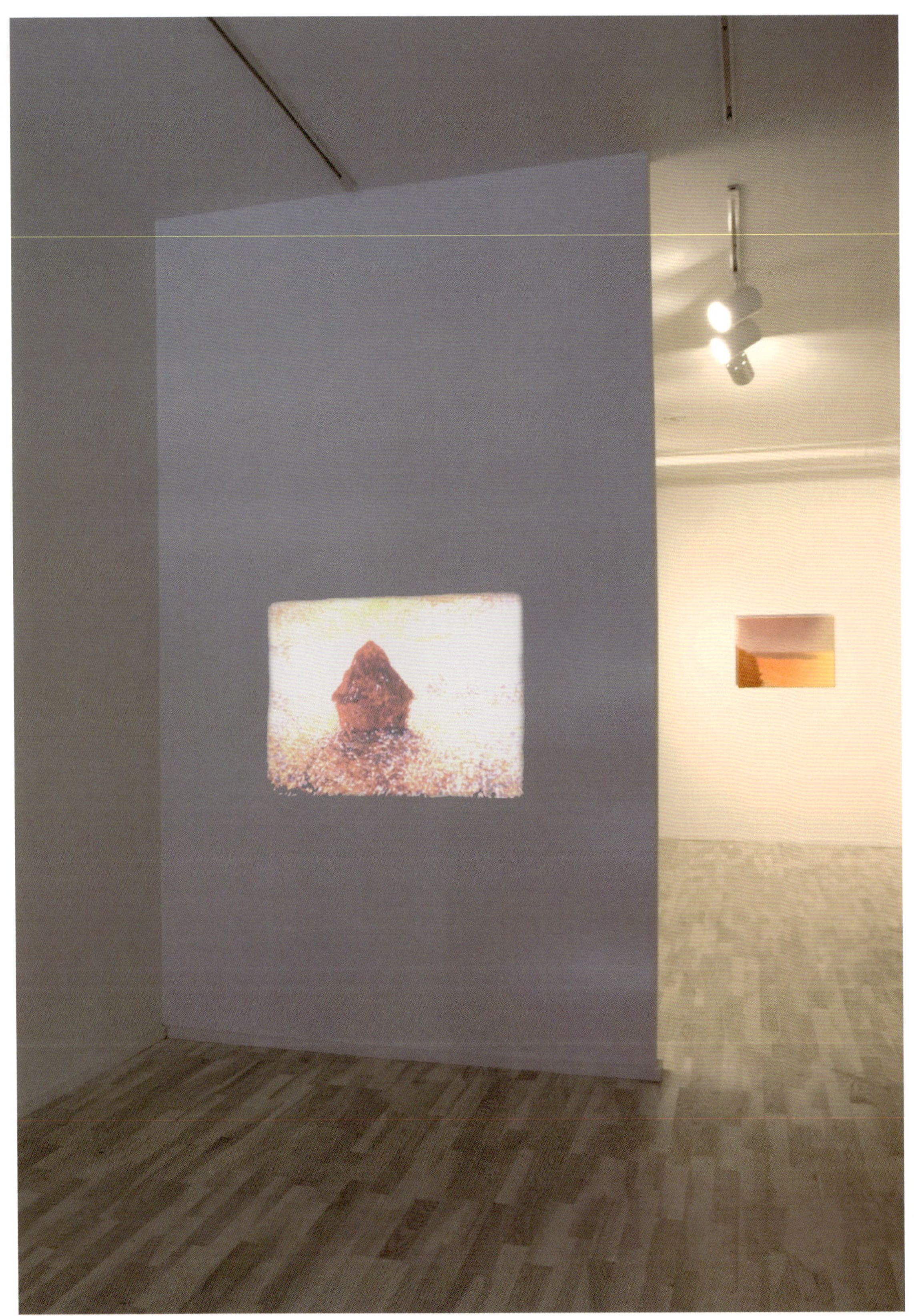

LES MEULES, 2011

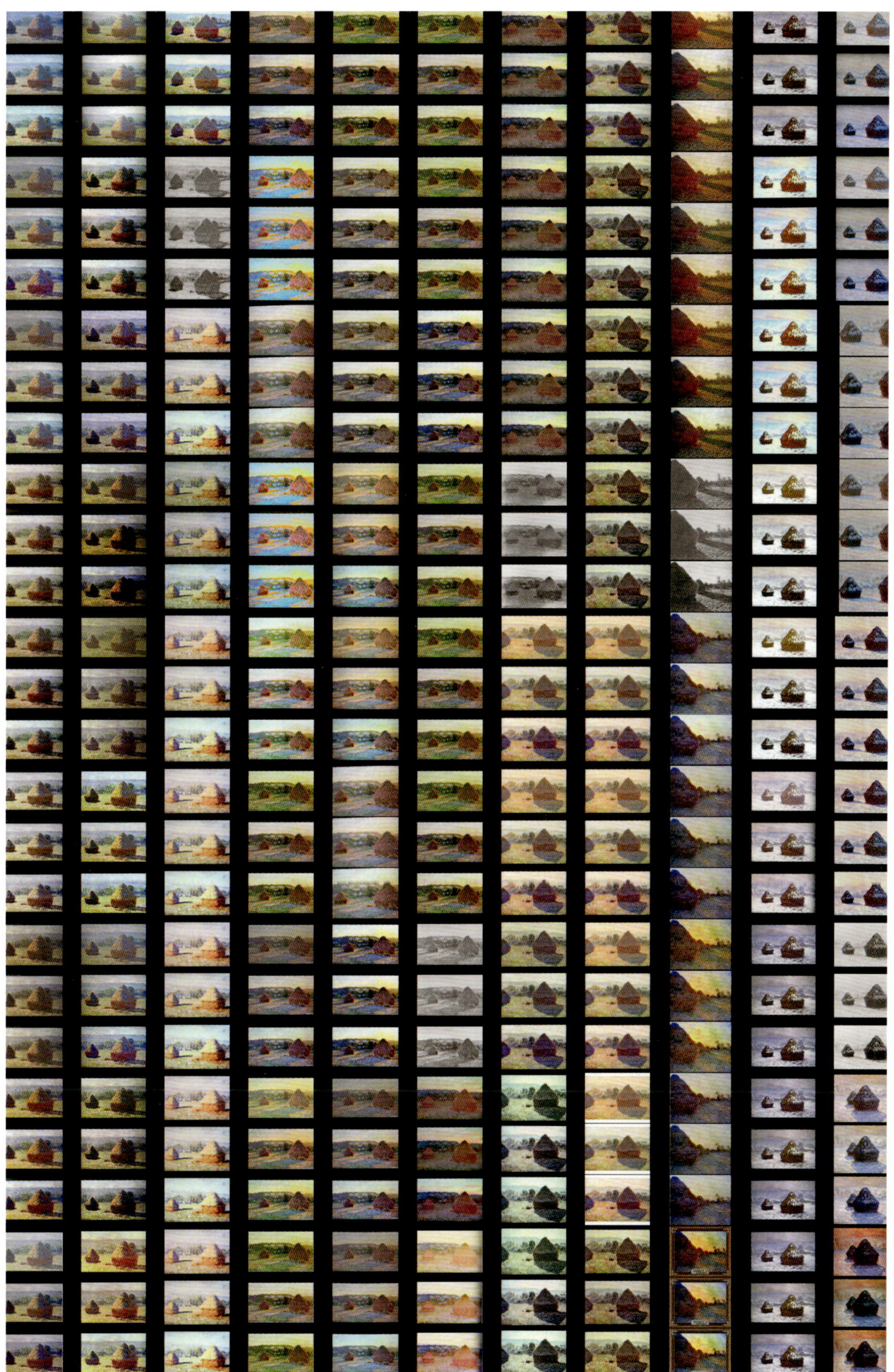

LES MEULES, 2011 (detail)

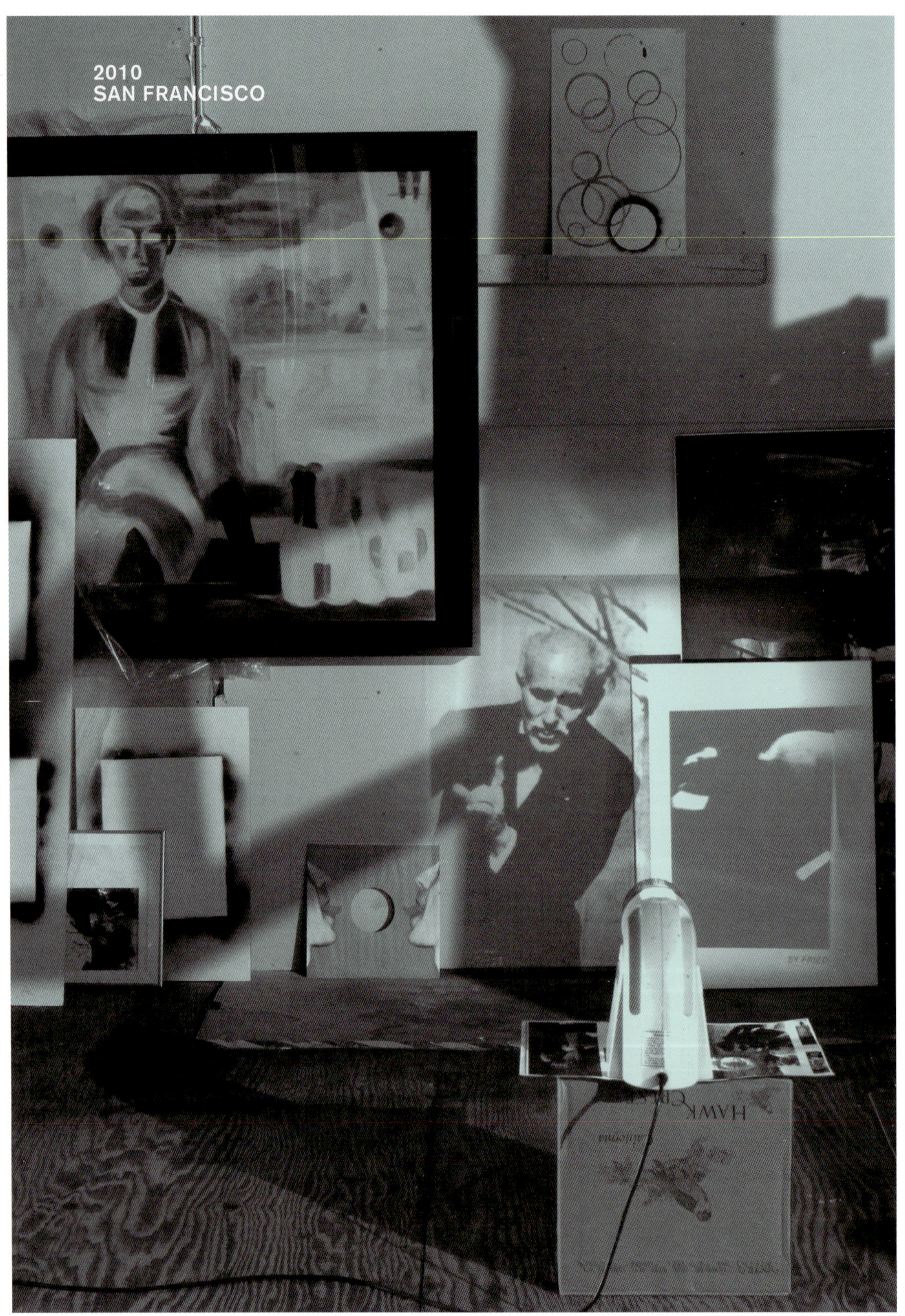

UNTITLED (STOREROOM INSTALLATION), 2010 (detail)

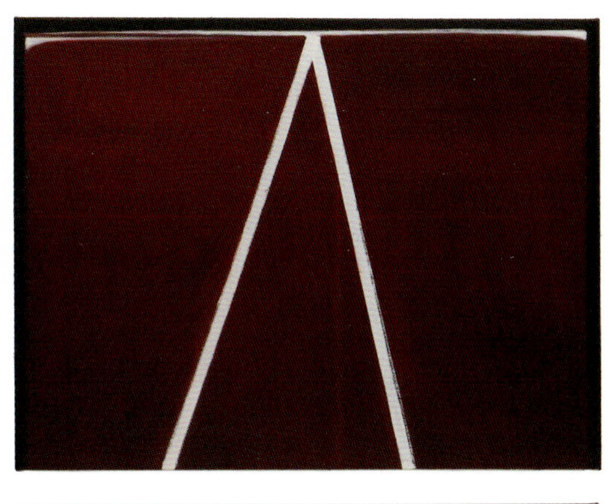

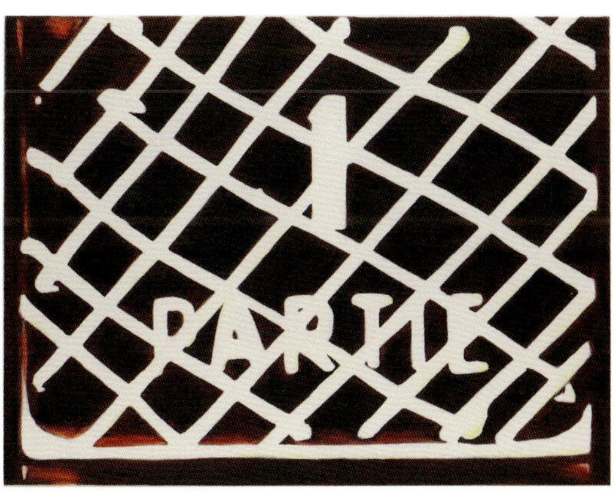

UNTITLED (FILM LEADER, RED 2), 2010
UNTITLED (FILM LEADER, RED 3), 2010
UNTITLED (FILM LEADER, PARTIE), 2010

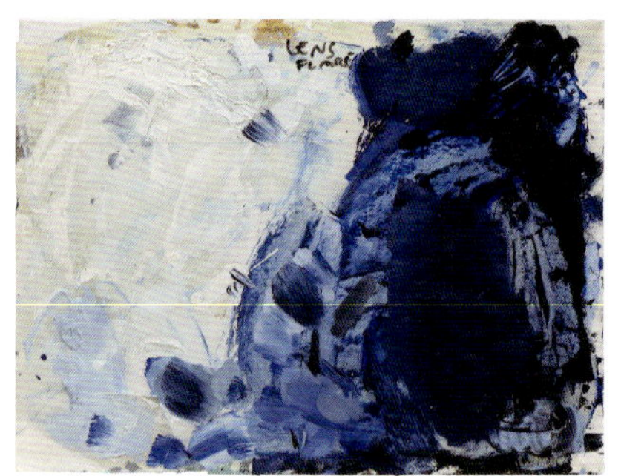
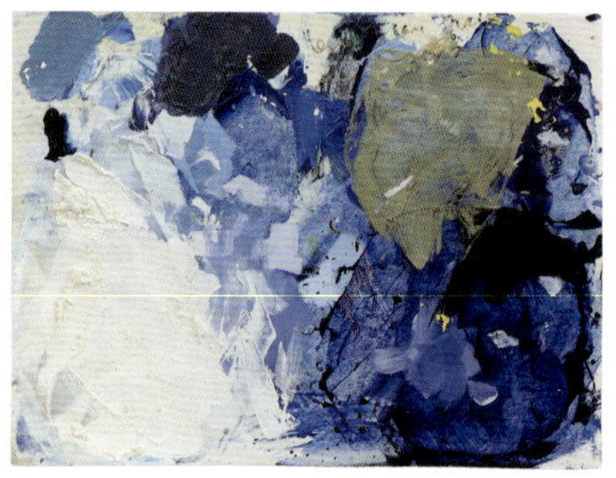

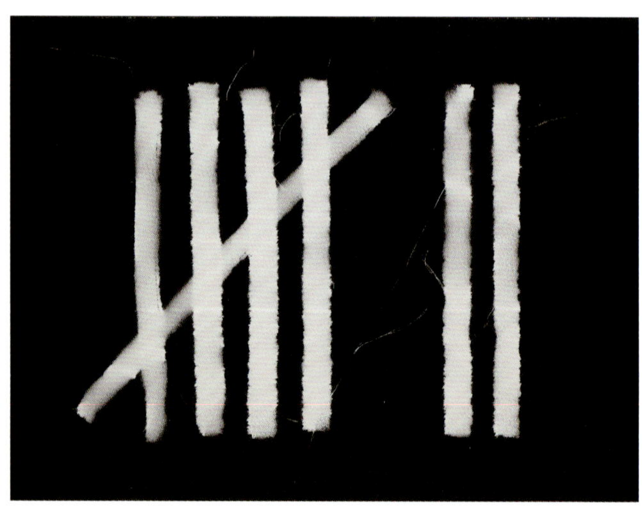

UNTITLED (LENS FLARE PALETTE), 2008–2009
UNTITLED (LENS FLARE TRIO PALETTE), 2008–2009
UNTITLED (LENS FLARE 5 & 6 PALETTE), 2008–2009
UNTITLED (COUNTDOWN 7), 2009

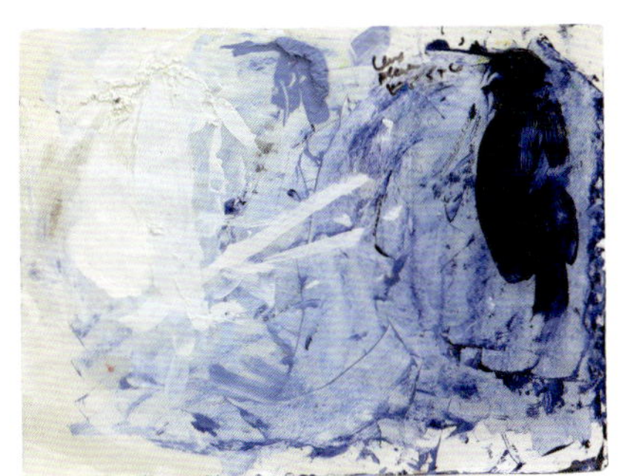

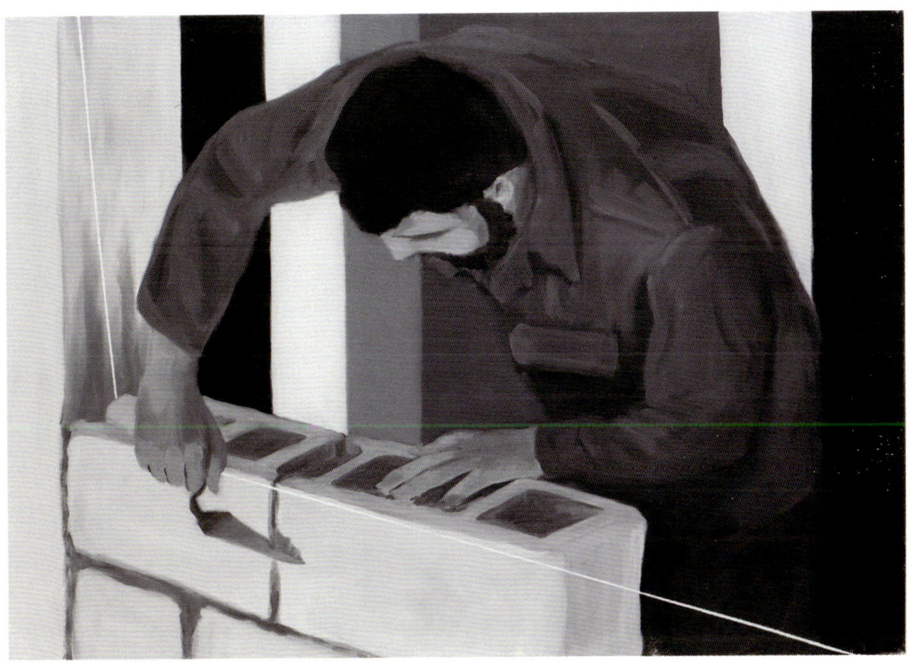

UNTITLED (BUILDER), 2006

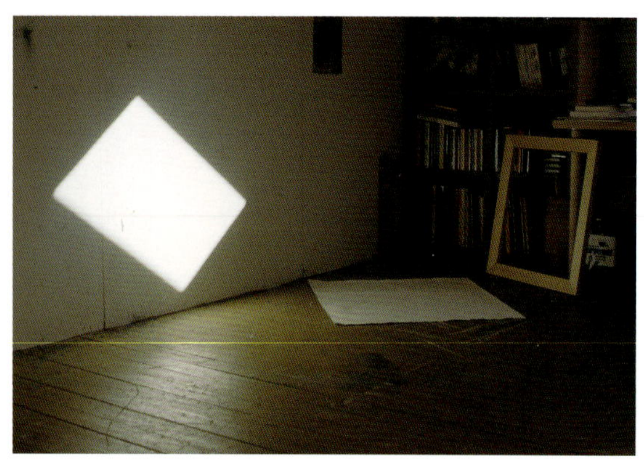

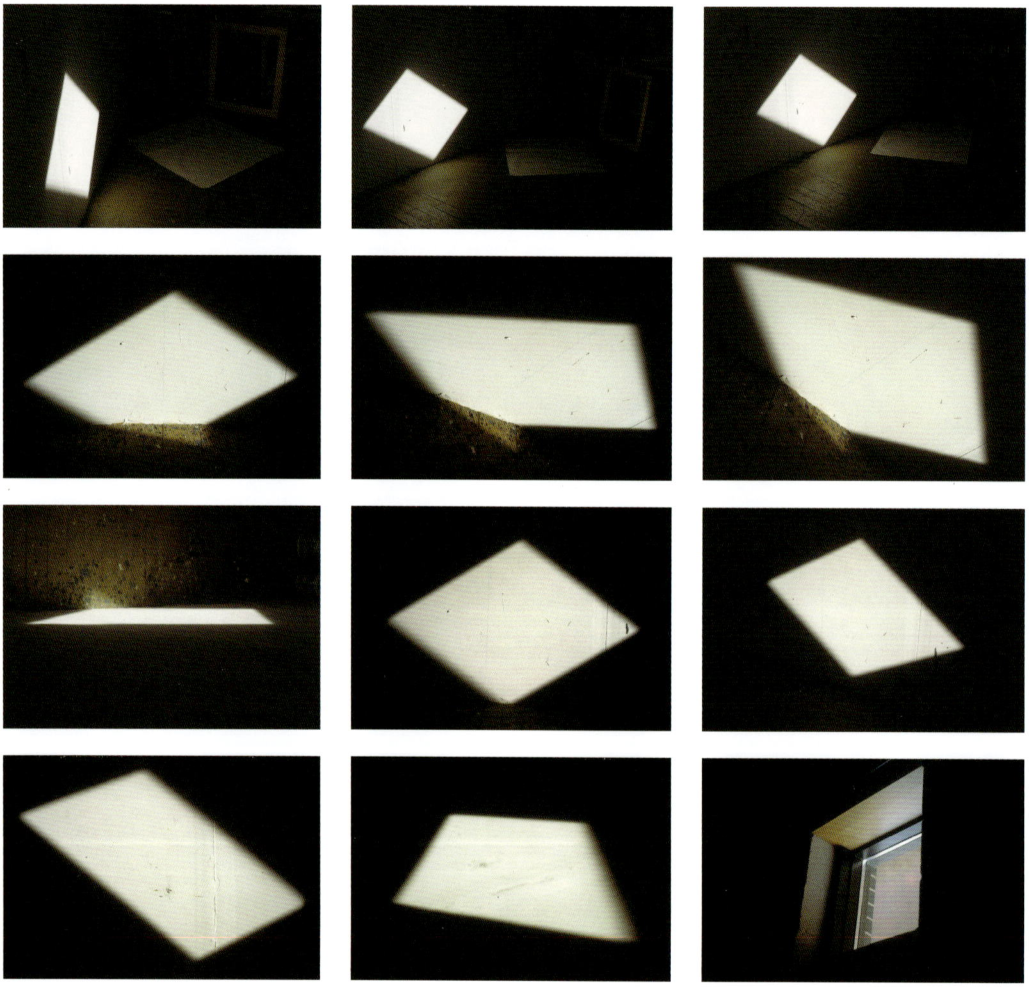

UNTITLED (STUDIO SHOTS, 1998), 1998–2010 (detail)

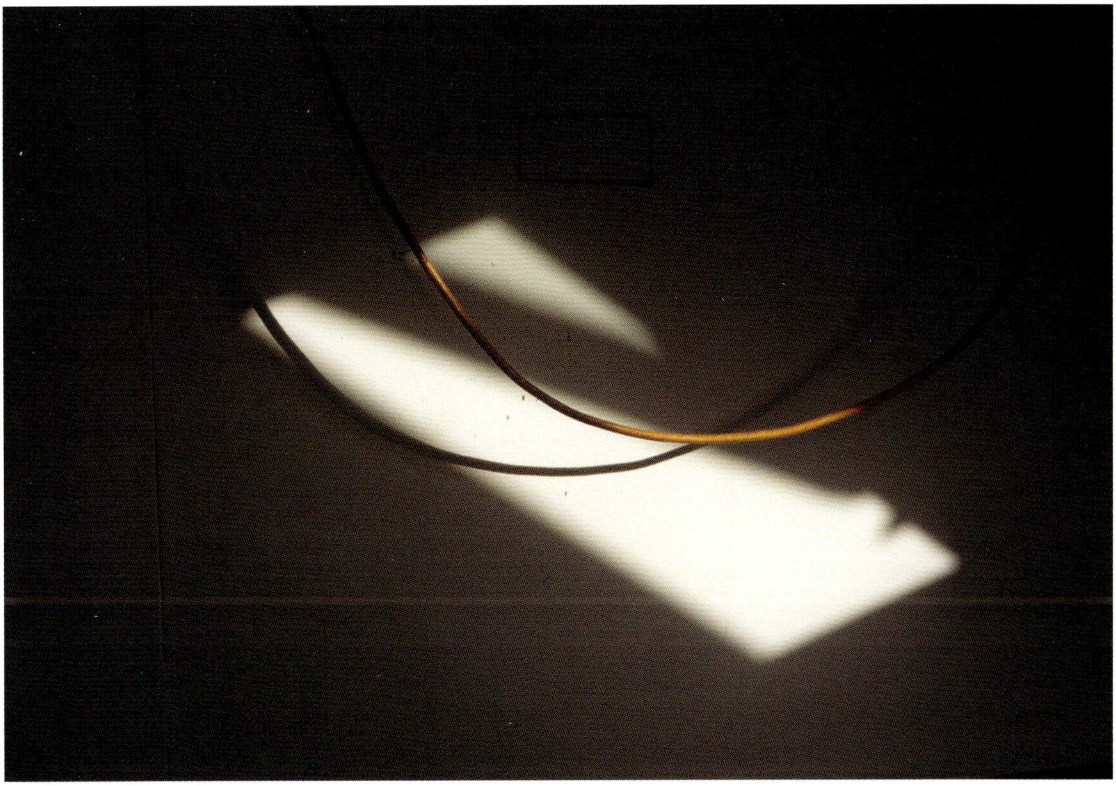

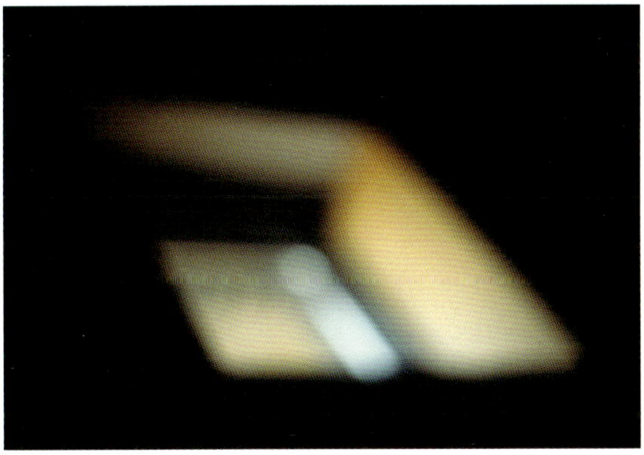

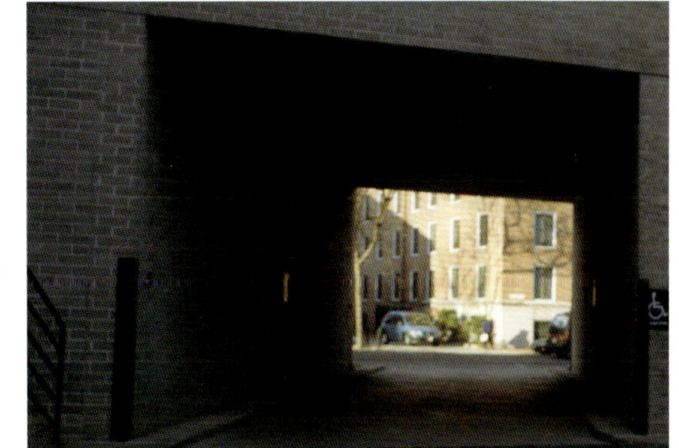

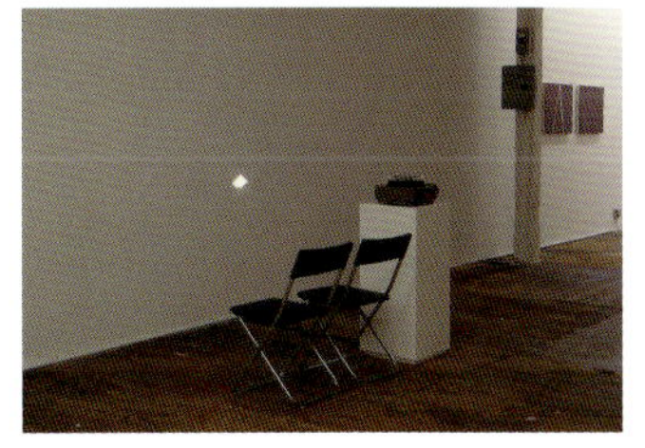

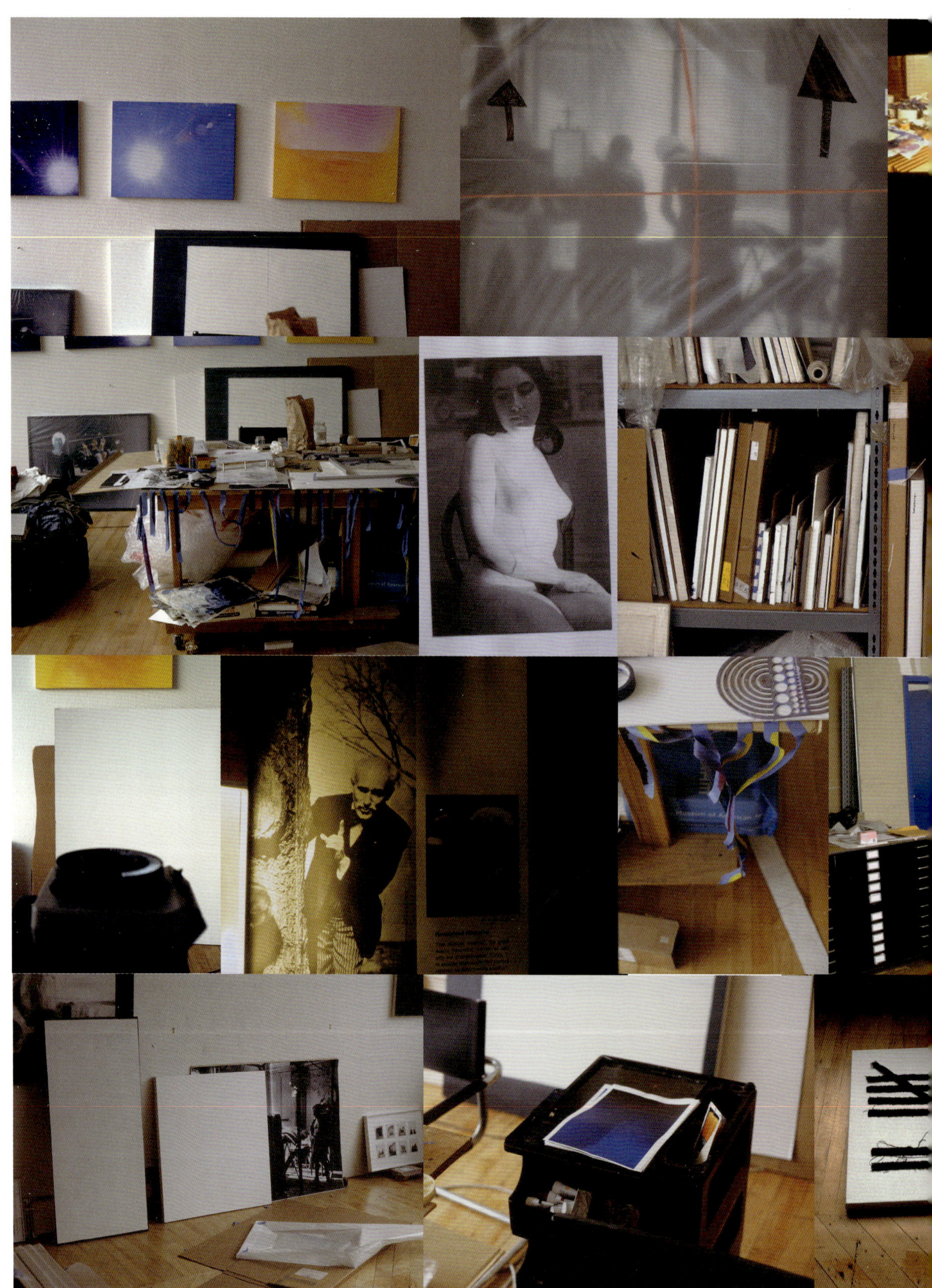

UNTITLED (STUDIO SHOTS, 2010), 2010 (detail)

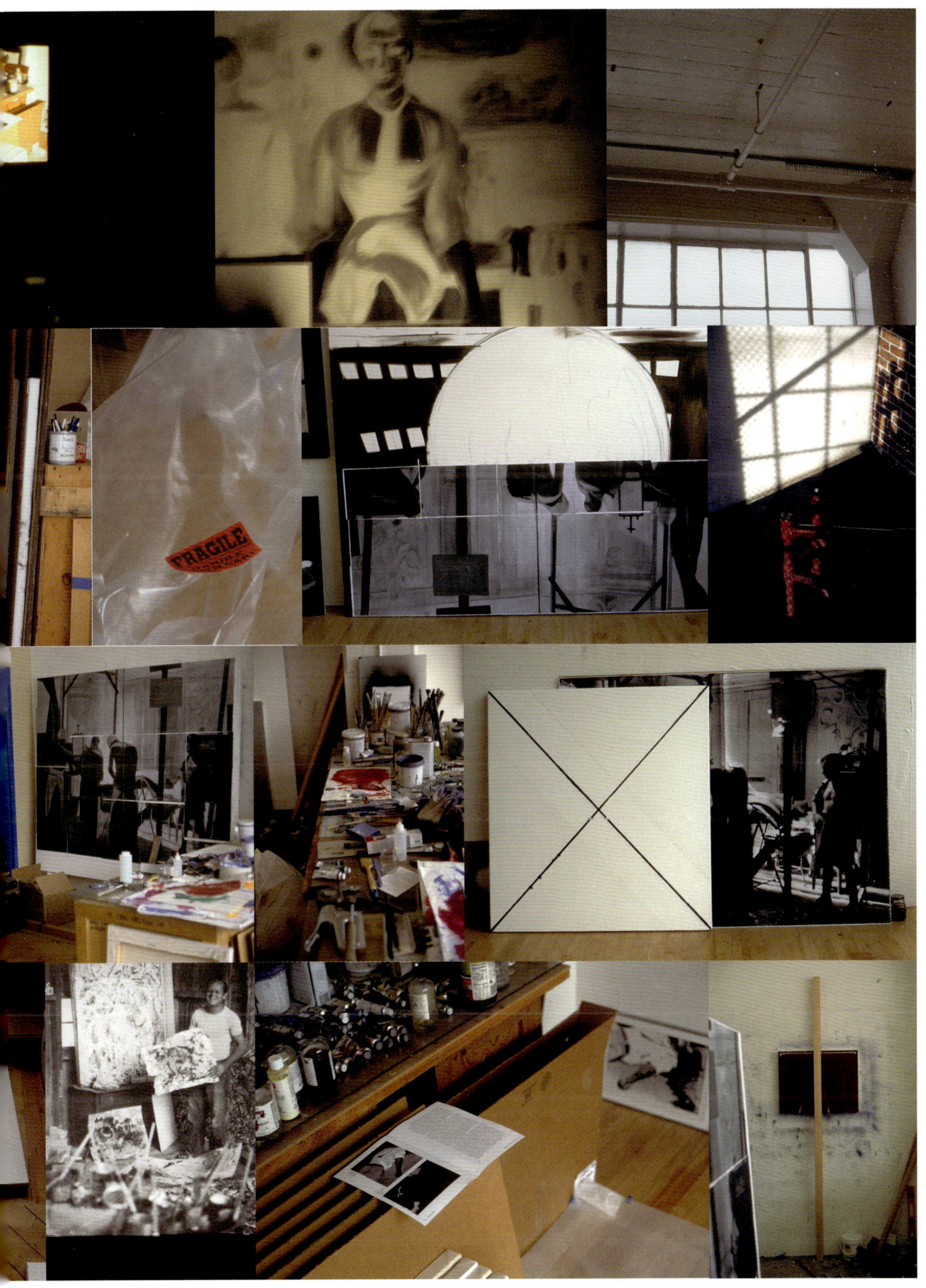

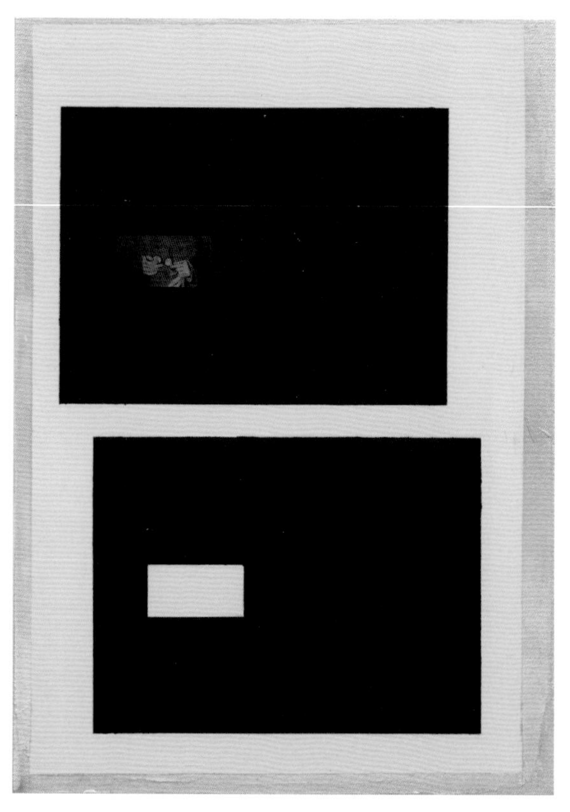

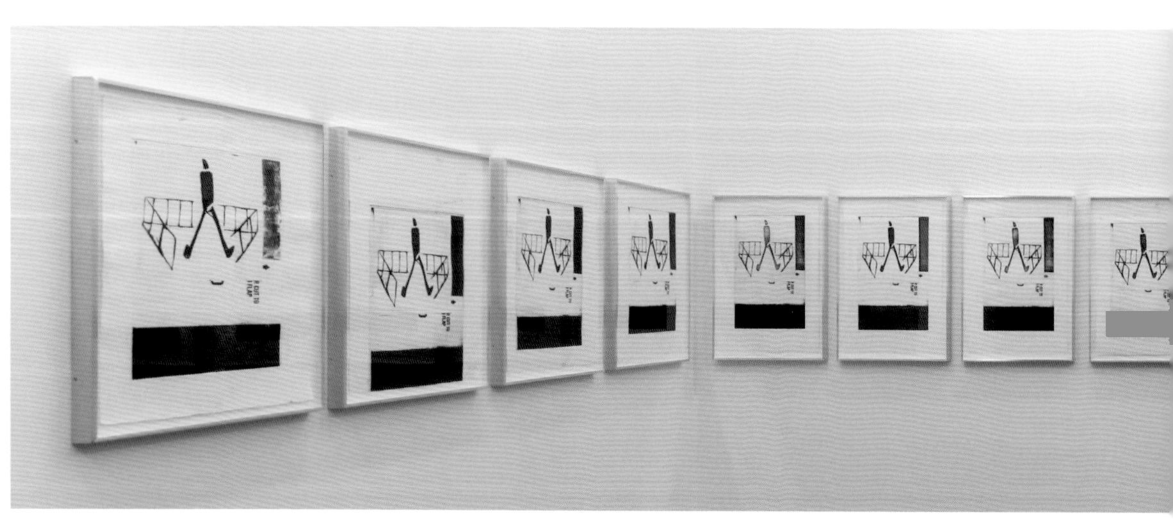

UNTITLED (COLLAGE PAINTING), 2007–2008
UNTITLED (WORKING SPACE), 2006/2009

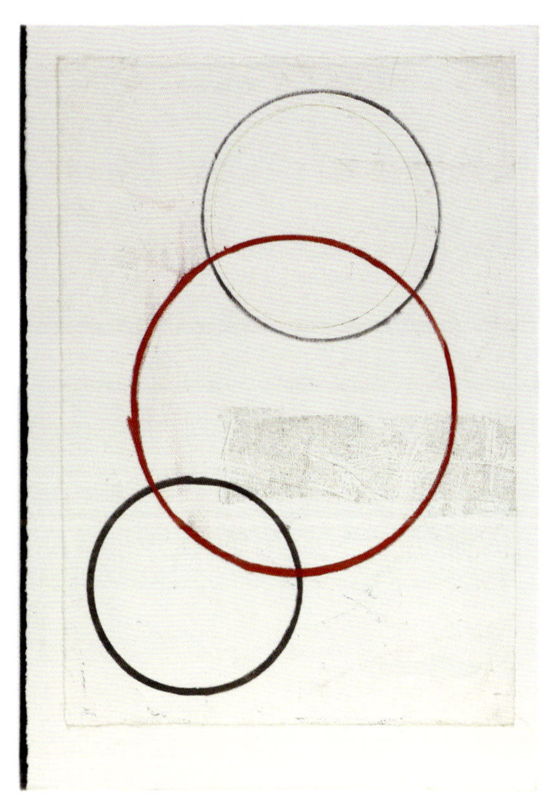

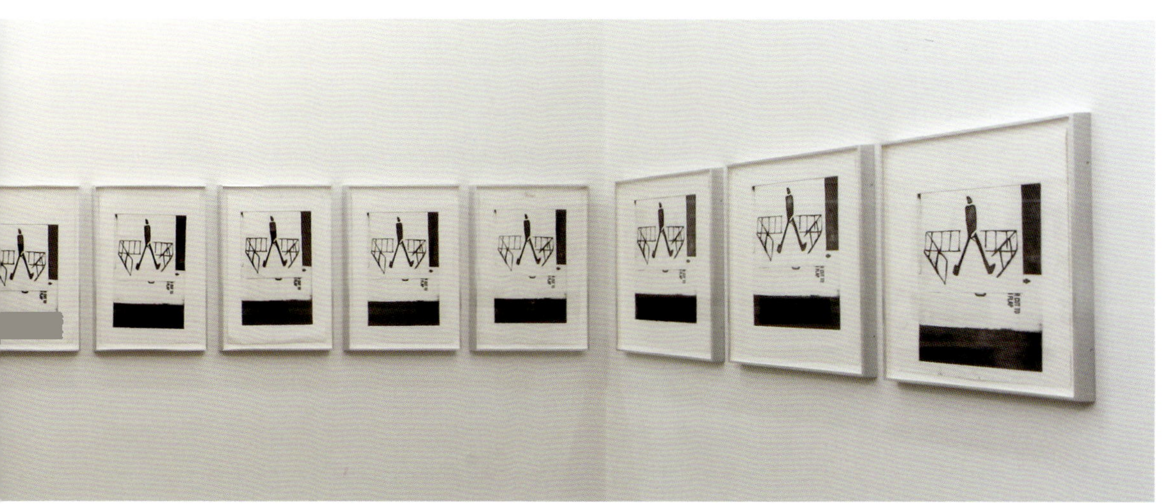

UNTITLED (RINGS), 2008

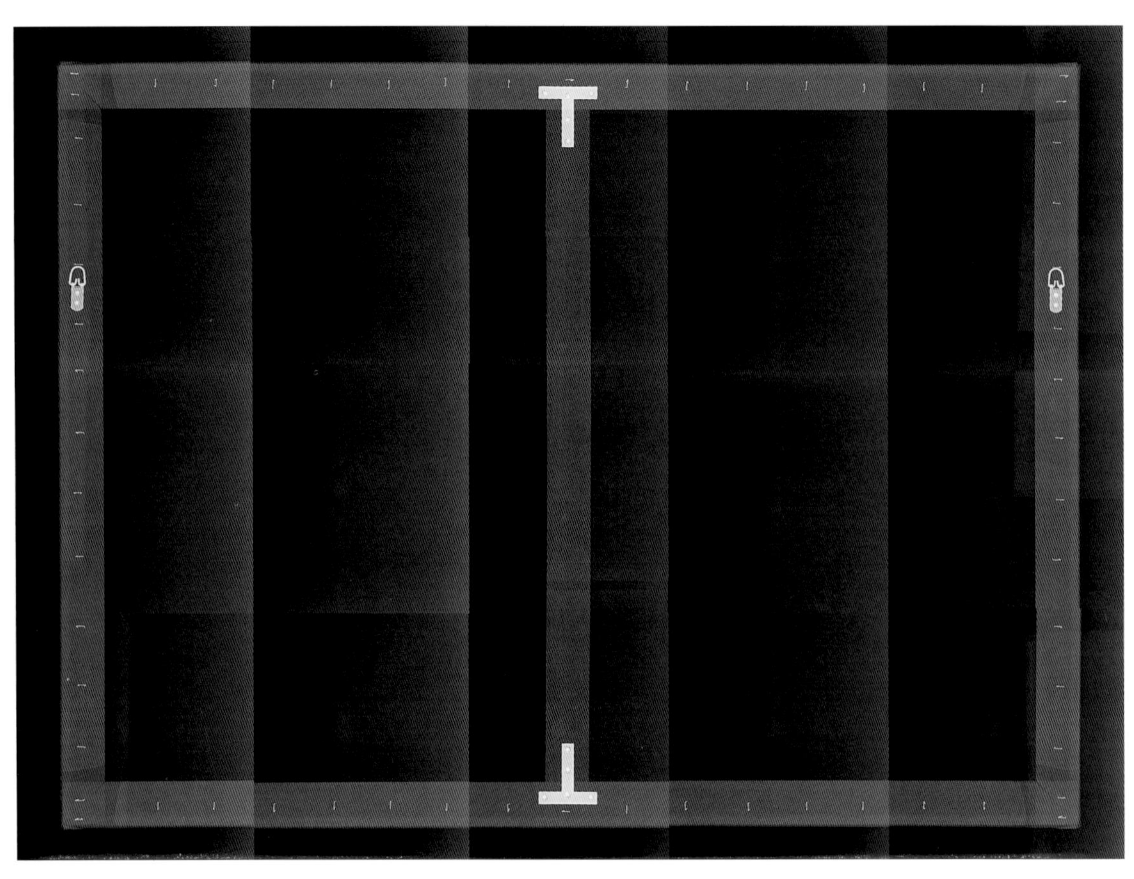

UNTITLED (X-RAY PHOTOGRAPH), 2009

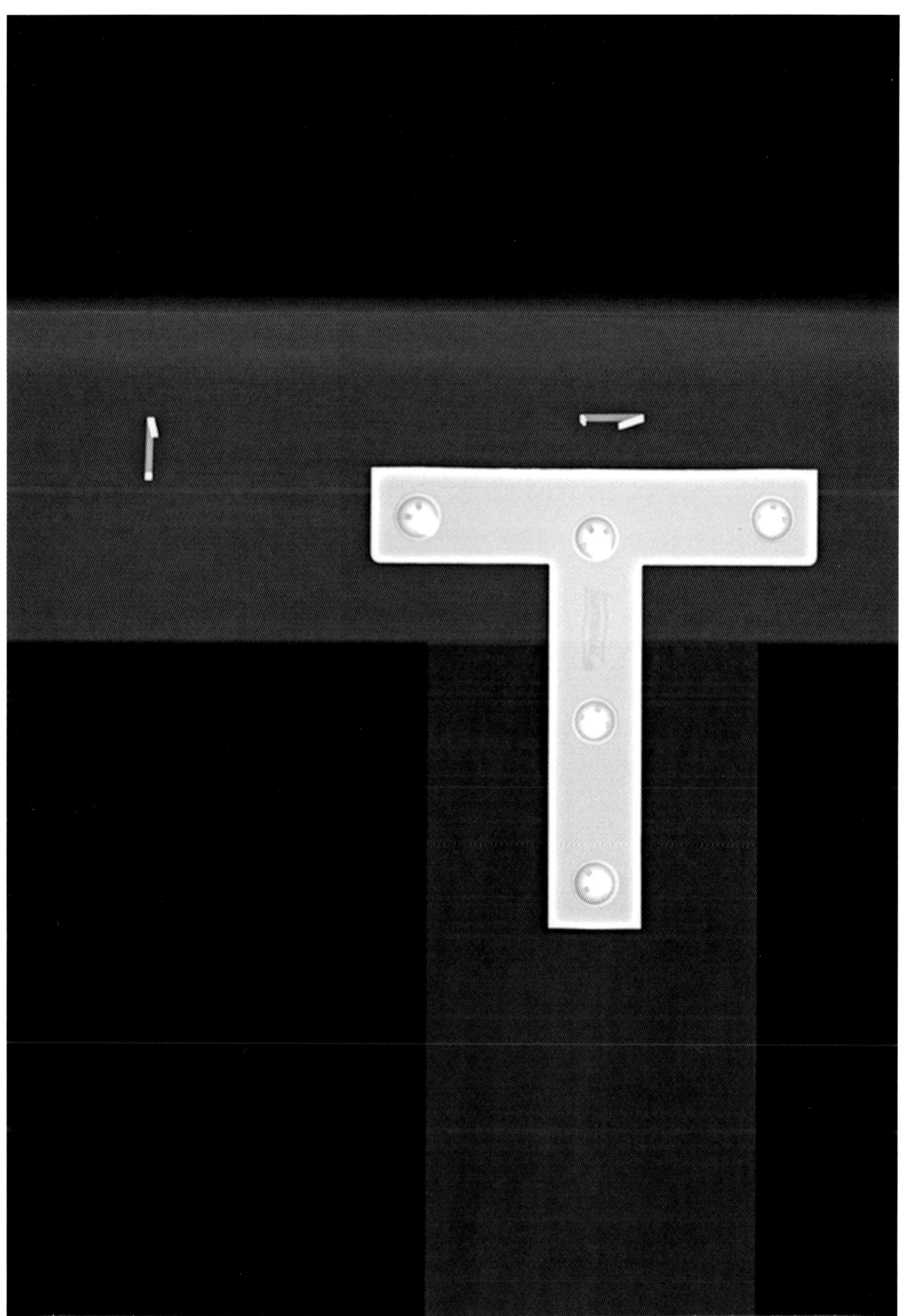

UNTITLED (X-RAY PHOTOGRAPH), 2009 (detail)

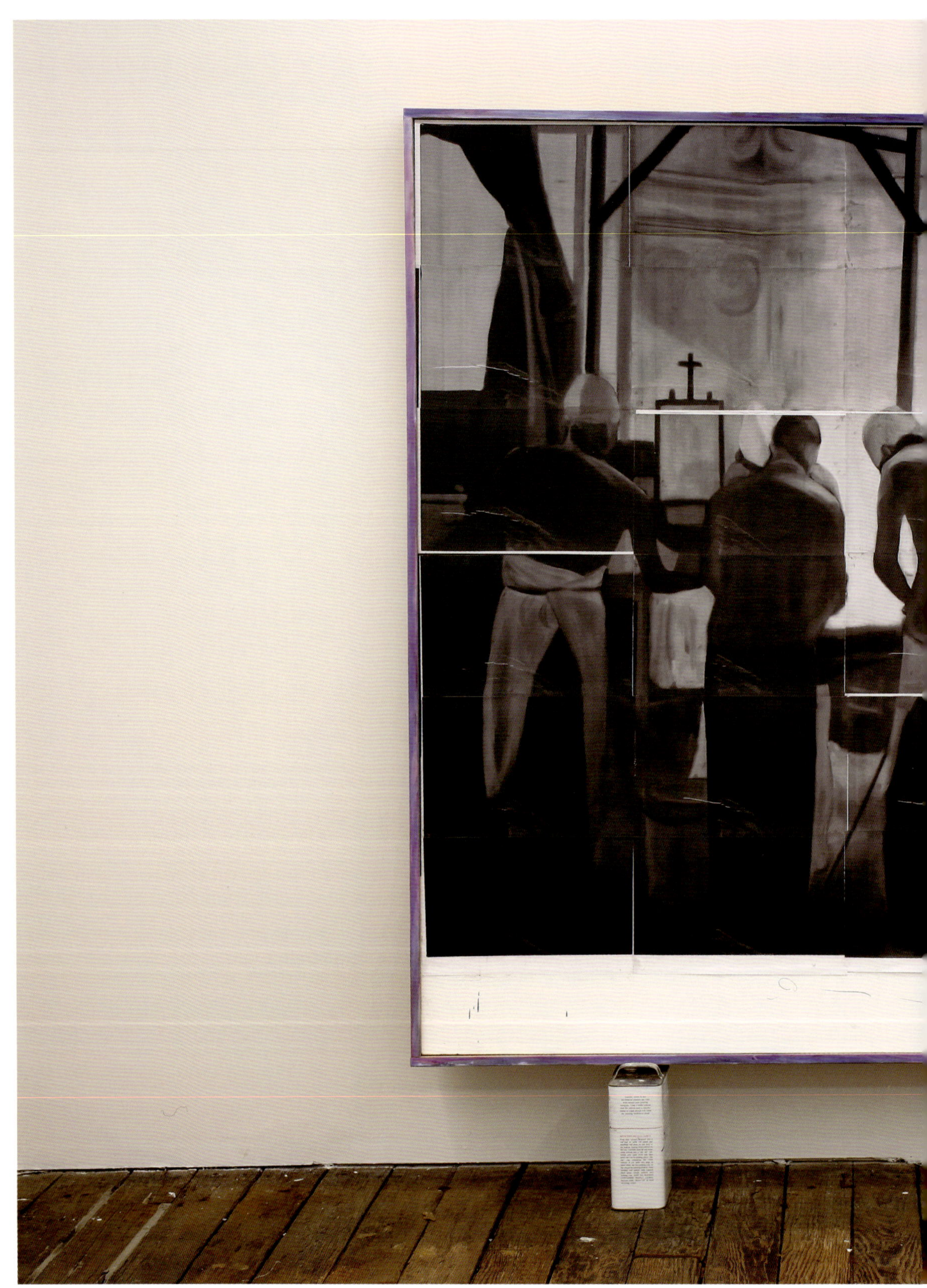

UNTITLED (SURGERY COLLAGE), 2009–2010

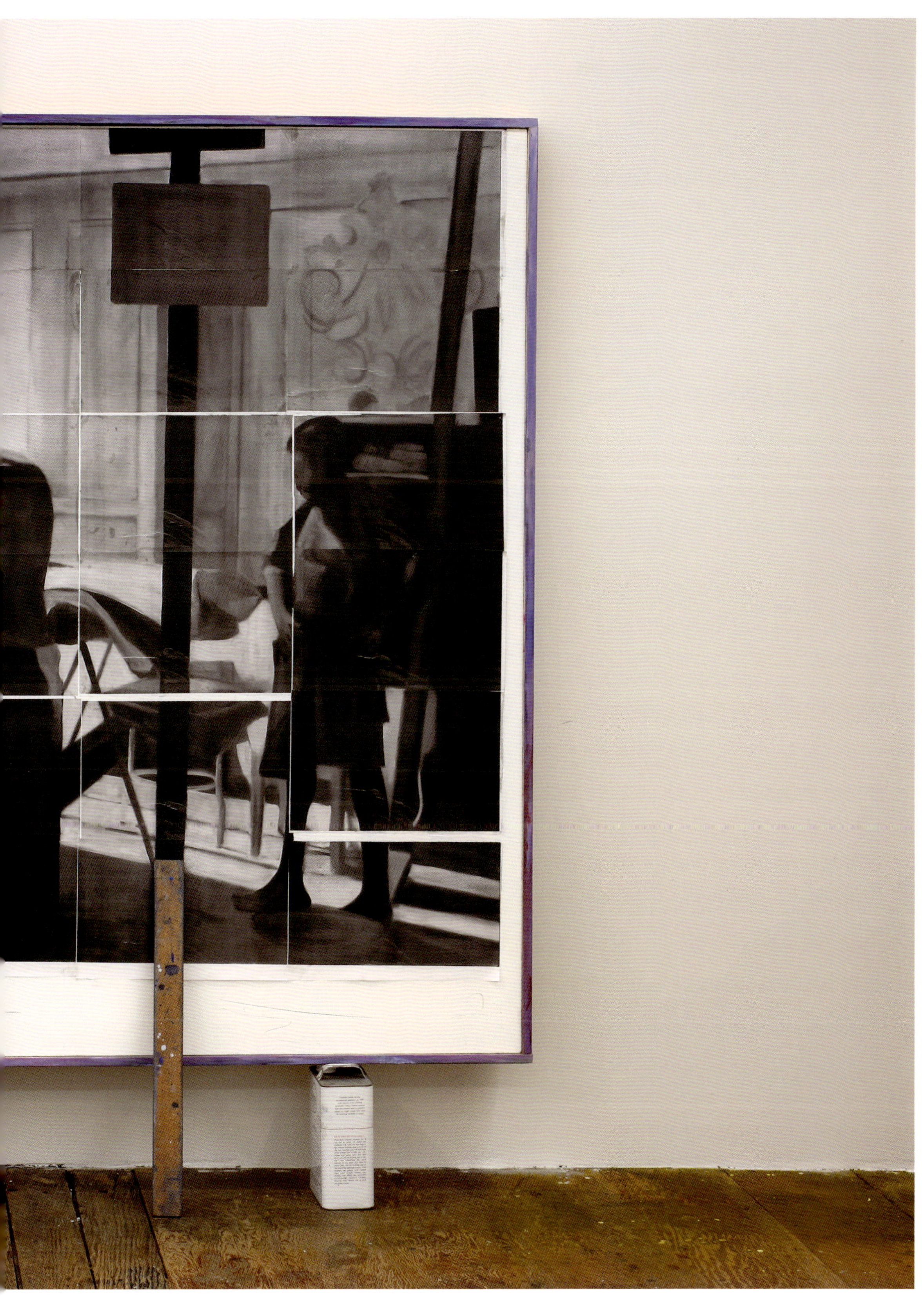

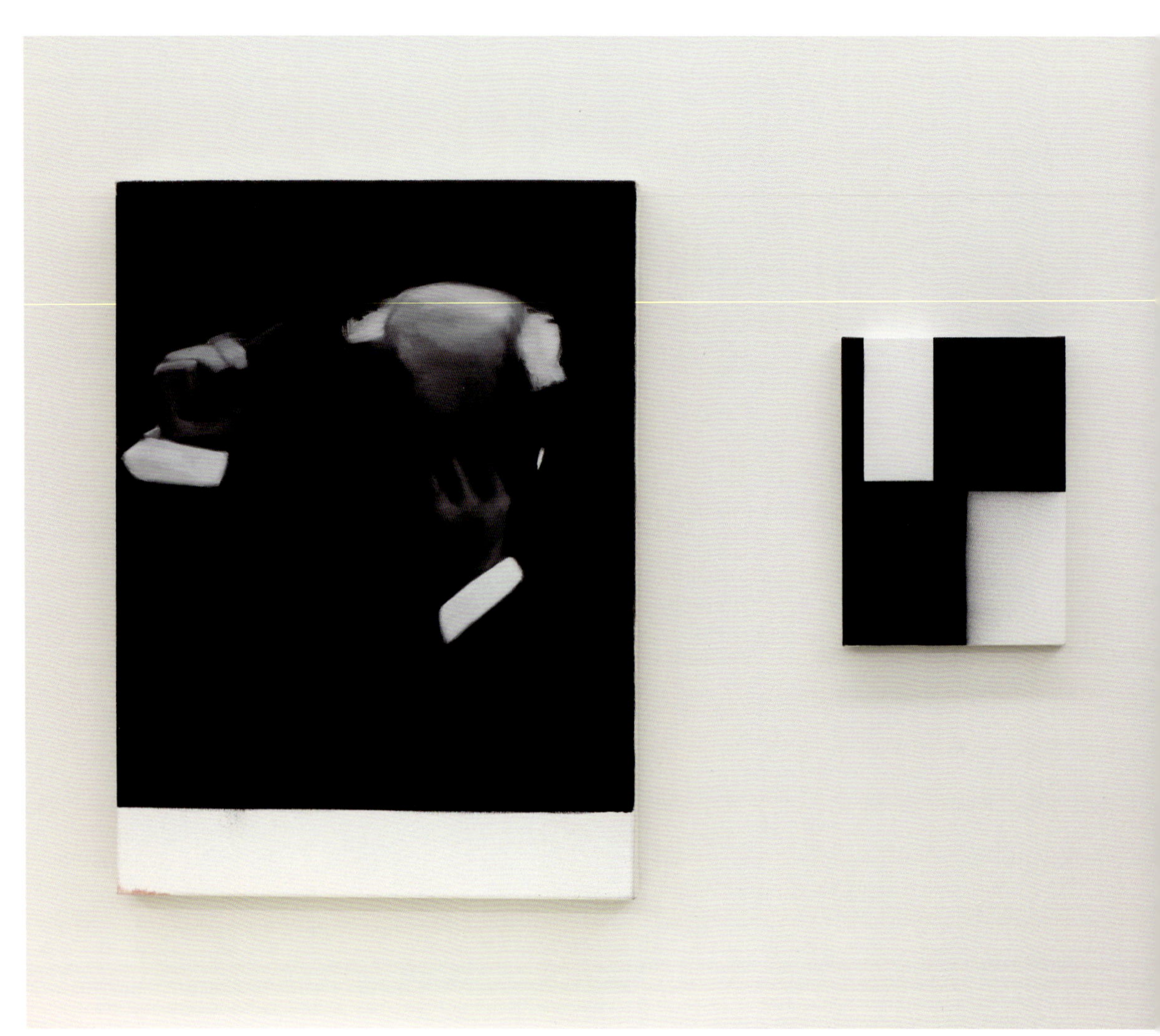

UNITLED (CONDUCTOR WITH MARGIN), 2010
UNTITLED (CANVAS WITH RECTANGLES), 2009
UNTITLED (CANVAS WITH RECTANGLES), 2009

UNTITLED (FILM LEADER, RED X), 2010

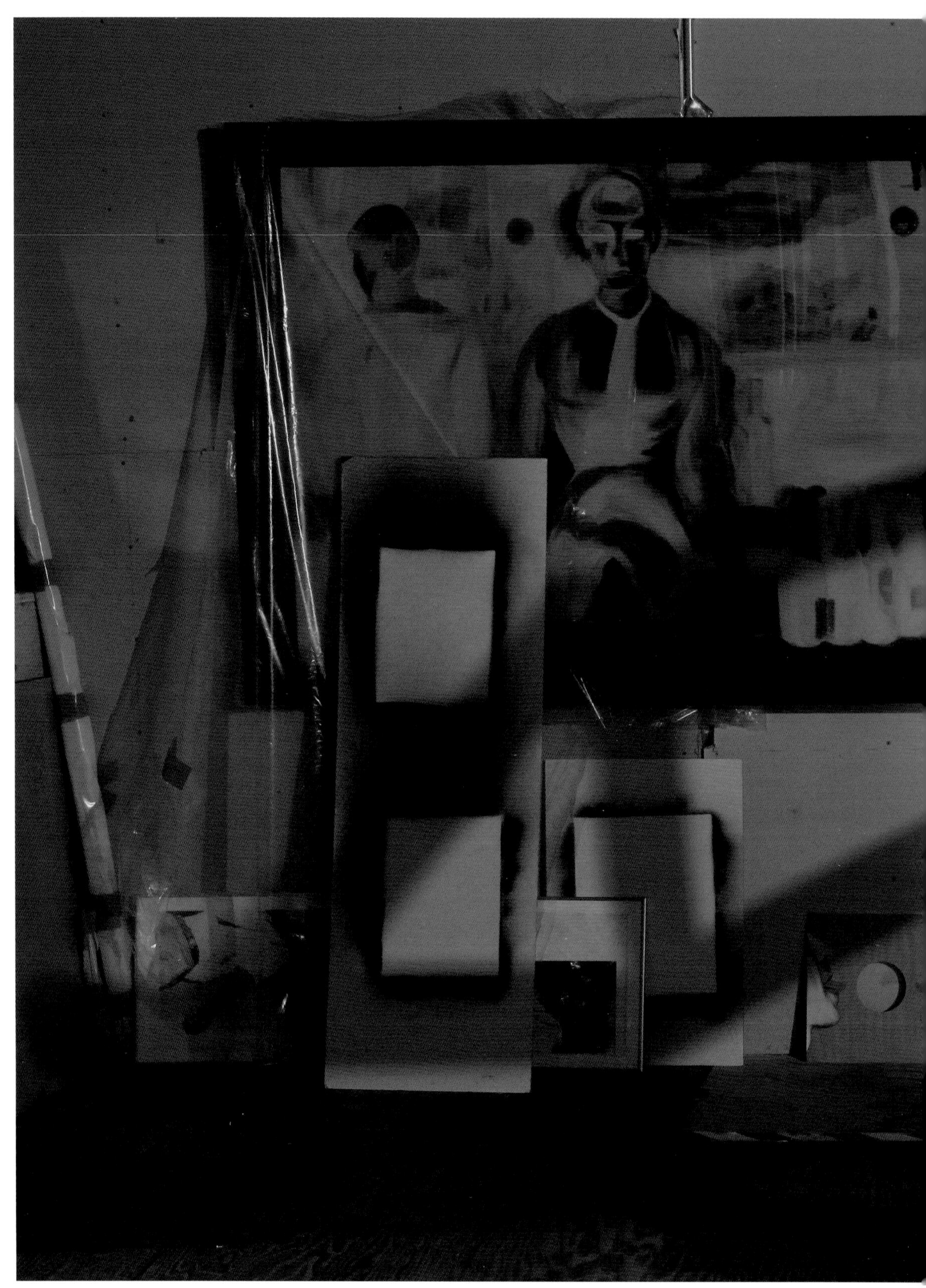

UNTITLED (STOREROOM INSTALLATION), 2010

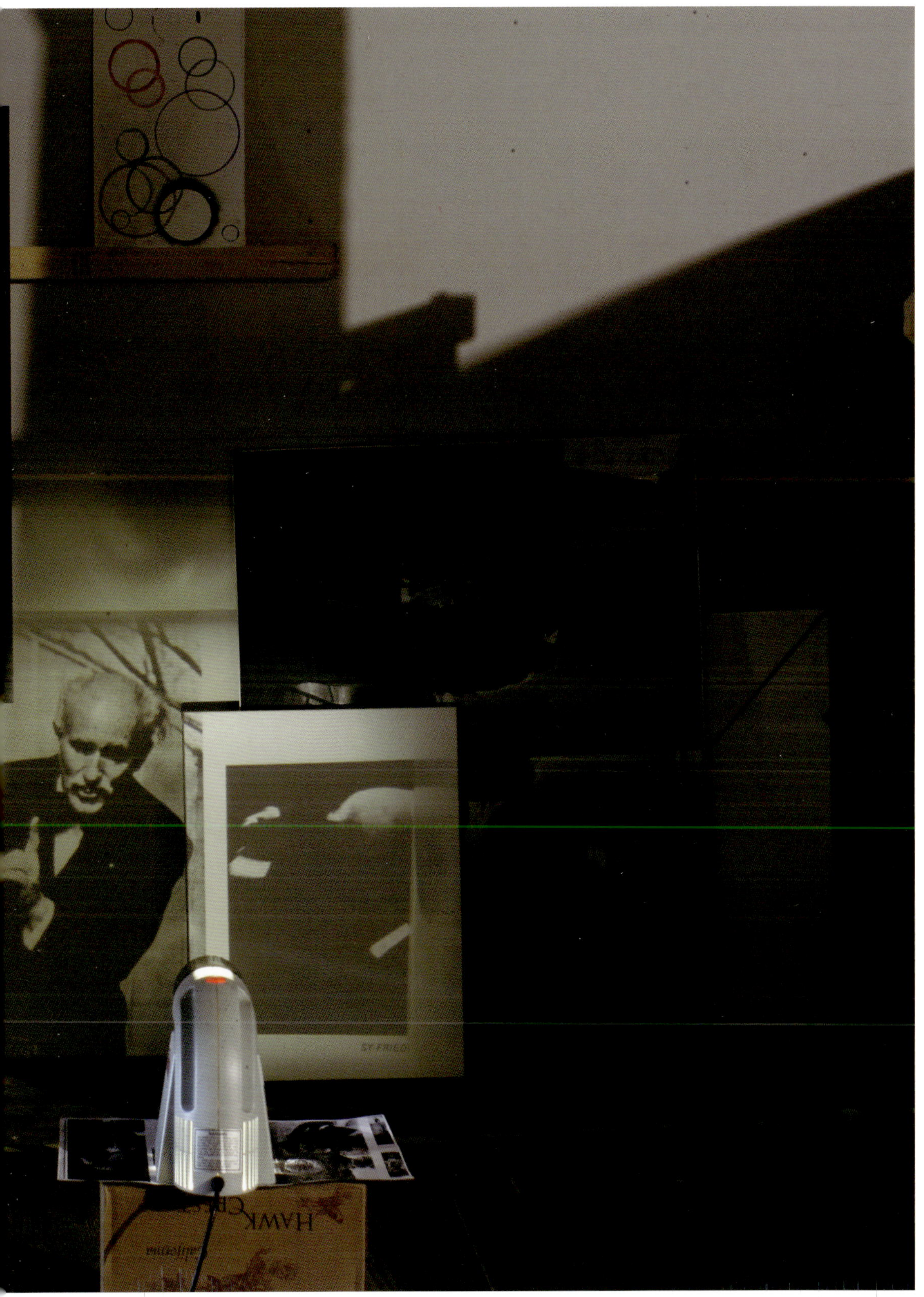

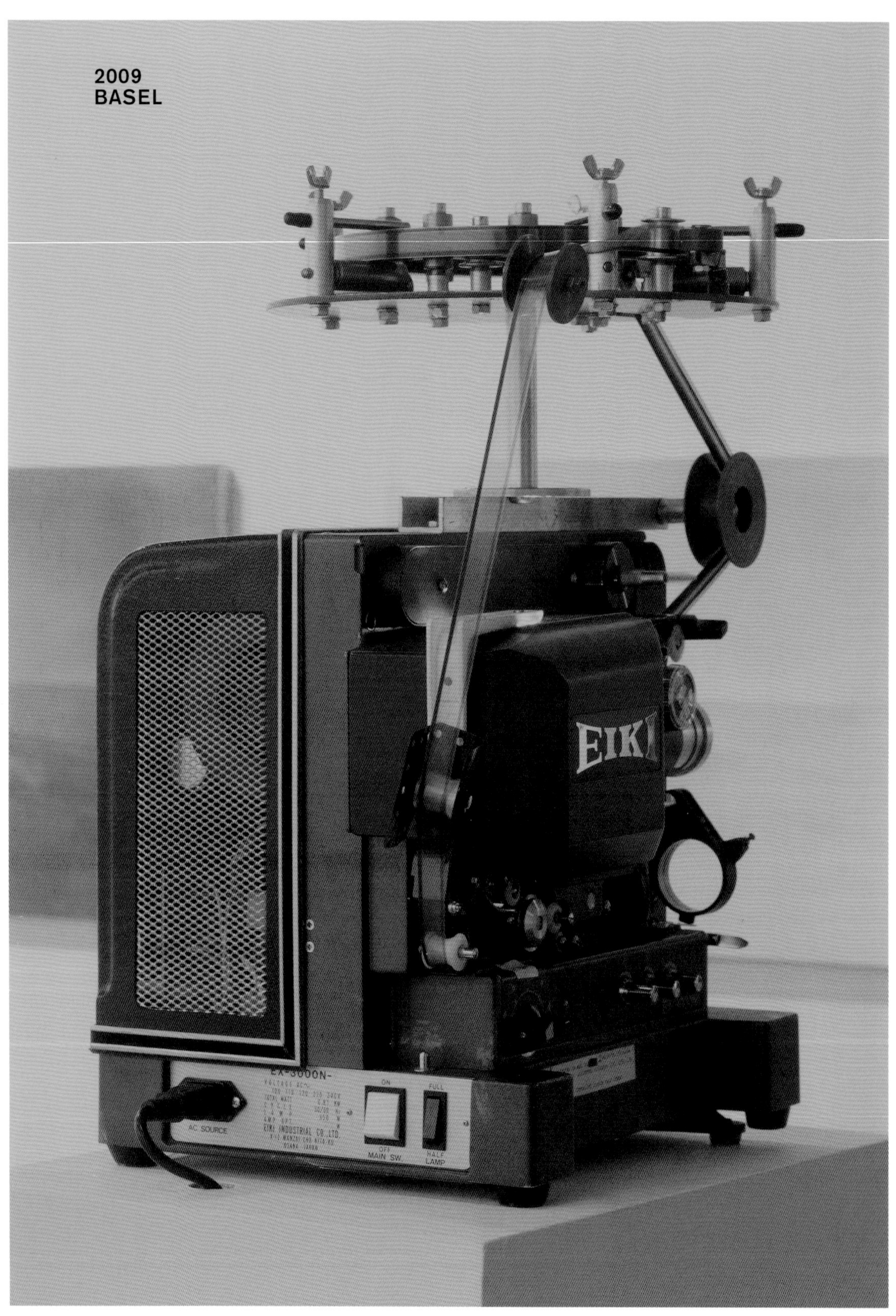

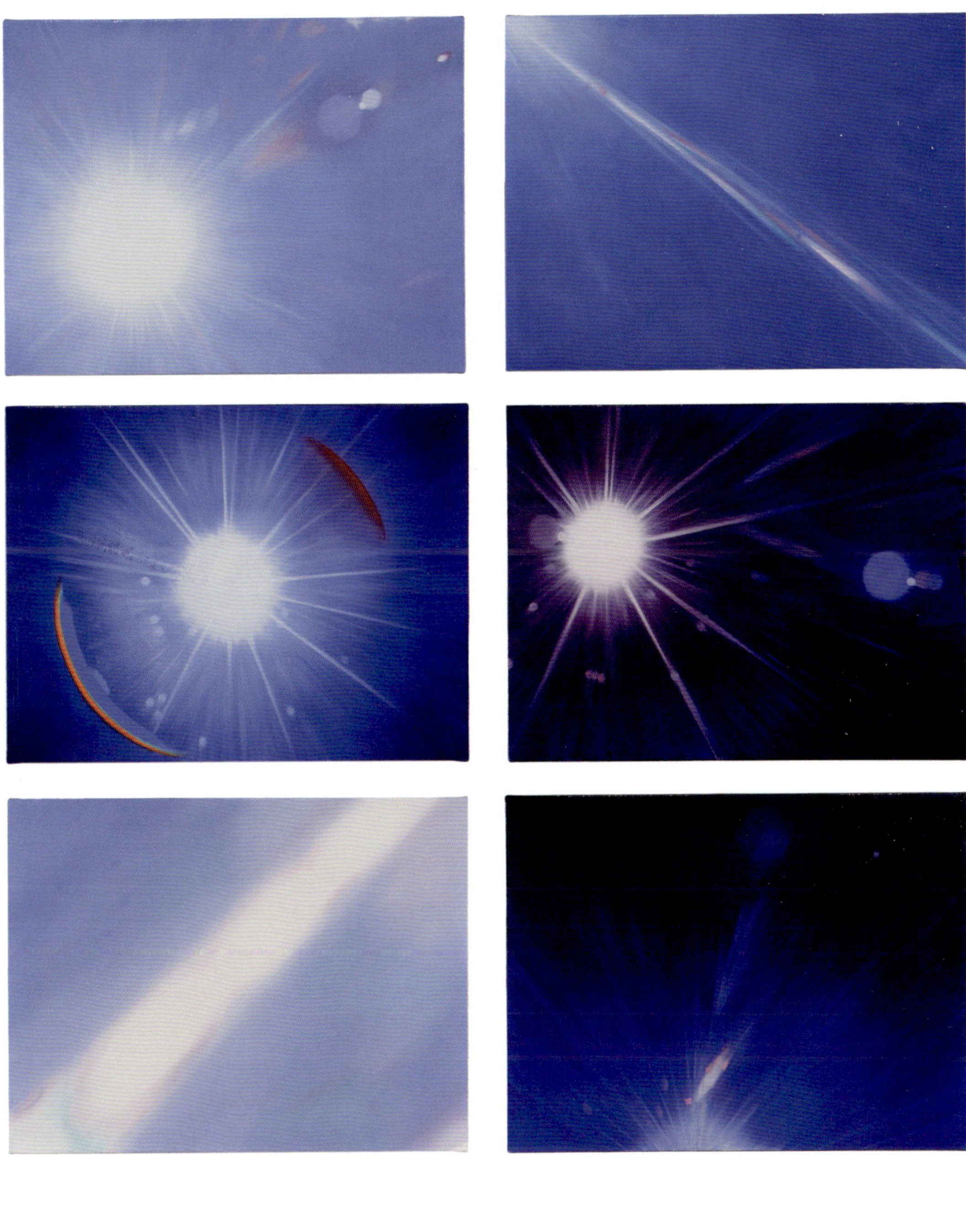

UNTITLED (BASEL LENS FLARE 3919), 2009
UNTITLED (BASEL LENS FLARE 4454), 2009
UNTITLED (BASEL LENS FLARE 4561), 2009

UNTITLED (BASEL LENS FLARE 4019), 2009
UNTITLED (BASEL LENS FLARE 4496), 2009
UNTITLED (BASEL LENS FLARE 5236), 2009

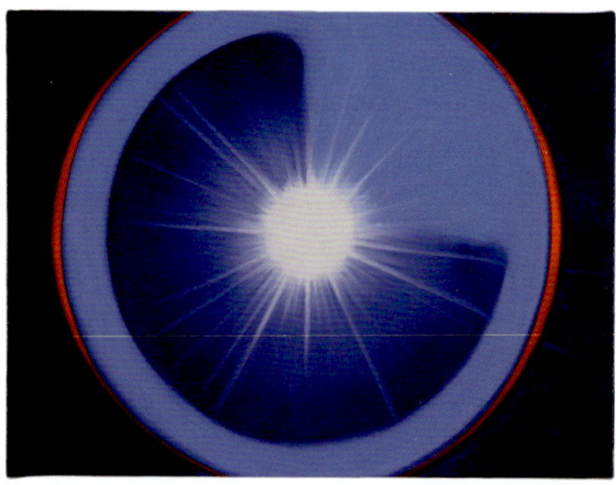
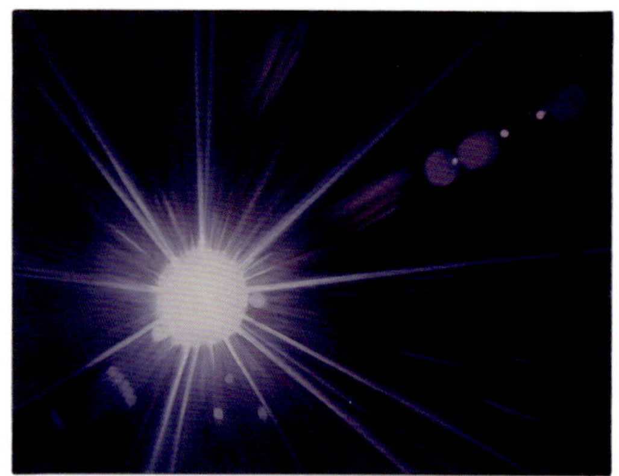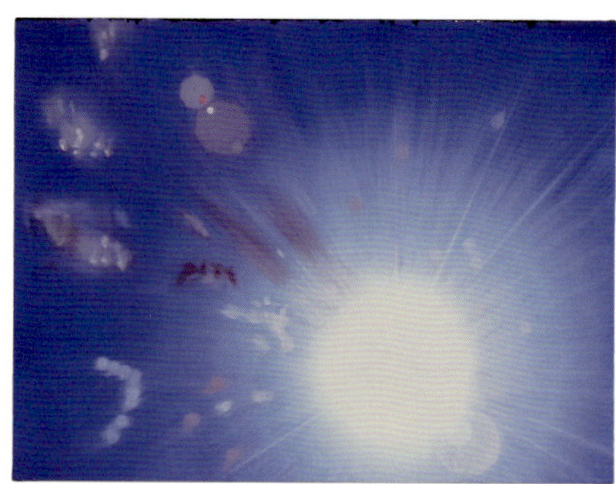

UNTITLED (BASEL LENS FLARE 5382), 2009
UNTITLED (BASEL LENS FLARE 6198), 2009
UNTITLED (BASEL LENS FLARE 5727), 2009
UNTITLED (BASEL LENS FLARE 6362), 2009

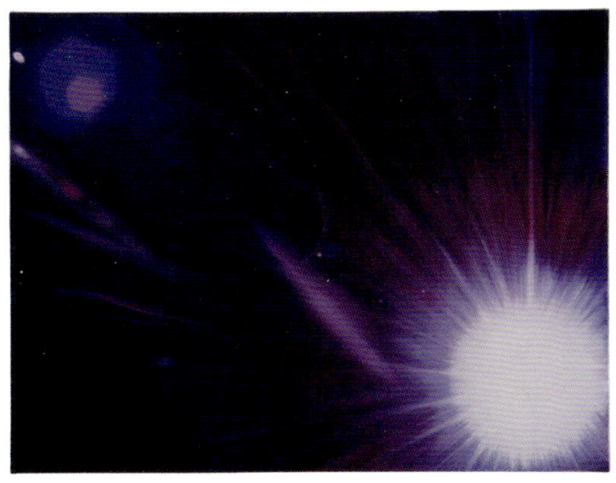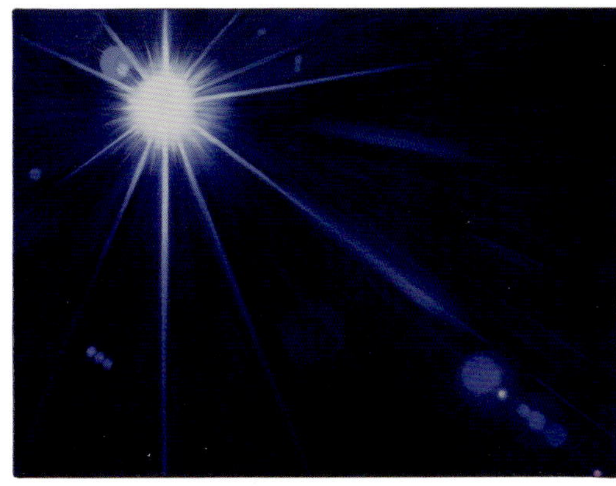

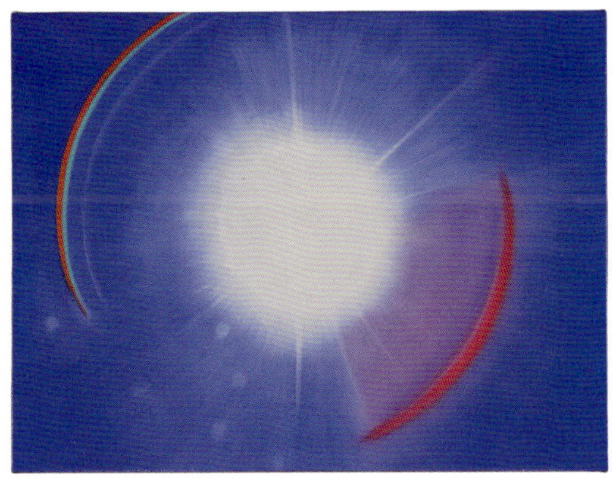

UNTITLED (BASEL LENS FLARE 5950), 2009
UNTITLED (BASEL LENS FLARE 6573), 2009

UNTITLED (BASEL LENS FLARE 6084), 2009
UNTITLED (BASEL LENS FLARE 6734), 2009

 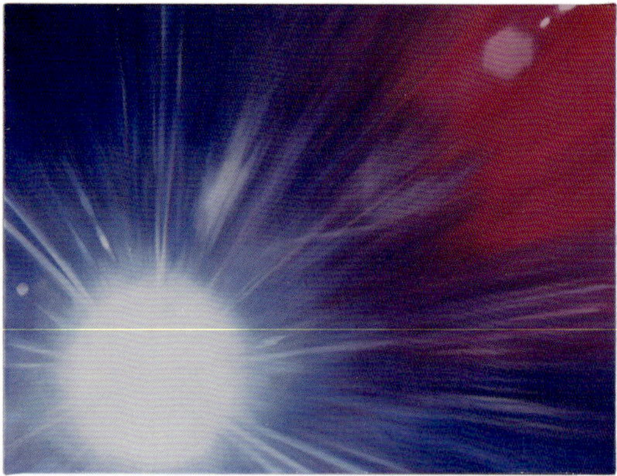

UNTITLED (BASEL LENS FLARE 6761), 2009   *UNTITLED (BASEL LENS FLARE 7497), 2009*

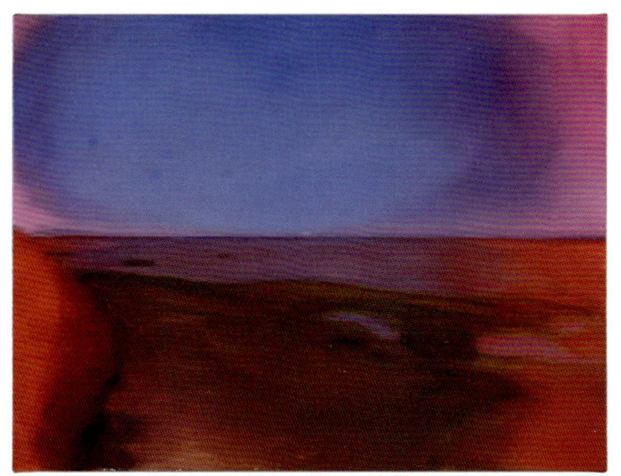 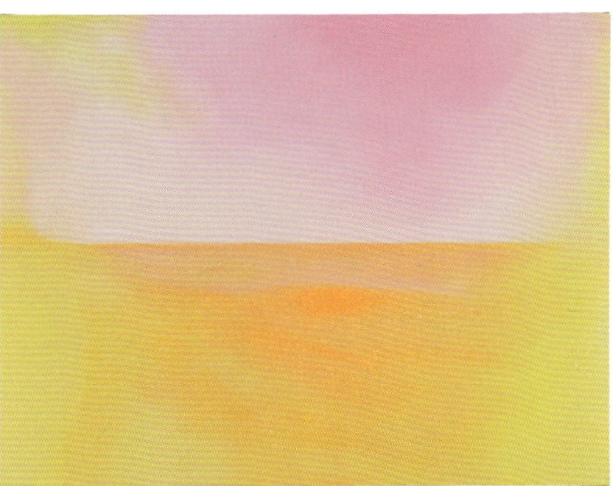

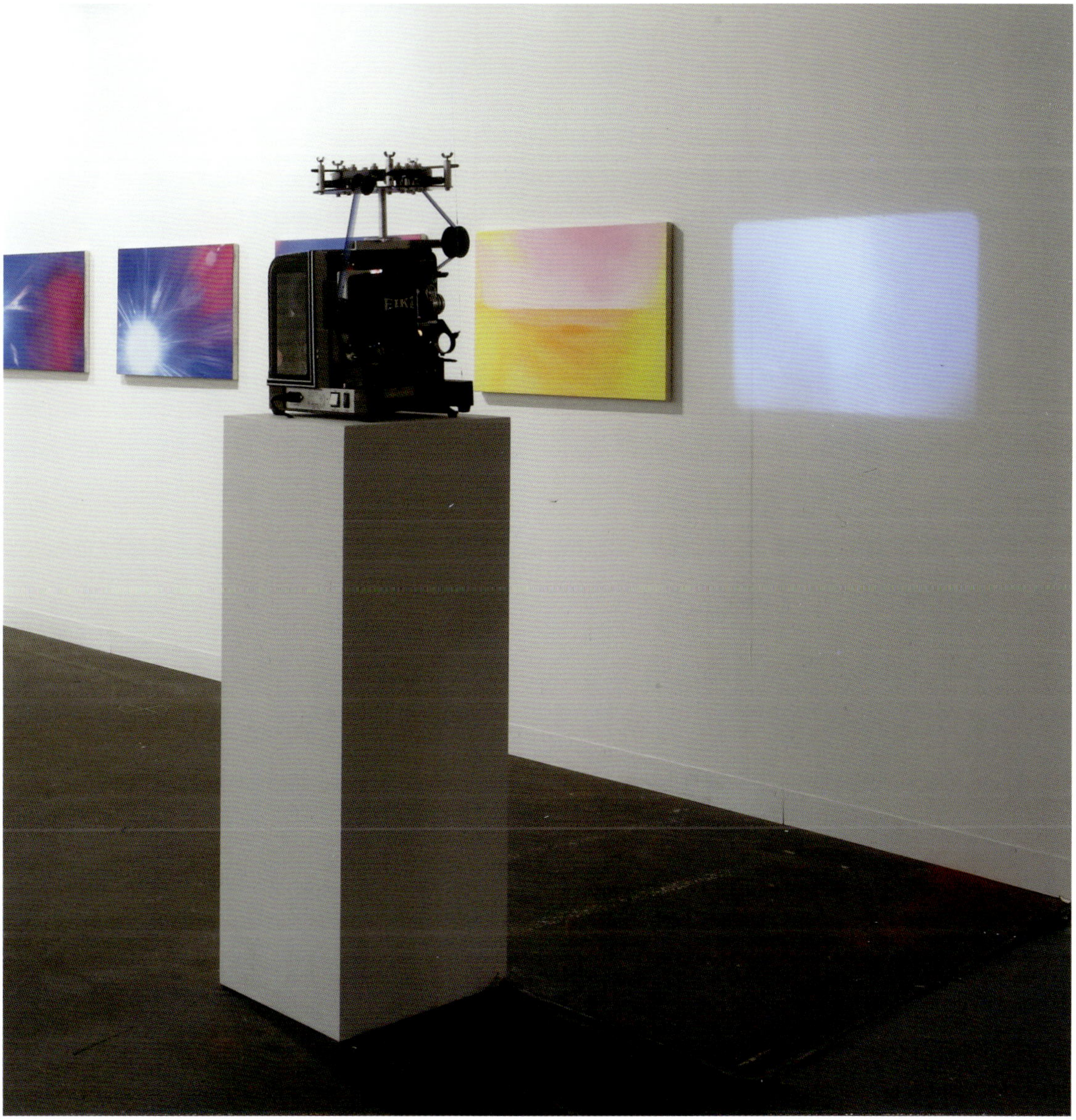

UNTITLED (BASEL LENS FLARE 7976), 2009
LENS FLARE, 2008–09

UNTITLED (BASEL LENS FLARE 8017), 2009

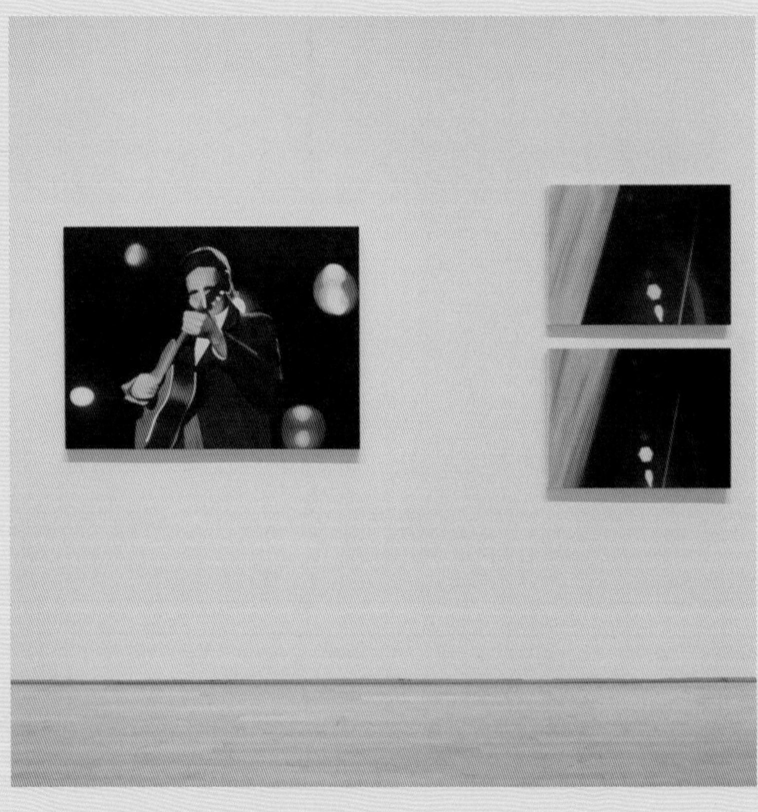

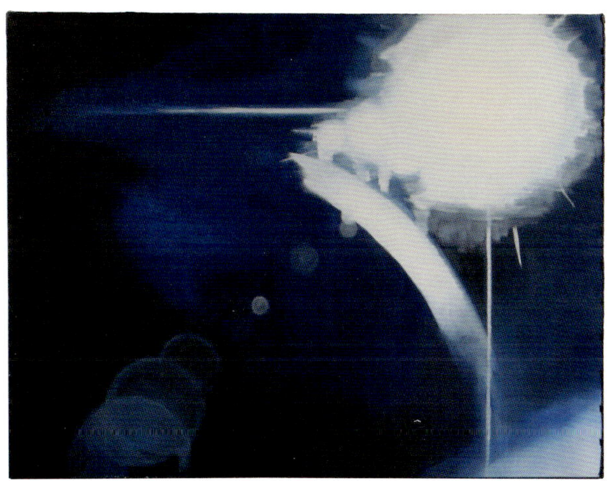

UNTITLED (LENS FLARE), 2008

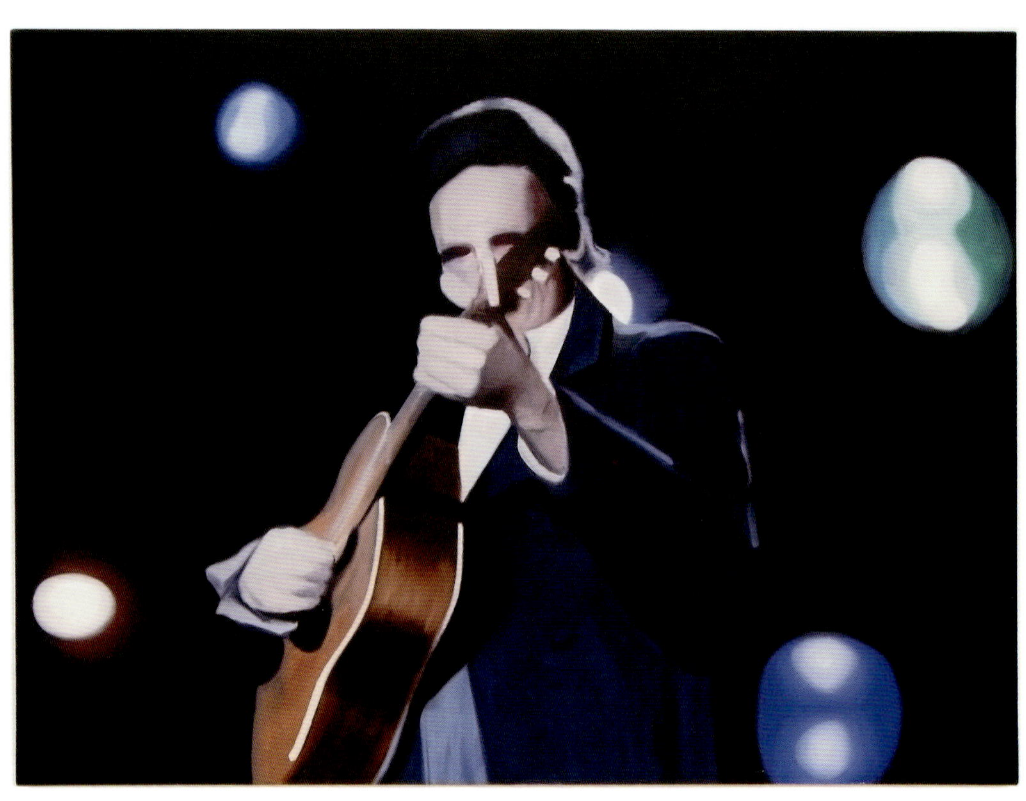

UNTITLED (THE GUITAR PLAYER), 2008

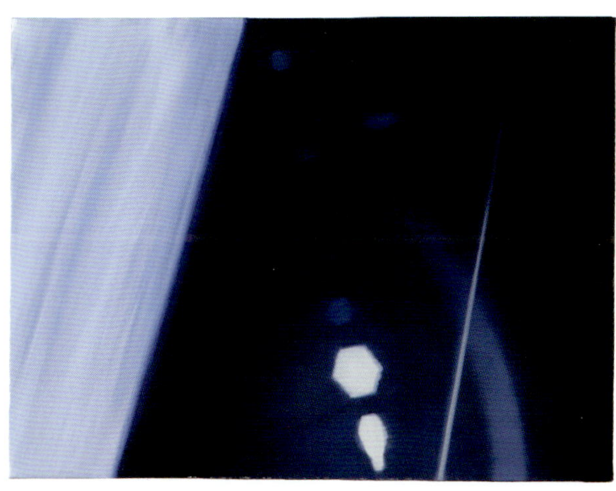

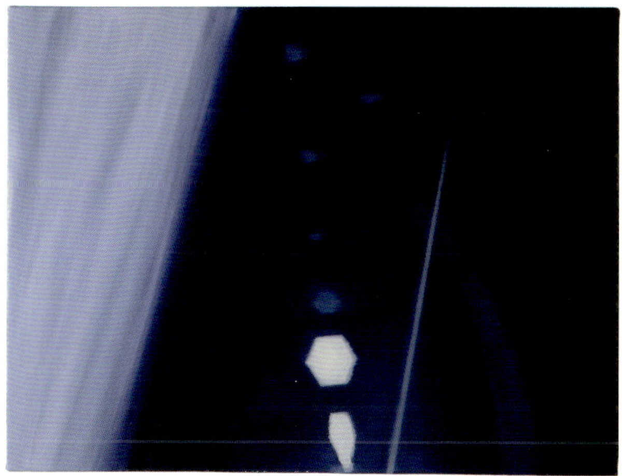

UNTITLED (LENS FLARE), 2008
UNTITLED (LENS FLARE), 2008

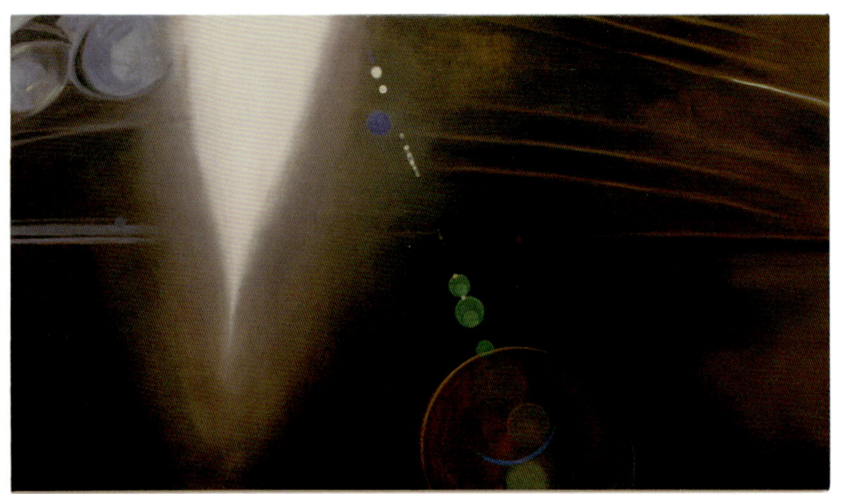

UNTITLED (HD LENS FLARE), 2008

These three works—an X-ray, a painting, and a photograph—take as their source Edouard Manet's iconic painting *A BAR AT THE FOLIES-BERGÈRE* (1882), a work deeply concerned with upending traditional notions of illusionistic representation. Kantor's appropriation and re-presentation of Manet's painting calls upon the fact of vision as subject matter as well as the history of the work itself as a subject of prolific critical discourse. In Kantor's artistic transformations the image becomes more significant as a point of art historical fascination than as a specific composition. Kantor used a conservation X-ray of Manet's painting, an artifact that represents a technological attempt to get beneath the original work's surface, as a starting point for his canvas—offering a view of this widely reproduced image not available via natural vision. This work itself then becomes the seed for a series that examines the structures of images as objects that provide different visual encounters with the same source. Kantor's photograph of his own painting is printed on metallic paper, creating a reflective plane, emphasizing its surface. The X-ray Kantor made of his own painting brings his process full circle. Here we literally get behind the image: seeing canvas attached to stretcher bars, staples, and screws (see p. 240).

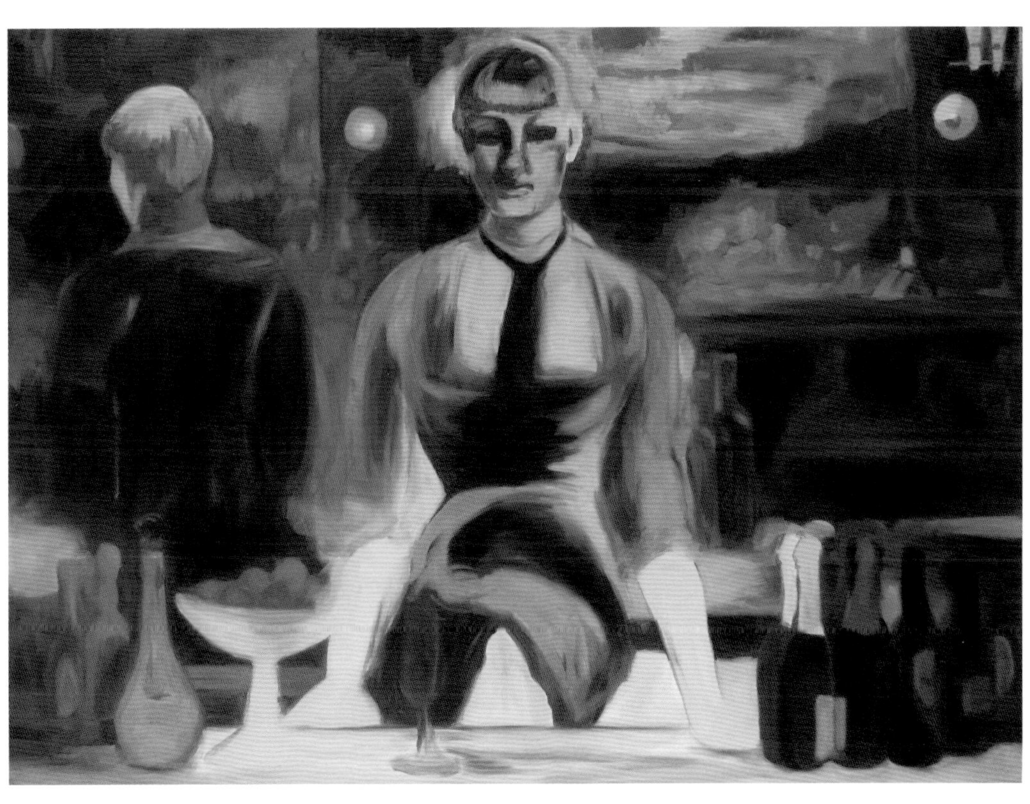

UNTITLED (THE BAR), 2007

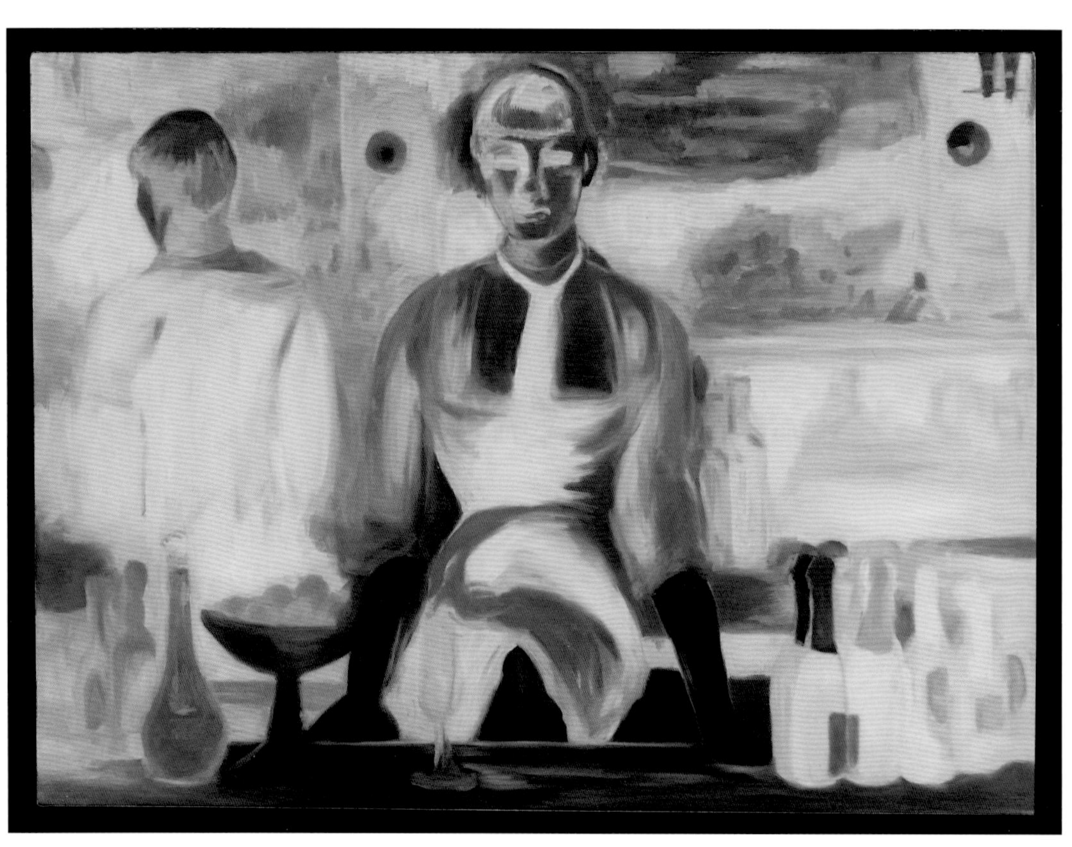

UNTITLED (THE BAR), 2009

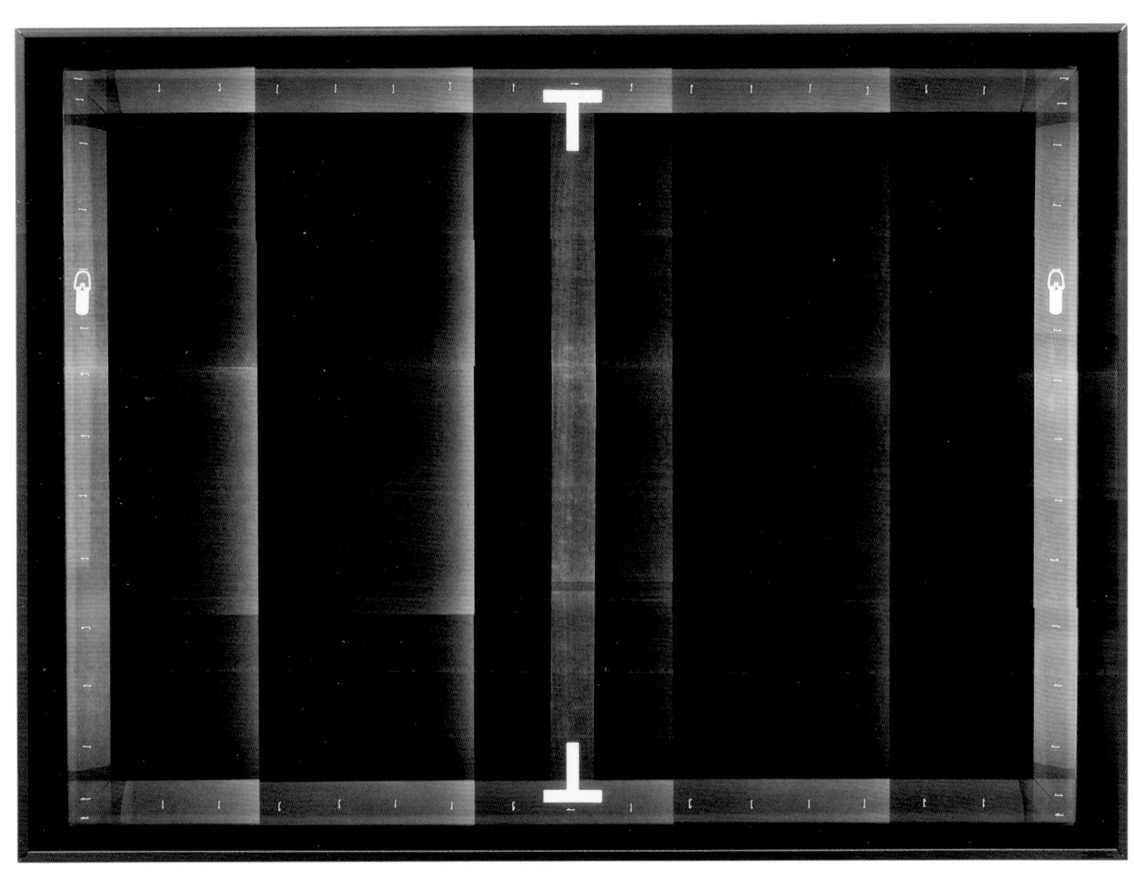

UNTITLED (X-RAY), 2009

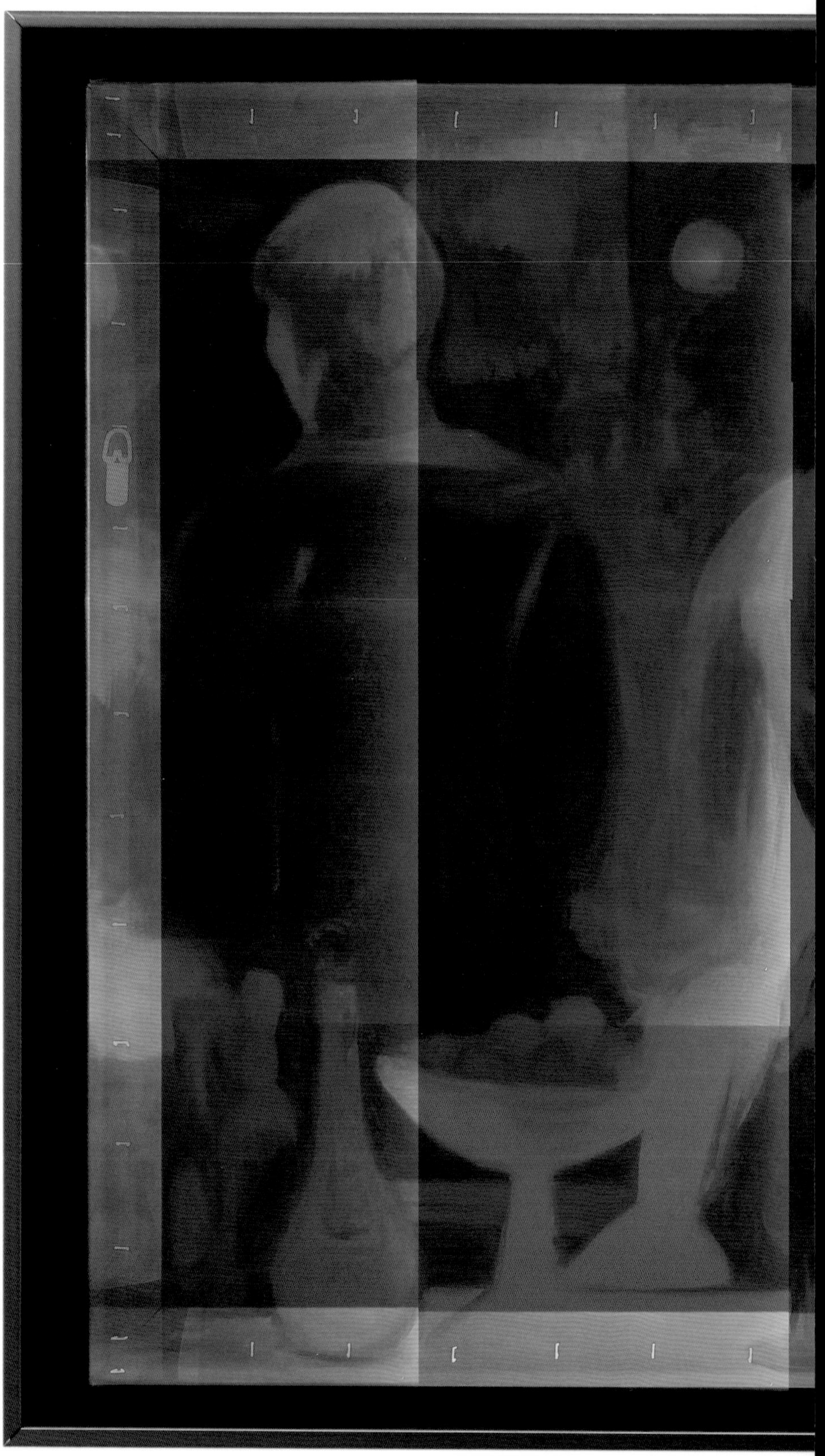

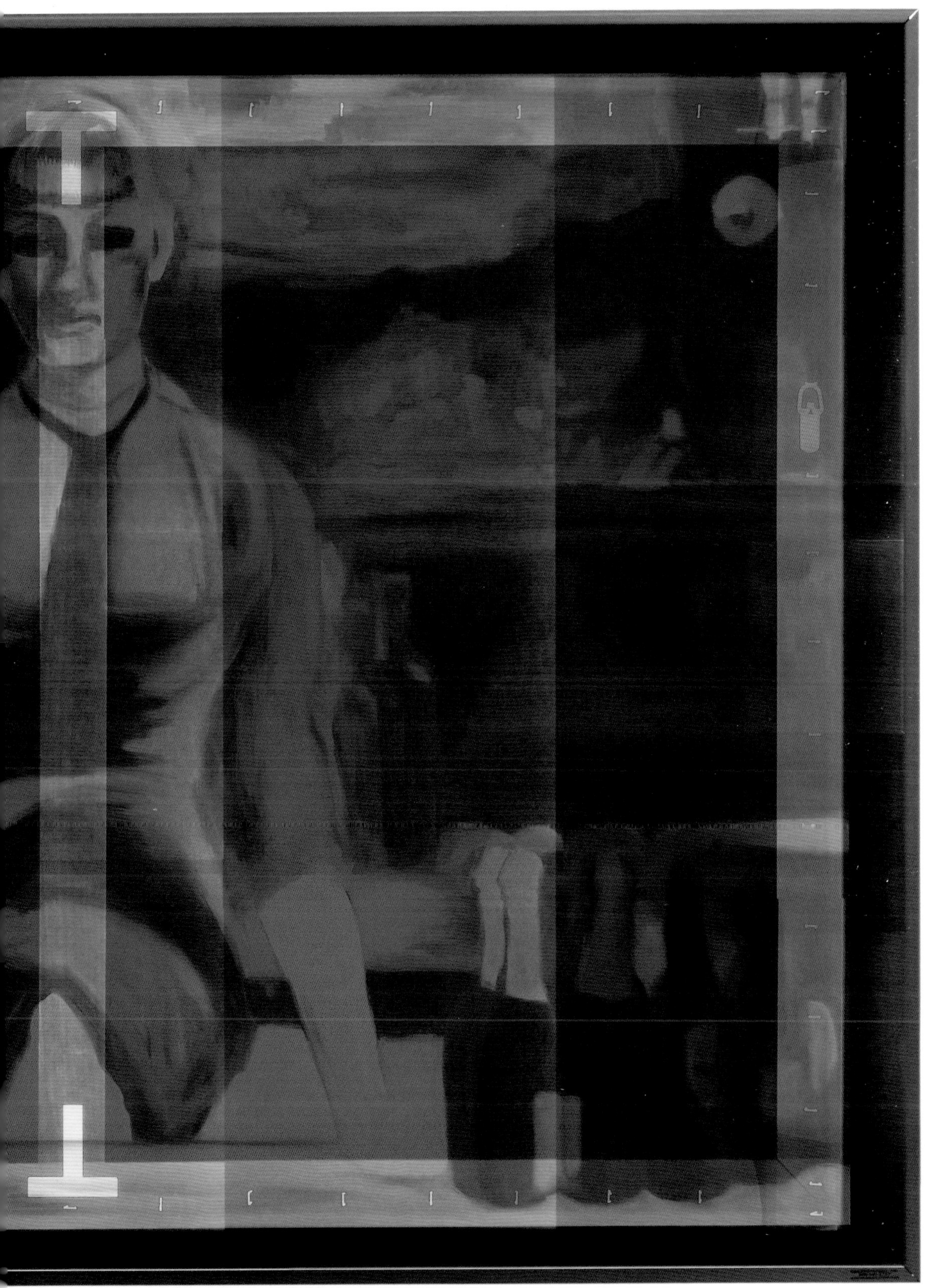

Composite image of *UNTITLED (THE BAR)*, 2007 and *UNTITLED (X-RAY)*, 2009

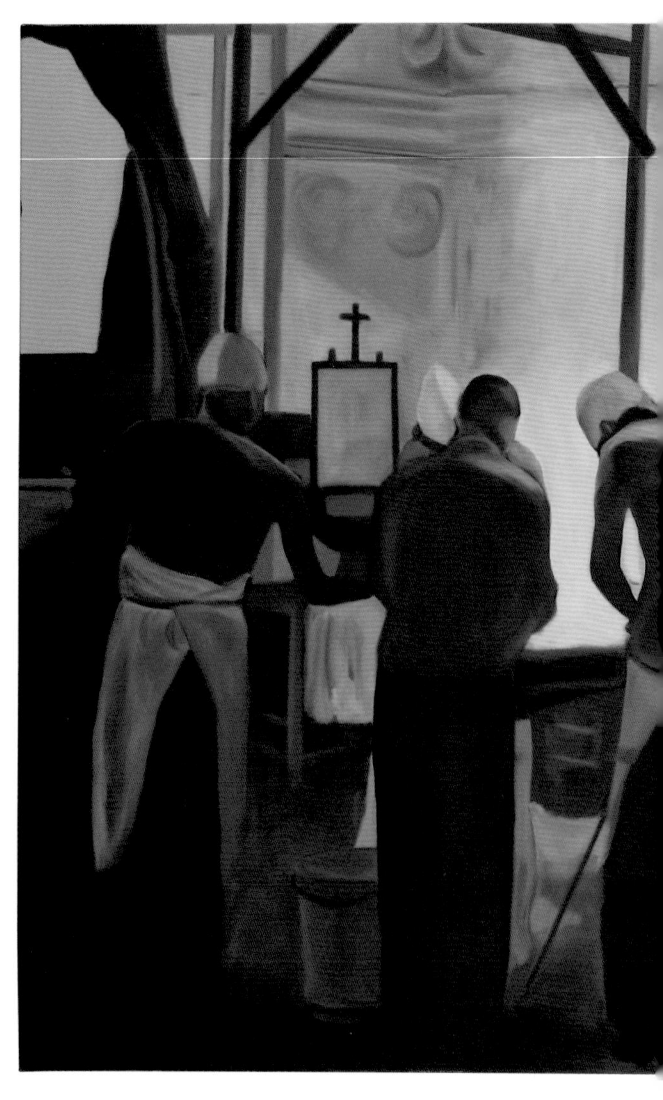

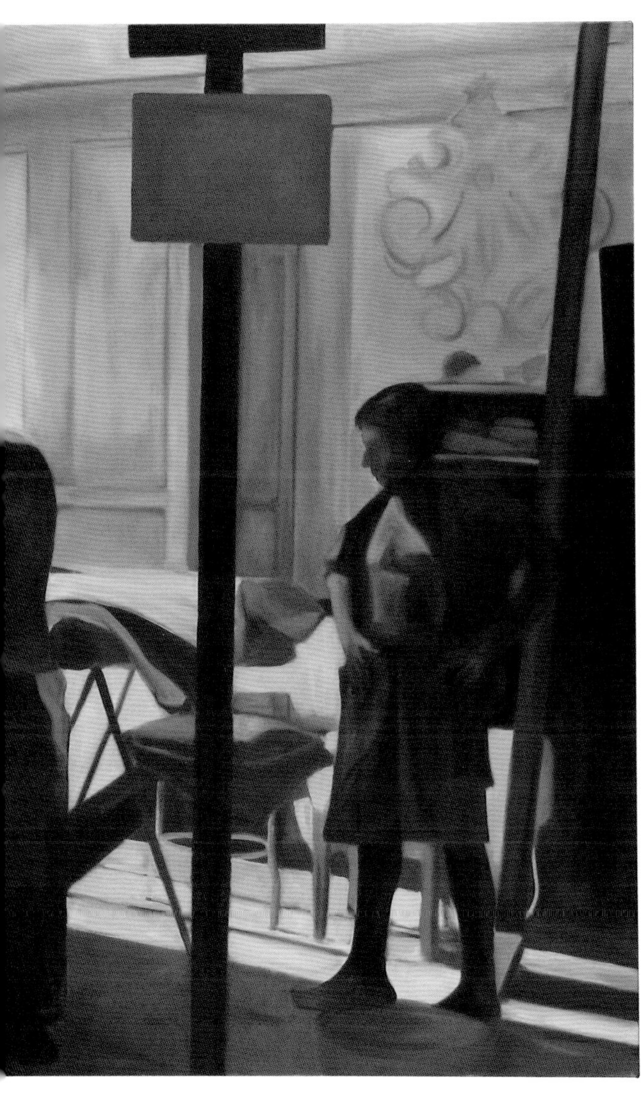

UNTITLED (SURGERY), 2006–07

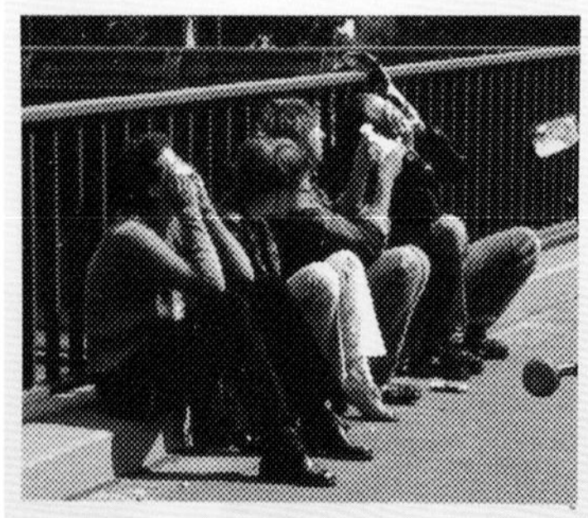
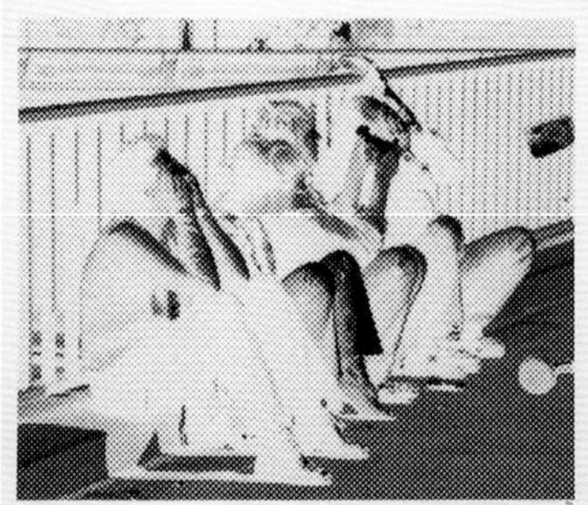

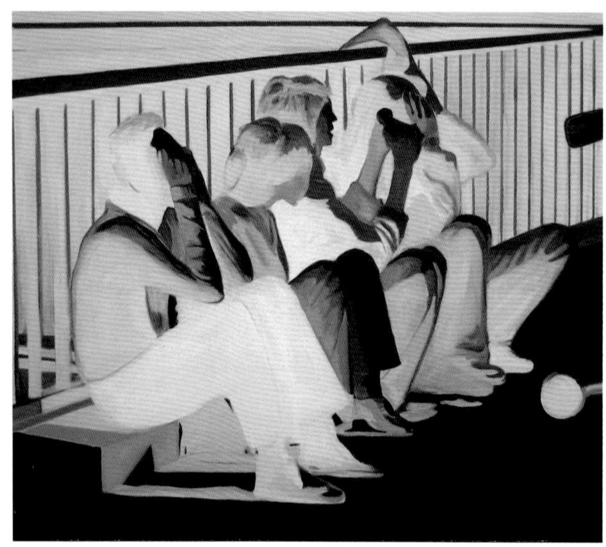

ECLIPSE, 2009
ECLIPSE, 2008

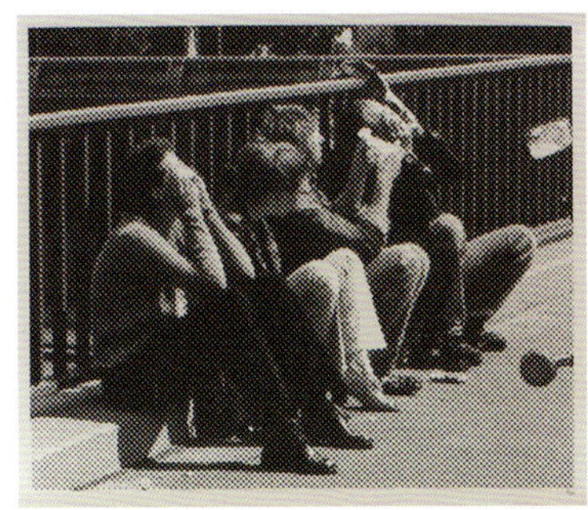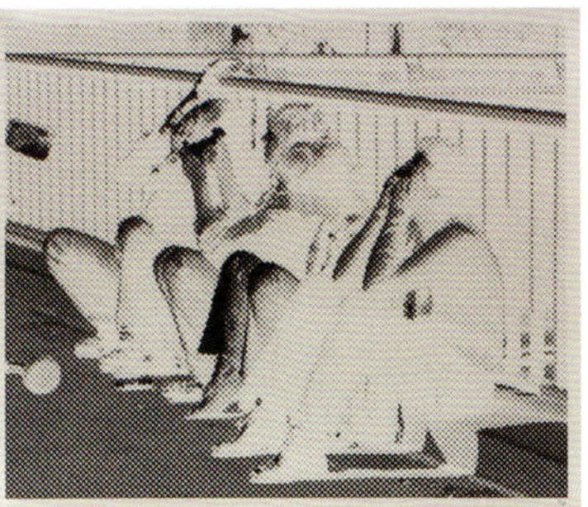

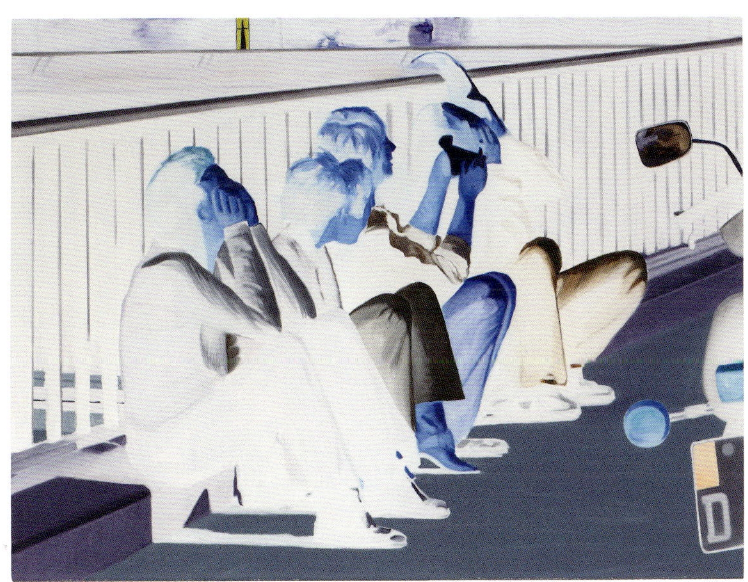

ECLIPSE (COLOR NEGATIVE), 2009

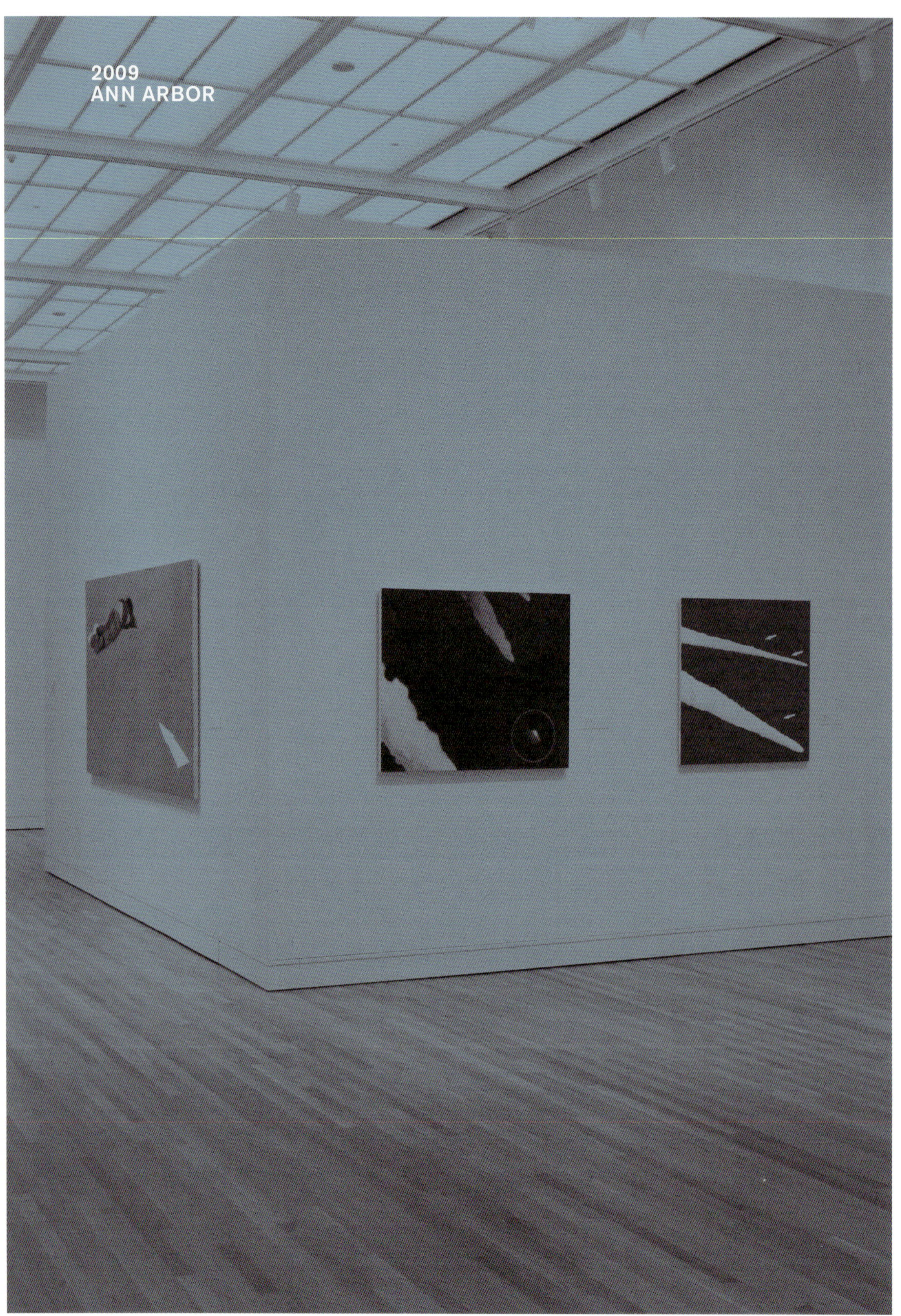

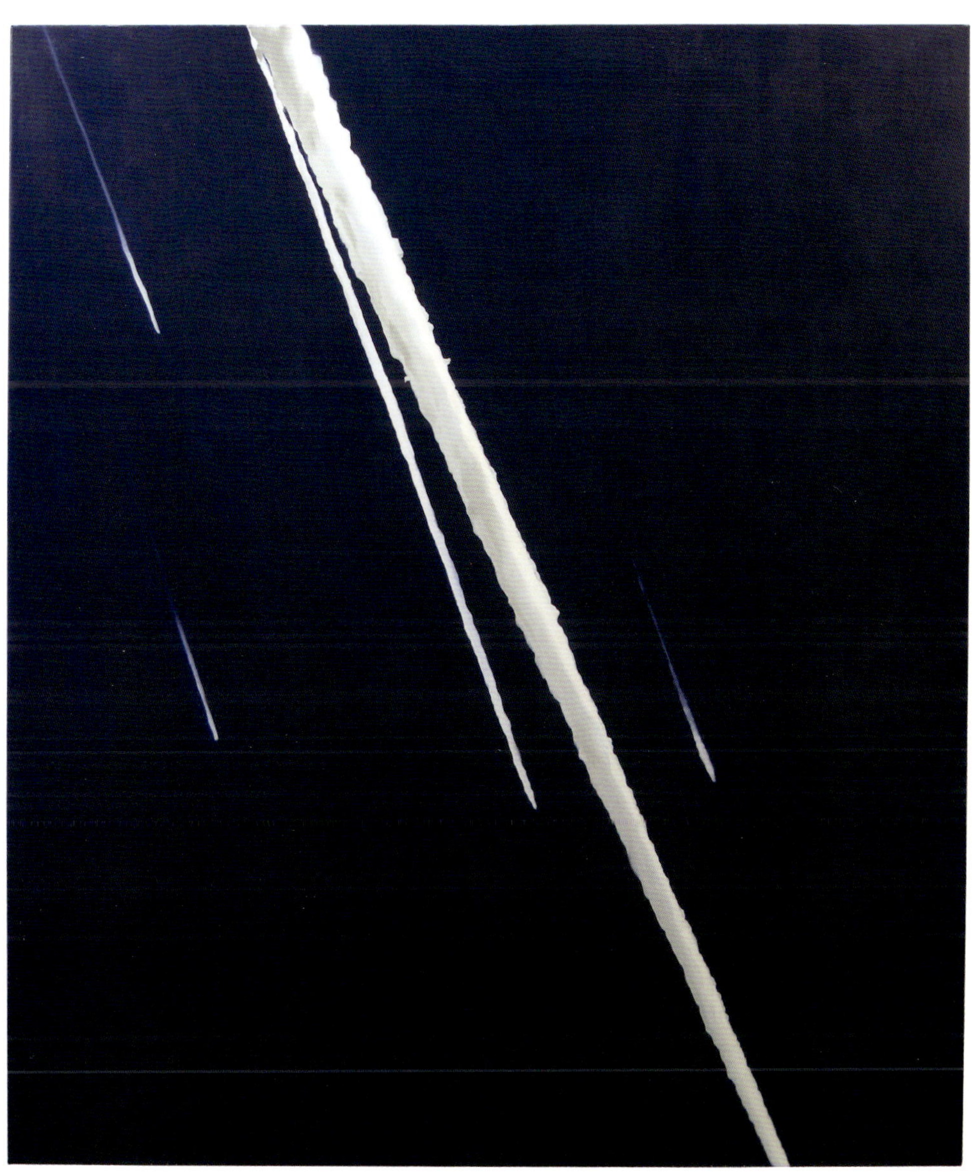

UNTITLED (CHALLENGER), 2007

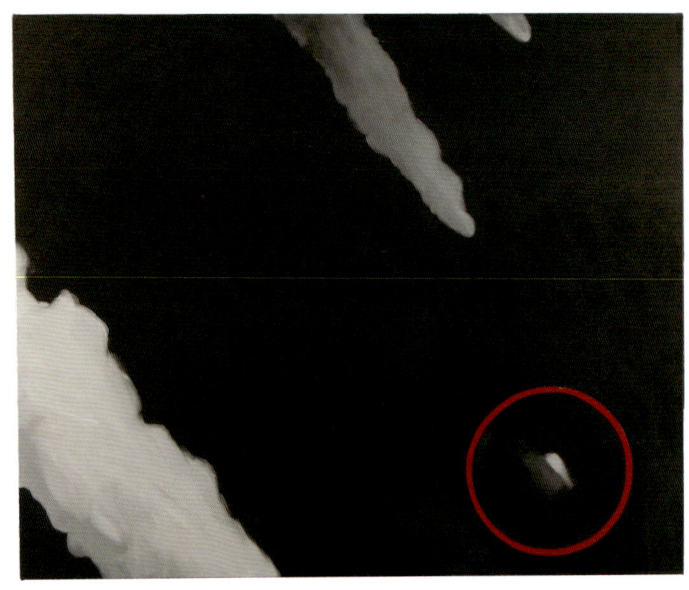

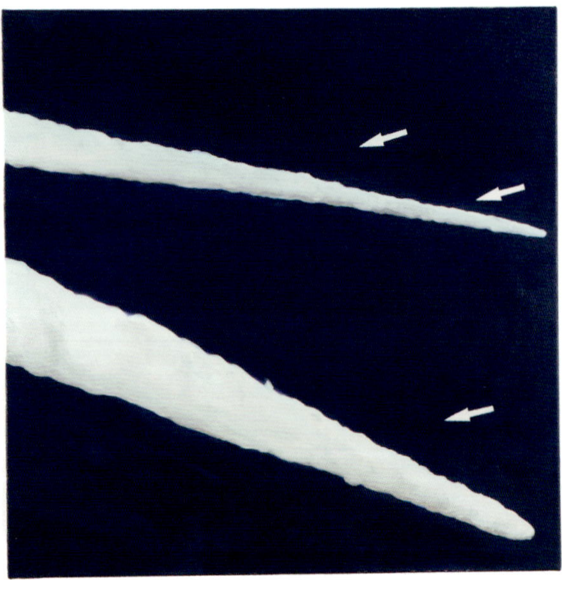

UNTITLED (CREW CABIN), 2007–08
UNTITLED (CHALLENGER), 2007–08

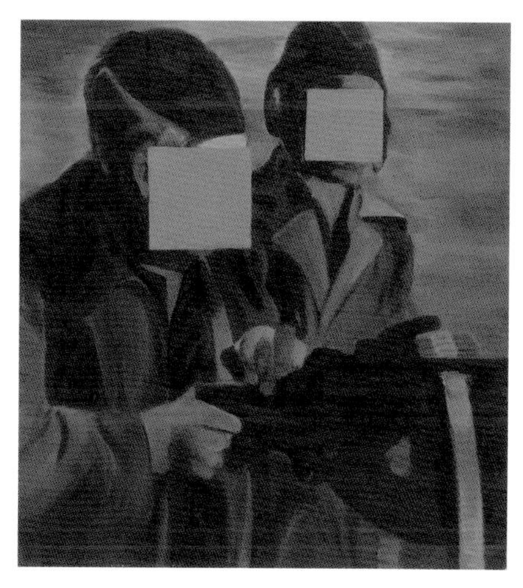

UNTITLED, 2004

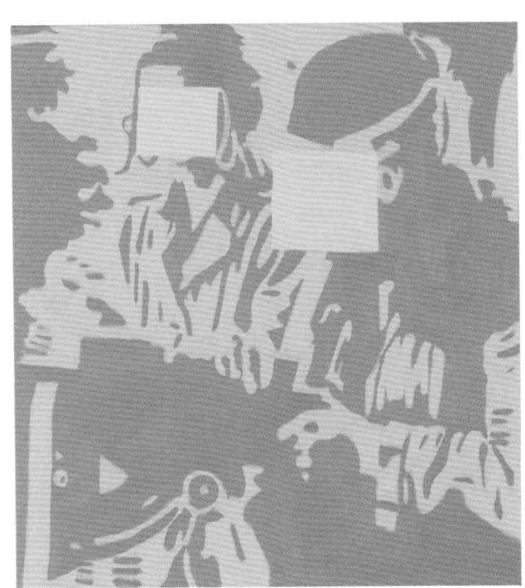

UNTITLED (GHOST IMAGE), 2006

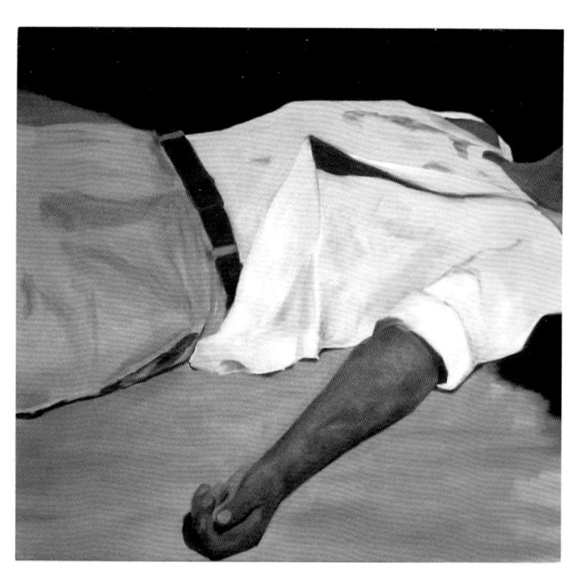

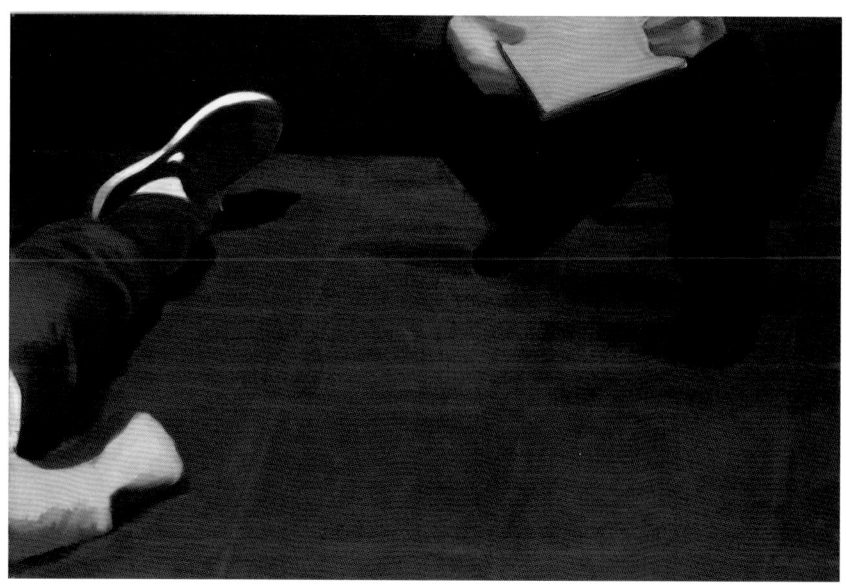

UNTITLED, 2004
UNTITLED (FORENSIC SCENE), 2004

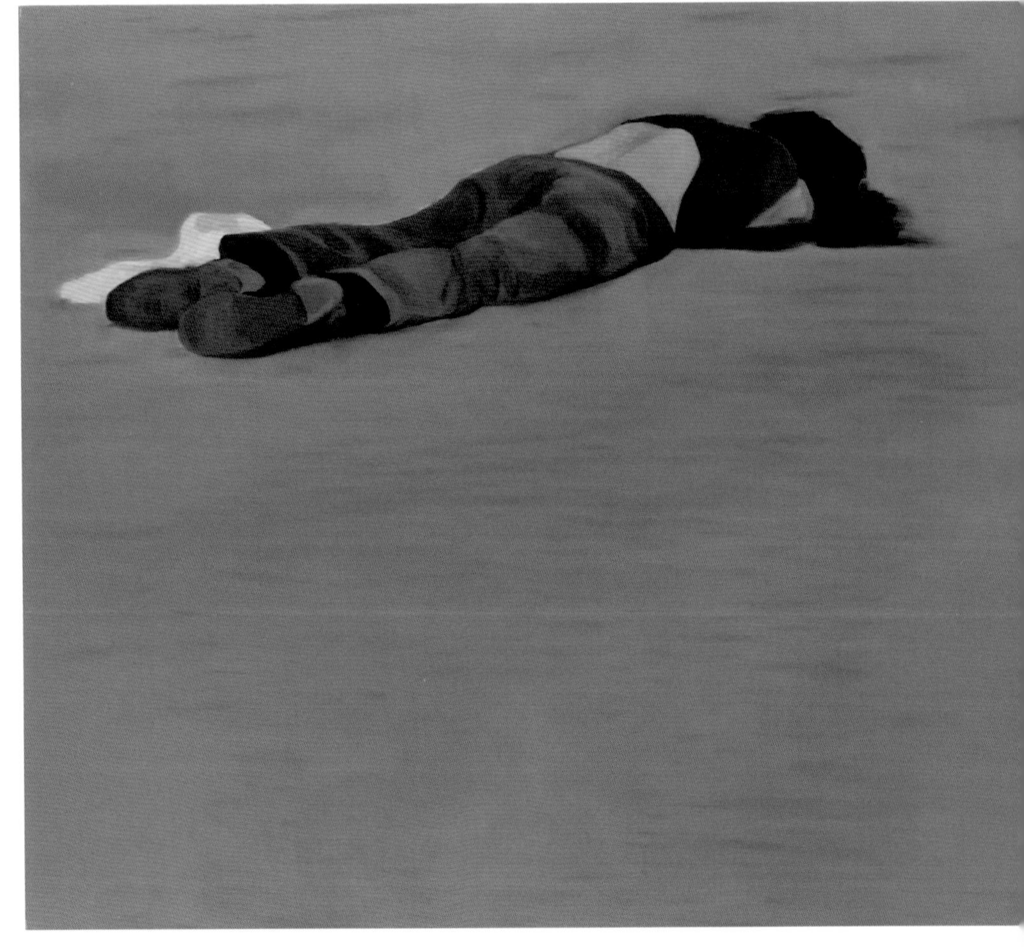

UNTITLED (PASOLINI), 2004

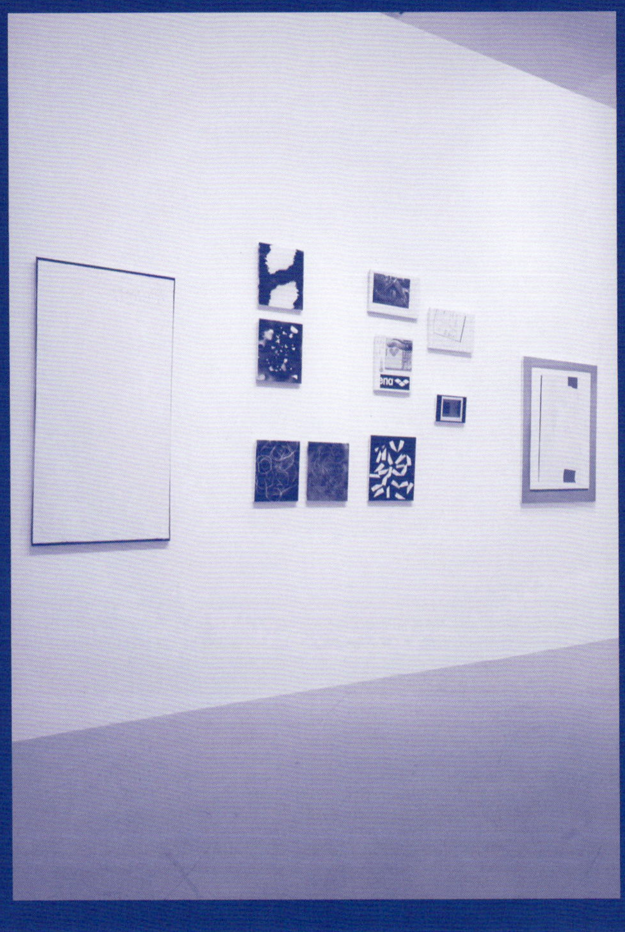

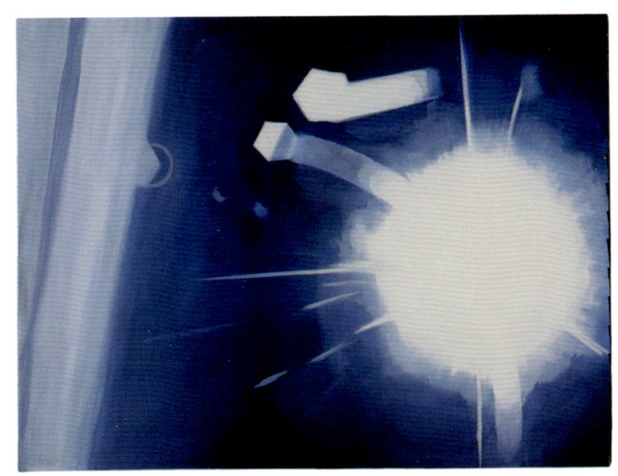

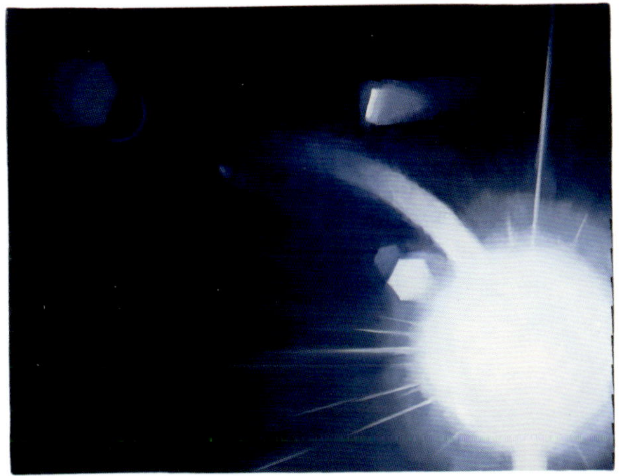

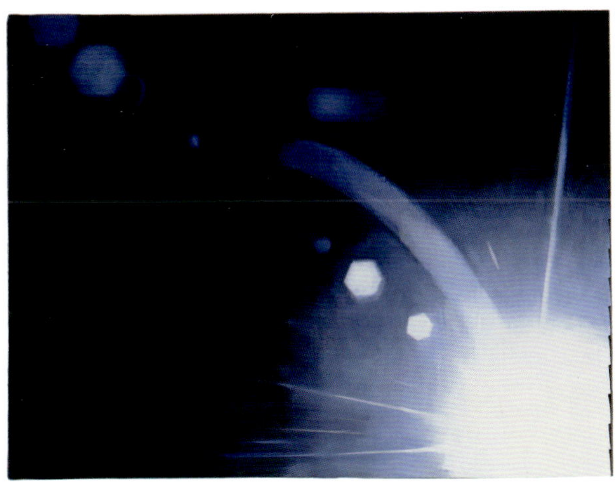

UNTITLED (LENS FLARE), 2008
UNTITLED (LENS FLARE), 2008
UNTITLED (LENS FLARE), 2008

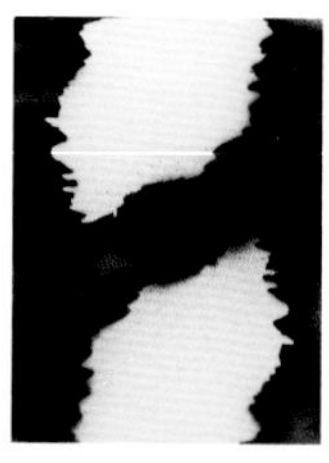

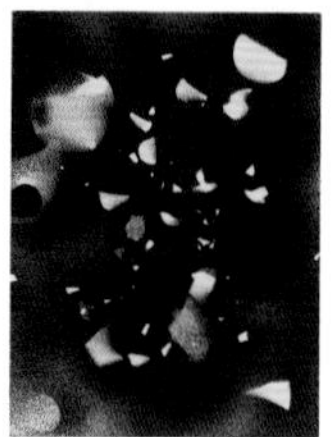

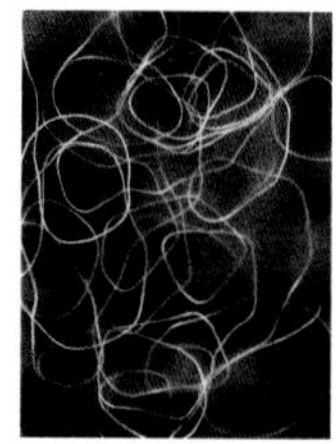

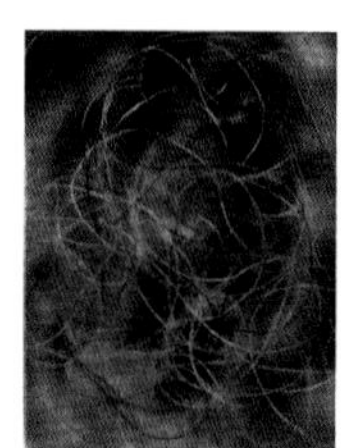

UNTITLED (CORRECTION PAINTING), 2007

UNTITLED (SPRAYED CUT OUTS), 2007
UNTITLED (BROKEN GLASS), 2007
UNTITLED (STRING PAINTING), 2007
UNTITLED (SILVER AND BLACK STRINGS), 2007

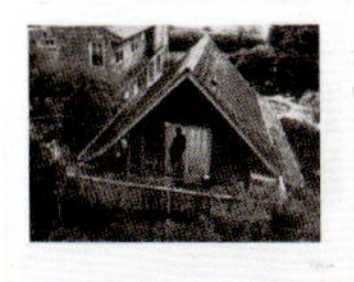
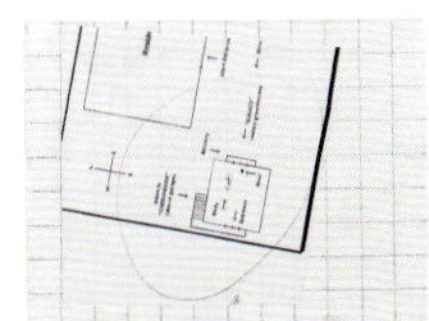
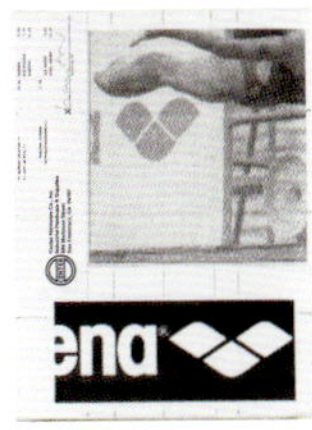
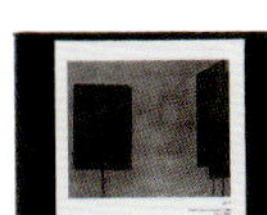

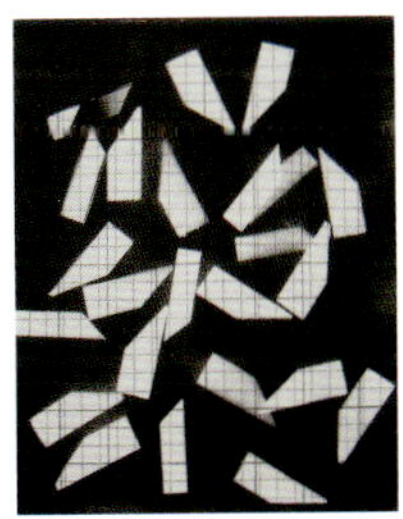

UNTITLED (GREENHOUSE), 2006
UNTITLED (GREENHOUSE DIAGRAM), 2007
UNTITLED (DIVING GIRL COLLAGE 1), 2007
UNTITLED (TWO MONOCHROMES COLLAGE), 2007
UNTITLED (GRID AND KEYS), 2007

UNTITLED, 2006

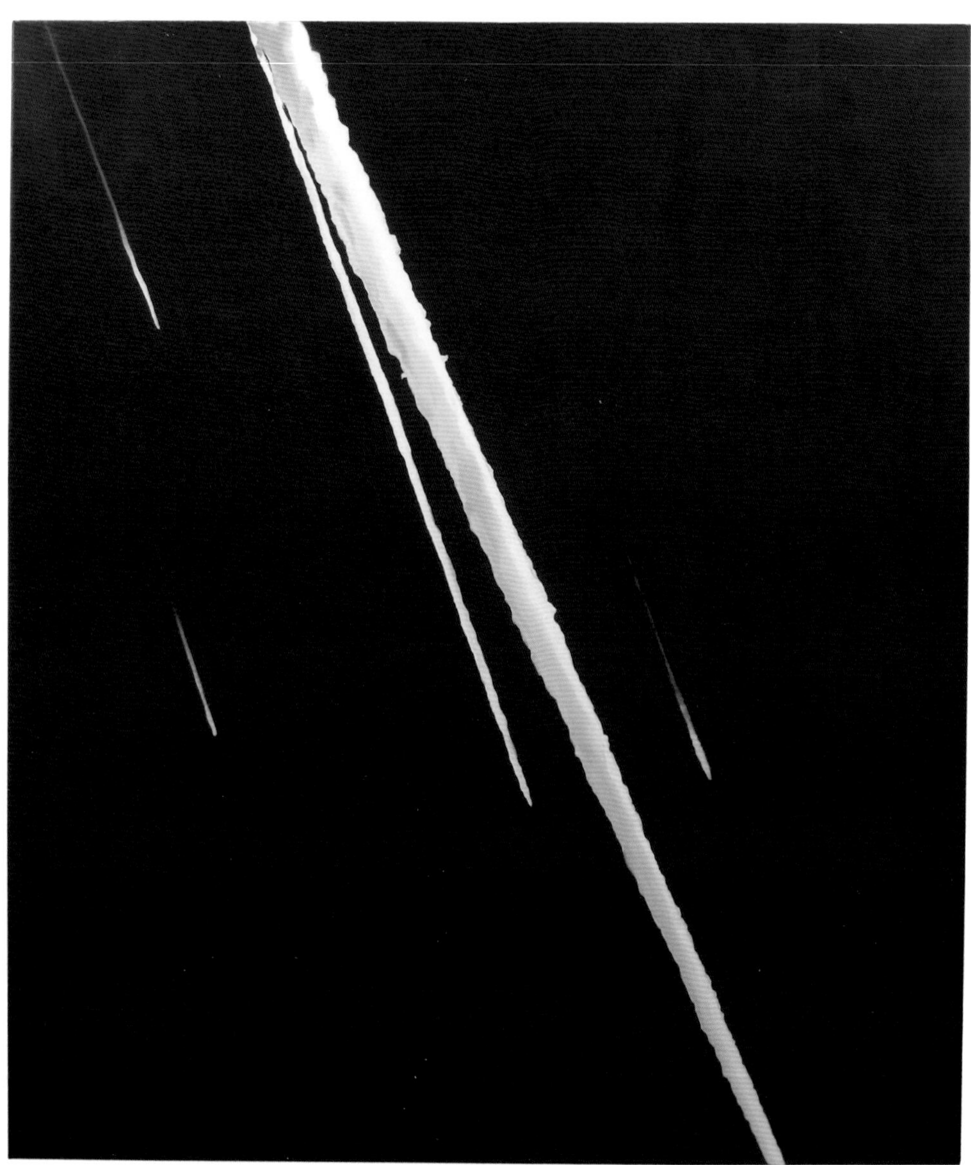

UNTITLED (CHALLENGER), *2007*

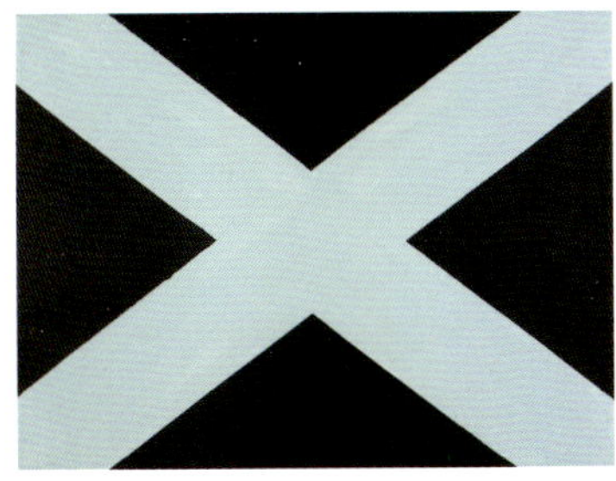

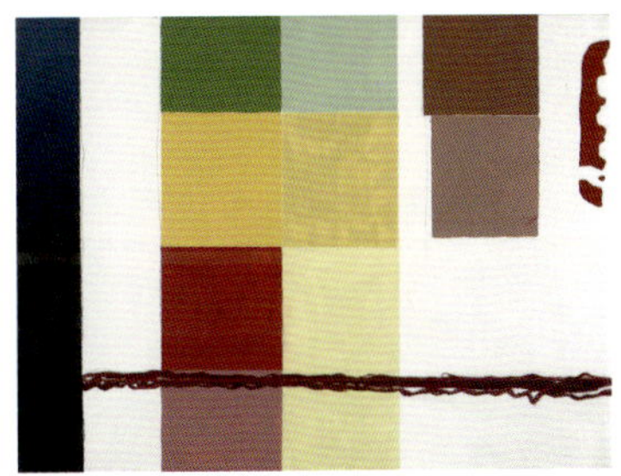

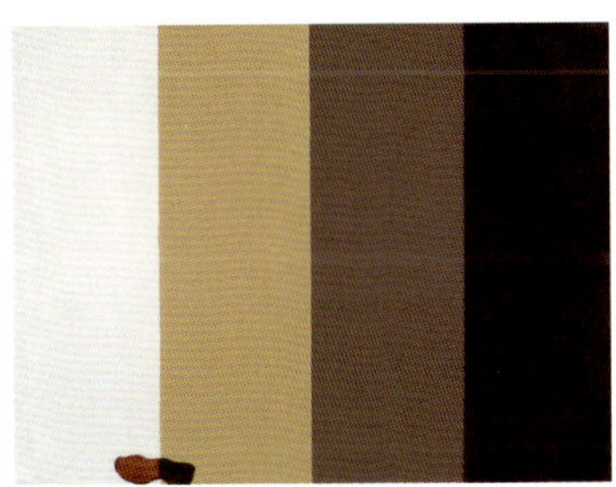

UNTITLED (FILM LEADERS #1–#4), 2007

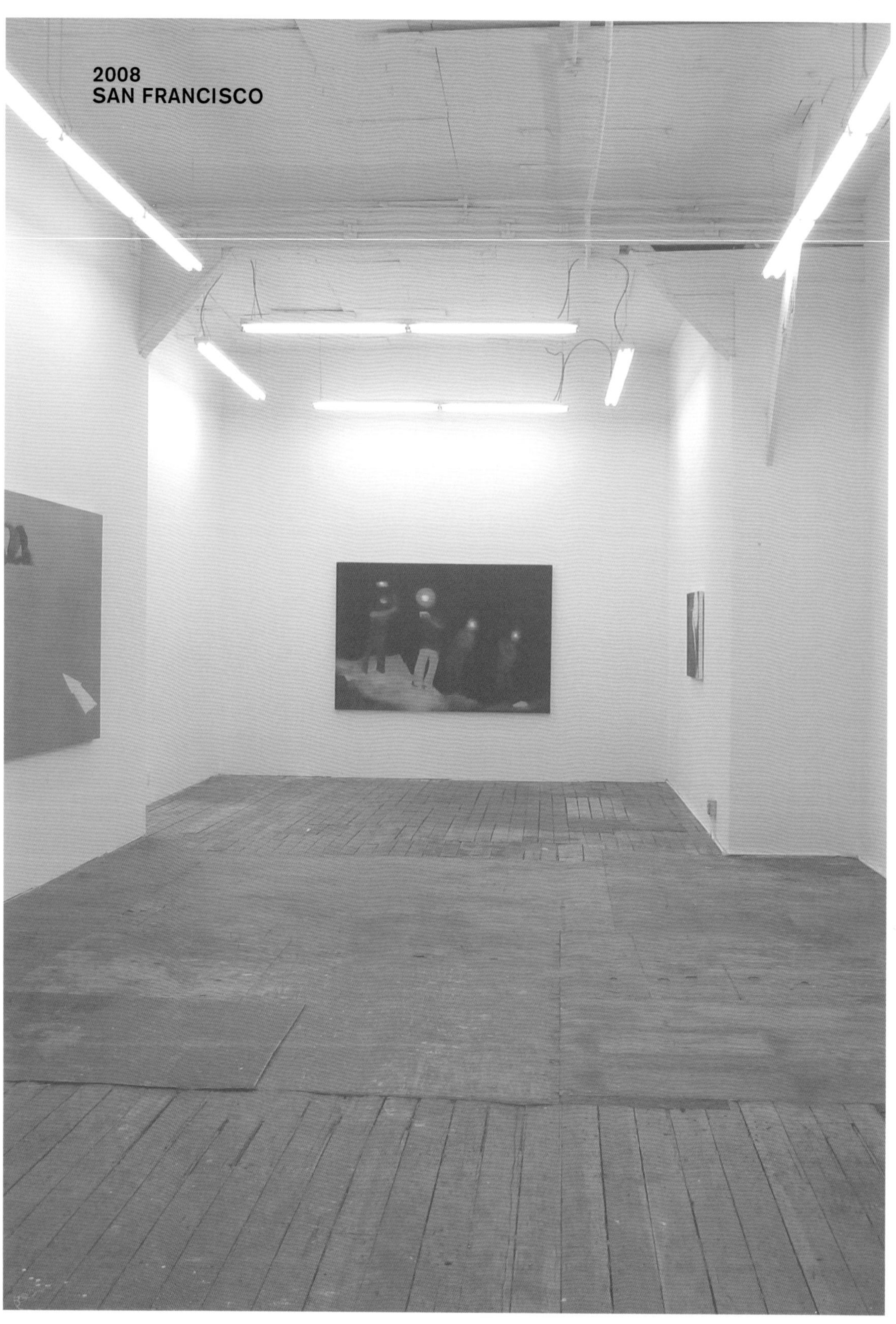

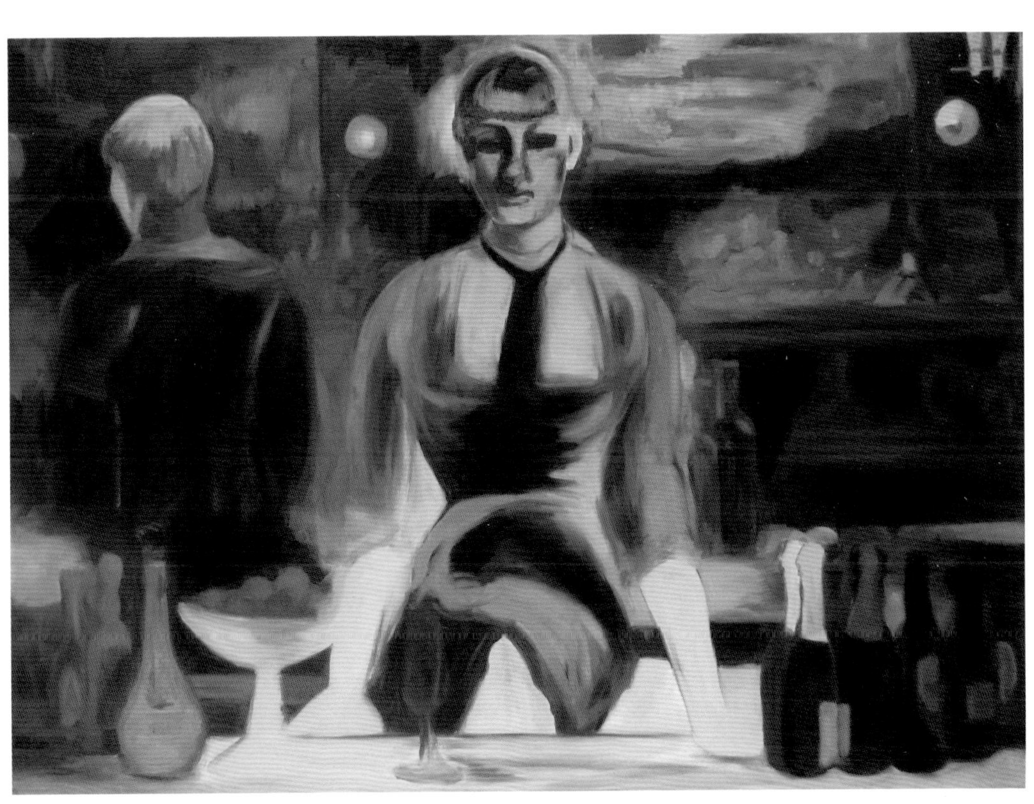

UNTITLED (THE BAR), 2007

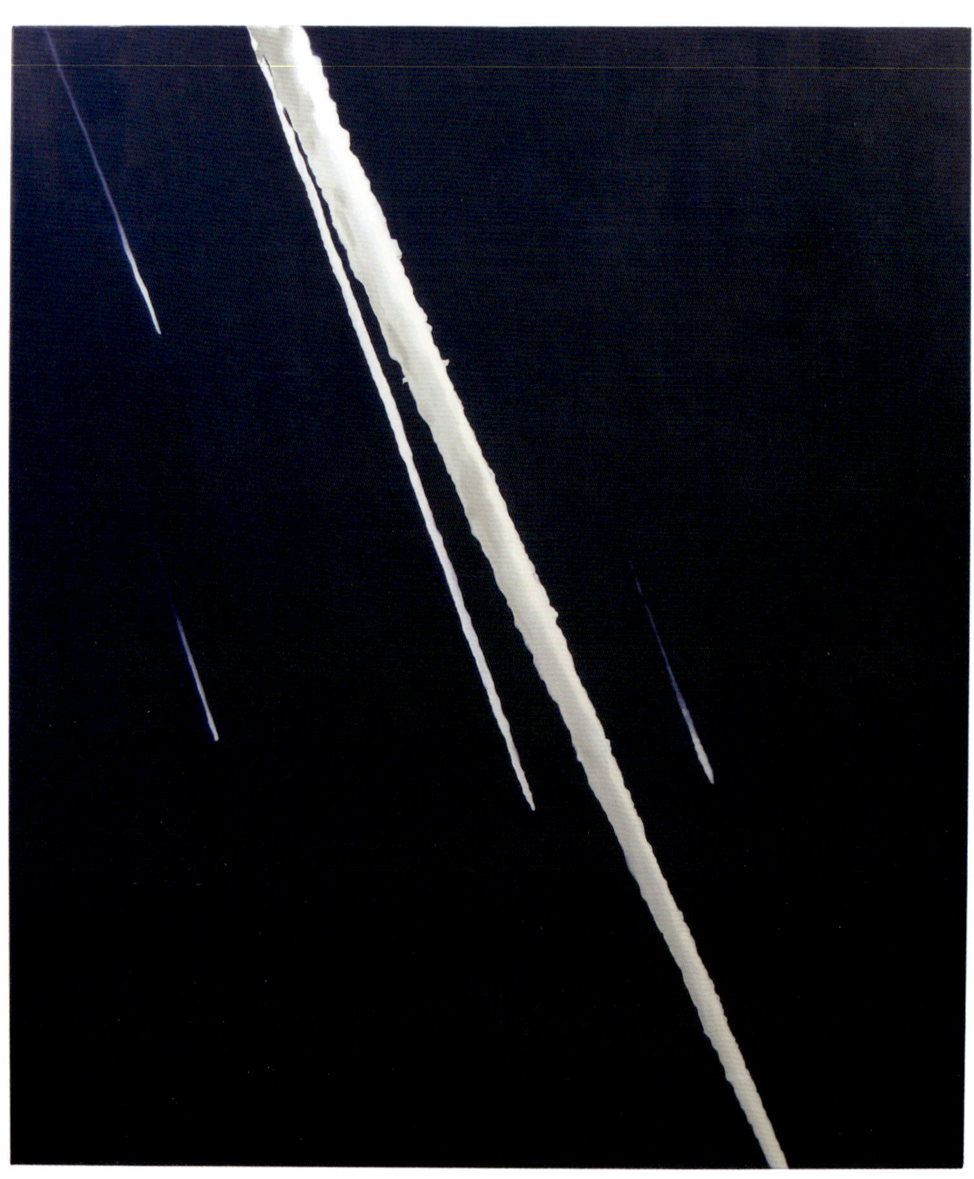

UNTITLED (CHALLENGER), 2007

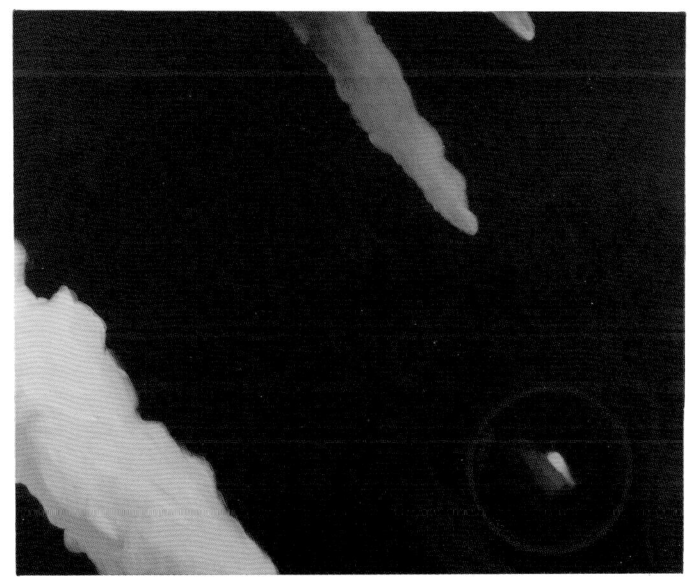

UNTITLED (CREW CABIN), 2007–08

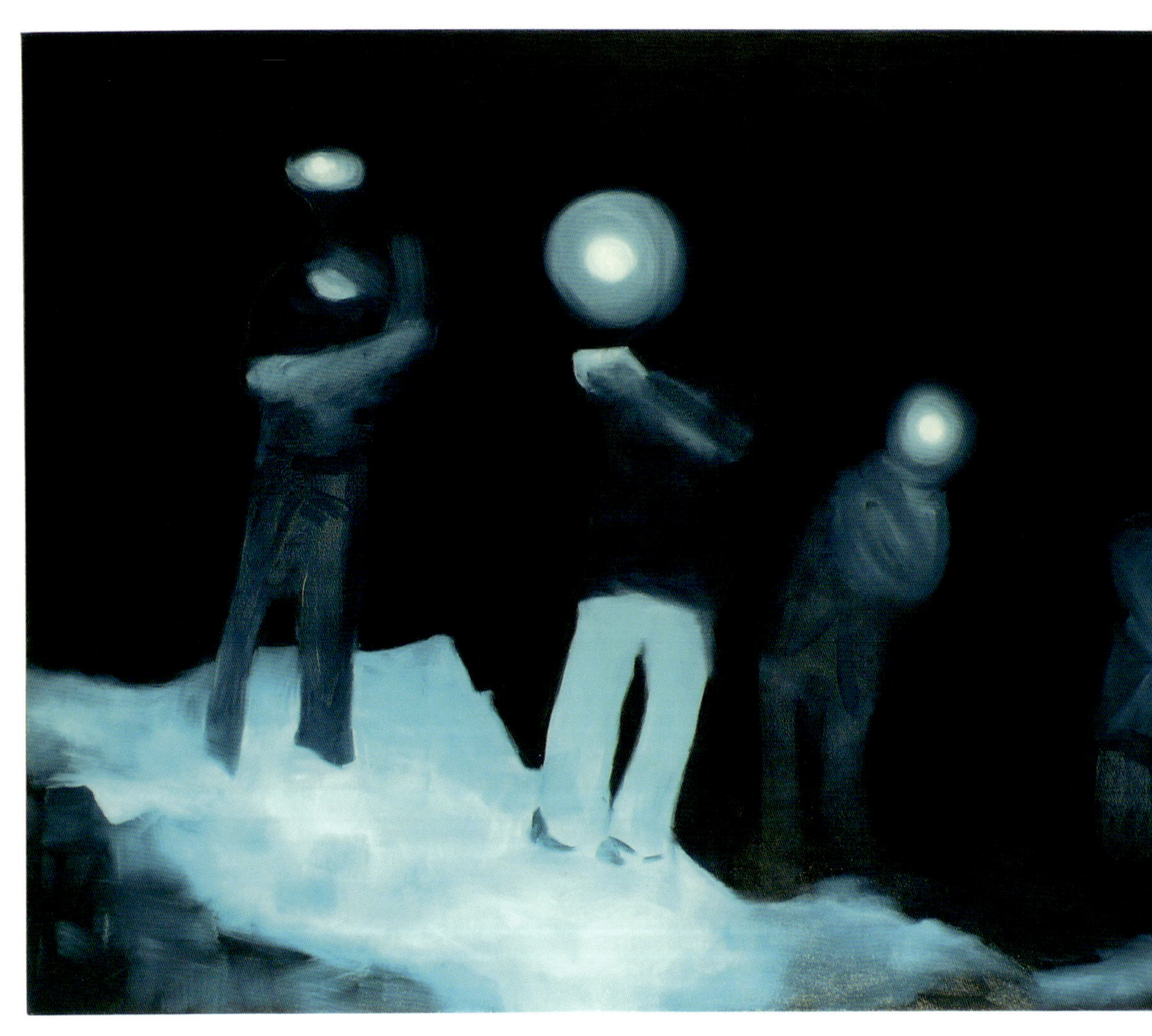

UNTITLED (FOUR SEARCHERS), 2007

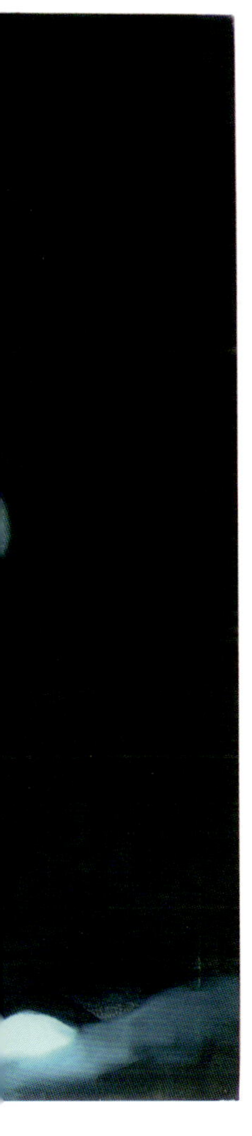

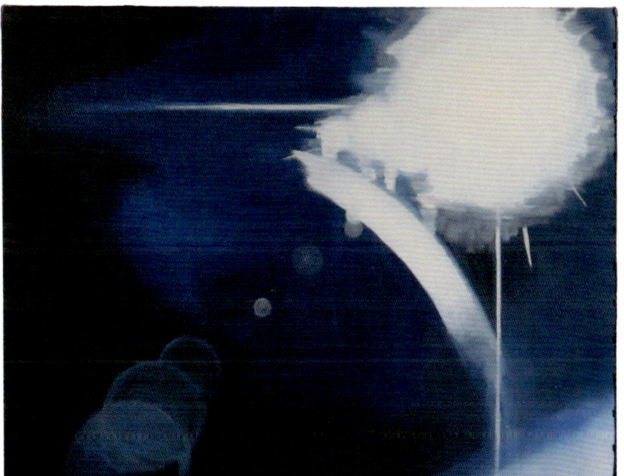

UNTITLED (LENS FLARE), 2008

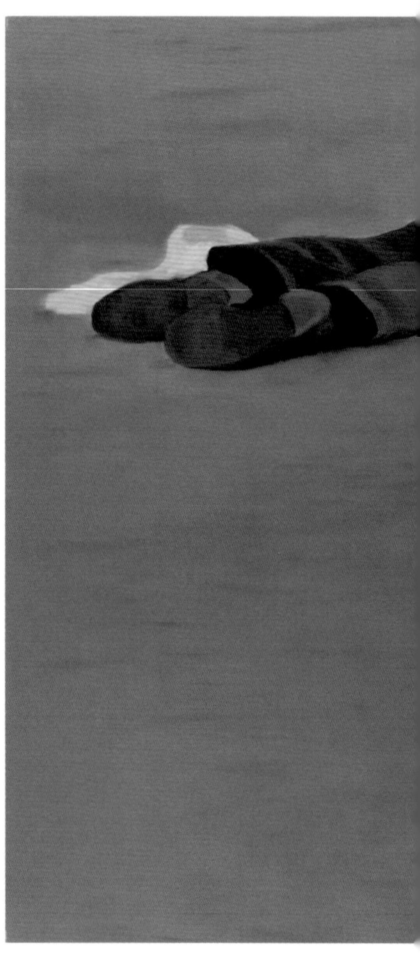

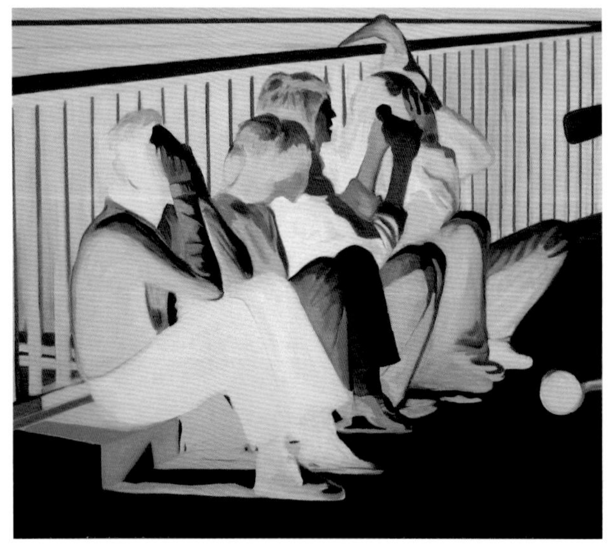

UNTITLED (PASOLINI), 2004
ECLIPSE, 2008

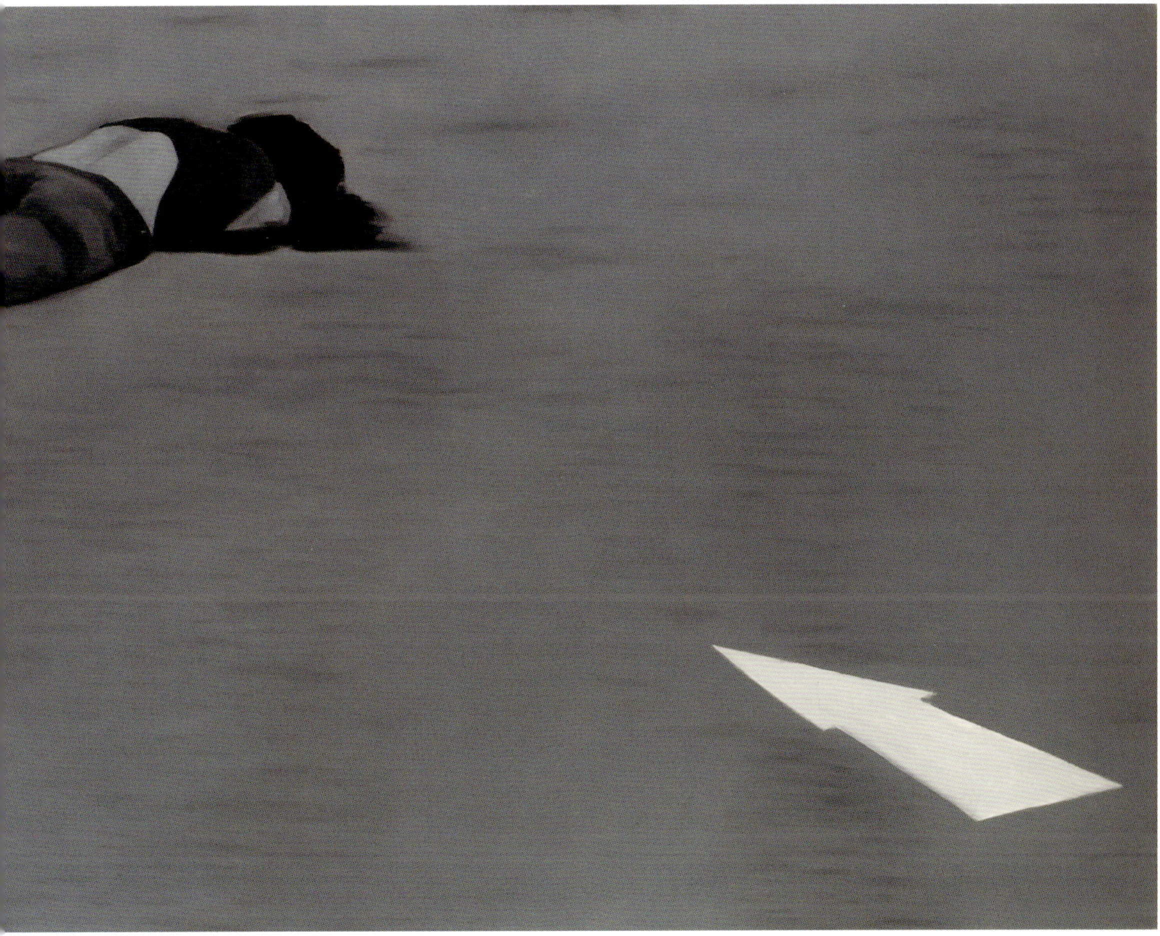

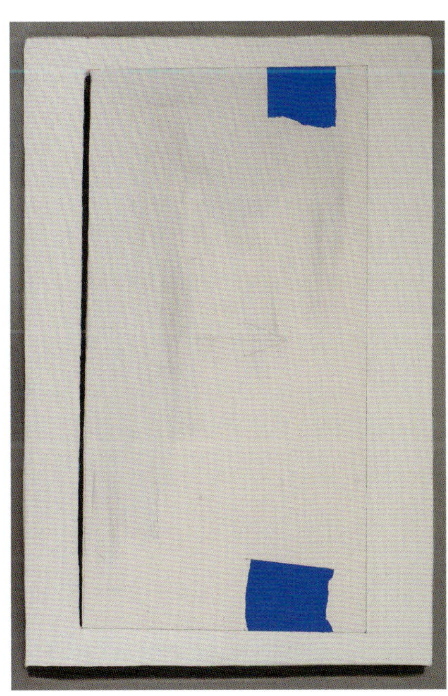

UNTITLED, 2006

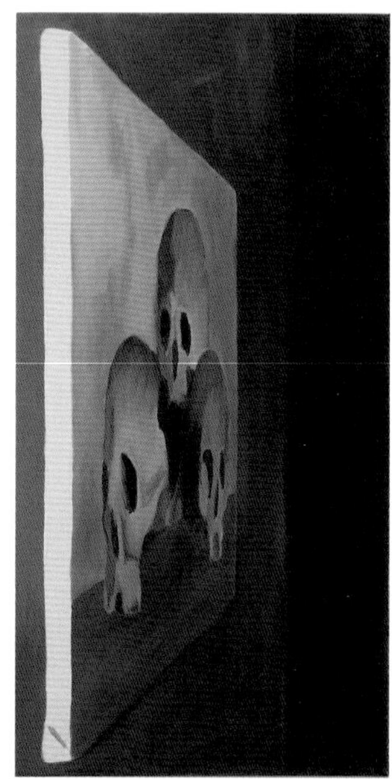

UNTITLED (WHITE PAINTING), 2007
UNTITLED (PERSPECTIVE SKULLS), 2005

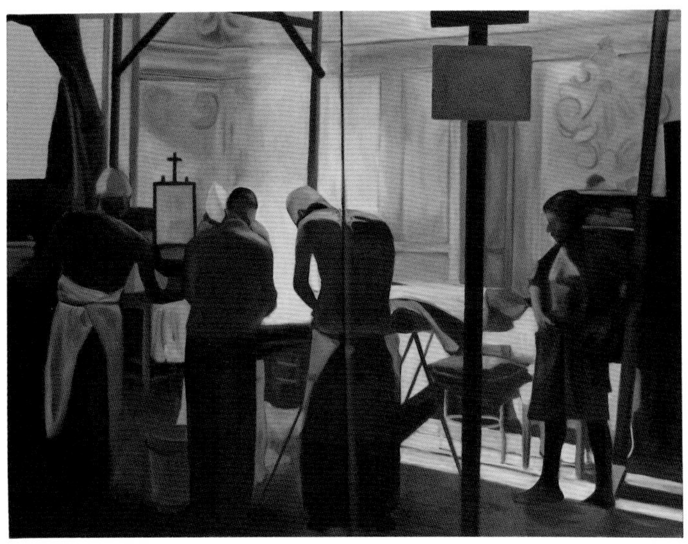

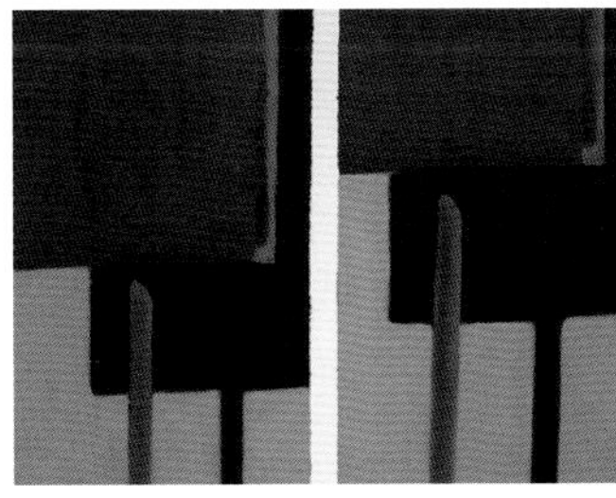

UNTITLED (CORRECTION PAINTING), 2007
UNTITLED (SURGERY), 2006–07, at reduced relative scale
UNTITLED, 2006

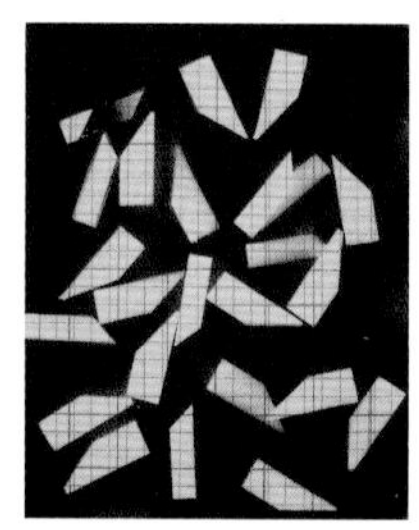

UNTITLED *(GRID AND KEYS)*, 2007
UNTITLED *(GRID AND KEYS)*, 2007 (detail)

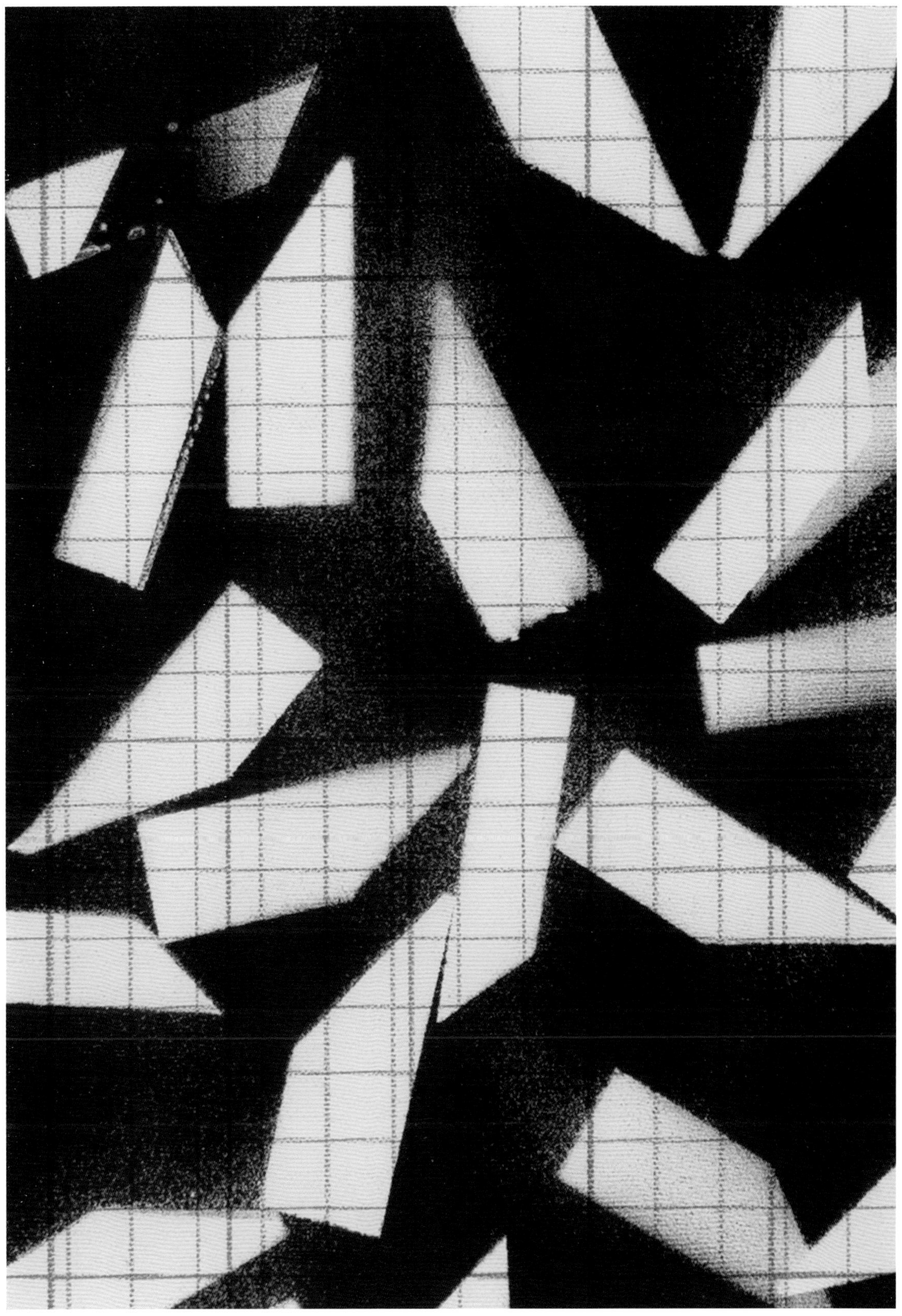

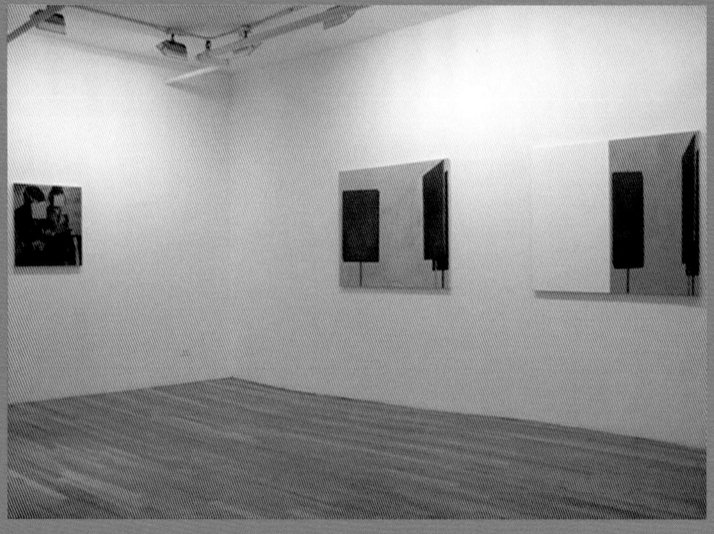

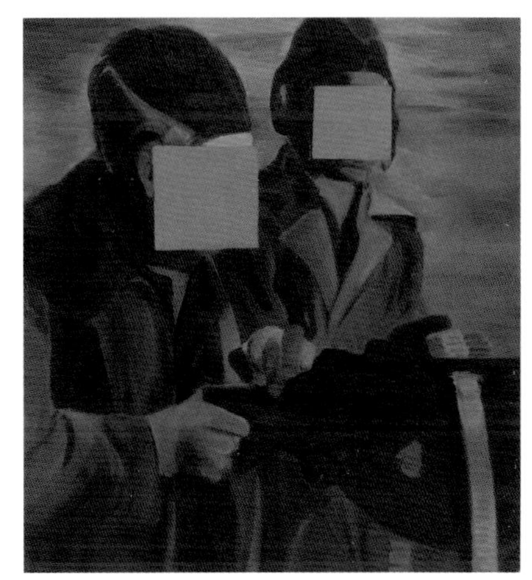

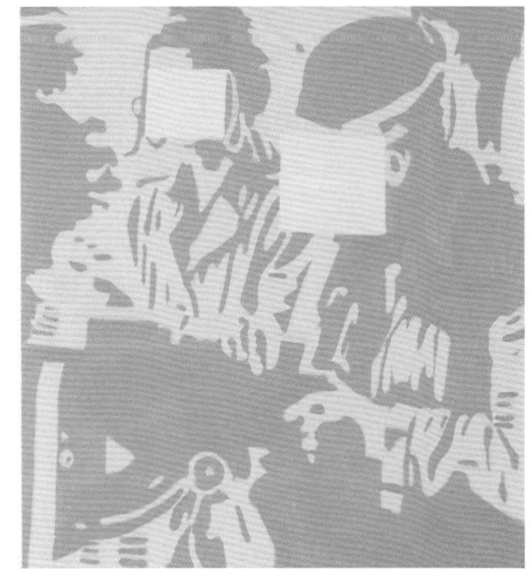

UNTITLED, 2004
UNTITLED (GHOST IMAGE), 2006

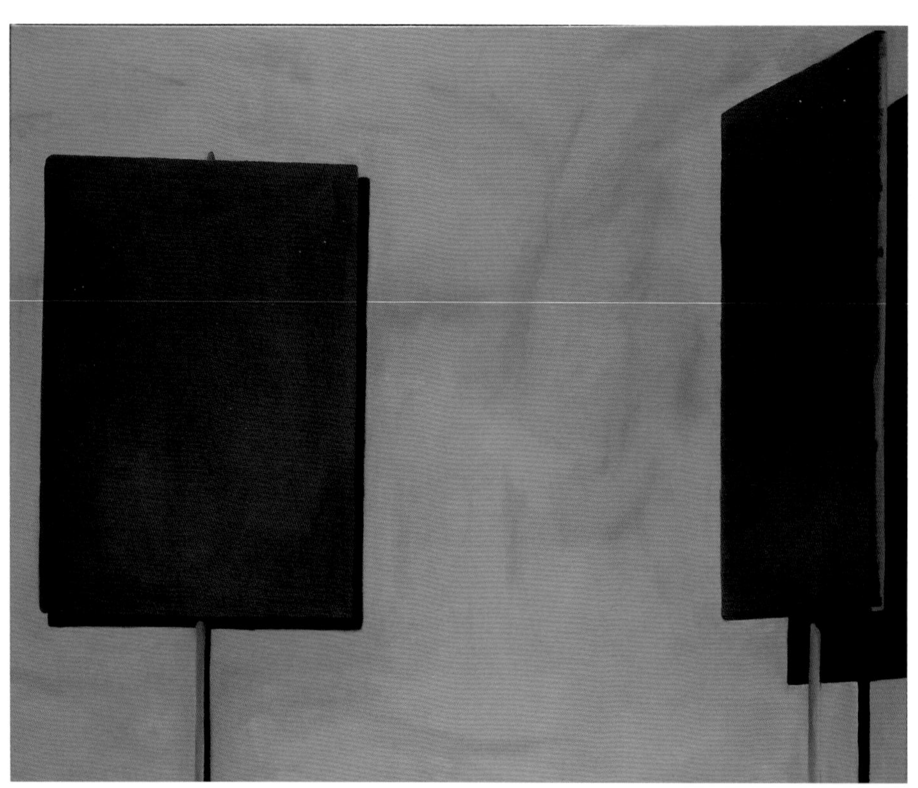

UNTITLED (TWO MONOCHROMES), 2006
UNTITLED (THREE MONOCHROMES), 2006

UNTITLED (MONOCHROME), 2007, at enlarged relative scale

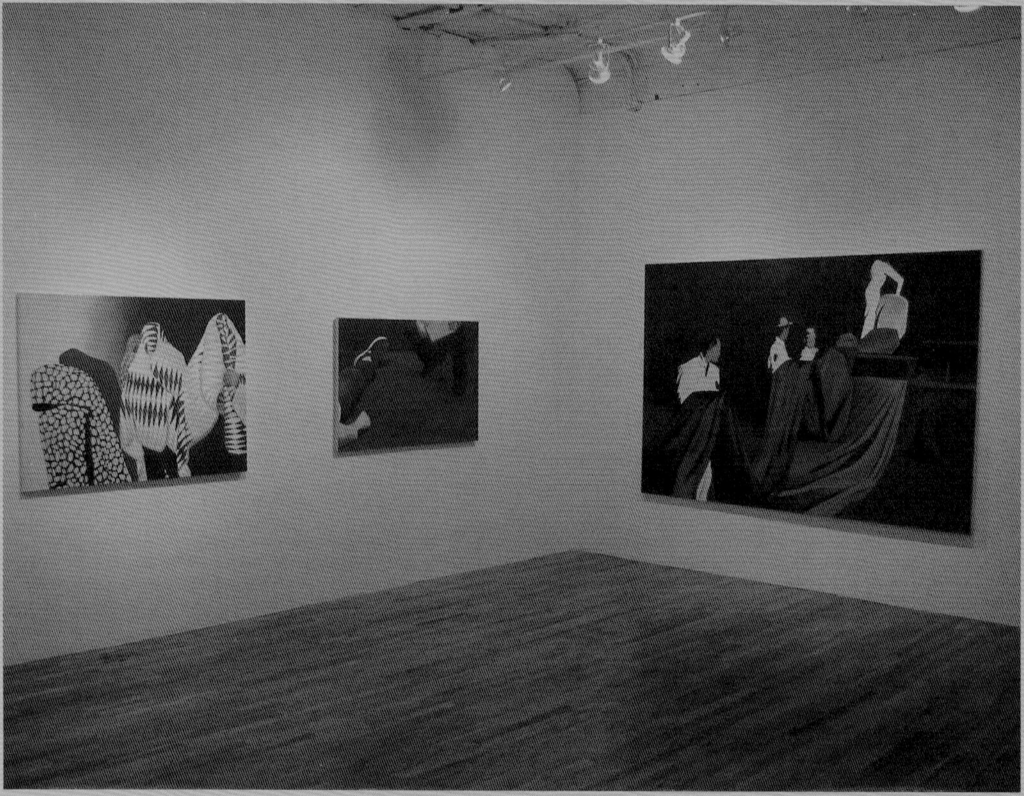

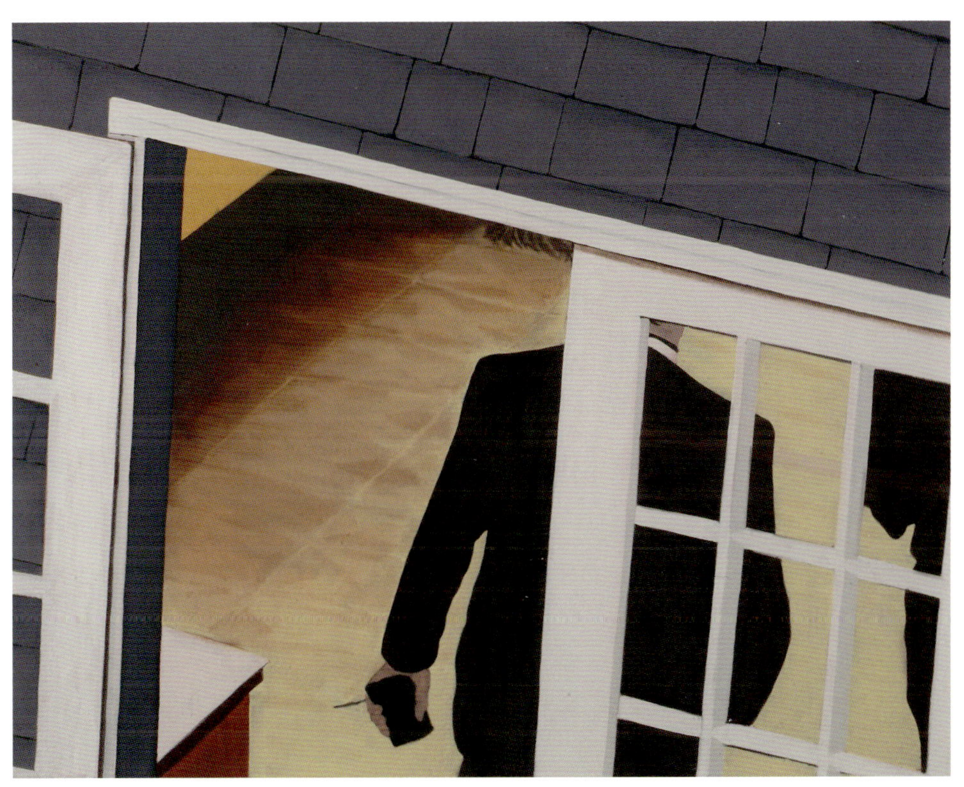

GREENHOUSE, 2006

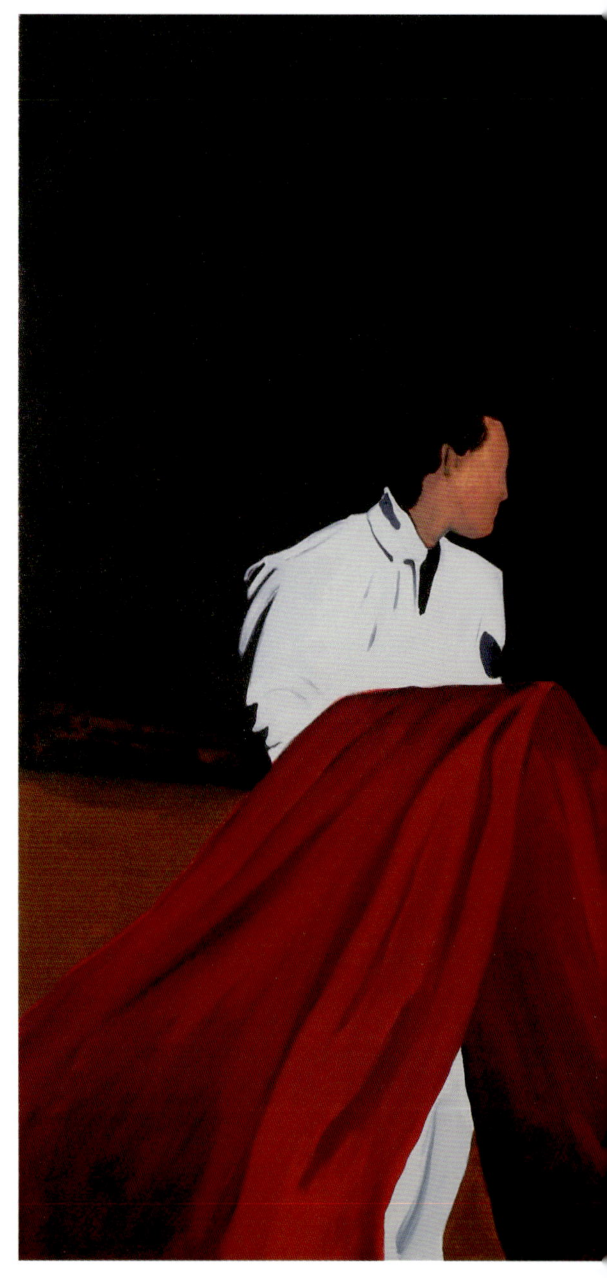

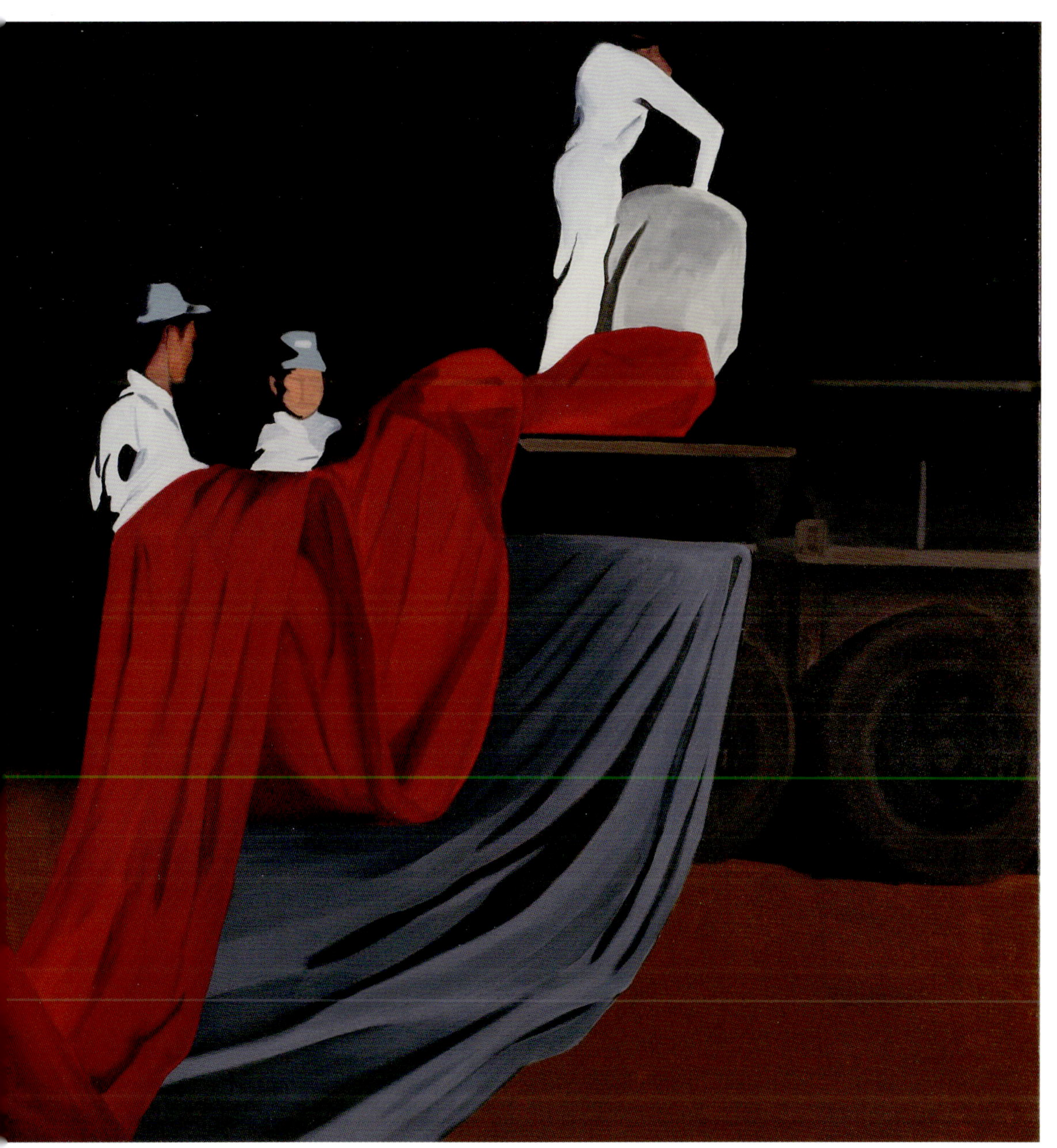

KITTINGER'S BALLOON, 2006

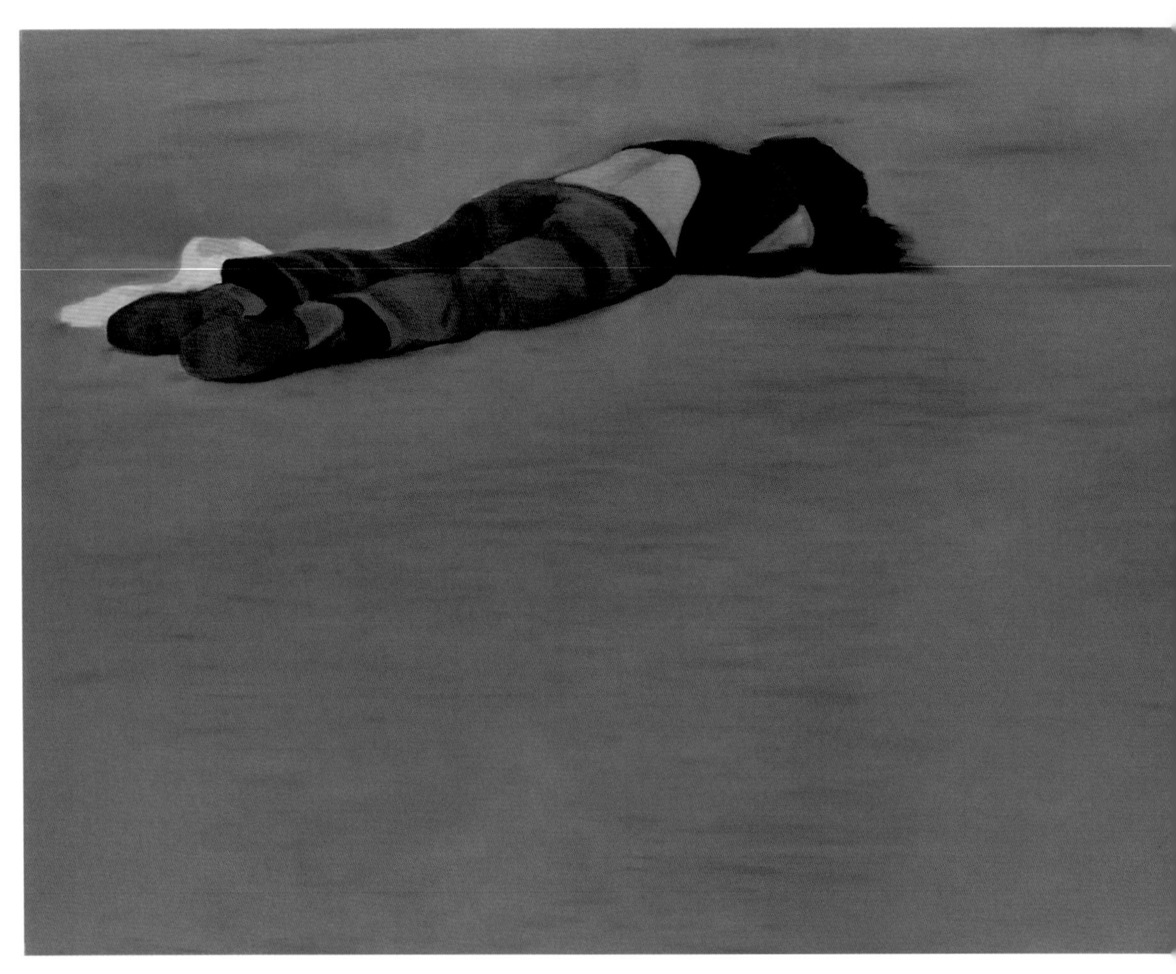

UNTITLED (PASOLINI), 2004

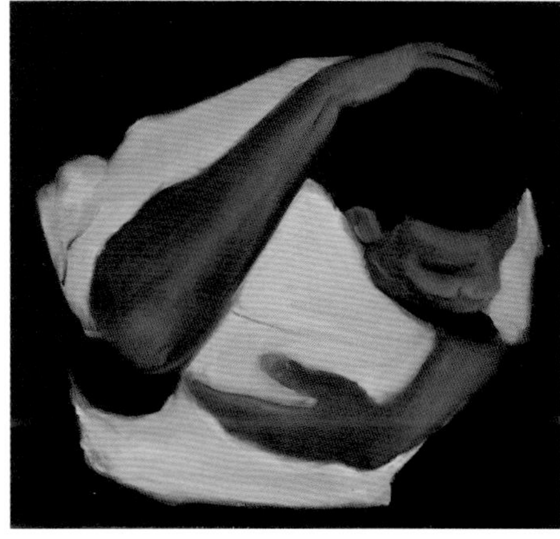

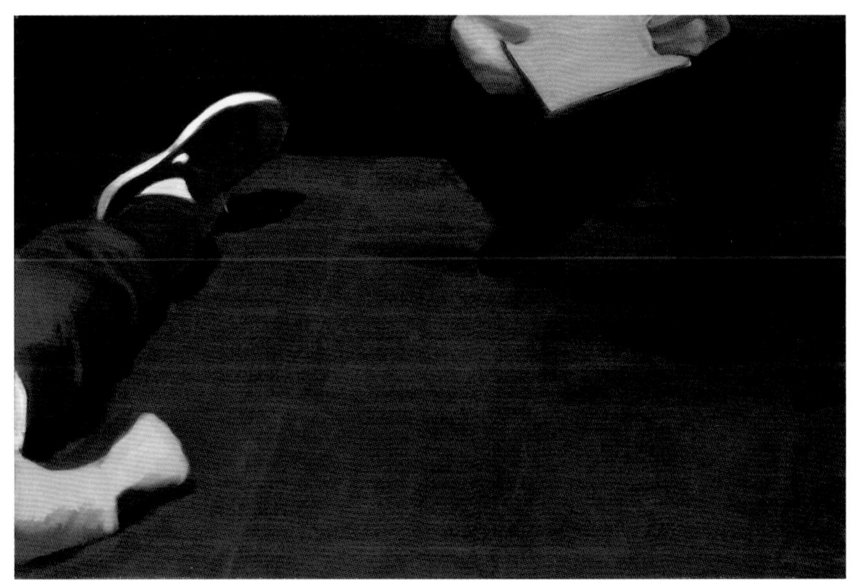

UNTITLED (FORENSIC SCENE), 2004   *UNTITLED*, 2004

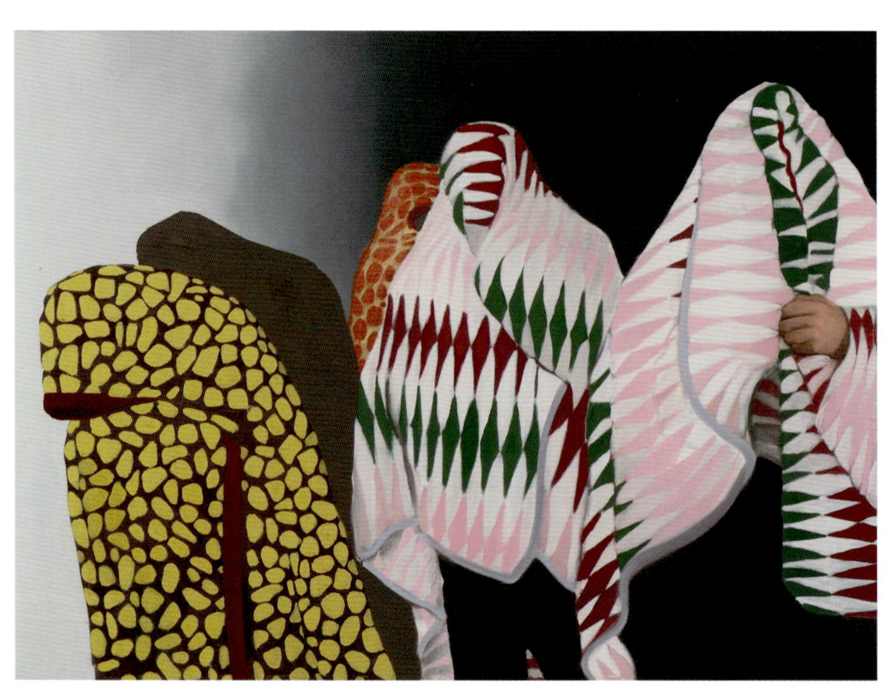

UNTITLED (INFORMERS), 2006

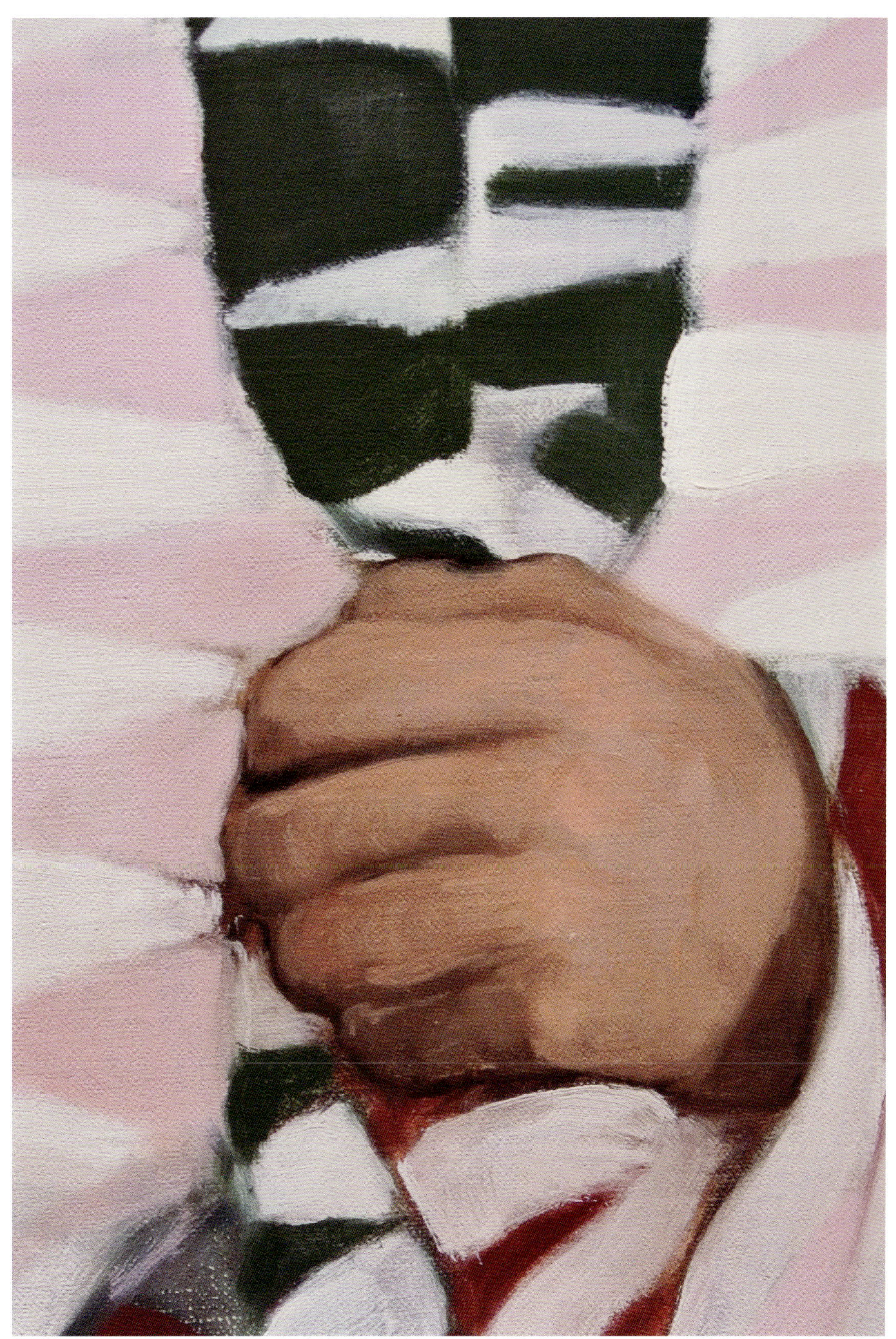

UNTITLED (INFORMERS), 2006 (detail)

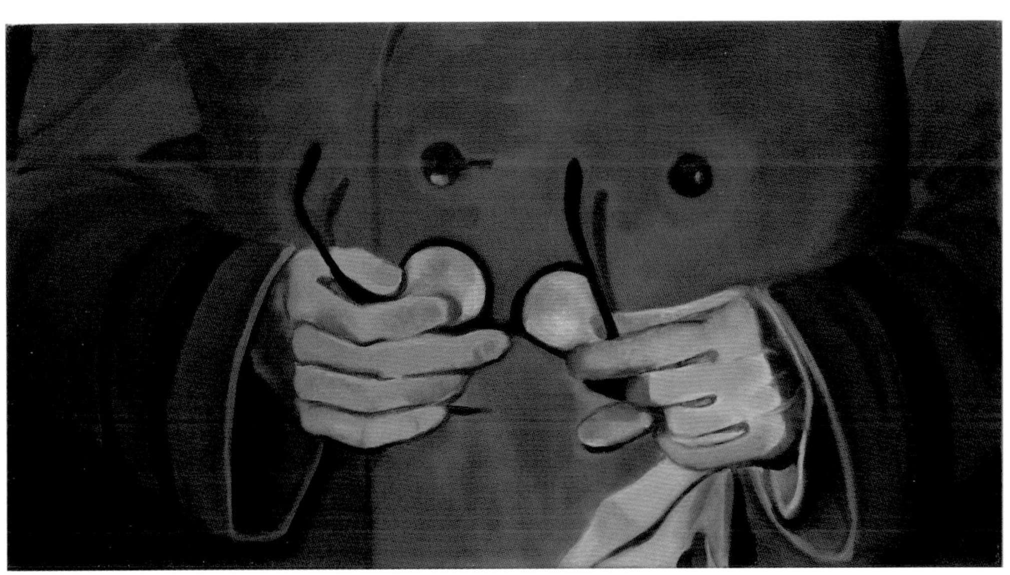

UNTITLED (HANDS WITH GLASSES), 2004, at enlarged relative scale

Jordan Kantor: We were just flipping though a mockup of this book here and talking about the apparatus; maybe now, with the recorder on, we could open with a discussion of some works in terms of the apparatus …

Yve-Alain Bois: Sure. There is a series in particular that seems relevant here: the lens flares. As you mentioned before, the lens flare is something created by the apparatus. These works embody a paradox of a realistic painting that represents something real, but that doesn't exist in the world except as the product of a photograph. That aspect is very interesting and puzzling.

JK: The lens flare works came from thinking about the historical argument about painting's representational function vis-à-vis photography. I wondered how to make a painting that would somehow confront this knowingly, that would acknowledge the old debate, and also gesture to painting's "lost" ability to represent the world. The use of lens flare imagery was one way to bring a kind of self-referentiality into the painting without entirely giving up the idea that paintings can also represent. The imagery of almost all the lens flare paintings is romantic—a picture of the sun or the sky or outer space, a clichéd idea of what an immersive painting would be—and the lens flares function like quotation marks that bracket the landscape with the mark of the apparatus.

The lens flare paintings are relatively early in the scope of the works in this book, and I think they set the tone for a relationship between surface and image, structure and projected space, and historical argument and contemporary object that runs throughout the subsequent works. I am interested in how to hold these tensions in an image.

YAB: What strikes me about those works is that the issue of the apparatus is not something that needs a lot of discourse to be unpacked. The apparatus of the camera is made visible in the image of the lens flare itself.

Let's go to another case: that of the negative/positive silkscreens on Mylar (*Eclipse*, 2009). When these works are presented in an exhibition, is it absolutely evident in the third print of the group that the black monochrome is created by putting the first two images of the series together, front to back?

JK: Yes, I believe so, if you are looking closely. It's something that you can see materially. The silkscreened images on the front and

back are necessarily slightly misaligned because of the
thickness of the transparent material onto which they are printed,
and this material support disrupts the perfect monochrome
from manifesting.

YAB: So when you move slightly sideways …

JK: When you move sideways, light catches in the Mylar, and the
image resolves. One part of the image is coming in front of another, and the relationship of your body to what you are seeing makes
the image contingent.

YAB: This is a good example of the materality of the process
being revealed.

JK: I hope so. I believe that the work makes this clear on its own,
especially when all five of the prints are shown together, and you
see the image in various aspects. It think that, with close looking,
it is clear that something is happening with this image that has
to do with its relation to its substrate, which changes across the
series. And since these five images belong together and are
shown together, the series tells some of its story on its own.

When we began discussing the apparatus earlier, you were
using the term in a very specific way, with a certain historical
context. Can you unpack that a bit?

YAB: When I talk about the apparatus, I mean all the technical
and ideological stuff that it takes to produce something. The
word "apparatus" first started to be used in the French context
in terms of Althusser's analysis of political discourse. Then it was
picked up in the *Cahiers du Cinéma* to describe the technical
aspects of cinema. Jean-Louis Comolli wrote a very famous
set of articles there, as did Jean Narboni. And then there was a
novelist, Jean-Louis Baudry, who also wrote about it, in response
to them, in a different journal *Cinéthique*. Comolli's argument
was that if you are a filmmaker, no matter what you do, you are a
prisoner of the apparatus. And the biggest part of the apparatus
is, of course, the camera, which will always force one-point perspective on you (except if you do something like Sharits or
Brakhage). In other words, even if you don't want to, you are
effectively doing work that rearticulates a Renaissance position.
I was very young when I read this argument, and I was very
impressed with it. The idea was that no matter how avant-garde,

how hard you worked to break the box as a filmmaker, as long
as you film, you are necessarily in the Italian Renaissance in a
fundamental way. This didn't mean that films couldn't be great or
even really innovative, but, as a filmmaker, you have to know that
your frame is imposing something on you. So I remember thinking
"well, is that the same for painting?"

JK: That's what I wanted to ask you: is it?

YAB: Of course, the issue is not one-point perspective anymore,
but, rather, what is the frame that we are forced to inhabit when
we start to paint?

JK: Exactly. Can you try to characterize that?

YAB: I don't know. That's probably why I left painting: because I
couldn't answer this question.

JK: Why you stopped making paintings?

YAB: Yes. It was too complicated for me!
  Perhaps now we can talk for a moment about another issue
your work brings up: the question of meta-discourse. In the works
we've discussed, the relation of the apparatus to the image is
visible in the work itself, but in many other pieces, there are a lot of
references outside the work that beg unpacking. For example, I am
thinking of your works that refer to Manet. I imagine that someone
who knows Manet's *oeuvre* very well would see the poses of the
figures in *Untitled (Clown Dance)*, 2012–13 or in *Untitled (The
Guitar Player)*, 2013–14—and having seen your exhibition invitation that is based on Manet's own invitation—would recognize
in these poses, sizes, and particular formats of the paintings a
reiteration of works by Manet. However, for the vast majority of
people seeing your show, the discourse would need to be pro-
vided somehow. That always has been an issue for me in a lot of
contemporary art with a conceptual bent: this necessity to have
a sort of meta-discourse.

JK: It's true, let's talk about the question of meta-discourse and
Manet together. First, Manet. He was, of course, himself obsessed
with the history of painting, and with Velazquez in particular. He
notably quoted Velazquez's paintings and poses again and again
in his own works. However, I don't think that our understanding of

Manet's work hinges on the artist explicitly unpacking this for his viewers. We don't rely on his "explanations" of his references or some such meta-discourse to approach his work. These connections emerge through interpretation and add layers to our readings of his paintings.

YAB: You don't think that the critics at the time knew that he was quoting Velazquez?

JK: Yes, indeed, they did, but I don't think he explicitly offered his relationship to Velazquez as a way to provide an explanation, or a meta-discourse for the interpretation of this work.

YAB: Yes, but I would imagine that the critics—I mean I would like to look more closely at the literature again to be sure— who saw his work, saw the link. It didn't need explanation to be visible …

JK: Let's agree there is a delicate balance to be struck about how artists attempt to direct a viewer's experience. For example, although, indeed, I did quote Manet extensively in my 2014 show (at Churner and Churner), I made sure that neither the press release nor any other material accompanying the exhibition addressed this aspect of the work as a way to provide "explanation." Nevertheless, as you note, the invitation we designed directly quoted the invitation to Manet's own 1867 self-organized exhibition. This was a significant clue, for it inhabited a specific historical document in the same way that many of my paintings recast some of the forms and imagery of his paintings. Further, the way I presented a diverse, almost anti-stylistic, range of works related to Manet's own exhibition strategy for that show. If a viewer were curious enough to pursue these leads and ask what this obviously anachronistic invitation design might point to, and perhaps even look into it, he or she might find one way to unpack my paintings—though certainly not the exclusive way. If we had included that information in a press release, I fear it would have implied that the only way to understand these paintings would be as historical quotations. That's not what I want to do. Then the work runs the risk of being seen as no more than an illustration of a concept, as opposed to something that can stand on its own. The references to Manet were more of a starting point for that work, than a node around which all interpretations might orbit.

YAB: Okay. How do outside references function in other works of yours? Would you say that most of your work is like this? What about the example of the two groups of five hands and the trellis *(Untitled (Color Test Hands #1–10)*, 2008-2012, and *Untitled (Lattice 1–3)*, 2012? I suppose that you can understand that each image is part of a sequence by looking at the series of paintings, but it would take a little longer to find out the relationship between the trellis and the paintings of hands.

JK: Yes. No doubt.

YAB: Is there anything in the show, or in the way that it is presented, that tells the story of the "China Girls"?

JK: Well, there was some information in the press release of the exhibition in which those works debuted (in 2013 at Ratio 3) that revealed that the hands depicted in the paintings come from footage of a woman shot for technical purposes of calibrating color in film. Even without this information, however, some of that story is alluded to in the parenthetical title of the piece: *Color Test Hands #1–10*. Also, you can get a sense of this from a close reading of the works themselves. Looking at the paintings as a group, you see a hand moving across a color spectrum, and you might further associate the color spectrum with some version of a degree zero of painting. From the previous room in the installation, which contained sludge paintings and rag paintings with monochrome wooden slats attached, you might recognize (at least, I hope you would) that this exhibition had to do, in part, with the process of painting and with deductive imagery. It might also be clear that this engagement was happening on the level of abstraction. So by the time you walked into the room with the color test paintings, the exhibition itself might hopefully have prepared you to surmise that, although very different from what preceded them, the relationships between the different works are structural rather than iconic.

Now, I don't believe it is necessary or even particularly important that a viewer would understand that the sequence of colors in the trellis slats relates to the sequence of the spectrum in the hand paintings *per se*, but I do think it is important that their presentation evokes a feeling of formal sympathy. I hope the fact that they are chromatically identical—in the sense that the colors on the canvas are exactly the same as those on the wood—would evoke a sense that they belong together.

It is less important to me that the viewer dissect the process and unpack the precise procedural relationships between the works. That's not my focus. I hope, rather, that in front of my works the viewer can encounter difference, but still experience kinship. All of this has to do with my still-evolving ideas about how to make exhibitions. I feel I am moving away from thinking of a show as a collection of autonomous objects towards considering instead the experience of the viewer. I am hoping to create an experience that may be fundamentally conceptual, but which comes out of a close material engagement with the work, and out of a narrative that is being constructed by how these objects are arranged in space …

YAB: I see.

JK: To return to what you were saying before, I wonder if it could be productive to consider the apparatus of painting as a filter through which to look at the other paintings in that show, the ones that incorporate rags and paint sludge. In the rag paintings, pieces of cloth that were used in the process of making "normal" figurative paintings are repurposed and presented on their own as found abstractions. These works were shown paired with monochromes painted from sludge, the material residue left over when you clean paintbrushes in solvent. Do you think that these works, which highlight the material remnants of process, could be understood relative to the apparatus of painting itself?

YAB: I'd say that they are certainly indexical signs of production. But are they themselves part of the apparatus? I don't know. Certainly they are tangible traces of the process of painting.

JK: So when you refer to the apparatus of painting, are you thinking more of the idea of an object that is on the wall, that is rectangular, flat, meant to be appraised with the eyes … these traditional qualities that pertain to most paintings?

YAB: Yes, maybe. These questions make me think of the group Supports/Surfaces. That's what they wanted to do, to work on the apparatus of painting. And, of course, they didn't really do it because it is hard. Or they make me think of someone like Robert Ryman. Basically, the best work of his for a good forty years had to do with painting's apparatus: What are the things that make a painting a painting? And, as his work demonstrates, these aspects are far more diverse than you would have thought.

JK: Yes. How to attach it to the wall? What kind of support is it on? How does the image work? It a field, or is it composed? Where does painterly touch fit in? All those kinds of things.

YAB: Yes, and with both Supports/Surfaces and Ryman there is the idea that the more you look, the more aspects appear to be part of painting's apparatus.

JK: I also was thinking about the apparatus in terms of image dis-tribution, specifically with regard to my haystack film, *Les Meules* (2011), which is comprised of a whole range of images of Monet's paintings culled from the Internet.

YAB: Distribution is certainly part of the apparatus today. It's a change that came with the web. These channels have become part of the apparatus of, let's say, pictorial knowledge, or pictorial distribution, and pictorial perception.

…

JK: I'd like to shift gears and return to the meta-discourse issue for a moment. Is it important to you that you eventually find out that there is a system governing an artist's project? That is, when you first encounter a bunch of disparate works that feel like they be-long together, but in other ways don't appear to belong together, is it important that you learn about the system, or meta-discourse, that connects them? That is, at what point do you need the figure of the artist to coalesce as an intentional character, to create a ground against which you can read that work as a creative and critical project? At what point is the singular subjectivity of the artist important to unify disparate work? As opposed to something, for example, that is unintentional, or the work of somebody that just doesn't make sense?

YAB: It is a good question. I suppose that once I sense that there is a system, then this is kind of titillating thing. System or not, I always want to try to understand what is at the core of a project. All my writing asks these questions. For example, with Matisse, I find the quality-quantity equation, which he speaks about all his life, in every single text. But people didn't notice it, and I thought, what does that mean? Mondrian speaks of destruction all the time. What does that mean? These are the questions that point to something at the core of what they do. It is not because I am fascinated by the intentionality of the artist *per se*, but rather that, in certain cases, a core unifies a practice. That's the role of the critic in a way: to identify and analyze this core. But it doesn't necessarily depend on what artists say. With some artists, it is very, very hard to ignore what they say. It's not that common. But it does happen. With Matisse, its unbelievable difficult to ignore what he says, because he is so eloquent.

Writing on Matisse is always a nightmare, because you try to avoid giving him the power of explanation. There is one text I wrote on Matisse, about his sculpture, in which I definitely said he is wrong about himself, that he completely misunderstands what he is doing. And what he is doing is much more important than what he thinks he is doing. But, in general, it is very hard to get out of Matisse's own ideas.

I always try to find something at the core of a practice, even if the work is extremely diverse. This is probably a result of my structuralist education, and is probably a very outmoded way of looking at and understanding things. So even though Picasso, for example, is like an endless cornucopia stylistically, I always try to understand what links all those things together. You know, sometimes it doesn't work. For example, for Matisse I invented this idea of a Matisse system that goes from 1905 to 1917, and picks up again in 1932 or 1931, and in between, he's against the Matisse system, it's like the anti-Matisse. It's Matisse trying to destroy what his work had been, and then coming back to it later and trying to revive what he had tried to kill for ten years. So, the Matisse system, for me, is chronologically split. There is a decade during which it does not apply.

JK: You used the concept of "return" there. Couldn't you frame the Matisse narrative as a dialectic, rather than as a return?

YAB: You could, but I have to admit that I have a strong distaste for Hegel—probably part of my education, it probably comes from Barthes.

JK: Because Matisse in part three is not the same as Matisse in part one …

YAB: No, of course not.

JK: … it bears the imprint of "reversal Matisse" in part two.

YAB: Oh, absolutely. I wrote an essay for a book on Matisse at the Barnes, which just came out. It's a hundred-page manuscript on Matisse from 1925 to 1935, about the crisis of the system, and then waking up with *The Dance* commission, and the Mallarmé book, and talking about the aftermath.

JK: Sounds a lot like Pollock from 1951 to 1956.

YAB: Yeah.

JK: Only Pollock doesn't get to live through the whole third act. Working through the crisis is a very interesting way to pose the problem. For Pollock, that involved some things that look to some people like reversals. But it is possible to provide a structural explanation that recasts them not as reversals, but as revisitations. Like an inventory of paths that weren't pursued.

YAB: Yes.

JK: When you are taking about Matisse, you are thinking in terms of an intentional system. I am interested in how this telescopes to larger questions about intention and interpretation. Maybe we can discuss this a bit—the different roles of the artist and critic—in the creation of meaning. Your writing often centers on artists in whose practices you identify systems, systems that either intentionally motivate their practices or that you define *post facto*.

YAB: Often.

JK: Let's take Ellsworth Kelly as an example. There are a number of memorable experiences that stayed with me from your Kelly seminar that I took (at Harvard University in 1999). First was our intense attention to what Kelly was doing on a material level. This mode of analysis was facilitated by the fact that we had his drawings on deposit there for us to look at in person each week. The experience of looking so closely and building analyses based on these observations impressed upon me a strong sense of how meaning could be unpacked from material gestures. Another important outcome for me was being introduced to your idea of the artist strategically introducing procedures to erase himself from the work. You identified a series of strategies of removal in Kelly's work: the transfer, monochrome, grid, collage, chance, readymade, seriality, non-composition, etc. Learning about these strategies was critical for me, and I saw them as an arsenal of sorts that I could take into my own studio practice. This was amplified by the fact that I was also thinking about deskilling in Pollock's work at that time. I thought these strategies could be recipes from which I could make work. I hoped that these strategies, precisely because they were impersonal, could help me couch a practice that was partially coming from a highly personal and non-intellectual place. I was hoping they could frame what I was up to with a set of concerns that were structural, as opposed to expressive. They were really helpful in that regard, especially since they were structural strategies, and I didn't feel like they belonged to Kelly alone. You and I have talked in the intervening years about the persistent "difficulty of erasing oneself," and about the fact that these strategies, and the systems artists devise to remove themselves from the work, almost always break down eventually. Despite their promise, they never create a tenable long-term practice. I think you have written on this in terms of Malevich, and Frank Stella ...

YAB: It breaks down for everyone ...

JK: ... everyone. So even though these strategies of erasure seem to offer such promise, they are never viable for long. Further, despite the pretense of its removal, the subjectivity of the artist always inevitably expresses itself, even, if ironically, through the act of erasure. Do you see that tension as a productive conflict or a dead end?

YAB: It's not a dead end, no. I don't know if you remember my essay "Painting: The Task of Mourning," which basically states that the entire history of modern art has always been a function of this fantasy of the end. The starting point is the fantasy of the end, and this produces a kind of productive contradiction. These artists constantly do things that are meant to resolve contradiction or questioning and in so doing produce more contradictions. It's like the endless recession of the end. But the end is posited at the beginning, as the origin. So I don't think that the contradiction between the desire to erase yourself and the impossibility to do so marks an impasse. The vector between those two basically accounts for the history of modern art, in general.

Let's think about the case of Francois Morellet, for example, who dreams of making systems that can produce his work without his intent. This is fine, but who designed the system? I visited Morellet with my kids about five years ago. They had not seen him for a long time, and he showed them his studio, and he explained what he is doing, how he is generating his work, and at some point he said, "Well, I don't know how long I will be able to survive…." He was 85 at the time. He said, "My wife and I decided that when I die, she can continue to produce the work. She'll put me in a fridge and nobody will know…." And my kids were like, "What!?!" They didn't realize instantly it was a joke. It would obviously be impossible. Because even with all these procedures—using chance and systems together—it doesn't prevent a Morellet from looking like a Morellet.

JK: And why not? How does an artwork which is ostensibly driven by systems always end up looking like it belongs as the work of the artist made it?

YAB: It is a very interesting paradox, and I don't know why exactly. Morellet would probably desire that this is not the case. I do remember that he and I had a real difference of opinion with regard to systems in Mondrian's work. Morellet believed that Mondrian's work would have been just as good if he had had a system. But I don't think that's true. Yes, in my use of the word "system" (as I speak of a Matisse system, for example), Mondrian has a system. That is, there are rules in Mondrian's painting, but only *he* knows the rules. This is not "system" as Morellet meant it, meaning something impersonally systematic, a set of rules than anyone could apply.

JK: Right, there is art that has a system and that obeys the logic of the system, but is not "systematic."

YAB: Exactly. Hence the big difference between Mondrian's grids—which are systematic, and he made only nine of them, and even within these there were parts that were non-systematic (like placement of color in the grids)—and everything else he did. After this short experiment with the modular grid, Mondrian's entire project was to go against anything that could be set systematically, and that jump-started the strategies of destruction throughout his life. Morellet thinks Mondrian was just a romantic dreamer, and his work would have just as good if he had had a system in the mathematical sense.

JK: Maybe that opinion is the engine of *his* practice.

YAB: Exactly! And I don't think its true: you can't make a Mondrian fit into a Morellet grid. It could never be the same. They are like two different conceptions of what painting should be, and two different ways of thinking about the disappearance of the artist. Mondrian, too, was thinking about the end. His entire theoretical apparatus, and the entire way in which he thought about his art and made his paintings, was to prepare for the end. For Mondrian, the end would mean there would no longer be a difference between artists and non-artists, between art and non-art, and all that utopian mish-mash that was very much part of the 1920s. It is a different way to think about disappearance, but it is not a way that has to do with systematic production of works that hide, or try to erase, the will of the artist.

JK: Here's another way to think about intention. In "Painting: The Task of Mourning," you use the psychological concept "mourning" to address the question of endless preparation for the end. I wonder if it's useful to revisit the issue of intentionality here. A psychological model can account for many things in an artist's practice that are beyond intention: things that are unconscious, or un-intentional, most notably. Can you talk a little bit about a fantasy about preparing for the end, a fantasy about death, mourning that death, or accepting that you will die, or that the system can end, in terms of the artist's psychology? Have you ever thought about that aspect?

YAB: At the end of that text, discussing the recurrent theme of the death of painting, I say something like "as long as there will be a desire to paint, painting will not die." It always returns, like a corpse. Every twenty-five years or so. Now its return is even quicker: every nine years or five, as things have accelerated.

JK: But the death of painting and the desire to paint are two totally different things. When we talk about the death of painting, we are usually talking about the death of this particular form as a viable and urgent means of public conversation about art. And this is connected to an idea, maybe now historical, of the avant-garde. That's very different from acknowledging that some people may desire to make paintings. The mere fact that some people still make paintings does not prove that painting lives on in a critical sense. Take the symphony or the opera, for example. These forms do not have the public life they once had at earlier moments in time. There still may be people who want to write symphonies and operas, but one would not argue that these forms remain vital and relevant in the way that they were in the nineteenth century, for example. So the question of the death of painting as a critical discourse that adds to our understanding of art and the fact that people persist in make paintings are not the same thing. One does not disprove the other.

YAB: That's true. There is death by exhaustion, which seems to be the model of the symphony and of the opera, as you say.

JK: Yes, and if one wants to construct a narrative of development to account for art, you cannot argue that painting is at the center of the conversation now. So painting does not continue to be reborn as a viable critical discipline every nine years, or every five years; just because the accelerated logic of the market demands paintings to sell to people who regard them as art by default, that doesn't mean it's viable or critical, really …

YAB: In that text, I traced three different strategies of modernism: the Duchamp model, the Mondrian model, and the Rodchenko model. Each of these strategies—represented by the readymade, the grid, and the monochrome—have to do with imagining the end. But I present these not as impasses but as paths of imagining the end; they are not the end itself. The argument is ultimately that if painting is to survive, it has to invent a new way to write its own death. That is the only motor for painting to continue to exist: to find new ways to die.

JK: The only motor for painting to continue to exist …

YAB: … is finding a new way to die.

JK: The idea that painting can exist only by imagining new ways to die presupposes two things, I think. First, it presupposes progress. It means we can recognize the past and accept new limitations based on what has already been done ...

YAB: … not necessarily progress. It has to recognize different categories, but these don't have to be progressive. It is not like Mondrian comes after Duchamp. It doesn't have be a chronological, linear sequence.

JK: Okay, let me take this from another angle: Is originality part of this conversation?

YAB: Yes, because you have to invent new ways of dying.

JK: And do you think that originality and invention are viable concepts today?

YAB: Well, I don't know if they are viable, but they are the ones that have to stick.

JK: Why do they have to stick?

YAB: It's my own taste, really. I don't like repetition. I mean, if I see something I've seen before, I lose interest.

JK: That's interesting, because, to my mind, a lot of the artists you like seem to be doing things that are very similar to each other. They might not repeat exactly what the others are doing, but they are all within a narrow band, let's say.

YAB: That is true. Although, I have written on things I didn't know I would be interested in.

JK: Like what?

YAB: Well, when Robert Pincus-Witten asked me to write about Ed Ruscha's "Liquid Words," I had no idea I would find them interesting.

JK: What was it that you found interesting about the "Liquid Words"?

YAB: Well, it's all in that text, which by the way, I wrote very fast. It was one of those rare texts where you read the documentation and then just sit down and write. I wrote it in two days, which doesn't happen that often in life. People think that I write fast. No way! And so, it was a happy text. Plus, I found a kind of pleasure in reversing the discourse on Ruscha, which always focuses on him being a Los Angeles artist, etc., etc. I don't care much about that. I have Russian formalists and Mallarmé and others entering my text, and Ruscha must have thought it absolutely crazy. He didn't like it, I found out.

JK: That last bit says something about the conflict between intention and interpretation. If you were to imagine yourself from an artist's perspective …

YAB: The way an artist sees his or her work and the way a critic does are often divergent. It happens all the time. Take, for example, the first people to write about Kelly in France. Michel Seuphor always presented him as a kind of true heir of Mondrian. This interpretation stuck for years, while his work had nothing to do with Mondrian. But what was he to do? Do you tell the people who defend you "no, no, you have it wrong?" What do you say when you are a young starving artist? You let it go.

JK: So let's talk about that in relation to, for example, your earlier line of questioning, which has to do with how much unpacking is necessary in the case of work that contains historical references. Is it your position that artists who work this way should be talking about their work? Or do you think its the art's job to stand and fall on its own, letting the references remain inexplicit?

YAB: I don't know if one has to have rules. Take Michael Asher: his work has always courted invisibility. The works that involve changing a gallery space slightly—moving a work that was there before, say—are only visible if you knew the place before. Otherwise, you don't see anything. Literally. There is nothing to see.

JK: It's only visible if you know Michael Asher's practice.

YAB: In a way, yeah. But if you knew that a particular sculpture was normally outside the Art Institute of Chicago, and then you saw it inside, you wouldn't need to be familiar with Michael Asher's practice to notice something had changed (*George Washington at the Art Institute of Chicago*, 1979 and 2005).

JK: But you need to know his practice to contextualize the gesture and to give it some meaning.

YAB: Yes, but to receive the information that the sculpture has been displaced, you only need to know where it was before. And a lot of his work is really enigmatic in that sense. It has a very light touch. The works of his that I prefer are those projects in which you instantly gather that something was added to the space. You see that something is out of place and you try to figure out what it is. And because you want to figure it out, you look for more information, which is usually found, minimally presented, on some piece of paper somewhere in the gallery. There was a show at the Santa Monica Museum of Art (in 2008), one of his last shows, in which Asher rebuilt the supporting structure of all the temporary walls that were designed for all the exhibitions ever held there. This created a labyrinth of metallic structures through which you could walk. (After you signed a document saying that if you got hurt, because those metallic posts were sharp, you would not sue the museum, of course!) Because of this multiplication of posts, the space was so crowded, so jam-packed, and it made you think, "Museums are crazy. Why do you have to redo all these walls from scratch all the time, in order to rebuild what amounts, basically, to the same spaces?" You felt a bizarre demonstration of the insanity and vanity of the art world. Asher's work, by underlining the strangeness of the space, showed very patently that for the museum industry exhibition de-sign has more to do with controlling the space than with the art it is supposed to showcase. This was very unlike most of his work. I was very struck by the piece for that reason. Because I always felt that the infinite discretion of his work had always come at the cost of invisibility.

JK: It seems that one reason that piece in particular functions so well is because it is very elegant. And it is very efficient. One deci-sion sets the whole thing in motion. It's elegant and efficient, and the means by which it solicits the interpretation you are outlining, has to do with exaggeration. Basically a single note has been turned up almost too loud, and because it is so loud, you then hear it differently. This relates to the typical modernist strategy of creating distance, or estrangement. There is kind of an alien-ation effect …

YAB: Absolutely. As well as a reduction to one given.

JK: Yes, and this efficient reduction to one given, which, through exaggeration and amplification, creates a distance that then pro-vides a space for critical reflection, right?

YAB: Yes.

JK: If estrangement is meant to create a critical space, then it is presupposed that it is indeed possible to occupy a privileged, critical space in relation to that gesture. Is that even an option today? Is it possible to think of a privileged critical space "outside"? Or, let me put it another way: Do you think it's possible to talk about anything like an avant-garde now? If not, if that term is now only useful historically, how would you describe practices today that you identify as being in that spirit of criticism, of distance, of alienation—those characteristics are that you identify with the Asher…? Can you call Michael Asher's work from less than a decade ago avant-gardist? If you can, can you tell me how? And if you can't, can you offer another term, or say how we might frame a critical practice, without using this historical terminology?

YAB: Yeah, it is very hard, because, of course, you know, in your own desire, you cling to that wish! (*Laughs.*) So it is very hard. I think that the old model of the avant-garde—represented by the daring artist or poet or musician who carries a torch, with humanity following behind—is really laughable today, especially within the new systems of production and distribution and globalism. That's just silly. But, in a kind of nostalgic way, you can't just deny the desire for something like that. As for Asher, I think in his own mind, he probably saw his project in avant-gardist terms. However, I think that one of the reasons his work succeeded in that particular moment was because, for the first time, it was spectacular as well. He understood that the condition of the spectacle had become central, viable conditions …

JK: … viable?

YAB: No, viable is not the right word. Necessary, rather. He realized the spectacle could be conveyed in a kind of reverse way. I was struck a few years ago by going to these big galleries in Chelsea, and seeing paintings that were not even one square foot on a huge wall. That is pure spectacle, too.

JK: Yes, of course. It is like Tiffany's putting a diamond ring spot-lit in a case in the middle of a huge room with double high ceilings.

YAB: Yes. The spectacle can be expressed in many different ways. That's hard to grasp, and even harder to accept, for someone of my generation … I think that someone's taste is formed fairly early and doesn't evolve that much. You always come back to that moment where you had you first big epiphany, even without knowing it. That experience structures you. But I do recognize that today,

in order for something to exist as a durational, meaningful angle
in the world, the dimension of the spectacle is not something you
can ignore. And some people can do it in a very effective way, I
mean, there are successes … it is not always horrible. But my own
taste is contra the spectacle.

JK: Can you think of contemporary practices that reckon with
the spectacle without indulging in it? Can you think of works that
engage that condition but which don't participate in it?

YAB: Yes. There are practices that participate in it, but also
provide a side view to it. I am thinking, for example, of Anthony
McCall's *Line Describing a Cone*, 1973. Okay, this work is not
contemporary in a strict sense, it is from forty years ago, but is
a good example. In order to recreate it recently he had actually
to change the apparatus, because, as you might remember, the
first iteration in the early '70s was in movie theaters where people used to smoke, and now he has to have a smoke machine to
create the effect. This is a perfect spectacle. It is extraordinary! Or,
there's Robert Irwin's installation at the Whitney just before they
moved (a 2013 restaging of *Scrim veil-Black rectangle-Natural
light, Whitney Museum of American Art*, 1977). They completely
emptied an entire floor of the Whitney, and he made this gorgeous
installation that was spectacular.

JK: Okay, these are good examples, but we are talking about two
different things here, and I'd like to distinguish between means
and ends. There is a famous line in "The Society of the Spectacle,"
in which Guy Debord says the only way to analyze the spectacle
is to speak its language. This is about creating disruptions. Both
the McCall and the Irwin examples are cases in which artists
are using the language of the spectacle to create a spectacular
experience that reflects on the conditions of the spectacle. It's not
to make the apparatus disappear so that your attention and vision
would be captured in the sense in which the Debord understands
the spectacle to operate …

YAB: … but it is still spectacular. You can see the way kids look at
the cone. They are in Luna Park! They put their hands through it
and say, "Oh, it disappears…." And you want to do it too! It's fun.
It's like we are at the circus. So it does participate in spectacular
aspects at the same time. That is why I think it is a brilliant thing. It
is both the spectacle and the demonstration of the spectacle.

JK: This is the argument typically used to locate criticality in Warhol's work—and in Jeff Koons's as well.

YAB: Warhol put his finger on the problems and the aporias of art production in the twentieth century in a very remarkable way. I mean, I think that Warhol was absolutely brilliant as a kind of diagnostician. But at the same time, he's like a doctor who sees the sickness and then gives you pills to make you even more sick. He was very good at this. He is a cynic, that's for sure. But he is also someone whose diagnosis made a lot of things change. Koons is in many ways repeating things that Warhol did, but he is more cashing in, rather than doing something new. I don't think there are a lot of new things in Koons.

JK: I want to shift gears here from questions of the spectacle and turn the conversation back to ideas of artistic intention, particularly as they are made visible through style and/or consistency. Can we start with your argument about Picasso and the Harlequin ("Picasso the Trickster," in *Picasso Harlequin 1917–1937*)?

YAB: Well, the Picasso Harlequin thing is something that is very interesting to me, because I struggled with it for a long time. I remember, a very long time ago, that I thought—like everyone else in my little pot, at least—that it was a "Return to Order" case. That is the way it was interpreted. But the more I read texts that defined what Picasso was doing as Return to Order, the more these arguments began to self-destruct. And the more I knew about Picasso and what he was doing, and the way he was doing it, my opinion changed. I remember seeing a work in the Musée Picasso: it's a grid and in some squares you have Cubist still-lifes and in others, Pompeiian hands (*Studies*, 1920–22).

JK: The painting of studies, with the face, and the hands, and the couple?

YAB: Exactly, and the Cubist still-life. I thought, this couldn't be Return to Order. These different painted parts—Cubist still-life and classical anatomic fragments—are contemporary: that's what he underscores in having them within the same canvas. He is telling us something about the range of painting.

JK: The range, and the mobility of style …

YAB: Yes, and that's something completely different from a return. And then, I had a conversation with Benjamin Buchloh about Richter. I was asking him, why do you say that Picasso of the '20s is part of a Return to Order? What about Richter's use of portraits? Isn't that the same? Benjamin said, "No, what Richter is doing with the use of portraits is showing the panoply of painting." I said, "Well, it seems to me that is exactly what Picasso was doing." Picasso wanted to fill all the possibilities on the chessboard of painting at the same time. At least that's what I think he was doing. Why he was doing this is complex and was difficult to find. I think it was a rescue mission for painting, so that it would not die. And especially, in Picasso's mind, not to die of abstraction. Contrary to Rosalind (Krauss)'s "Picasso/Pastiche" argument, I don't think that anxiety about Dada and Picabia and the readymade was what was going on with Picasso. I don't think it was really so fundamental for him. But preventing painting from dying—and for him, abstraction would have been the death of painting—that is surely part of Picasso's motivation.

JK: And so what he does is present a dictionary of painting's possibilities.

YAB: Yeah. And I think that is what Richter is doing, too, in a different way, later on.

JK: I think Richter's dictionary is much narrower. It includes the monochrome and gestural abstraction …

YAB: … and seriality, and the grid, but also the "history paintings," the landscapes, the nudes, the portraits, etc.

Many, many years ago I wrote an essay called "Historization or Invention: The Return of an Old Debate," which is not translated into English. Perhaps I should revisit it. In the essay, I was thinking about the modernist telelogy. I was fascinated by several texts, one of which was by Robert Klein. Do you know who that is?

JK: No.

YAB: He was a brilliant art historian. I think he was from Bulgaria. He didn't have a passport for whatever reason, and he was exploited like hell by the French art historian André Chastel, the great specialist of the Renaissance, who was like the king of art history in France at the time. Klein was Chastel's assistant for a lot of things, but he was also a philosopher, a follower of Merleau-Ponty, steeped in phenomenology and all that. Very, very interesting guy. Klein wrote several essays about the aesthetic attitude. He made a fantastic comparison between the car mechanic and the art connoisseur. It was very funny. And there was another one in which he argues that chronology and historicization have become part of aesthetic criteria. That is, when a work of art is made and how it relates to other—past, contemporary, or posterior—works of art, this has become part of our taste, and date and sequence become part of the aesthetic judgment. I was very struck by that because this certainly is not something that is part of the intention of the artists.

JK: That story reminds me of something, maybe a more radicalized version of that. It's a short text that fascinates me by Borges called "Kafka and His Precursors." Do you know it?

YAB: I vaguely remember it.

JK: In the text, Borges gives four examples of historical material that preexisted Kafka: Zeno's paradox against movement, a text by Han Yu, the work of Kierkegaard, and a poem by Browning. And then Borges says all of these examples can be said to hold in them elements that we identify as "Kafkaesque." Borges also notes that none of the examples have anything in common with each other. And the fact of this unity and difference is remarkable, because it means that Kafka, a writer who lives chronologically later than the examples Borges cites, creates meaning in his predecessors' work that we only see retrospectively and that we can't then unsee. And so this reverses the model of influence. Instead of saying that these four examples "created" Kafka in a classical sense, Borges argues that Kafka writes his precursors.

This creates a model of understanding history that I think is germane to the history of painting, and particularly strong in the history of critical, self-referential painting practices. I am particularly interested in this idea of a subsequent artist "creating" aspects of his or her precursors, especially in Manet's rewriting of Velazquez. This is also is something that I am trying to address in my own work.

YAB: Well, you are at a moment in which there is no easy course forward in painting. Manet was also in a crisis. So what did he do? He decided to look back to see what he could change. It's like *The Terminator*, you go back to prevent …

JK: … your own death. And I think that Manet is a particularly potent reference for me personally. Not only because he is a great artist, and I want to spend my time thinking about great art, but because I think that the moment that he inaugurates, in terms of painting's encounter with other technical means of representing the world, as a crisis position, relates to our own time. It inaugurates a moment that is now ending. The terms of that encounter—between painting and photography, say—have now totally changed. We are in a new era. Our understanding of photography is completely different. For Manet, it represented a new means of truth-telling that threatened painting's priority for picturing the world, whereas now we've already witnessed an intense critique of photography's naturalizing function. My feeling is that the "death of photography," that we are witnessing, if you could call it this, could be connected to rebirth of painting in postmodernism. That is, if photography didn't do what it claimed it was doing vis-à-vis painting—that is, mechanically and dispassionately representing the world—then perhaps painting's relative weaknesses weren't insurmountable. This type of thinking certainly informs my interest in showing the apparatus of the lens flare in a "romantic" painting. It's to say if we acknowledge that the thing that was supposed to kill painting—i.e., mechanical reproduction in photography—is in fact as much an ideological instrument as painting, then, ironically, this might open a space for one of the oldest and most durable disciplines of all.

Which leads me back to Barthes. I've been meaning to ask you about "Death of the Author"—about his relation to that text, and your relation to it, as well as your relation to him—as a way to discuss what it really means to take biography so radically out of the equation of interpretation. I understand "Death of the Author" was meant as a kind of polemic, and it presents an extreme counterpoint to a specific brand of biographically driven hagiography that characterized literary and art criticism in the '60s …

YAB: Well, as you know, Barthes came back to the notion of biography later on. His notion of the "biographeme" takes biography as a piece of fiction. So it's not that he was returning to the kind of biographically driven interpretations from before. What he resented, and which is constant, even today, is the tendency to explain the work by maker's life, even when many artists said, "No, no, no. You shouldn't do that." Barthes really resented biography as a kind of heuristic explanation of the work. When he reintroduced biography it was in terms of little blips of fiction, as another element of writing, almost like a haiku. It was not as an explanation of the work, at all. I remember when he reintroduced this idea. It was in the preface of *Sade, Fourier, Loyola*. The book is a collection of essays about three "Logothetes," as he called them: that is, inventors of languages. Anyway, I can tell a story about that. So, the book appeared, and we had a seminar just like a week or ten days later....

JK: How many people were in the seminar?

YAB: About fifteen.

JK: And what year was this?

YAB: It must have been '72 or '73, something like that. Students were not forced to do presentations in his seminar. (In fact, I never did one; I was always too anxious to do it. But you could.) Anyway, someone had asked to make a presentation and was talking about the poetry of Arp. Now Barthes and poetry: forget it. It was not his cup of tea. And this student's presentation was unbelievably boring. At the end, Barthes, with his normal generosity, said something like, "Well, if I were you, I would have spoken a little more"—and, by the way, the guy had not spoken of it at all—"about all the dualities here: we have someone with two names 'Hans' and 'Jean', two languages, two addresses, two dates of birth, two practices, as a *plasticien* and a poet, etc." The guy was scribbling all these things down in his notebook, and at some point another student, a Brazilian woman, erupted. She said, "How can you go back to this thing? You wrote *Sur Racine* against biography!" It was obvious that she was the only one of the entire group who had not read the new book. We all looked at her. And Barthes—of course, he could not tolerate violence—he was completely shocked at her outburst. I had an appointment with him to discuss my work (I was quite stuck, I remember, and really needed his guidance), and we went to this café, and he said, "Yve-Alain, I can't do it. I am so annoyed at this woman." He was furious at her. And it was interesting that she had not understood what he was trying to do. He was not trying to explain Arp's work by this duality, he was trying to say there is some basic pattern there, that is interesting in itself. Given this, it makes sense to ask, what do we do with it?

JK: Yes, he clearly had a more nuanced way of considering biography—it returned as a text in its own right, not as an explanation.

YAB: Exactly. It's not explanatory at all. It is as an element. I remember another time spotting him in a café, reading a book, and I waved hello to him, and he invited me over and showed me the book he was reading. He said, "I will show it to you," but it was clear he was not going to show it to everyone. It was a memoir written by Proust's maid with the help of someone, full of all these anecdotes.

JK: It was gossip, basically. Biographical gossip.

YAB: And he said, "I adore it!" (*Laughs.*)

JK: Well, it's very nice to hear that not every position is so rigid.

YAB: With regard to several things, Barthes could be surprisingly traditional. Even though he was a Marxist early on, he had always been very opposed to and skeptical about the endless explanation of a work of fiction or whatever through the lens of what was at that time a very vulgar Marxist type of analysis. Refusing the idea that the class position of the writer explains everything. He had such a complex conception of what meaning is. That is something all his students learned. All the people who studied with him can never hear the word "meaning" without thinking, "Well, you know...."

JK: He had very complex conception of what meaning is.

YAB: Indeed. For example, when people discuss abstract art as if it has no meaning; this is not true, of course. It has a lot of meaning. But perhaps not what they intend by "meaning," which is usually "referent," because most people don't know the difference. Barthes was against any explanation a work of art of any kind that is simple, whether it be biographical, socio-political, or even psychoanalytic. I mean, he was very interested by psychoanalysis, but the explanation of a work of art through that grid alone was something he found ridiculous.

JK: Where does that leave artistic intention? Was it meant to be completely excluded, or could intention be considered as one element amidst a constellation of elements?

YAB: It could be brought in, but only as one element. I mean, it is very complicated. I am very interested in the fact that when you do a catalogue raisonné, like I am doing on Kelly, you become

an arch reactionary historian! (*Laughs.*) You do! It like a rule. You
have to transform yourself. So often I have thought, after I have
written a paragraph, Poor Barthes! If he were to see me now, he
would be very disconcerted by what I have to do: to sort out the
"true" intention.

JK: Oh no. I can imagine. Perhaps we can connect this back to the
idea of self-erasure. Can you comment a little bit on why you believe self-erasure emerges in certain self-aware critical practices?

YAB: You cannot ask this question without specifying historical
parameters, because the impetus changes several times and is
dependent on context. The desire for impersonality was very clear
at the moment of Mallarmé and Seurat, for example, as a kind of
rebellion against a Romantic view of art. And it was very strong at
the moment of Dada, as well. Jean Arp, for example, is particularly
clear about it, at least in a retrospective text in which he clearly
associates impersonality with the collages he made with Sophie
Taeuber: both the modular grid ones, with the rectangles made
using scissors, and those arranged by chance. Arp believed both
strategies worked against a certain conception of subjectivity
based on a Cartesian ideal of free will, which, as he saw it, had
brought about WWI. You can also see a drive for impersonality after WWII as a kind of rebellion against the war. Then the
pendulum swings again, and tendencies emerge against Abstract
Expressionism. The will to self-erasure changes according to the
times. For example, the reasons that would motivate such practices in Soviet Russia—as being against the entire subjective, com-
positional aesthetic bourgeois baggage—has nothing to do with
Arp, just a few years before in Europe. Similarly, neither has much
to do with, let's say, the Minimalists. Because all these moments
have different motivations, I don't think that you can say there is
any single reason "why." It does seem an important point about all
these instances, however, is that in each, the cult of personality
is thought to lead to disaster: either to aesthetic disaster or to
socio-political disaster.

JK: Of course, contextualizing these different signal moments of
self-erasure within a bigger socio-political frame helps immensely.
Perhaps then for our purposes, we can focus on the most recent
manifestations. To that point, I am thinking about instances from
the postwar period into the present, in which self-erasure—
and even more specifically, strategies of deskilling—is theorized

in political terms as a response to global capitalism. Here we could return to the example of Richter, whom we discussed briefly previously. My understanding of deskilling in Richter's practice has to do with a desire to move beyond personal taste, which, by implication, represents the traditional model of the artist as an exceptional expressive figure constructed by bourgeois ideology. That is, Richter is understood to work towards a counter-position of a role inherited by a capitalist system geared towards valorizing individual achievement in the market.

YAB: Sure. It's interesting to see this as a counter-move. As you know, the "return to painting" in early '80s (in America, at least) was framed in the most bravado way, with figures like Julian Schnabel as exemplary. At the time Richter was clearly distanced from such a return to big, neo-Romanticism by everyone around him. He himself was not that vocal about it, as far as I remember, but it was clear that a conceptual anchor was very important to his practice. I didn't get the feeling that he was specifically de-nouncing the art market as a false, artificially created force behind the new painterly, pictorial cult. I don't think that he was himself saying that his work was battling against that, rather that he was maintaining a certain degree of ambiguity, let's say, which was probably rather strategic. I am speaking only about his reception in America. But even here it was clear that since he was working on so many different genres and in so many different guises that he was up to something different than, say, Anselm Kiefer. For any kind of public to have an artist that does these abstract paintings, monochromes, portraits, landscapes (well, the landscapes came later), this is always somewhat strange. The diversity of his prac-tice was so extravagant that it prompted people to begin ask what he was doing. It was obvious that he knew his twentieth-century stuff. It was not like he was coming out of nowhere; he was not the Douanier Rousseau. Given this, his work obviously exhibited some kind of construct. And so the fact that he seemed to be executing a plan in an orderly fashion became clear very quickly, especially when compared to the other painters at that time.

JK: So, Richter was pitted against models in which a singular style is being pursued, because that style is meant to expressively attend to an individual subject. By using many different modes, Richter's practice demands his viewers consider the meta-project and its overarching parameters …

YAB: What about Picasso then? He tackled absolutely everything. But you always see the seed of his personality. I think that Richter is different. Specifically in his landscapes and portraits, he avoids the idea of a real underneath the representation. He is not painting in a style. He just picks up something and paints it in a way that is almost cliché.

JK: Okay, but even when you are working in a multitude of modes, each of these modes bears the imprint of your subjectivity. In your mind, does the self-erasure model—which pushes the expressive subject back one degree—seem effective, at least inasmuch as it signals an awareness of the political problems of romantic subjectivity? Does this take the question into a different, more productive, order, or does it merely move the same problem onto a conceptual level?

YAB: I think it makes it of a different order. And doing this, it keeps the question alive. It keeps contradiction alive. And so, if you are a Marxist, or you believe that contradiction is good, it works.

JK: It keeps the contradiction alive, okay, but it does so against a backdrop that conservatively still expects an individual subject will express him- or herself in only one way and in only one style. But what if you are no longer wedded to this clichéd ideas of a single style anyway?

I also wonder how you understand strategies of self-erasure to change across different mediums. In literature, for example. Can we talk a little about such strategies in literature, in Oulipo, for example?

YAB: Oulipo certainly had the idea very early on to have a literature that would be completely programmed. It started in the '50s, and I think musicians were related to it. Pierre Schaeffer and others pursued the idea of programmed music. Schaeffer wrote a big book in the early '50s called *In Search of a Concrete Music*, and he was the king of the particular branch of the French Radio System, a research branch called Groupe de Recherche de Musique Concrète. It is amazing to think that the French government paid these avant-garde musicians to do their stuff for at least a good twenty years. You know, Morellet was also part of Oulipo at some point. Not closely linked, but he had some friends in that circle. Oulipo is part of a long tradition that had the idea of introducing specific problems in literature. The most famous, of course, is

Georges Perec's *La Disparition*. It is a whole novel without the letter "e." Which, in French, is almost impossible to fathom. It is just crazy! "E" is the most important letter. So to write a novel with no "e" means a lot of juggling. It means that you can't use many, many things. The funny thing was that when he published the book, he never mentioned it. He never said the letter "e" was "the disappeared" of the title. There were, I don't know, two months of reviews, and not a single one mentioned the absence of the letter "e." Finally he said, "I didn't know it was that good! Nobody realized…." So that was Oulipo: Literature as math problem, a problem to be solved.

JK: And do you think that any of those strategies have any traction now, or do you just see them as part of a historical avant-garde?

YAB: I think they are historical. These strategies don't seem to attract anyone right now. I mean it's not that it would necessarily be a return to high-falutin Romanticism, but … I don't know.

JK: I think that there are a lot of artists returning to this idea of self-erasure as a strategy, and maybe looking toward formulas and methodologies like those of Oulipo as a way to temper an expressive impulse, but also to demonstrate a critical awareness, like we were discussing with Richter. I know I am! The question of how to be an artist who pushes back against what is expected by the market seems a pressing problem. This can mean low visibility. By contrast, those who are seen are seen because they most successfully fulfill the role they're being asked to perform. Fewer people are given the platform to do things like, I don't know, make a novel out of a chess script, or something. The question is, do you think that all art in which the artist appears as an individual expressive subject or is recuperated as an individual subject, even if it is on the level of the critical meta-project, is inherently tainted by the way that capitalism asks us to perform individuality? Is that an inescapable problem?

YAB: You know, there was a moment where this same question was asked at the end of the structuralist movement in France. There was a real, clear return to subjectivity. It was not yet identity politics, which came later from America, but rather it was subjectivity that emphasized bodily presence. This really returned as a backlash after the abstraction of the structuralist ethos. Funnily enough, at that time, it was not at all understood as a kind of capitulation in front of the force of the market. Now, after nearly twenty-five years, and I am speaking about French literature, the endless publication of autobiographical fiction is totally exhausted. People are just fed up with it. But it took a long time for the market to pick up, and for this to become the standard thing to do. I think capitalism is so strong that nothing can escape it. It's a dream, an infantile, naïve, cute dream, to think that you can develop the means to escape the hydra of the market. You aren't going to escape it.

JK: Maybe it's a naïve fantasy to think that you could escape the market. Is it equally naïve to think that there could be any critical space in which to operate?

YAB: Yes. I think that it might be naïve. But, at the same time, its important to keep that naïveté alive.

JK: There is a word for that.

YAB: (*Laughs.*) It's called "hope."

JK: It's called "utopia!" (*Laughs.*)

YAB: Yes!

July 2015

INSTALLATION PHOTOGRAPHS AND CATALOGUE OF WORKS EXHIBITED

Jordan Kantor: Selected Objects (from some time ago until now) assembles a large collection of works by Jordan Kantor, conceived and installed by the artist specifically for CCAD. Comprising works spanning over fifteen years, the exhibition highlights the diverse and interdisciplinary nature of Kantor's practice and includes painting, photography, drawing, and printmaking, among other artistic mediums. Drawn exclusively from the artist's own collection—with the selection principle that all pieces be black, grey, or white—the exhibition features many works never before shown, including a new group of large-scale paintings. *Jordan Kantor: Selected Objects (from some time ago until now)* provides a singular opportunity to survey the artist's materially-diverse, conceptually-driven practice to date.

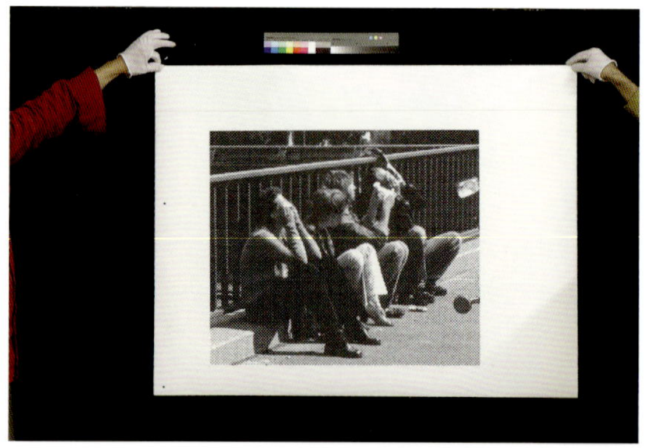

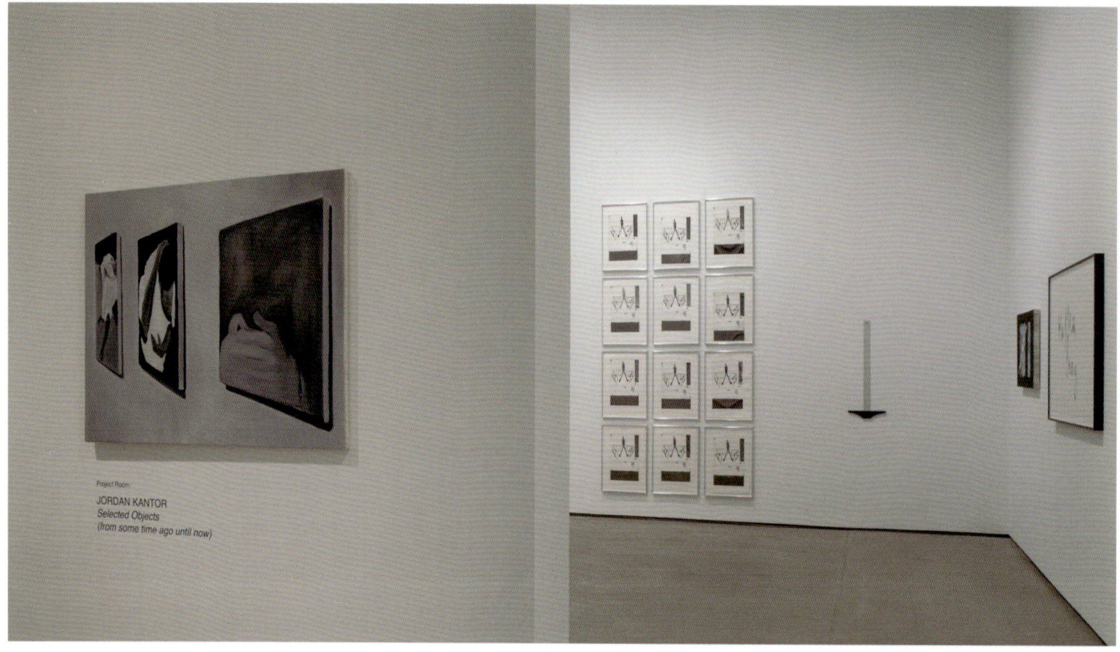

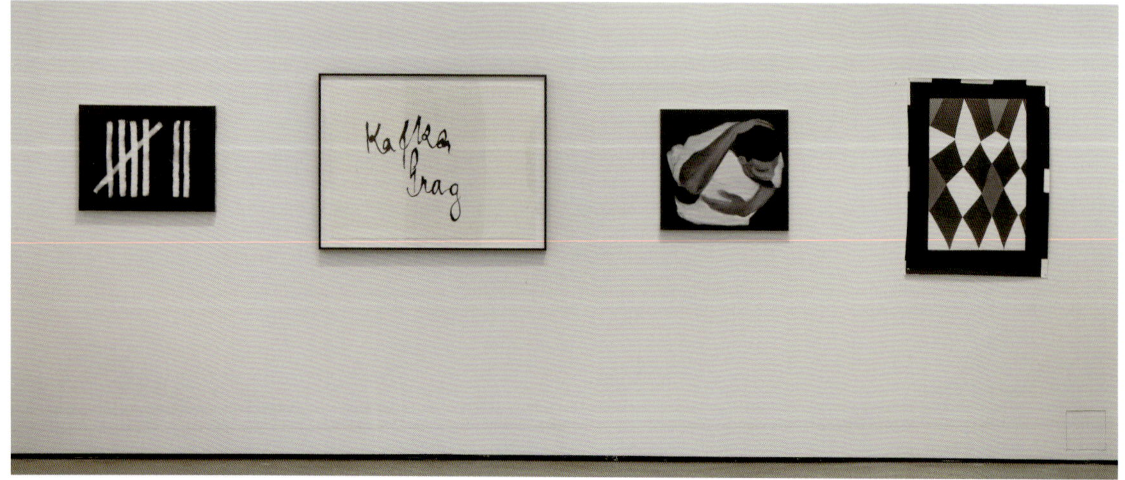

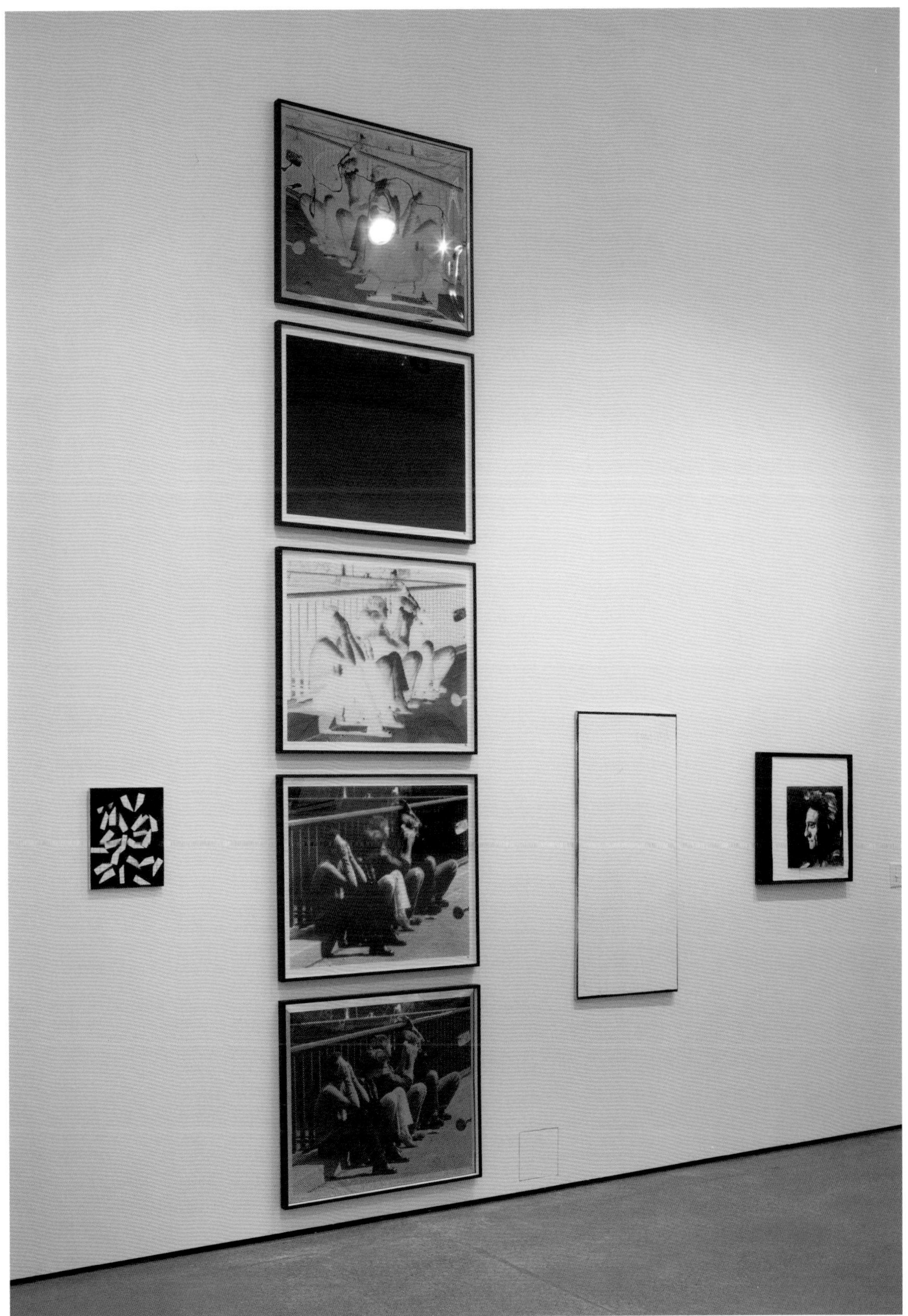

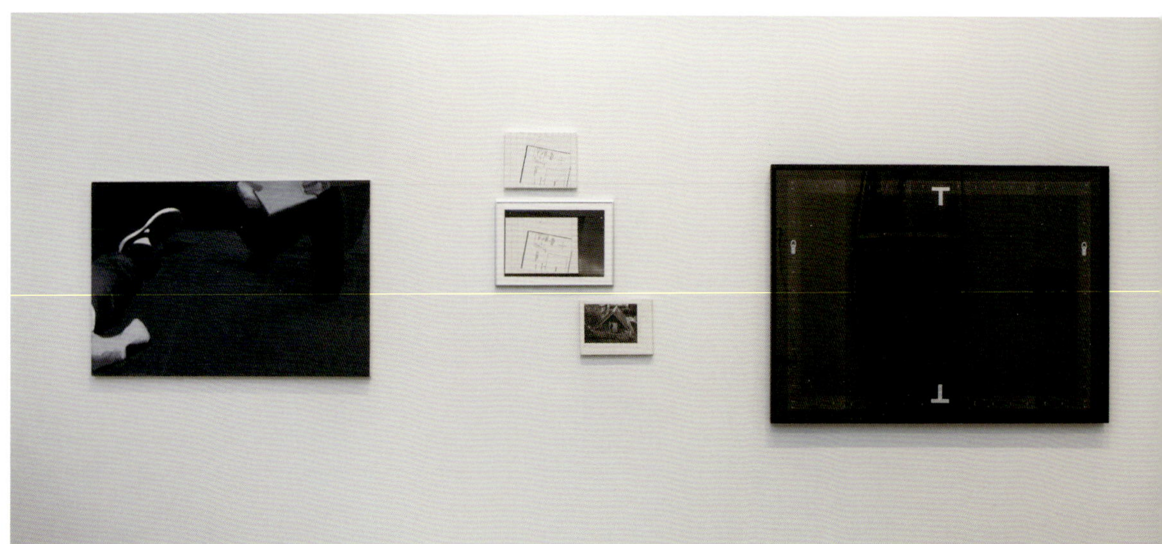

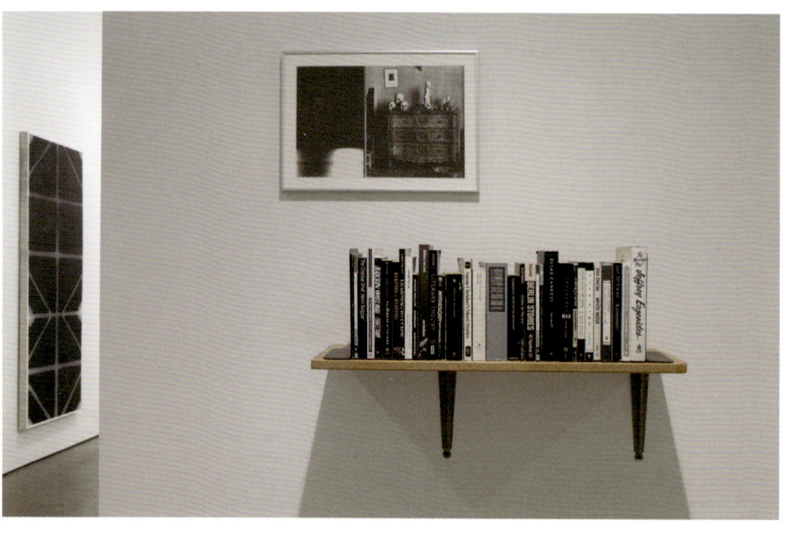

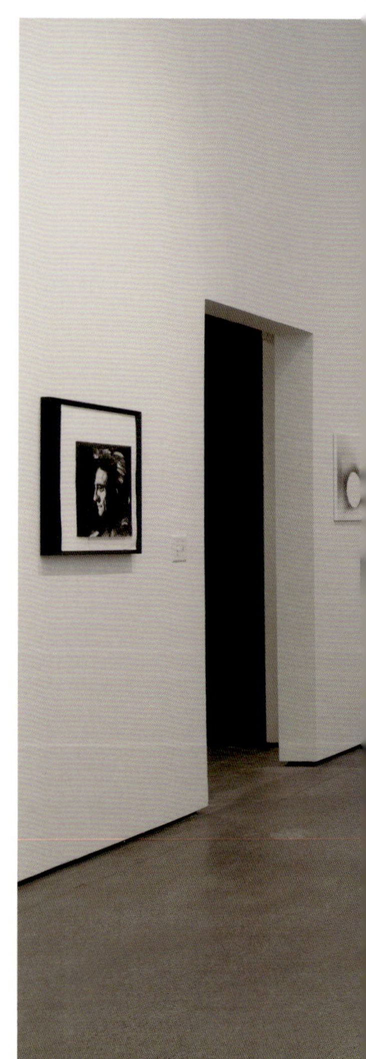

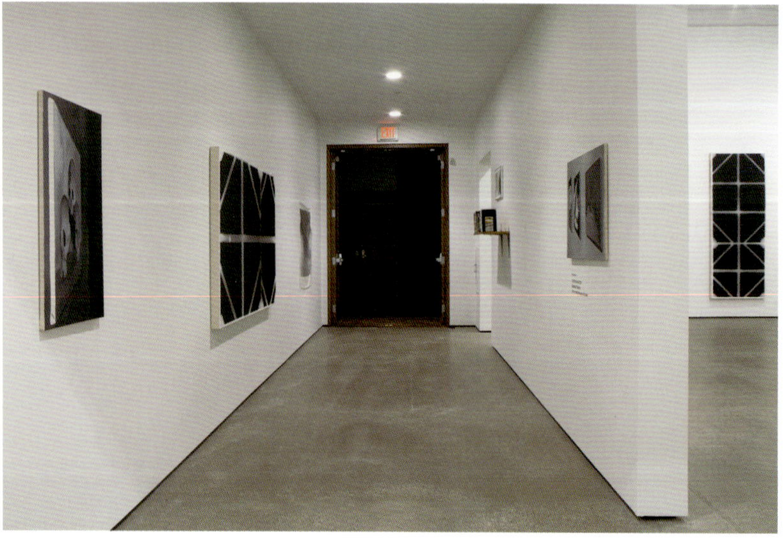

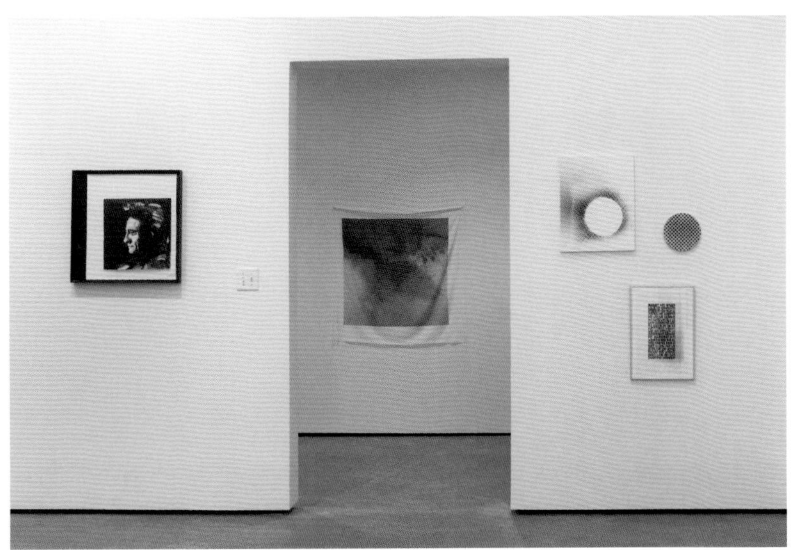

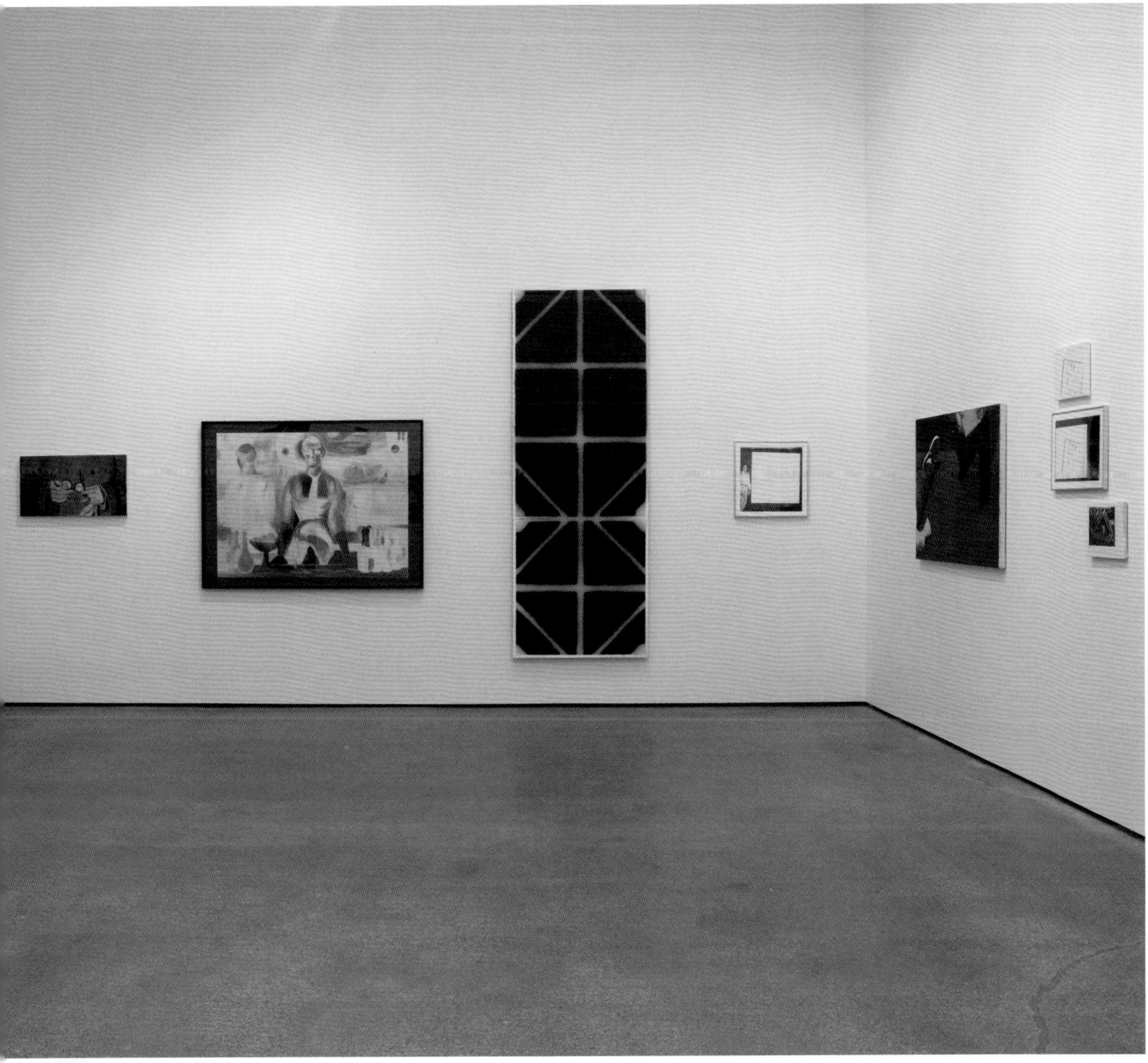

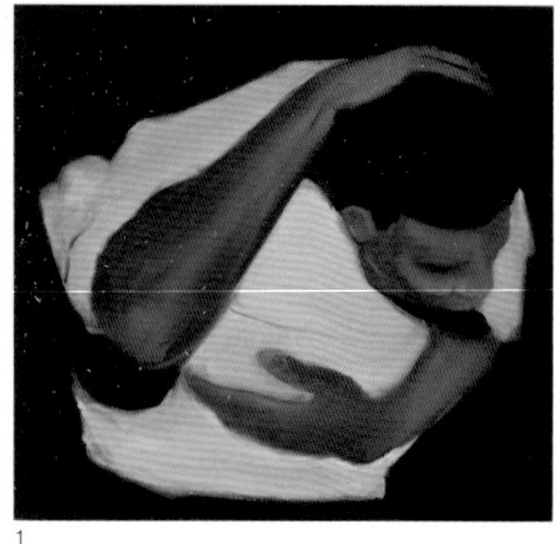

1

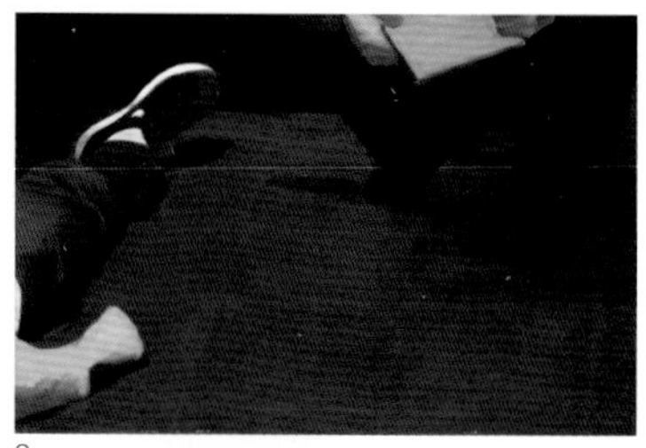

2

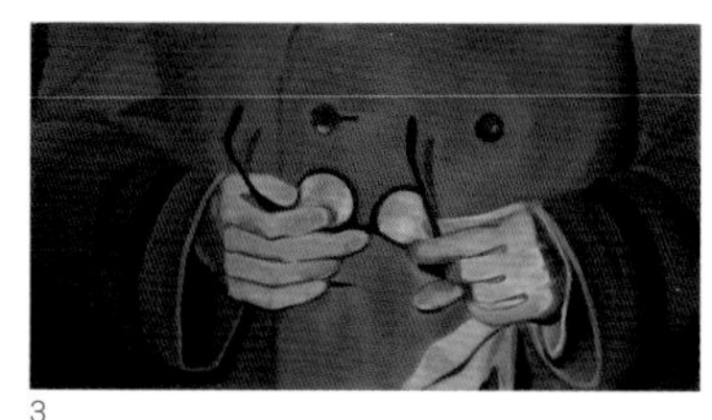

3

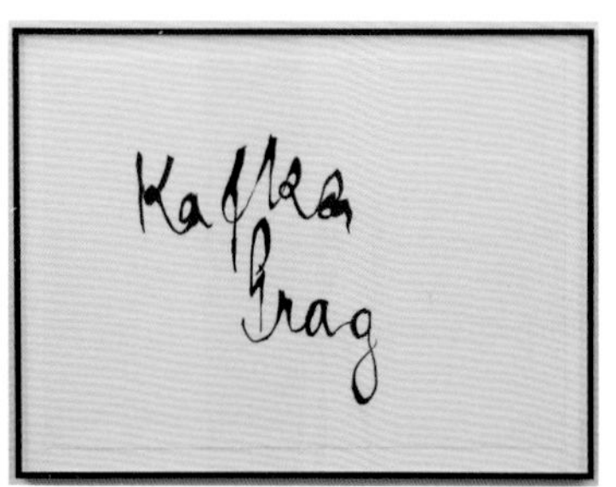

4

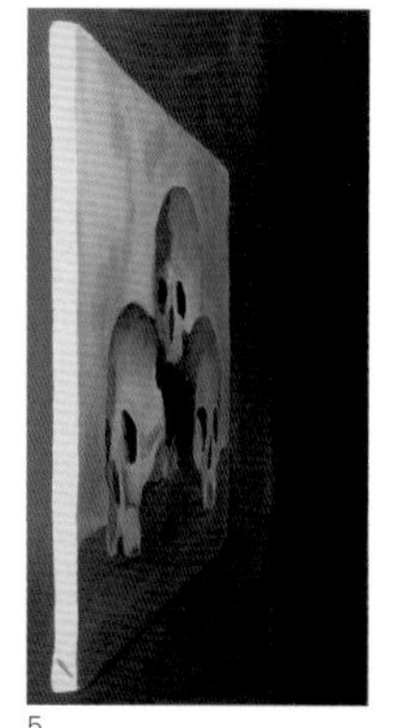

5

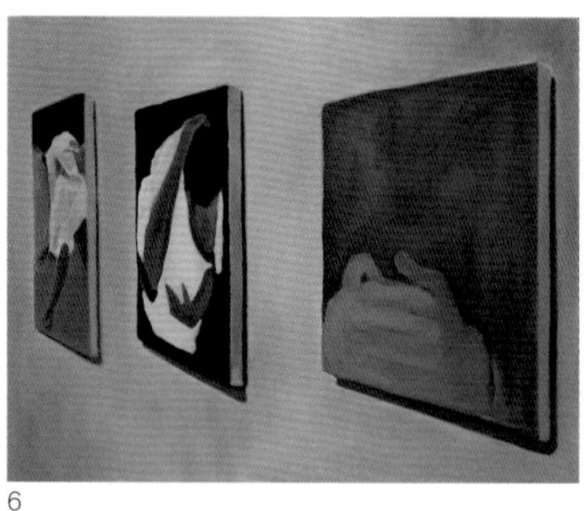

6

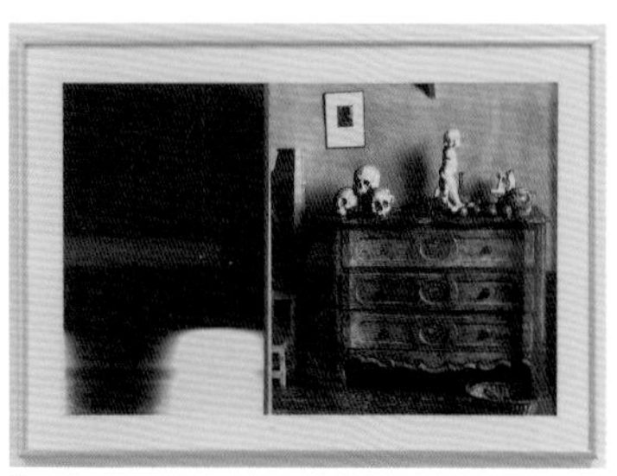

7

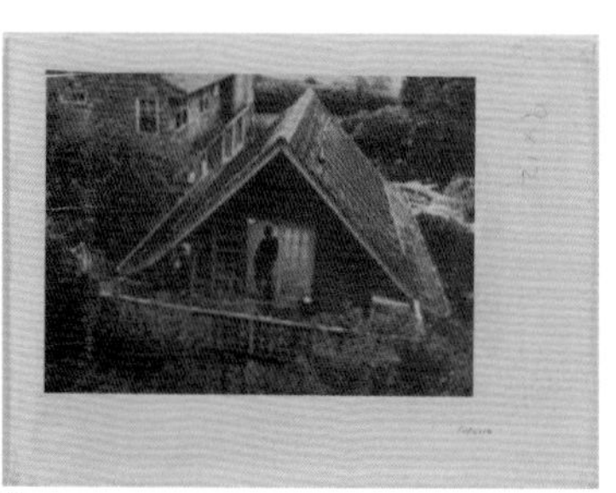

8

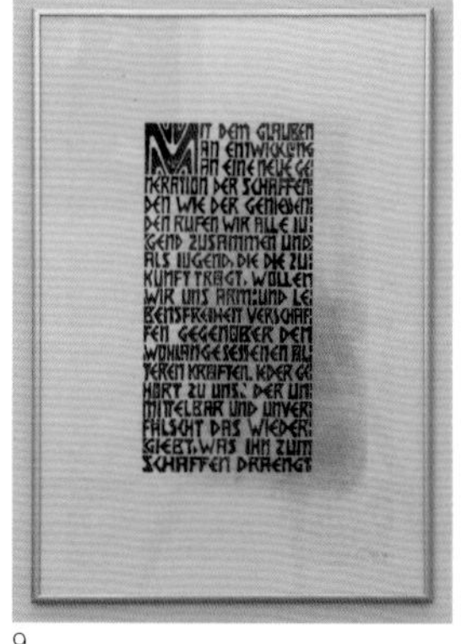

9

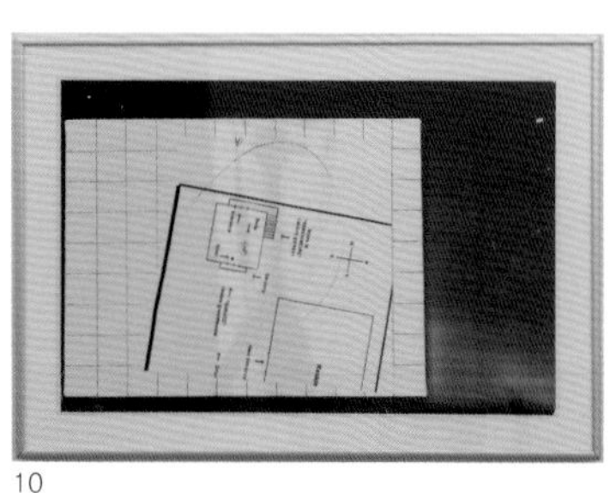

10

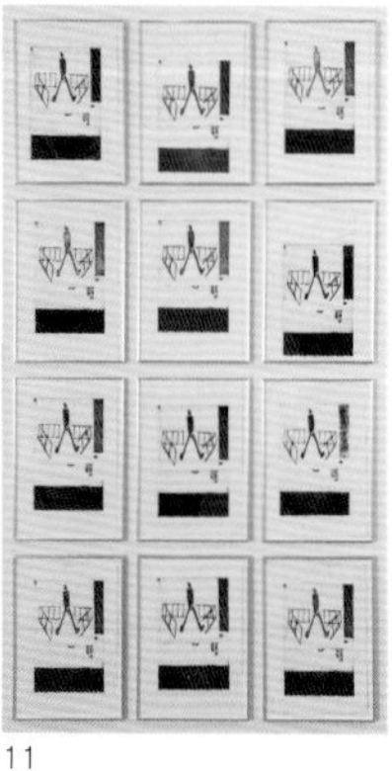

11

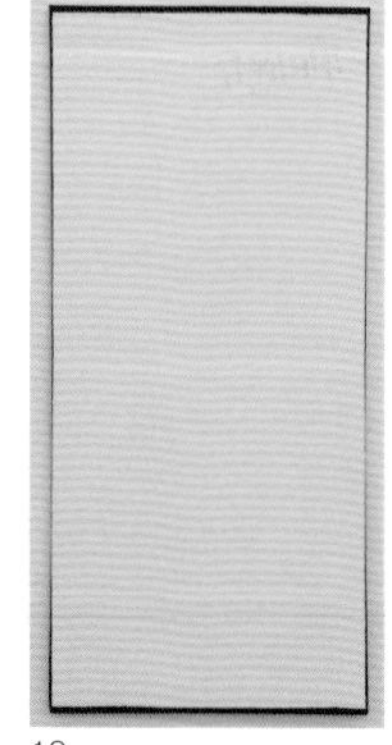

12

1
Untitled, 2004
Oil on canvas
24 × 26 in.
2004.1.004

2
Untitled (forensic scene), 2004
Oil on canvas
32 × 48 in.
2004.1.006

3
Untitled (hands with glasses), 2004
Oil on canvas
16 × 30 in.
2004.1.007

4
Kafka Prag, 2004
Charcoal on paper
30 × 42 in.
2004.2.001

5
Untitled (perspective skulls),
2005
Oil on canvas
34 × 17 in.
2005.1.007

6
Untitled (three paintings), 2005
Oil on canvas
24 × 30 in.
2005.1.008

7
Untitled (Cézanne's studio), 2005
Photocopy on paper
13¾ × 19¾ in. (frame);
11 × 17 in. (sheet)
2005.2.004

8
Untitled (greenhouse), 2006
Photocopy, synthetic polymer varnish,
and graphite on canvas
9 × 12 in.
2006.1.015

9
Untitled (Manifesto), 2006
Photocopy on paper
19¾ × 13¾ in. (frame);
17 × 11 in. (sheet)
2006.2.011

10
*Untitled (greenhouse diagram clear
photocopy)*, 2006
Photocopy on clear mylar
13¾ × 19¾ in. (frame);
11 × 17 in. (sheet)
2006.2.015

11
Untitled (working space)
(selections), 2006/2009
Soft-ground etchings in brushed
aluminum frames, sixteen pieces
(12 pieces shown)
24 × 16¾ in. ea. (frame);
22 × 14¾ in. ea. (sheet)
P2006.003.1-16

12
Untitled (correction painting),
2007
Oil and graphite on canvas
48 × 22 in., irreg.
2007.1.002

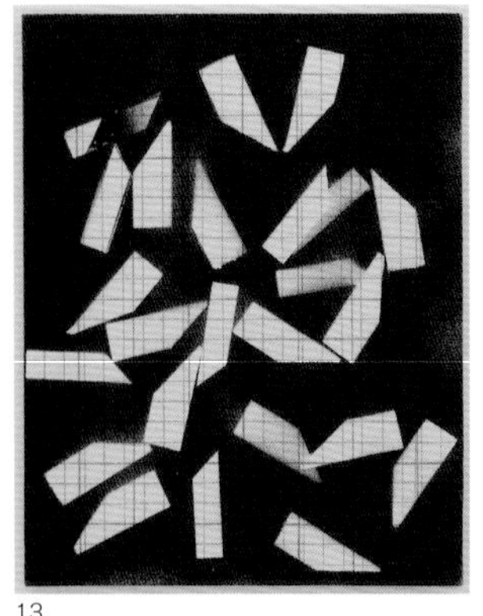

13

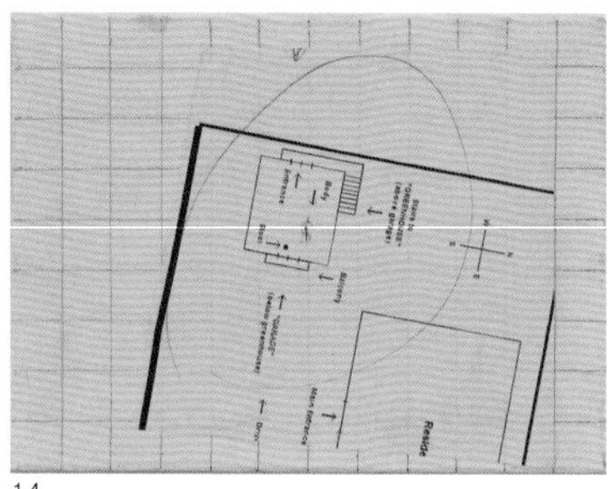

14

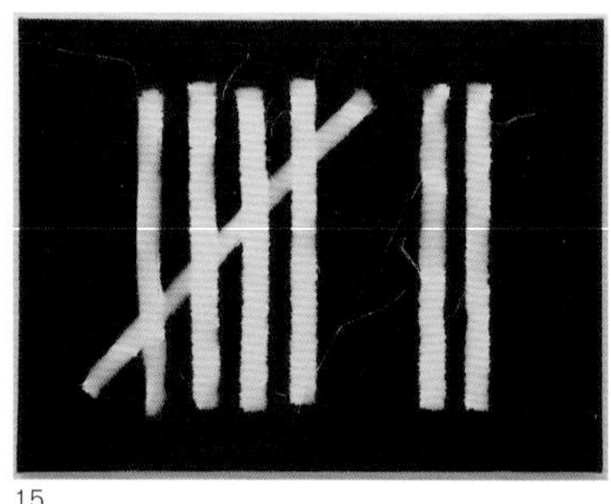

15

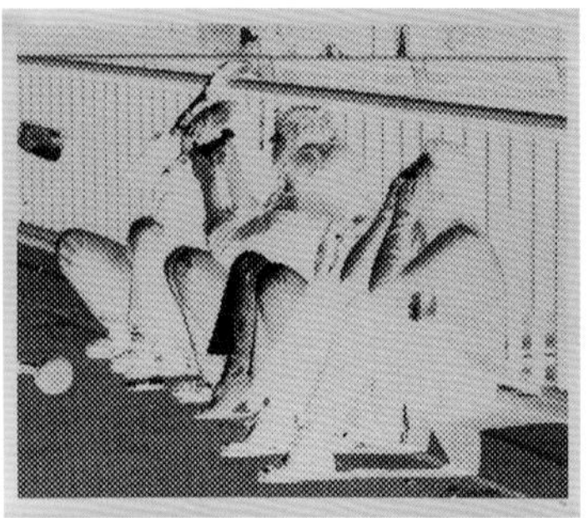

16

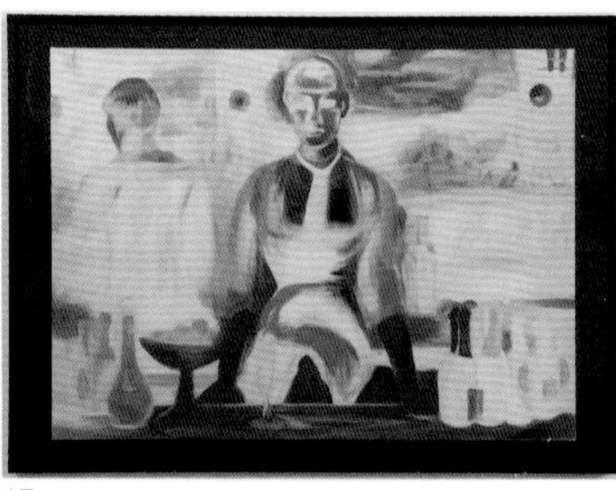

17

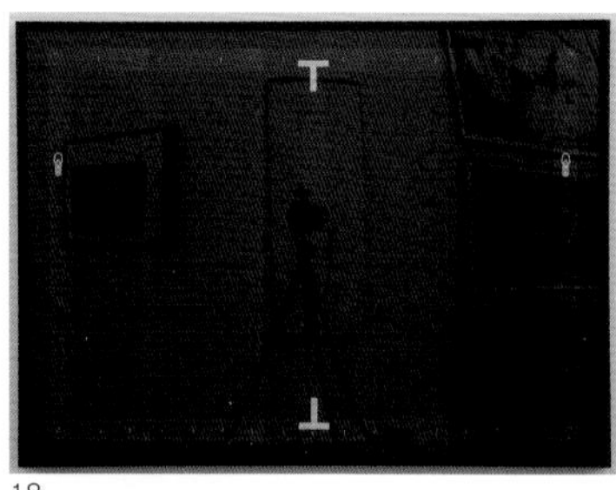

18

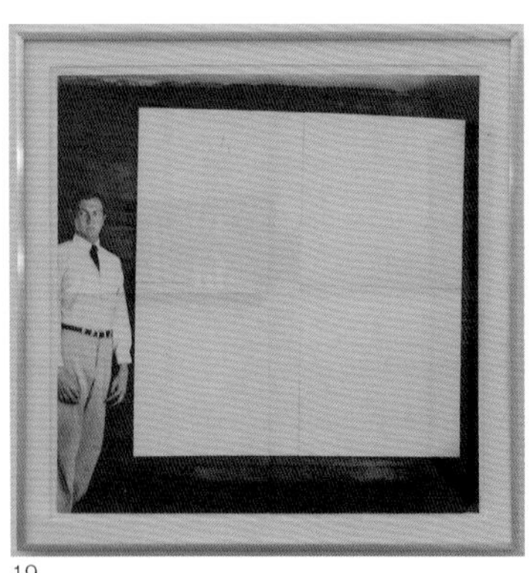

19

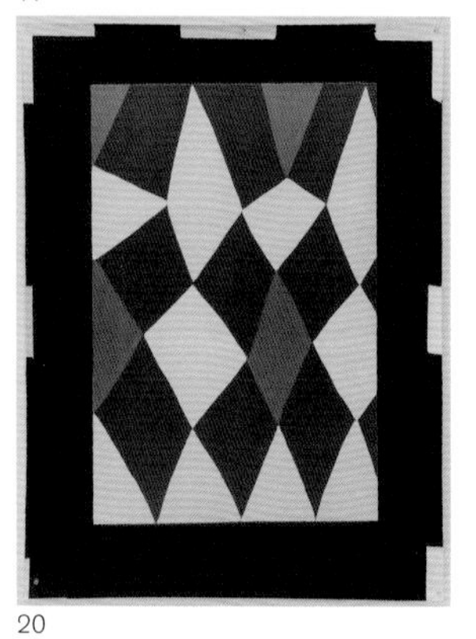

20

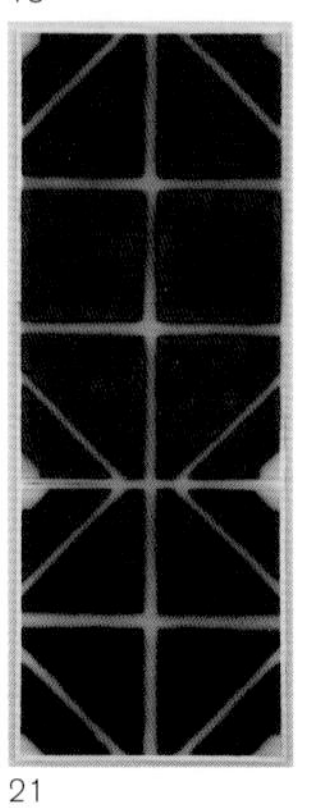

21

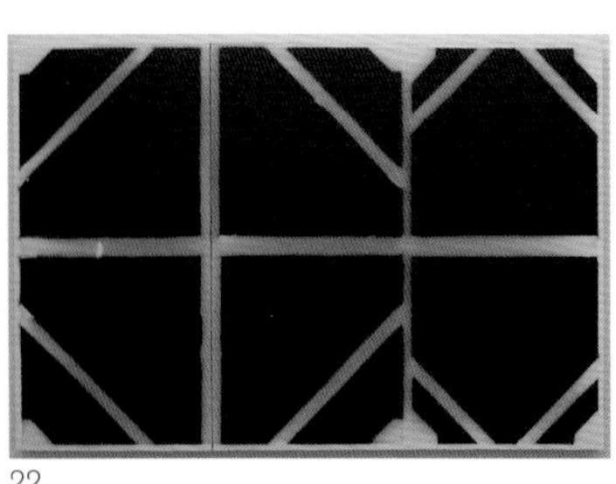

22

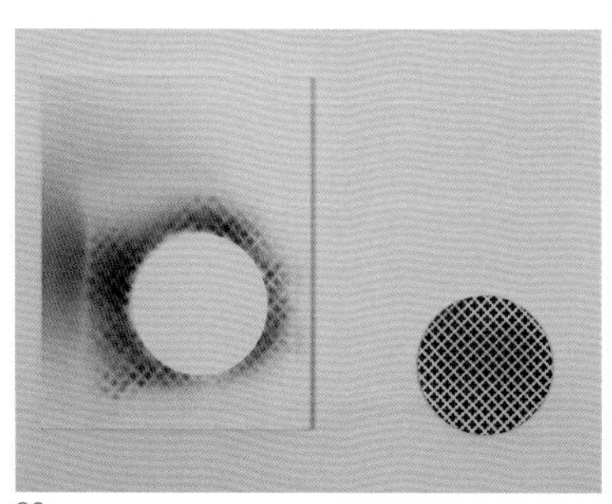

23

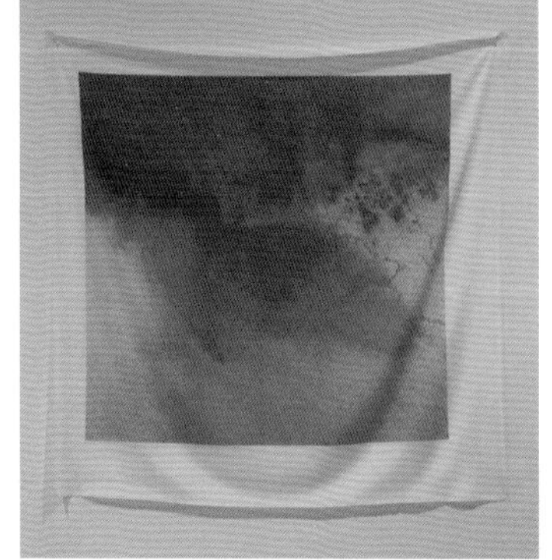

24

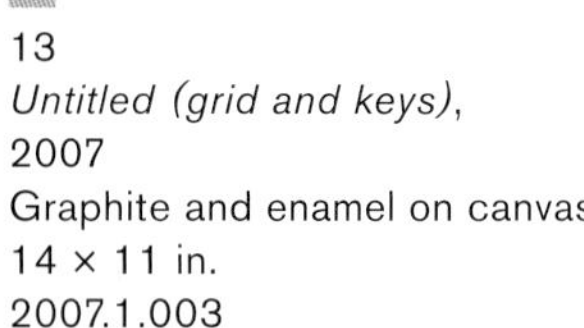

13
Untitled (grid and keys),
2007
Graphite and enamel on canvas
14 × 11 in.
2007.1.003

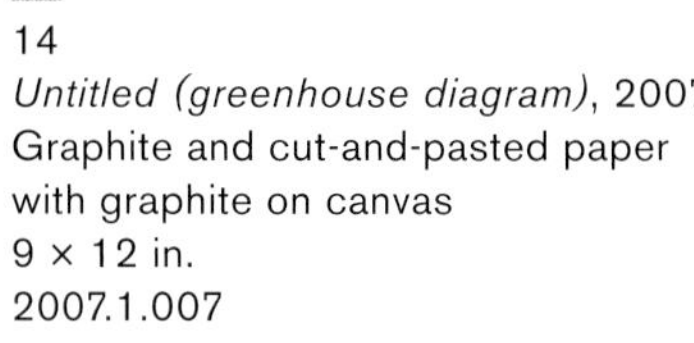

14
Untitled (greenhouse diagram), 2007
Graphite and cut-and-pasted paper
with graphite on canvas
9 × 12 in.
2007.1.007

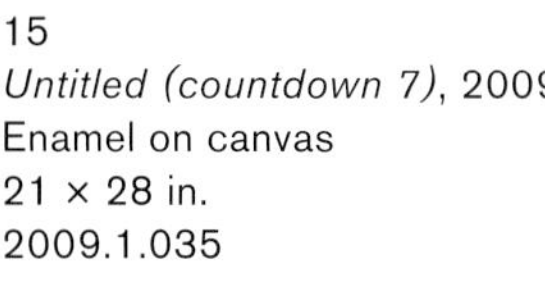

15
Untitled (countdown 7), 2009
Enamel on canvas
21 × 28 in.
2009.1.035

16
Eclipse, 2009
Portfolio of five screenprints
31½ × 35 in. ea. (frame);
30 × 34½ in. ea. (sheet)
P2009.001.04.1-5

17
Untitled (The Bar), 2009
Chromogenic color print on metallic
paper, mounted on gatorboard
43 × 59 in.
Ph2009.001.01

18
Untitled (X-Ray photograph), 2009
Chromogenic color print,
mounted on gatorboard
40¾ × 55¾ in.
Ph2009.003.001

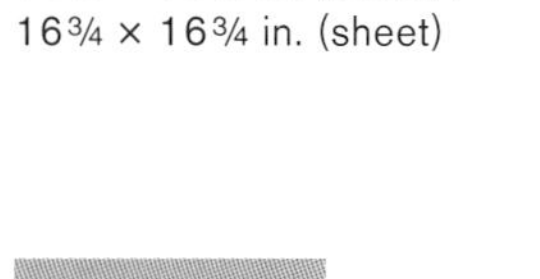

19
Untitled (Rauschenberg Poster),
1968/2015
Commercially-made offset print
19¾ × 19¾ in. (frame);
16¾ × 16¾ in. (sheet)

20
Untitled (Harlequin), 2015
Collaboration with Jason Kalogiros
Unique gelatin silver photograph
40 × 30 in.
2015.1.010

21
Untitled (Number 1), 2015
Enamel on canvas, in two parts
96 × 36 in.
2015.1.011

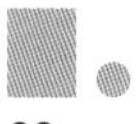

22
Untitled (Number 2), 2015
Enamel on canvas, in two parts
48 × 72 in.
2015.1.012

23
Untitled, 2015
Enamel on canvas, in two parts
Overall: c. 20 × 35 in.
2015.1.016a-b

24
Untitled (Void fabric), 2015
Ink on Organza
image: 36 × 36 in.;
fabric: 43 × 42 in.
2015.1.020

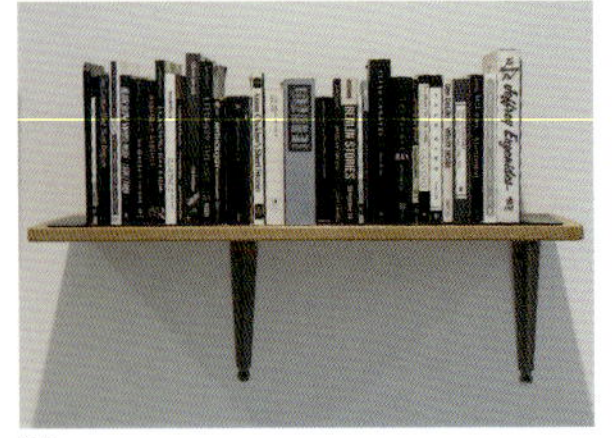

25

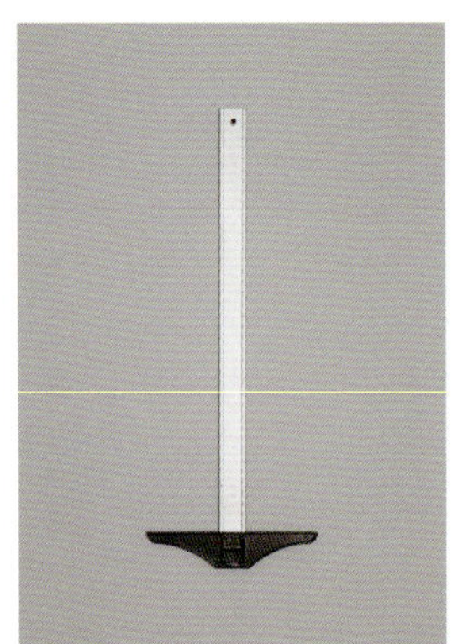

26

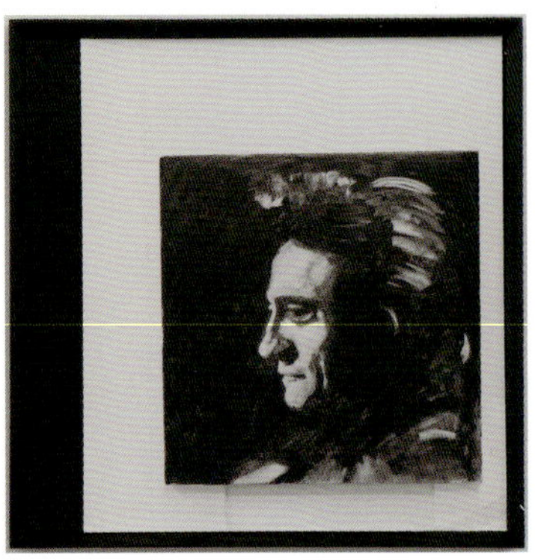

27

25
Untitled (B/W Shelf Piece), 2015
Printed books, wood shelf,
metal brackets
Overall: 24 × 31 ½ × 11 ¼ in.
2015.3.002

26
Untitled (T-square), 2016
Commercially-made 30 in. T-square
32 ¾ × 12 ½ in.
2016.1.001

27
Untitled (JC/VM photo), 2016
Cut-and-pasted silver gelatin print,
mat board, enamel, in artist's frame
24 × 24 in.
2016.1.002

This exhibition will comprise a wide-ranging selection of interconnected works, indicative of the artist's diverse studio practice. Figurative paintings that merge contemporary photographic and art-historical sources, geometric and gestural abstractions, as well as a large group of collages that incorporate mechanically produced and handmade gestures will be included. All of the works are shown here for the first time.

Informed by both historical research and studio improvisation, Kantor's newest works revisit several touchstone debates of modernist painting within a twenty-first century context. By reframing some of the signal strategies by which the medium has incorporated photography, abstraction, and contemporaneous subject matter, the exhibition revolves around questions central to discourses in painting—unified by conceptual logic rather than a singular style, format, or aesthetic approach.

TABLEAUX

BY

M. JORDAN KANTOR

EXHIBITED

CHURNER & CHURNER

28 Feb – 30 Mar 2014

OPENING RECEPTION: THURSDAY, 27 FEB, 6–8PM

—

NEW YORK

205 TENTH AVENUE, 10011
(212) 675-2750
churnerandchurner.com

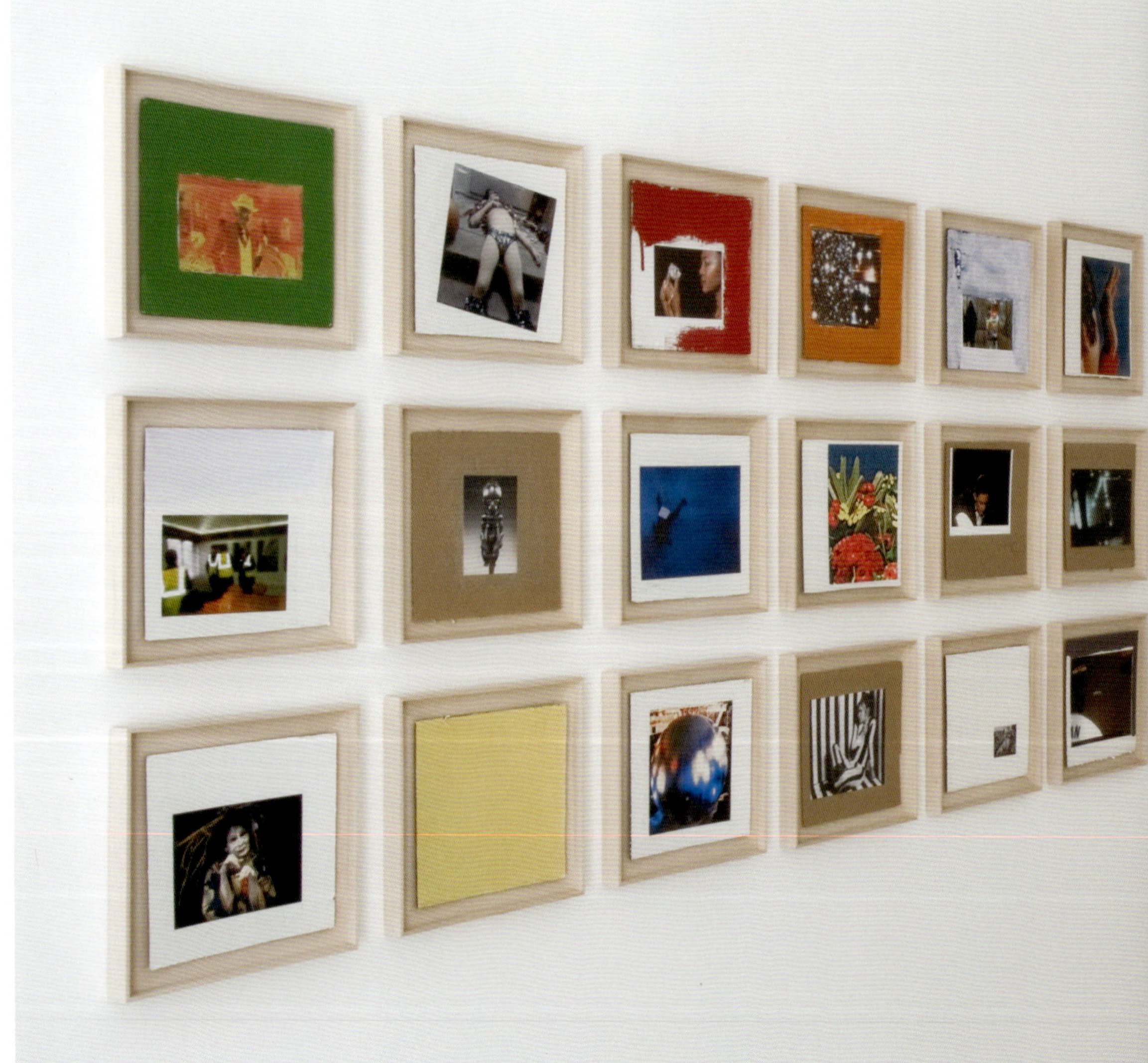

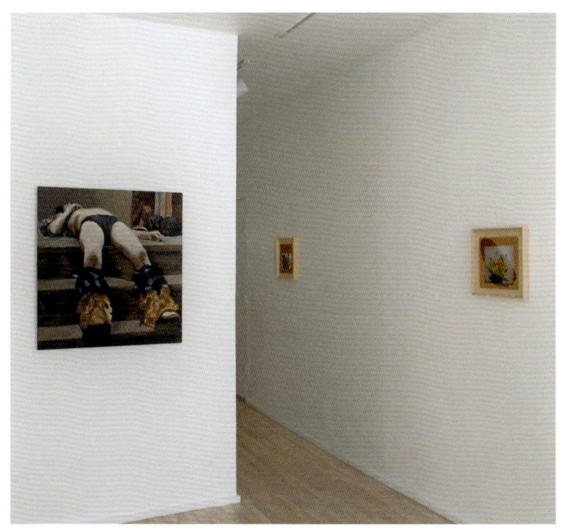
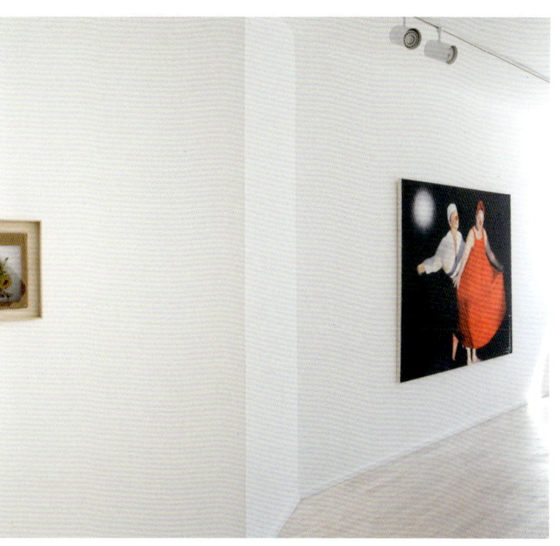

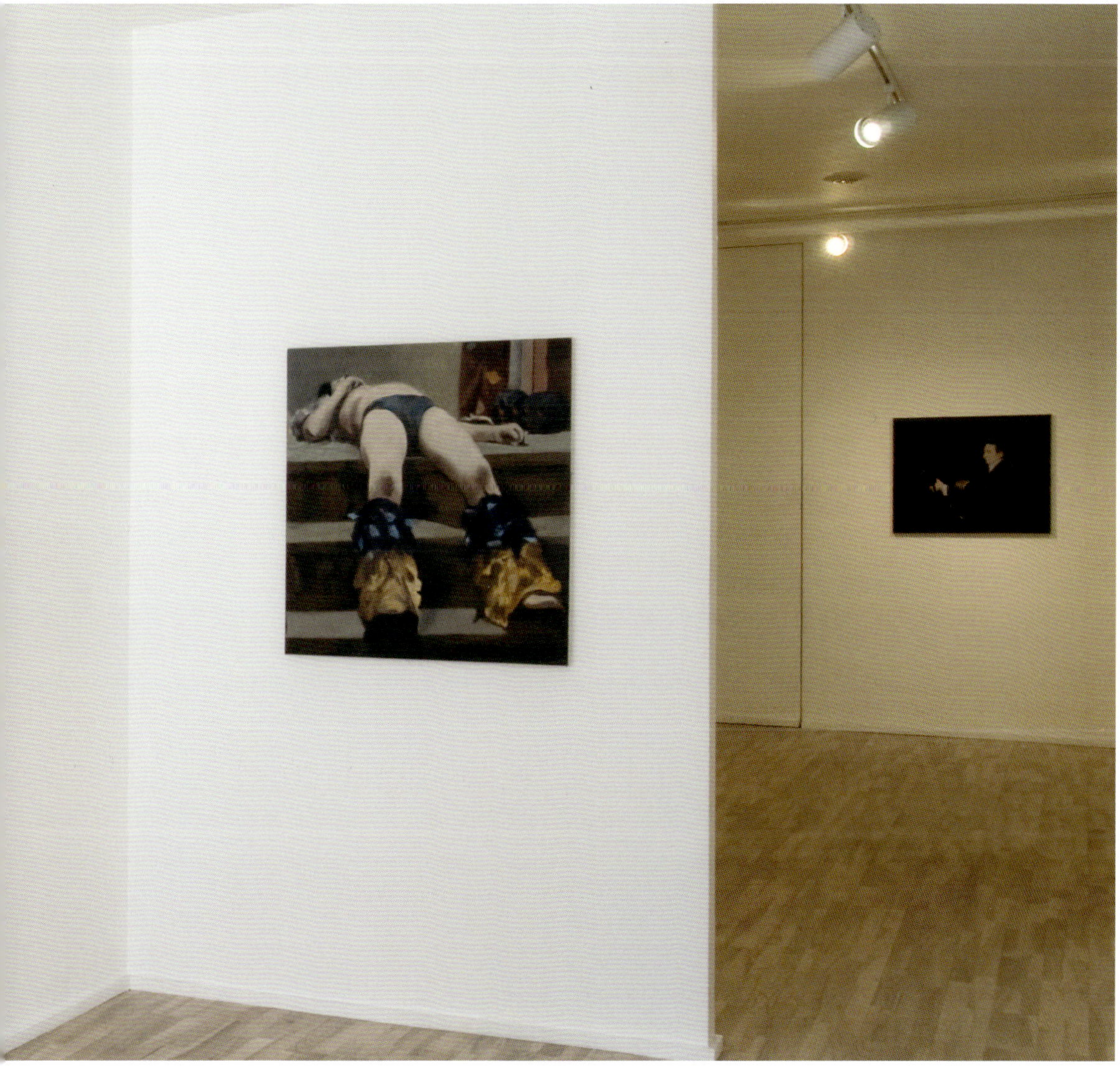

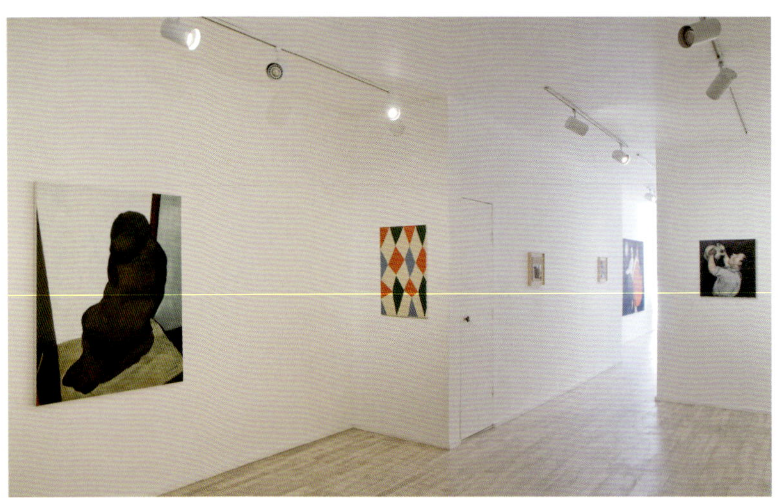

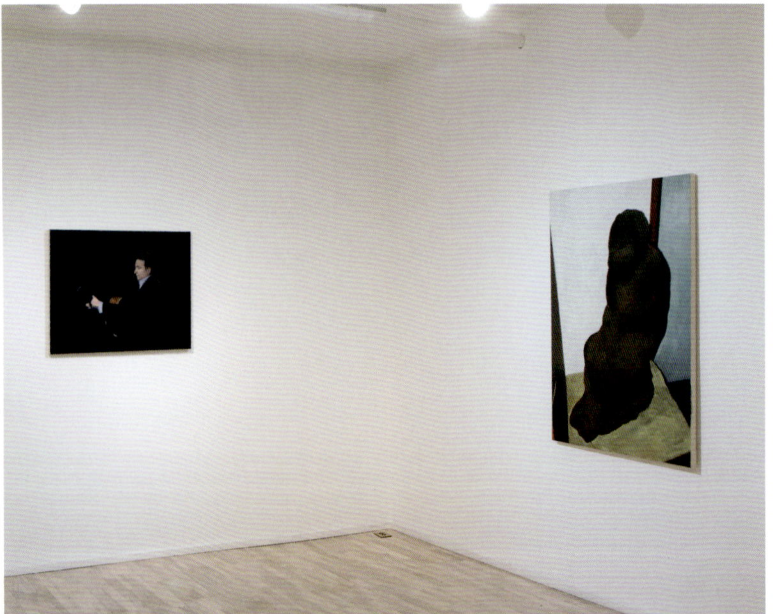

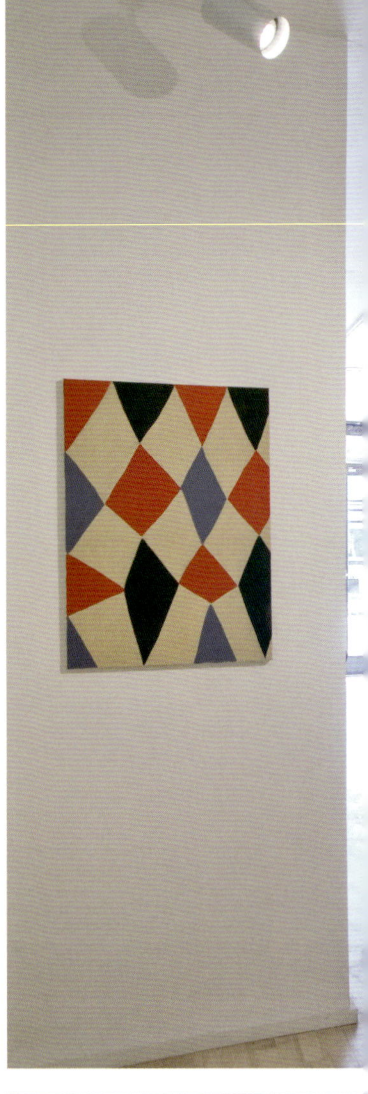

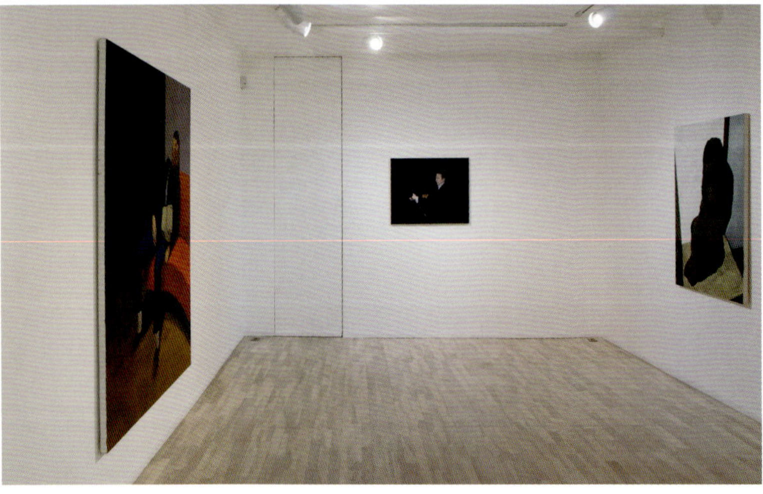

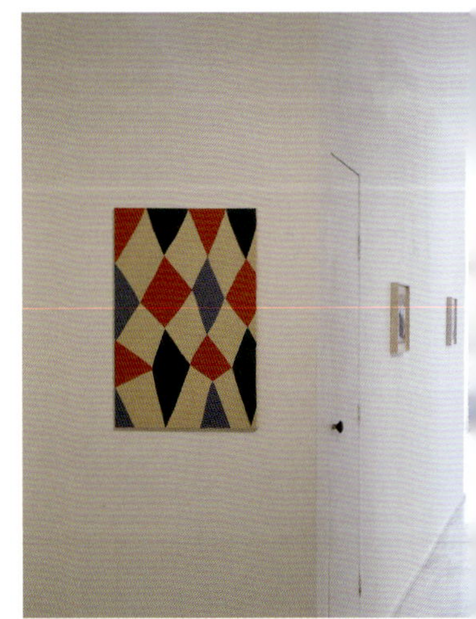

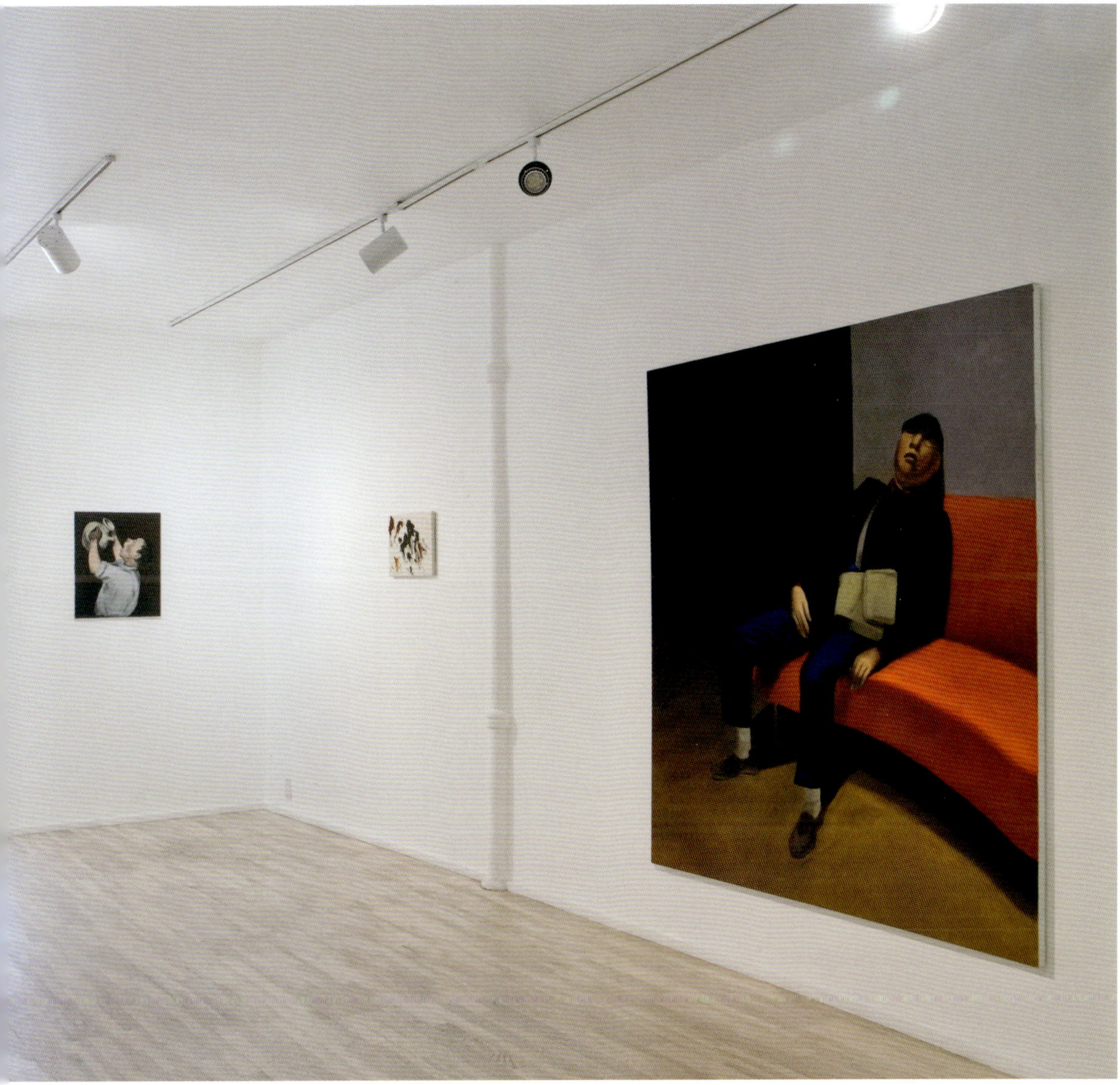

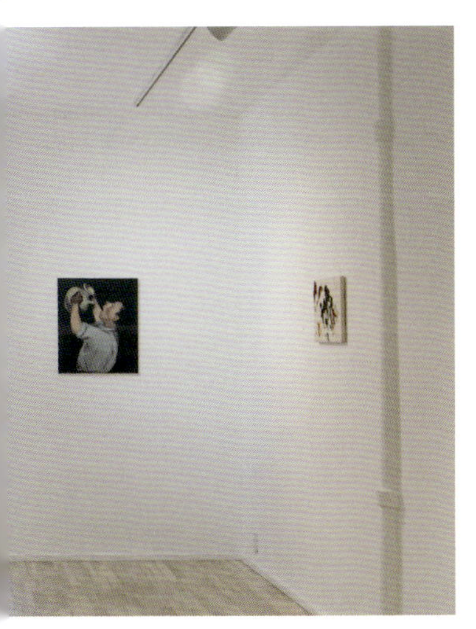

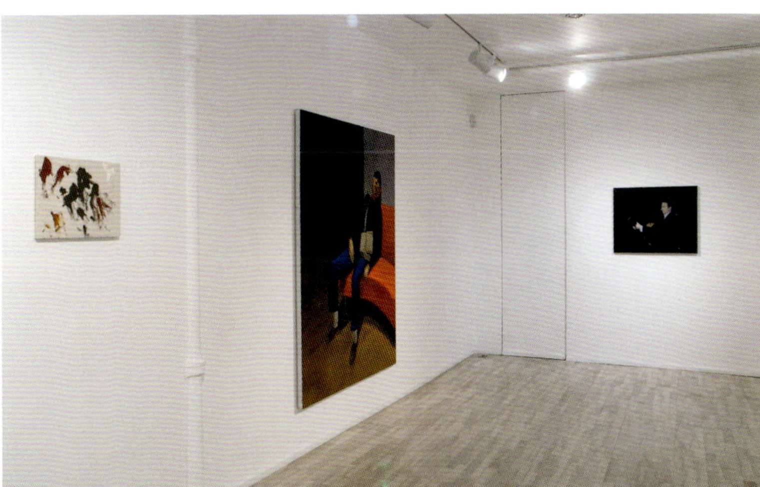

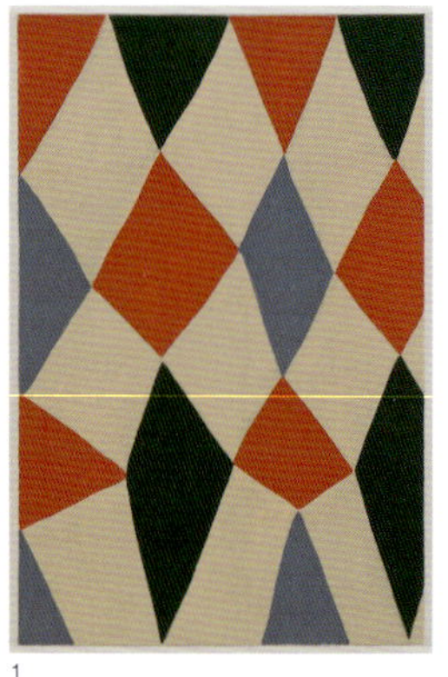

1

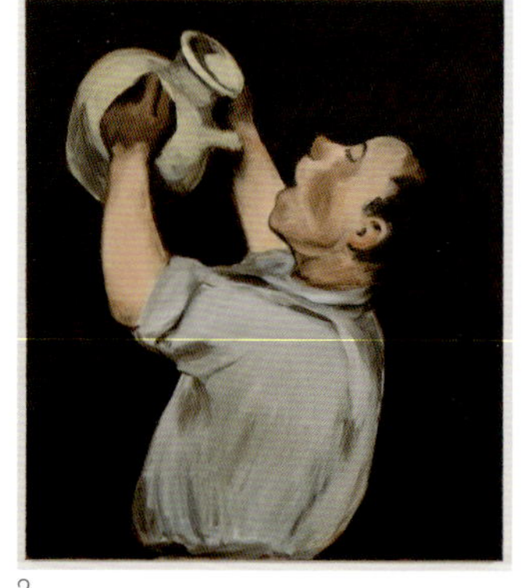

2

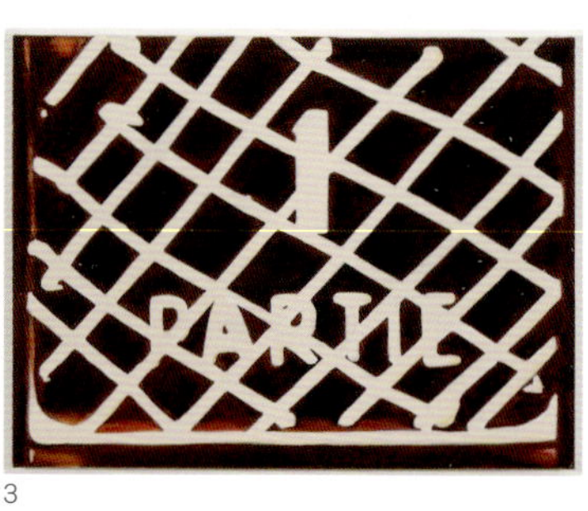

3

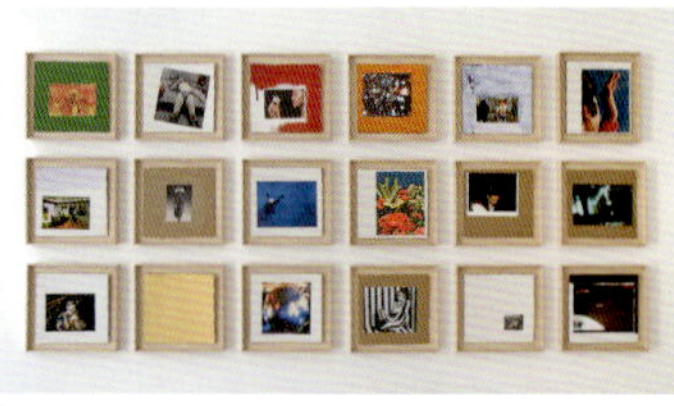

4

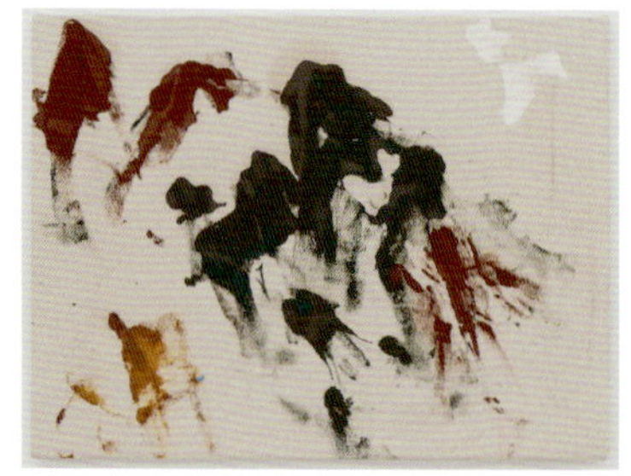

5

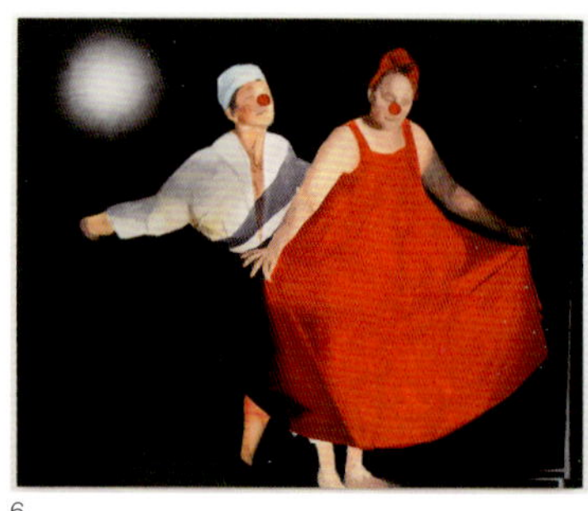

6

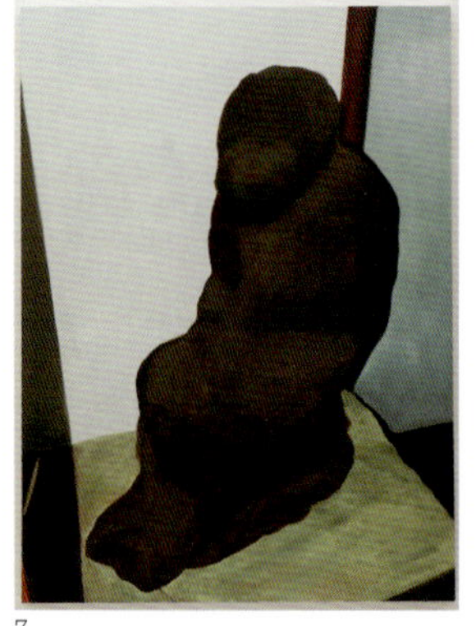

7

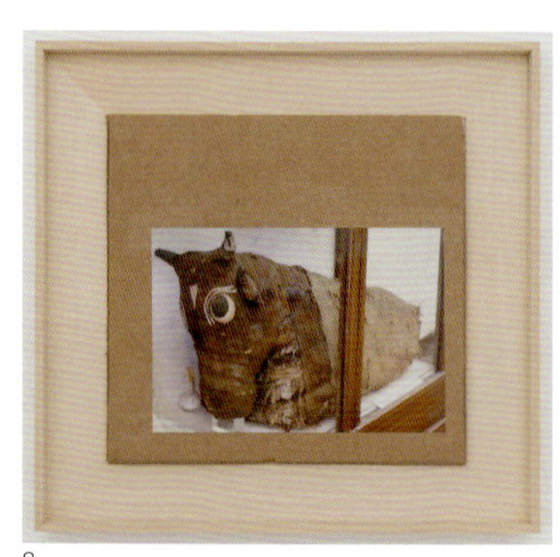

8

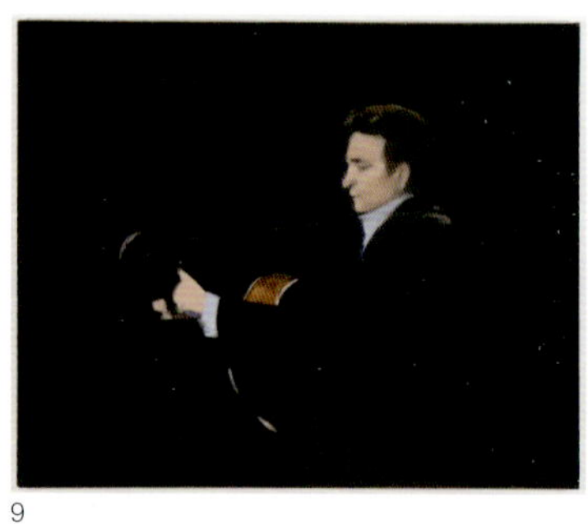

9

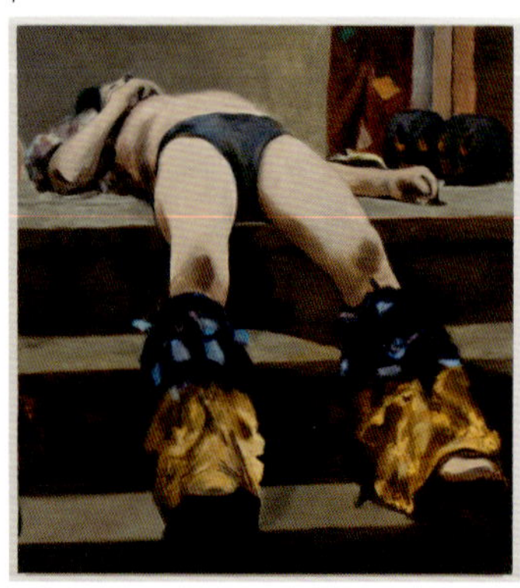

10

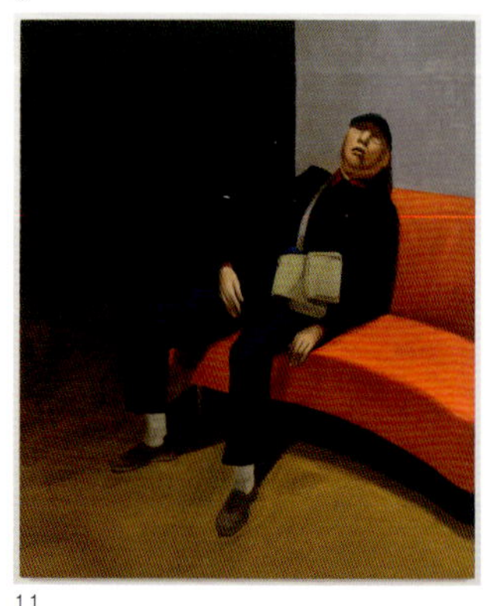

11

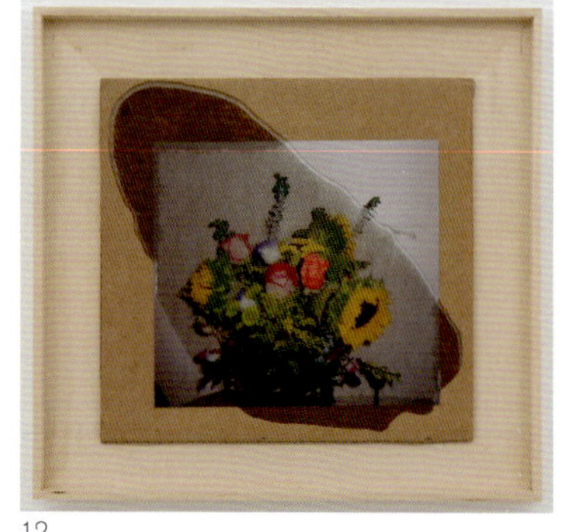

12

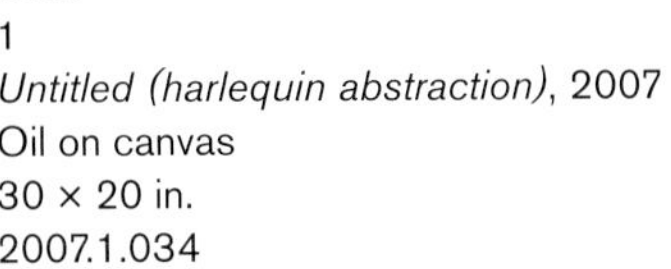

1
Untitled (harlequin abstraction), 2007
Oil on canvas
30 × 20 in.
2007.1.034

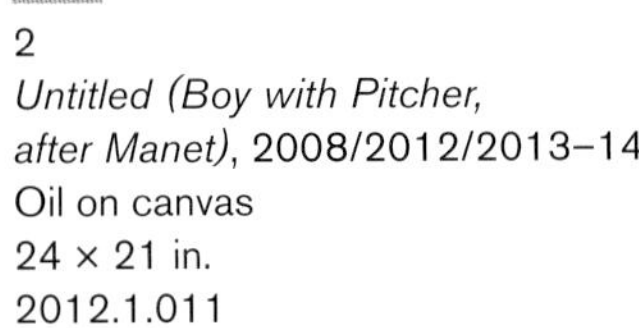

2
*Untitled (Boy with Pitcher,
after Manet)*, 2008/2012/2013–14
Oil on canvas
24 × 21 in.
2012.1.011

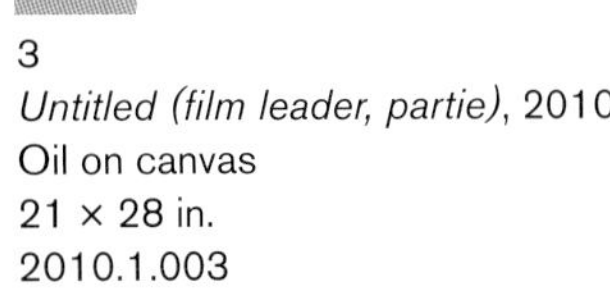

3
Untitled (film leader, partie), 2010
Oil on canvas
21 × 28 in.
2010.1.003

4
Untitled (collage wall), 2011
Cut-and-pasted paper, acrylic,
and oil on cardboard, eighteen pieces
13 11/16 × 14 7/8 in. ea. (frame);
c. 11 × 12 in. ea. (board),
overall dimensions variable
2011.1.013.a-r

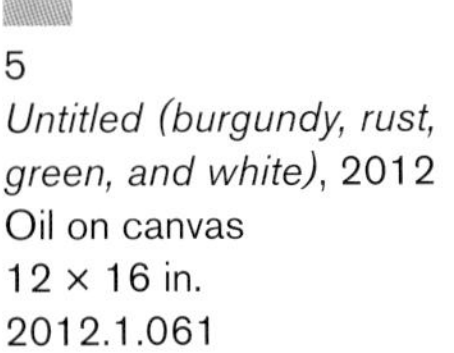

5
*Untitled (burgundy, rust,
green, and white)*, 2012
Oil on canvas
12 × 16 in.
2012.1.061

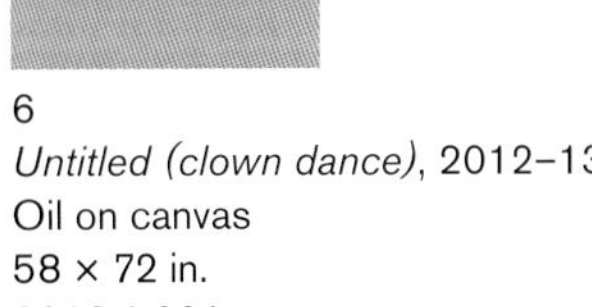

6
Untitled (clown dance), 2012–13
Oil on canvas
58 × 72 in.
2013.1.001

7
Untitled (Baboon mummy 2), 2013
Oil on canvas
48 × 36 in.
2013.1.002

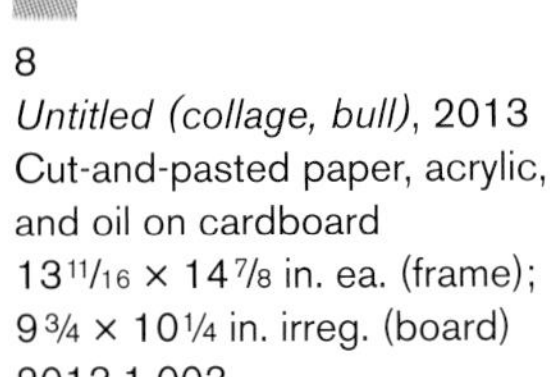

8
Untitled (collage, bull), 2013
Cut-and-pasted paper, acrylic,
and oil on cardboard
13 11/16 × 14 7/8 in. ea. (frame);
9 3/4 × 10 1/4 in. irreg. (board)
2013.1.003

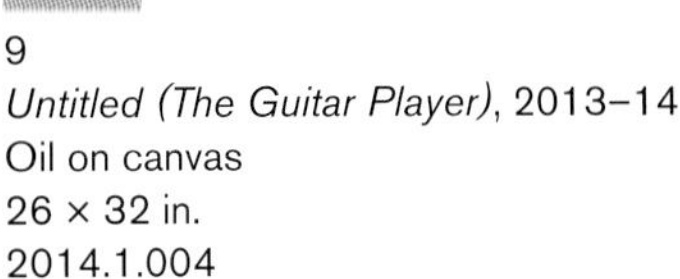

9
Untitled (The Guitar Player), 2013–14
Oil on canvas
26 × 32 in.
2014.1.004

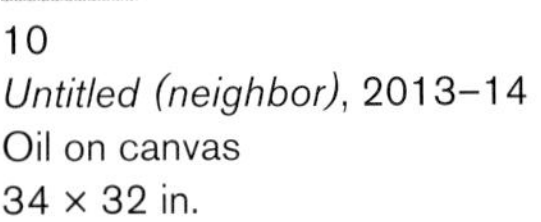

10
Untitled (neighbor), 2013–14
Oil on canvas
34 × 32 in.
2014.1.001

11
Untitled (Paris, asleep), 2014
Oil on linen
72 × 60 in.
2014.1.007

12
Untitled (collage, flowers varnish), 2014
Cut-and-pasted paper and epoxy
coating on cardboard
3 11/16 × 14 7/8 in. ea. (frame);
10 × 14 5/8 in. irreg. (board)
2014.1.008

The exhibition will feature an installation of works that re-purposed materials employed during the process of painting but which are not typically considered the end result. A series of colorful abstractions on cotton rags sewn to canvas comprises one such group of works shown here.

Rags, once used for removing color from a painting-in-process or for cleaning a paintbrush, were collected, sewn to un-primed canvas, and stretched. A wooden slat, painted a single color found in the cotton rag, was attached to each side of the stretched rag-canvas to complete the piece.

These rag paintings are shown with a group of dark, monochromatic paintings made with paint sludge, the usually-discarded pigment sediment that gathers at the bottom of a vessel containing mineral spirits employed to remove paint from used brushes.

In the second gallery, a sequence of ten paintings, based upon film stills shot in a studio setting, depict a woman's hand passing in front of various colors of cloth. Based on imagery from a film test used by technicians to calibrate how color is captured and presented on film, these works extend the investigation into how color is used and interpreted. An installation of painted wooden structures suspended from the gallery ceiling and hung on the wall elaborated this color study. As with the painted slats ringing the rags in the first room, the colors of the painted lattice are derived from colors found in the film still paintings. Also included in the show is a signal canvas from seven years prior, which is re-contextualized in the company of the newer work.

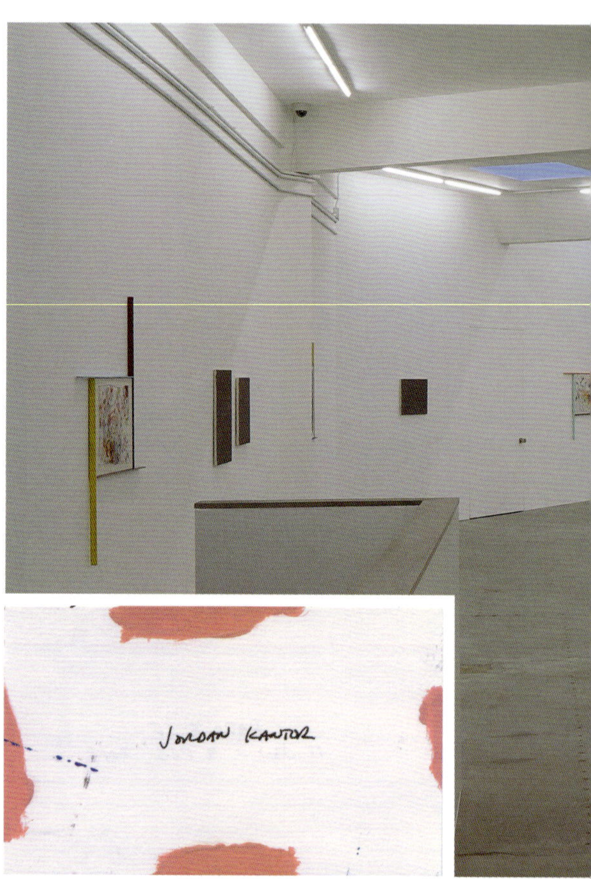

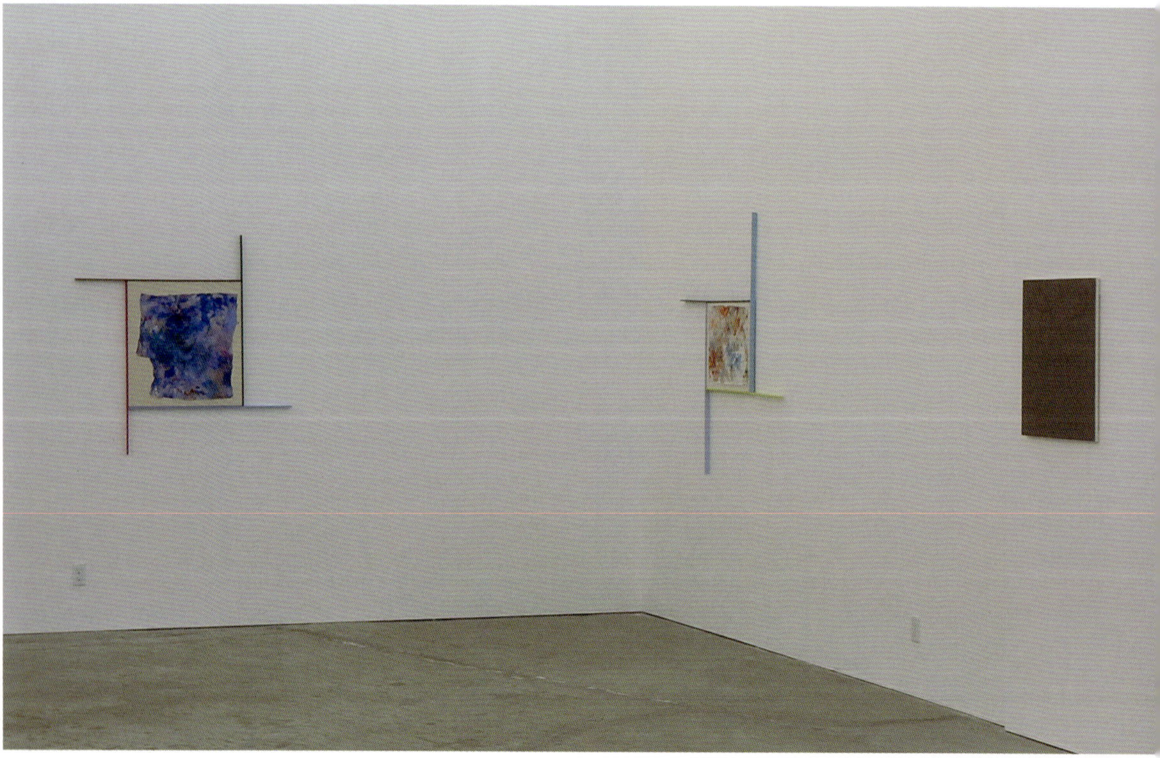

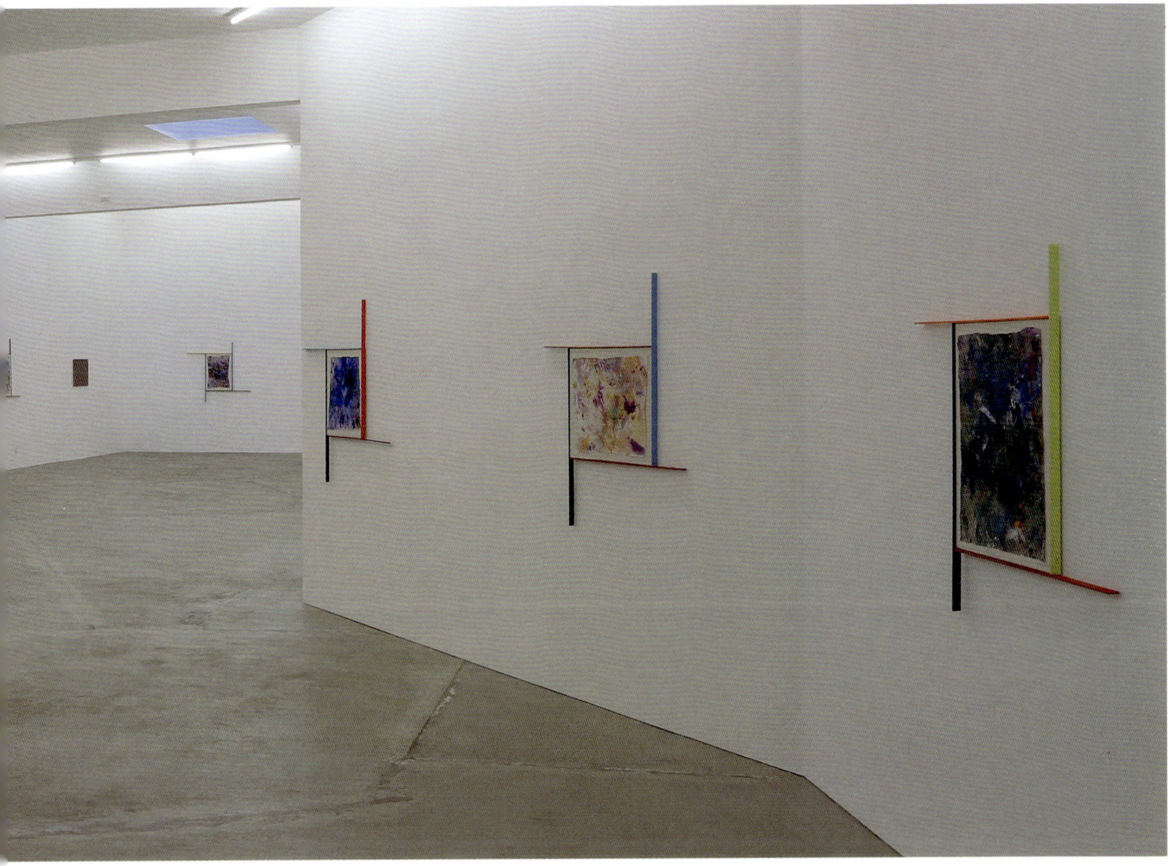

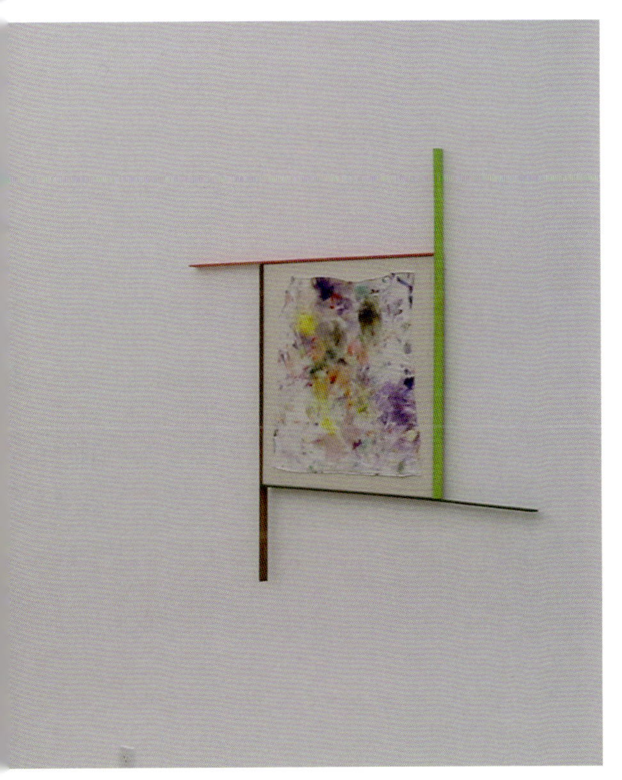

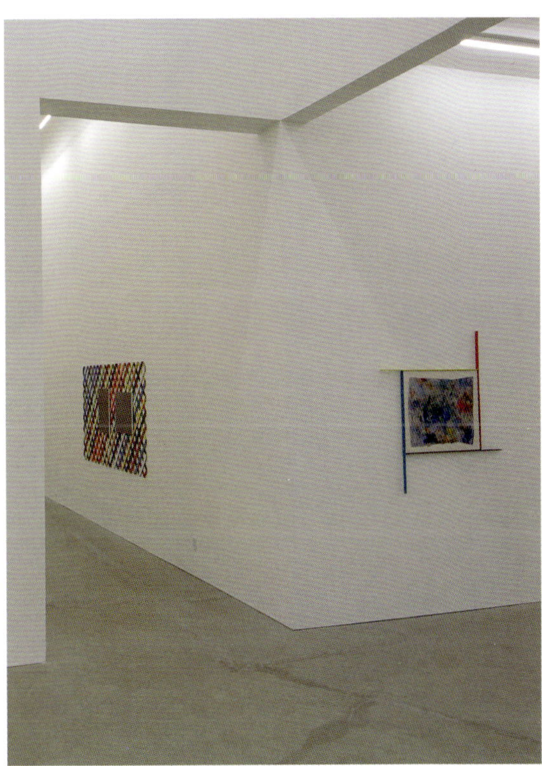

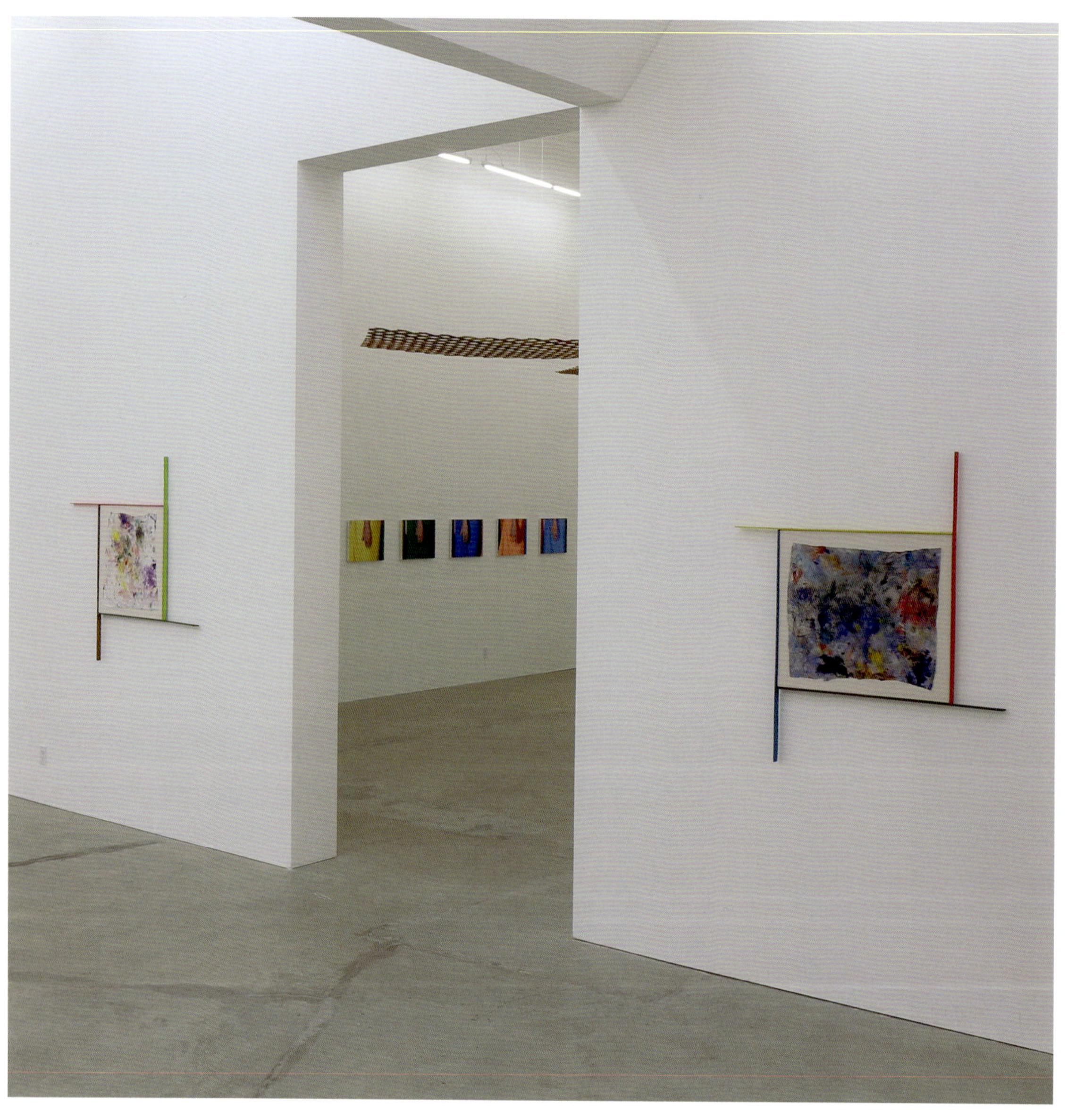

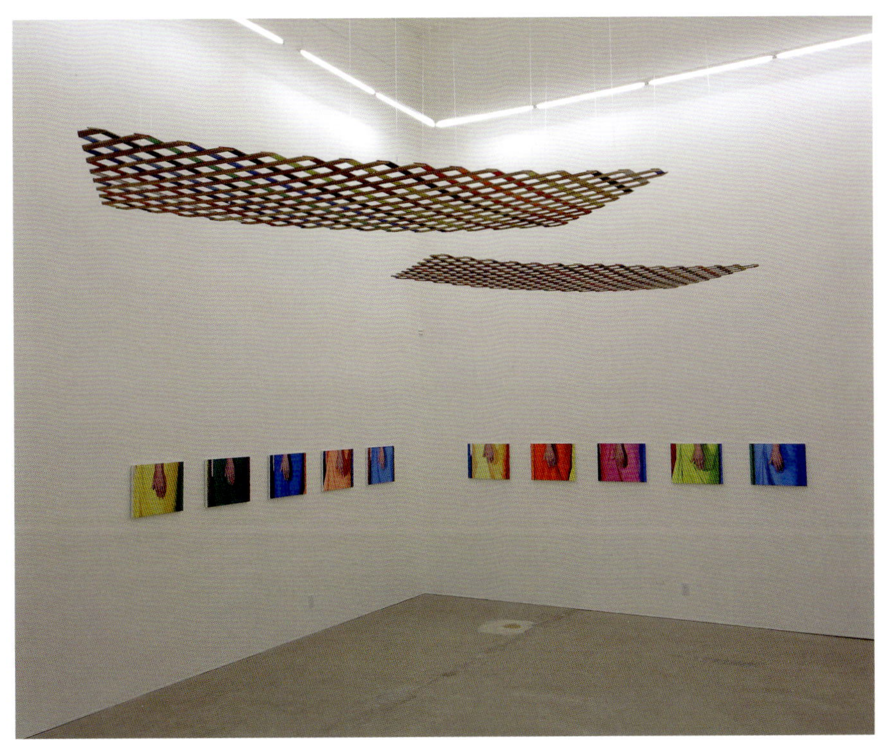

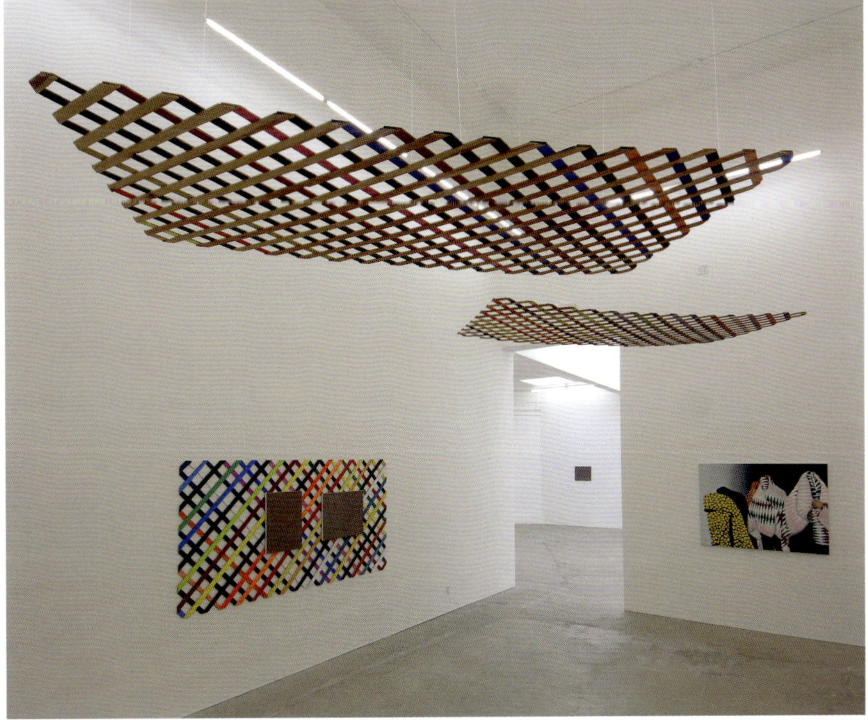

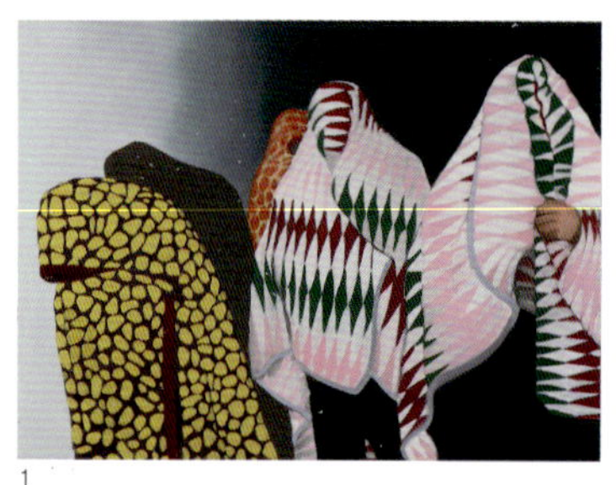

1

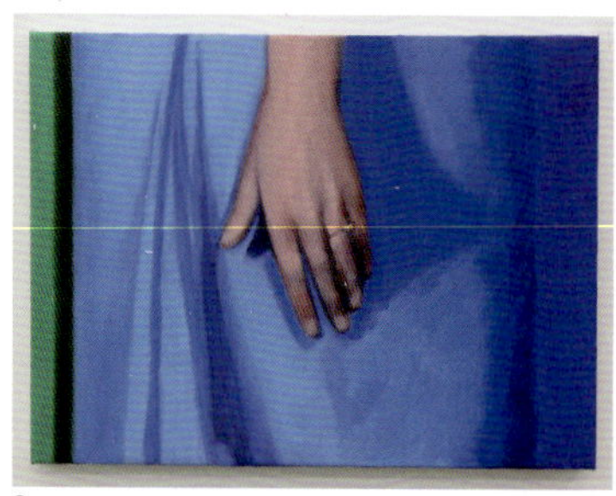

2

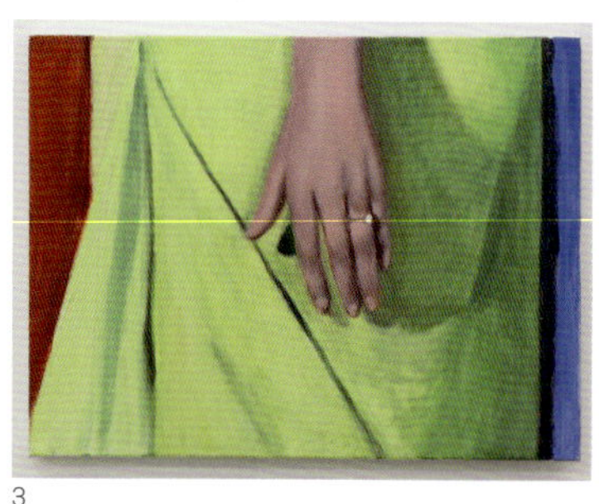

3

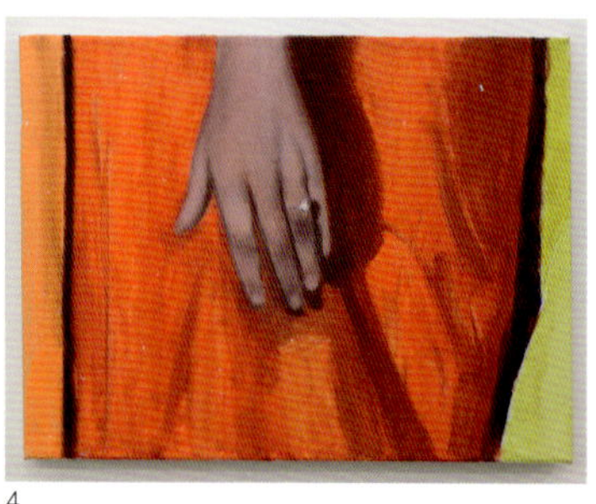

4

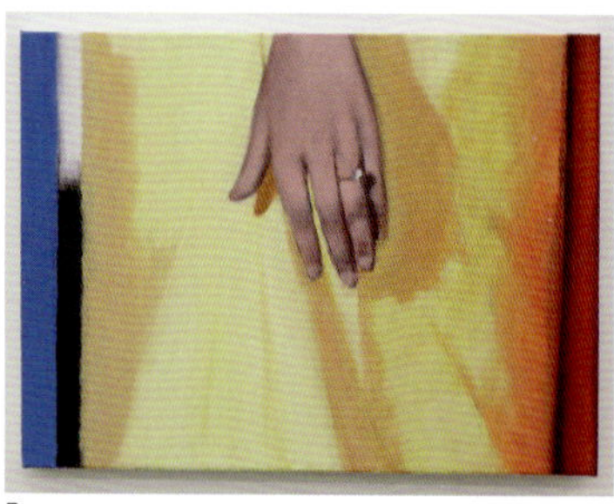

5

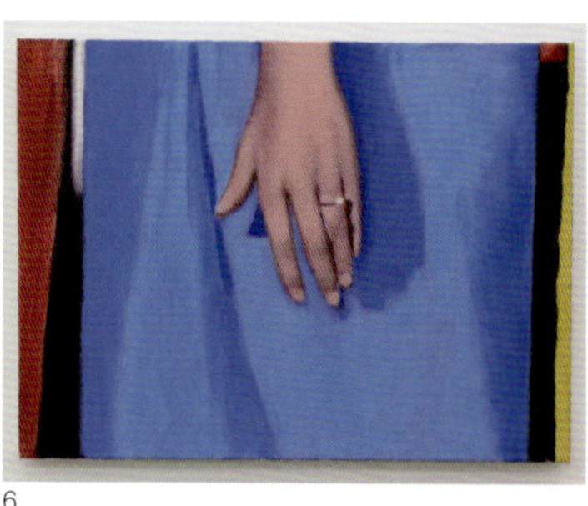

6

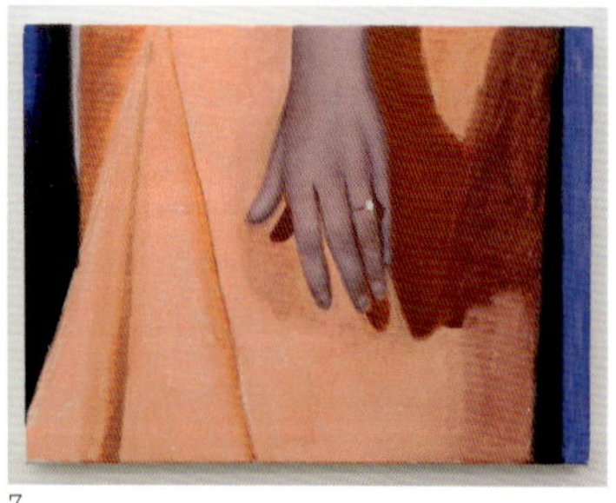

7

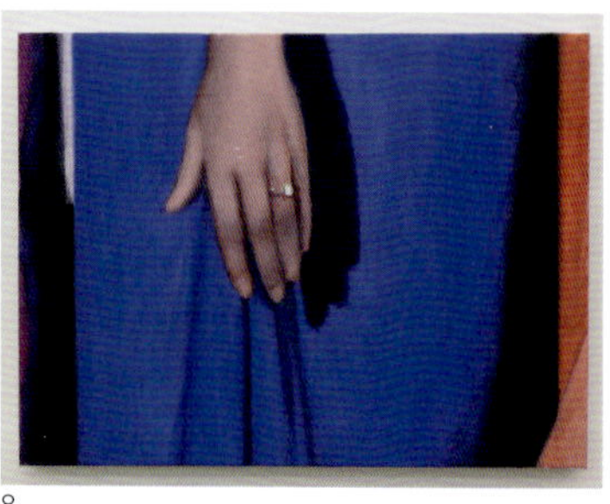

8

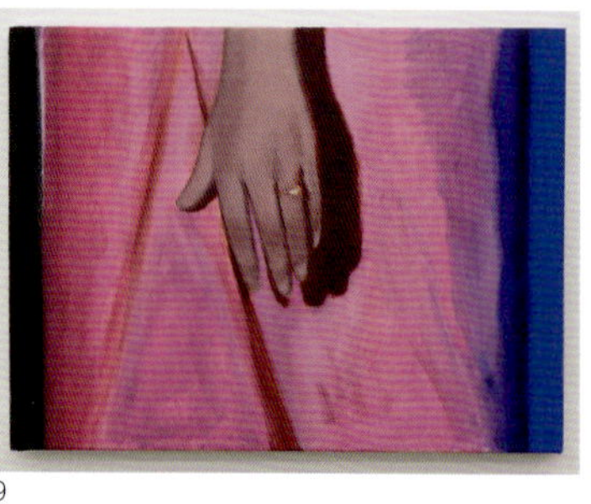

9

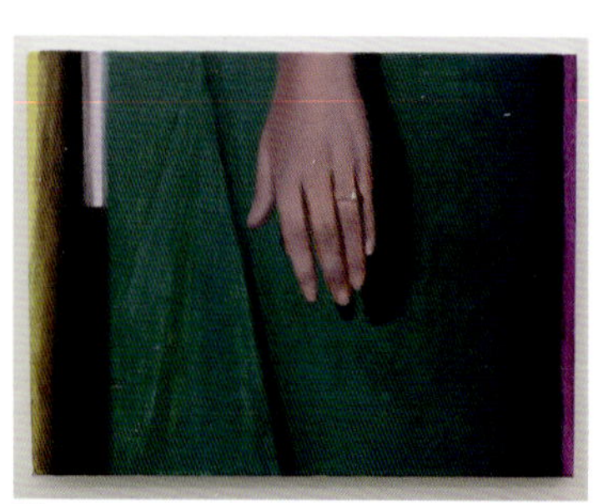

10

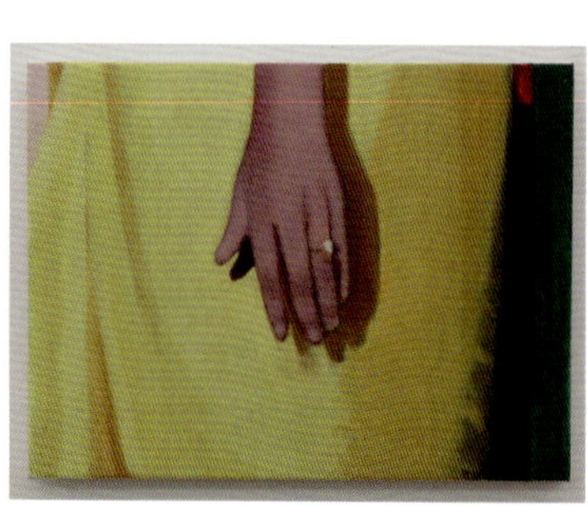

11

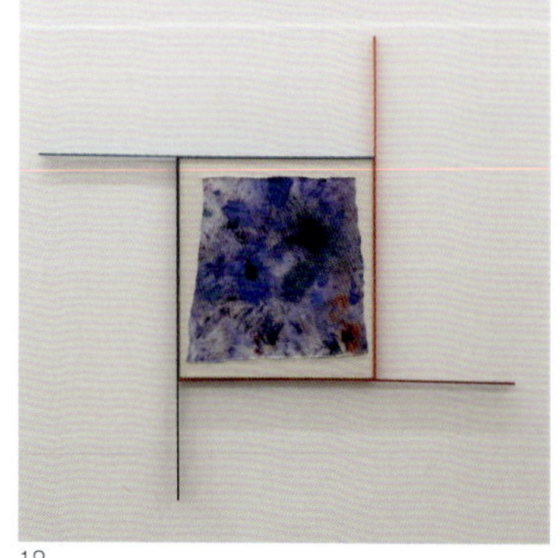

12

1
Untitled (Informers), 2006
Oil on linen
38 × 52 in.
2006.1.012

2
Untitled (color test hand #1),
2008–12
Oil on linen
15 × 20 in.
2012.1.001

3
Untitled (color test hand #2), 2012
Oil on linen
15 × 20 in.
2012.1.002

4
Untitled (color test hand #3), 2012
Oil on linen
15 × 20 in.
2012.1.003

5
Untitled (color test hand #4), 2012
Oil on linen
15 × 20 in.
2012.1.004

6
Untitled (color test hand #5), 2012
Oil on linen
15 × 20 in.
2012.1.005

7
Untitled (color test hand #6), 2012
Oil on linen
15 × 20 in.
2012.1.006

8
Untitled (color test hand #7), 2012
Oil on linen
15 × 20 in.
2012.1.007

9
Untitled (color test hand #8), 2012
Oil on linen
15 × 20 in.
2012.1.008

10
Untitled (color test hand #9), 2012
Oil on linen
15 × 20 in.
2012.1.009

11
Untitled (color test hand #10), 2012
Oil on linen
15 × 20 in.
2012.1.010

12
Untitled (1A), 2012
Oil on cotton and pencil
on canvas, oil on wood
Overall: c. 49 × 51 in.;
canvas: 23 × 21 in.
2012.1.014

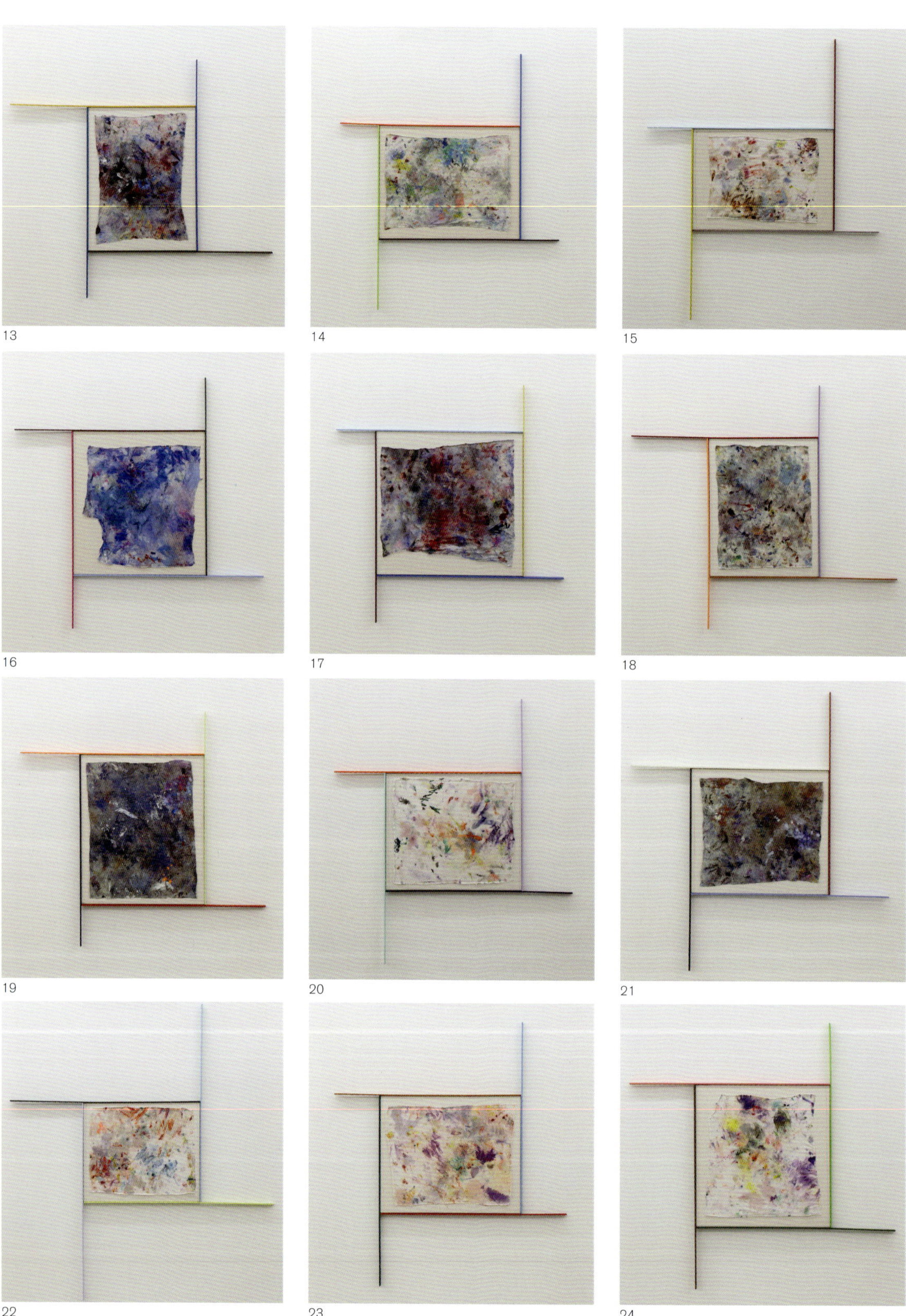

13

14

15

16

17

18

19

20

21

22

23

24

13
Untitled (2A), 2012
Oil on cotton and pencil on canvas,
oil on wood
Overall: c. 45 × 51 in.;
canvas: 27 × 21 in.
2012.1.015

14
Untitled (3A), 2012
Oil on cotton and pencil on canvas,
oil on wood
Overall: c. 50 × 44 in.
canvas: 22 × 28 in.
2012.1.016

15
Untitled (6A), 2012
Oil on cotton and pencil on canvas,
oil on wood
Overall: c. 53 × 45 in.;
canvas: 19 × 27 in.
2012.1.019

16
Untitled (8A), 2012
Oil on cotton and pencil on canvas,
oil on wood
Overall: c. 46 × 47 in.;
canvas: 26 × 25 in.
2012.1.021

17
Untitled (11A), 2012
Oil on cotton and pencil on canvas,
oil on wood
Overall: c. 45 × 44 in.;
canvas: 27 × 28 in.
2012.1.024

18
Untitled (13A), 2012
Oil on cotton and pencil on canvas,
oil on wood
Overall: c. 46 × 51 in.;
canvas: 26 × 21 in.
2012.1.026

19
Untitled (14A), 2012
Oil on cotton and pencil on canvas,
oil on wood
Overall: c. 44 × 48 in.;
canvas: 28 × 24 in.
2012.1.027

20
Untitled (16A), 2012
Oil on cotton and pencil on canvas,
oil on wood
Overall: c. 50 × 46 in.;
canvas: 22 × 26 in.
2012.1.029

21
Untitled (18A), 2012
Oil on cotton and pencil on canvas,
oil on wood
Overall: c. 50 × 47 in.;
canvas: 22 × 25 in.
2012.1.031

22
Untitled (19A), 2012
Oil on cotton and pencil on canvas,
oil on wood
Overall: c. 54 × 50 in.;
canvas: 18 × 22 in.
2012.1.032

23
Untitled (20A), 2012
Oil on cotton and pencil on canvas,
oil on wood
Overall: c. 50 × 45 in.;
canvas: 22 × 27 in.
2012.1.033

24
Untitled (21A), 2012
Oil on cotton and pencil on canvas,
oil on wood
Overall: c. 47 × 48 in.;
canvas: 25 × 24 in.
2012.1.034

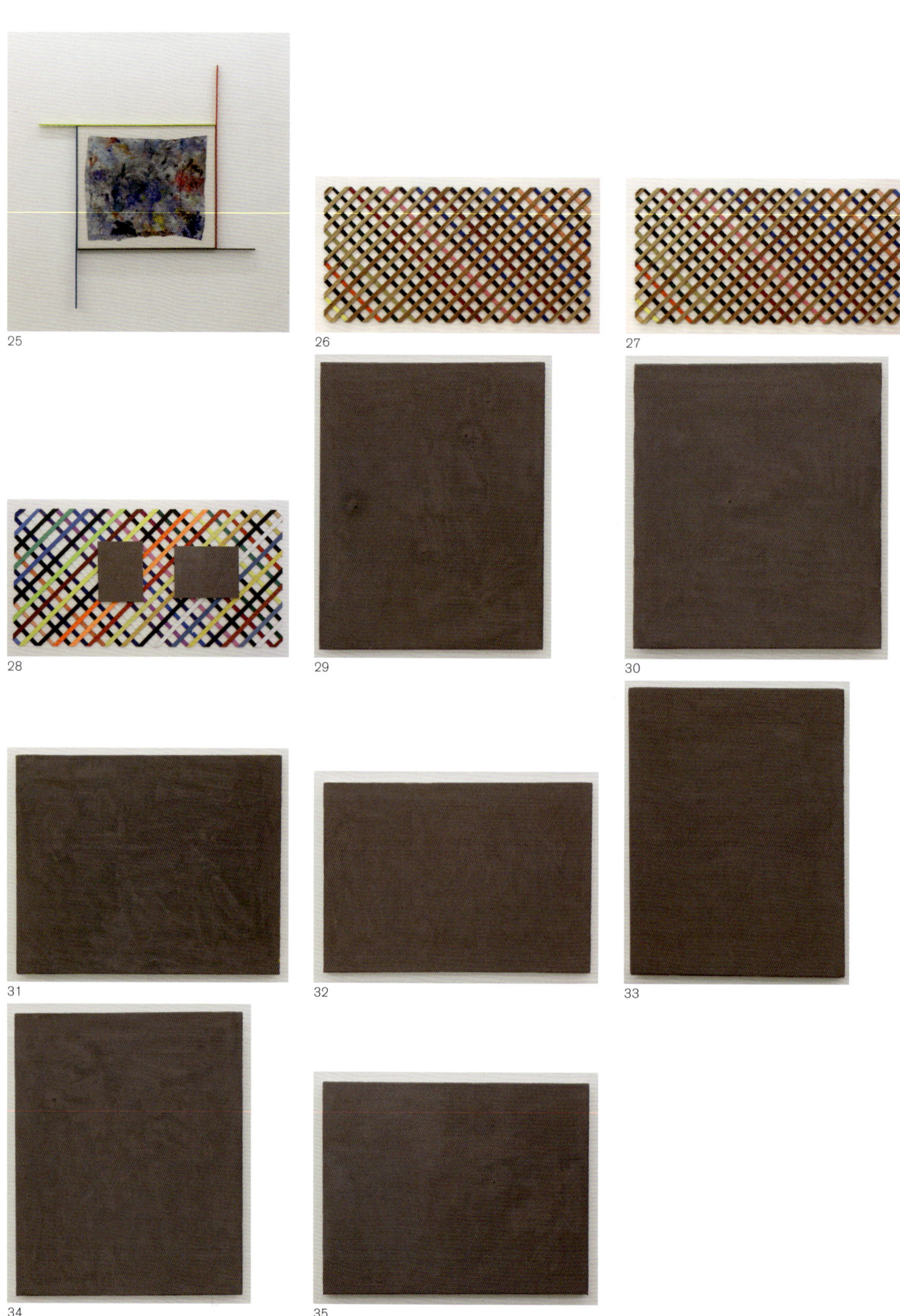

25

26

27

28

29

30

31

32

33

34

35

25
Untitled (24A), 2012
Oil on cotton and pencil on canvas, oil
on wood
Overall: c. 48 × 44 in.;
canvas: 24 × 28 in.
2012.1.037

26
Untitled (lattice 1), 2012
Oil on wood
48 × 96 in.
2012.1.056

27
Untitled (lattice 2), 2012
Oil on wood
48 × 96 in.
2012.1.057

28
Untitled (lattice 3), 2012
Oil on wood
48 × 96 in.
2012.1.058

29
Untitled (14B), 2012
Oil on canvas
25 × 20 in.
2012.1.048

30
Untitled (1B), 2012
Oil on canvas
19 × 17 in.
2012.1.040

31
Untitled (17B[1]), 2012
Oil on canvas
16 × 20 in.
2012.1.051

32
Untitled (5B), 2012
Oil on canvas
19 × 27 in.
2012.1.042

33
Untitled (10B), 2012
Oil on canvas
21 × 16 in.
2012.1.044

34
Untitled (12B), 2012
Oil on canvas
24 × 20 in.
2012.1.046

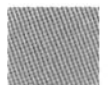

35
Untitled (23B), 2012
Oil on canvas
18 × 23 in.
2012.1.055

For the exhibition, Kantor has produced *Les meules*, a four-minute 16mm film that takes Claude Monet's haystack paintings as its impetus and visual content. Comprised of over 1,000 photographs of the Impressionist's paintings and projected at the same size as the original canvases, *Les meules* presents an image of the temporal changes in season and time of day brought up to mechanical speed; color changes now arrive through camera settings and monitor calibrations rather than the location of the sun and subjective interpretation of the artist. Digital images of the paintings culled on-line have been turned into single frames in the film, and thereby returned to physicality and to the photographic process that was a principal concern of Monet and his contemporaries.

This transition—from painting to photograph to film-still—is then further mediated, as Kantor produces new paintings from digitally manipulated photographs. The new paintings maintain the 3:4 aspect ratio of 16mm film, and evoke *Les meules* in their composition, scale, and vibrant color palette, only in the end to frustrate their references to the natural world. For as in his previous Lens Flare series, the paintings are freeze-framed instants, visible only via a technological apparatus: the lens flare as an effect caused by the refraction of light through a camera's lens, and the manipulations of colors as a Photoshop tool.

When in 1891 Monet exhibited fifteen paintings of haystacks, friend and critic Camille Pissarro wrote that the paintings "breathed contentedly"; the interchangeable and repetitious nature of the paintings, their sameness in difference, is given a faster breath in Kantor's artwork, fueled by the reciprocal interaction between film and painting, digital and analog, and the mechanical and the handmade.

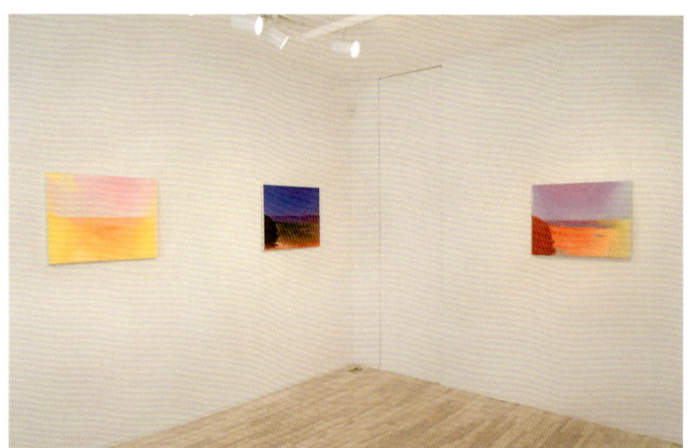

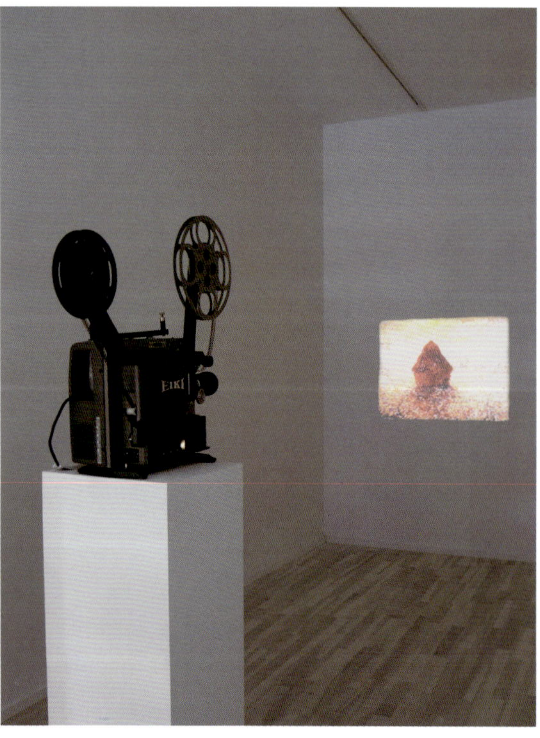

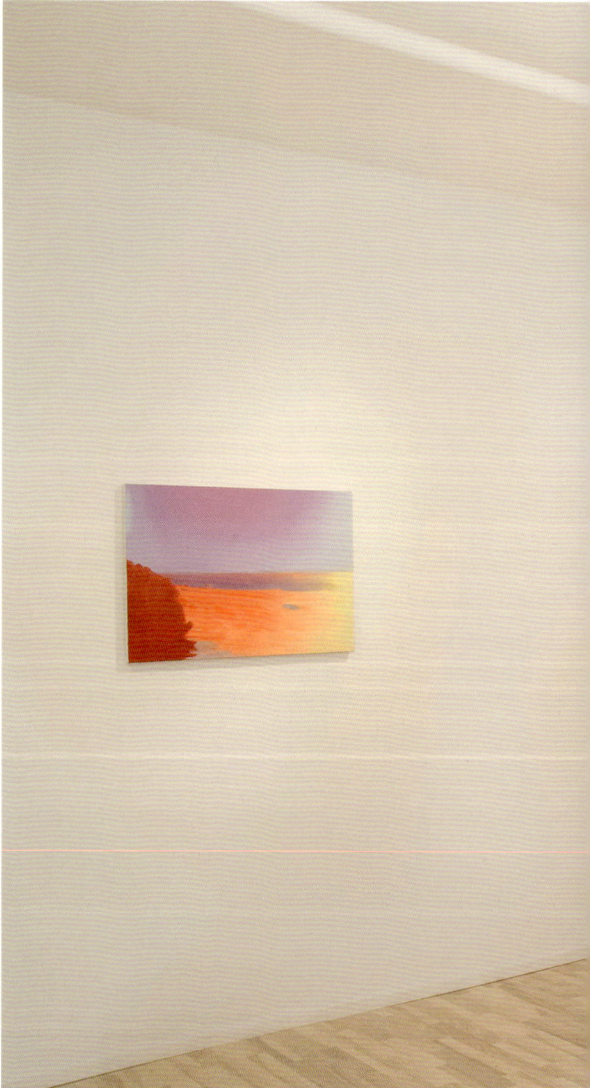

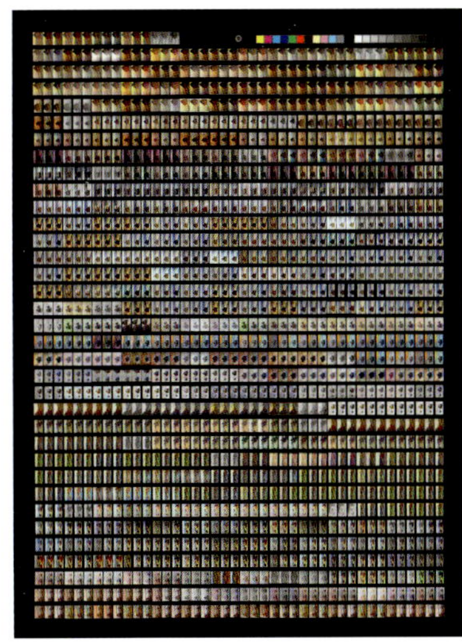
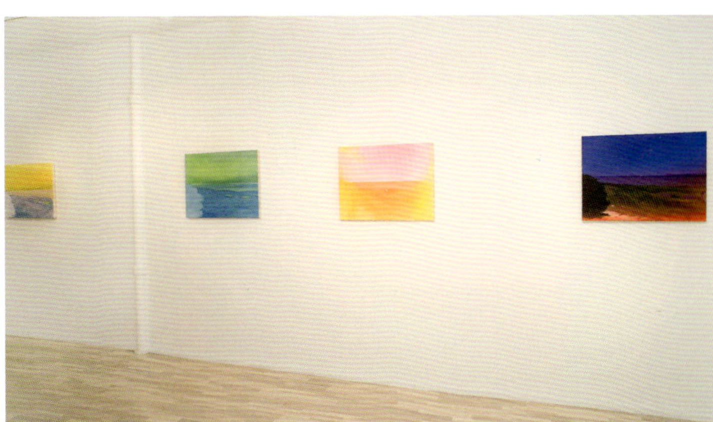

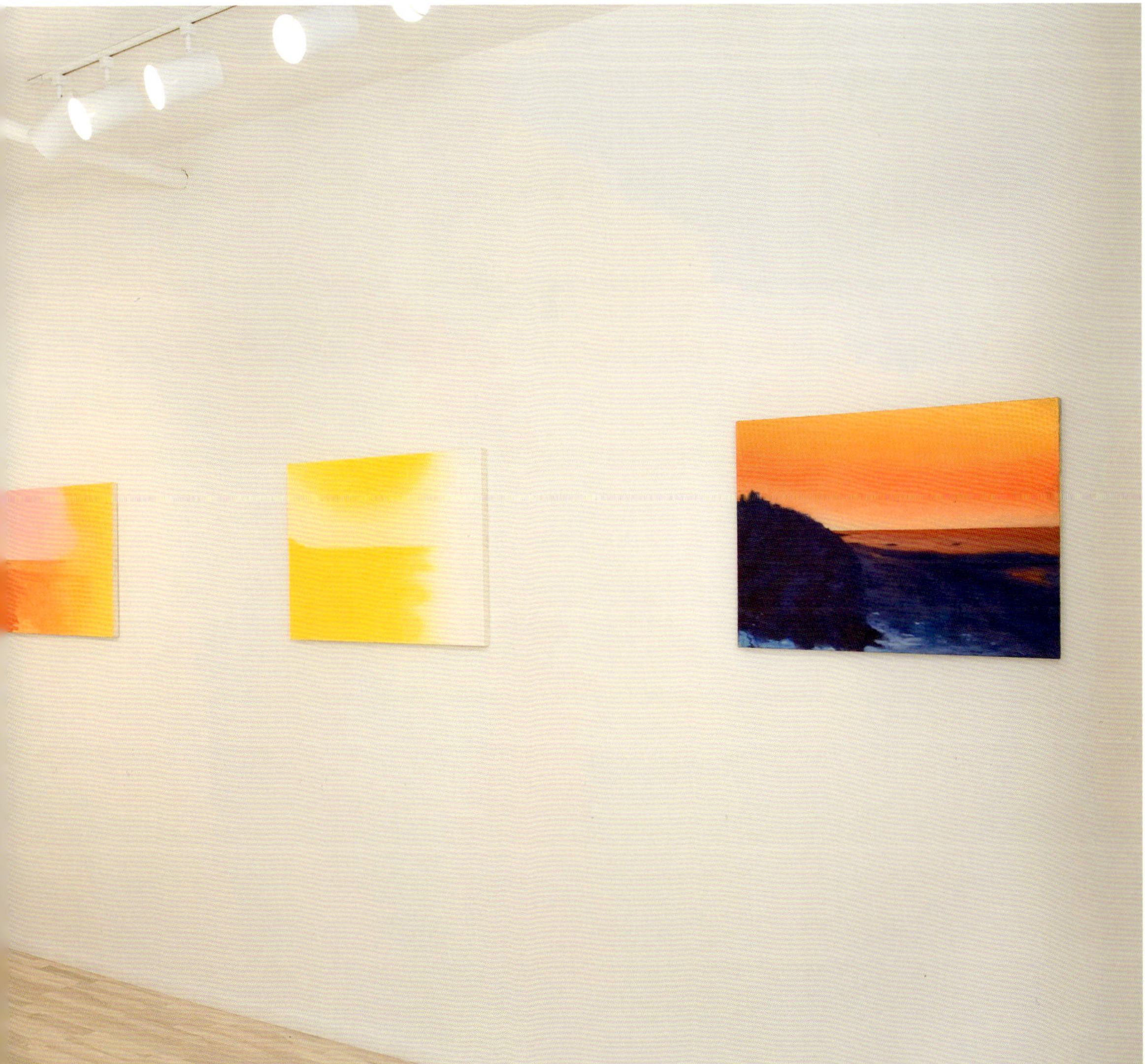

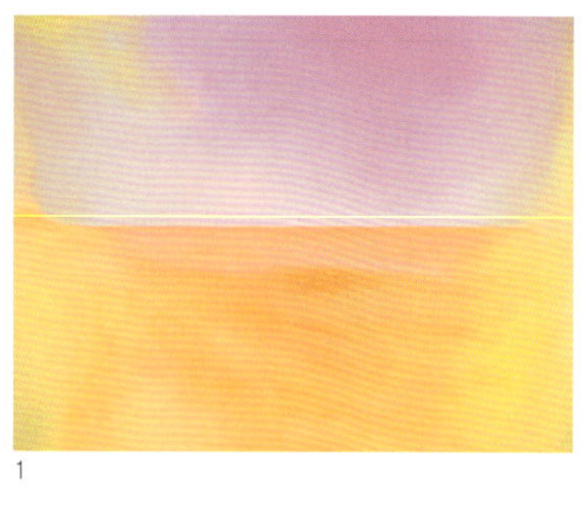

1

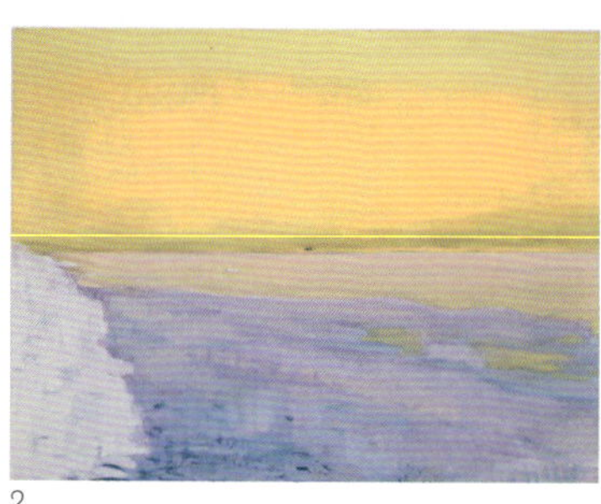

2

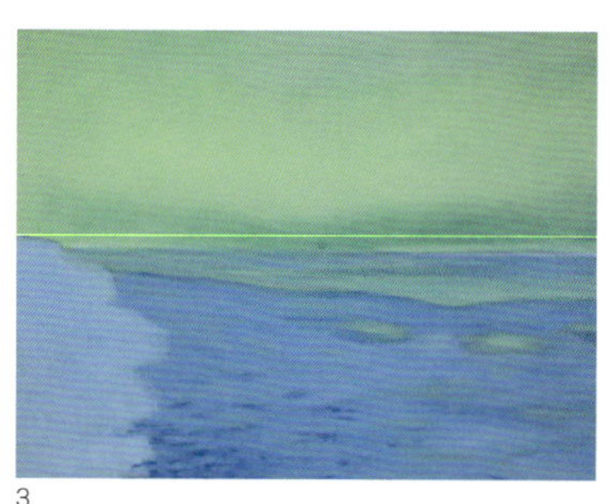

3

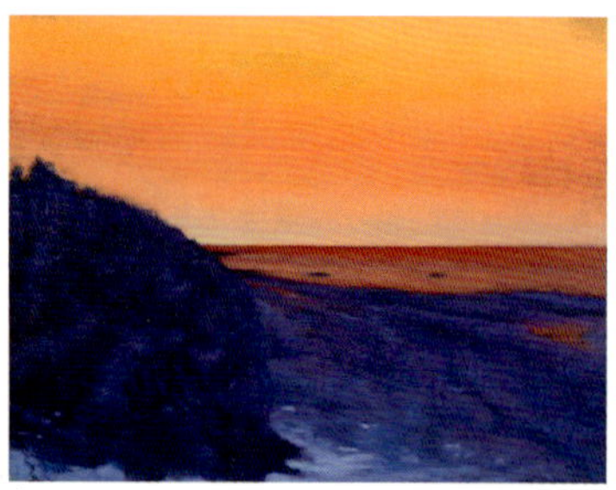

4

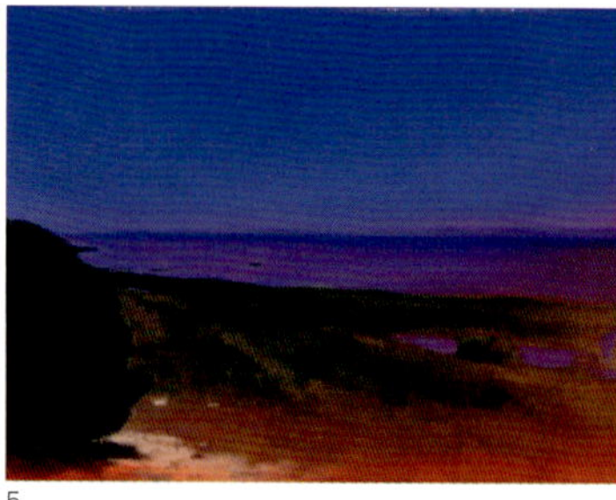

5

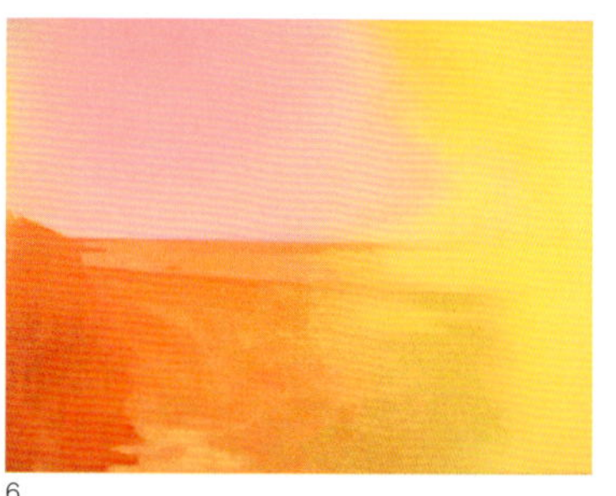

6

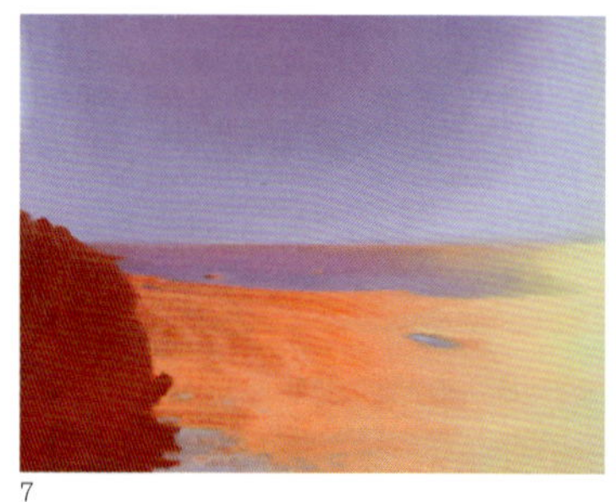

7

8

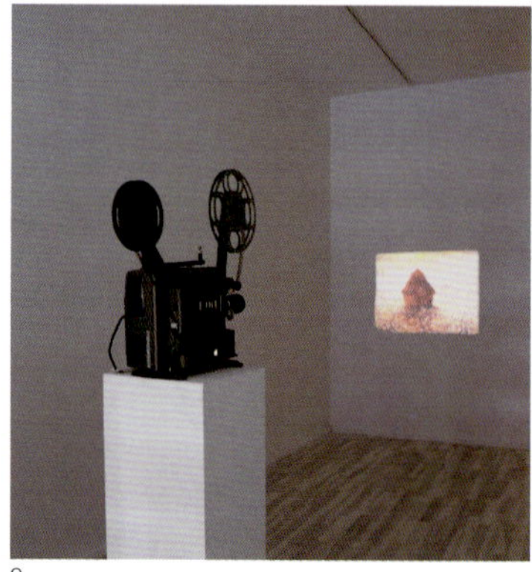

9

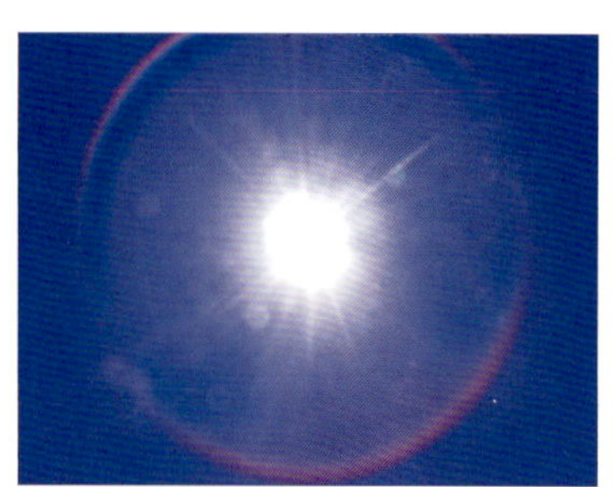

10

1
Untitled (Basel lens flare 8017), 2009
Oil on canvas
21 × 28 in.
2009.1.025

2
Untitled (lens flare 7867i), 2010
Oil on canvas
21 × 28 in.
2010.1.009

3
Untitled (lens flare 8005i), 2010
Oil on canvas
21 × 28 in.
2010.1.008

4
Untitled (113590 rev 1), 2011
Oil on linen
21 × 28 in.
2011.1.005

5
Untitled (113557), 2011
Oil on canvas
21 × 28 in.
2011.1.006

6
Untitled (113577), 2011
Oil on canvas
21 × 28 in.
2011.1.002

7
Untitled (113590 rev 2), 2011
Oil on linen
21 × 28 in.
2011.1.004

8
Untitled (113606), 2011
Oil on canvas
21 × 28 in.
2011.1.003

9
Les meules, 2011
16 mm film (color, silent), 3:18 min.
F2011.1.001

10
Lens Flare, 2008–2009
16 mm film (color, silent), 3:20 min.
F2009.1.002

**2010 SAN FRANCISCO
RATIO 3
APRIL 30–JUNE 12**

Ratio 3 is pleased to announce Jordan Kantor's second solo
exhibition at the gallery. The exhibition will feature all new
works, debuted here. These will include:
• several paintings on canvas, some in oil, others in enamel
• two looping slide projections
• a group of unique etchings with aquatint, in brushed finish
welded aluminum artist's frames
• three wax paper palette/paintings
• a large cut-and-pasted paper collage on canvas in a
hand-painted artist's frame with objects.
Though comprised of individual pieces, this exhibition is
conceived as a constellation of works to be seen together in
the space in which they are shown.

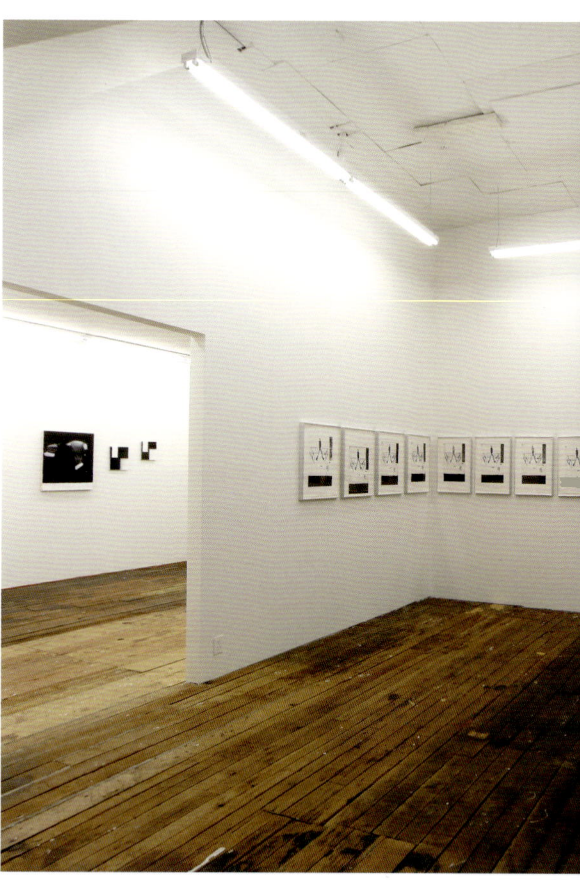

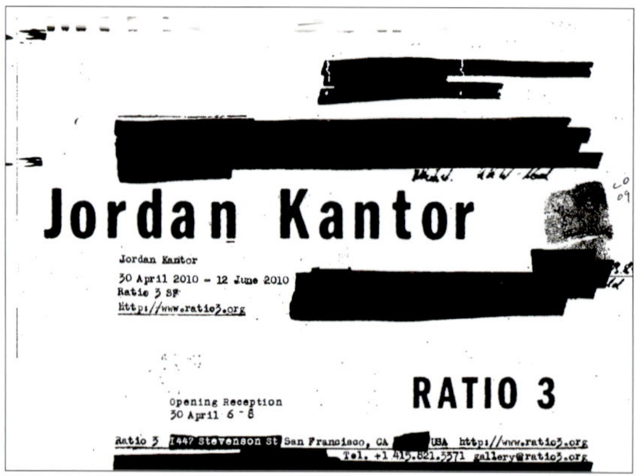

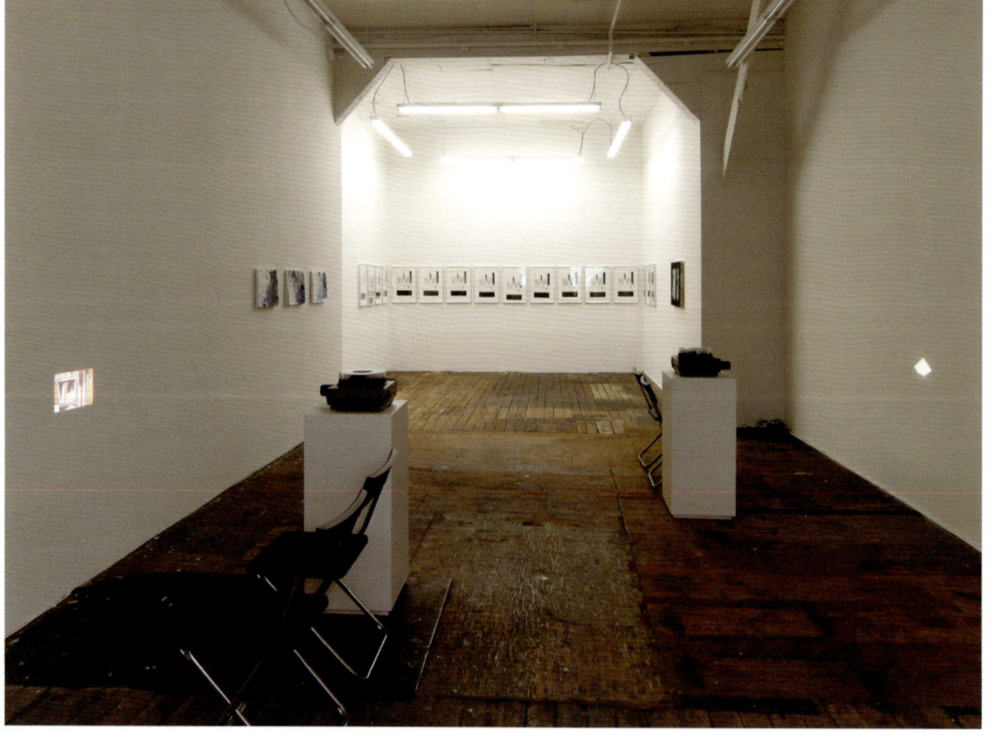

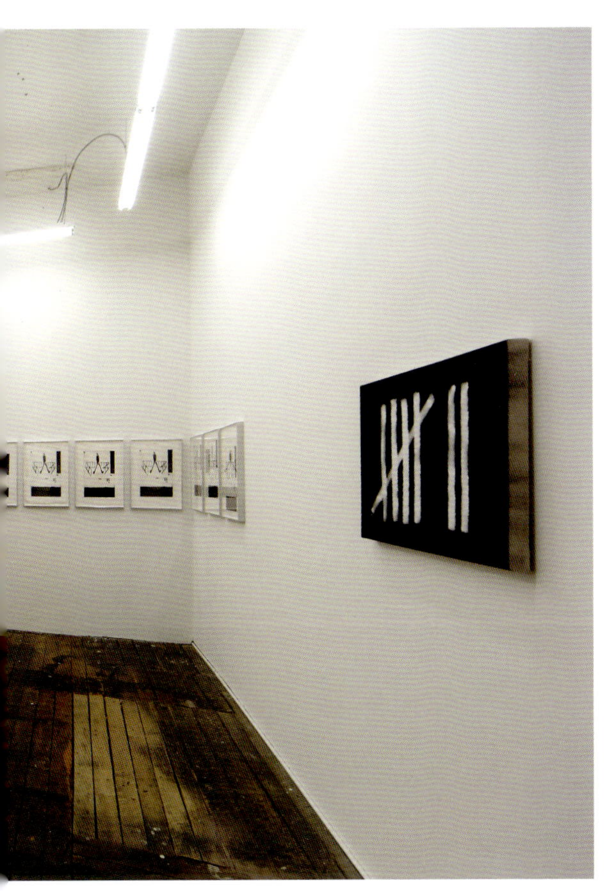
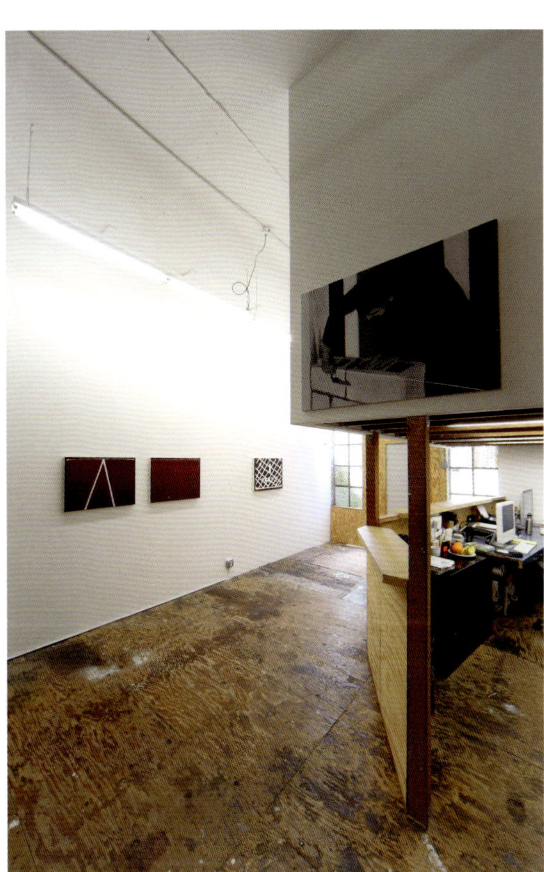

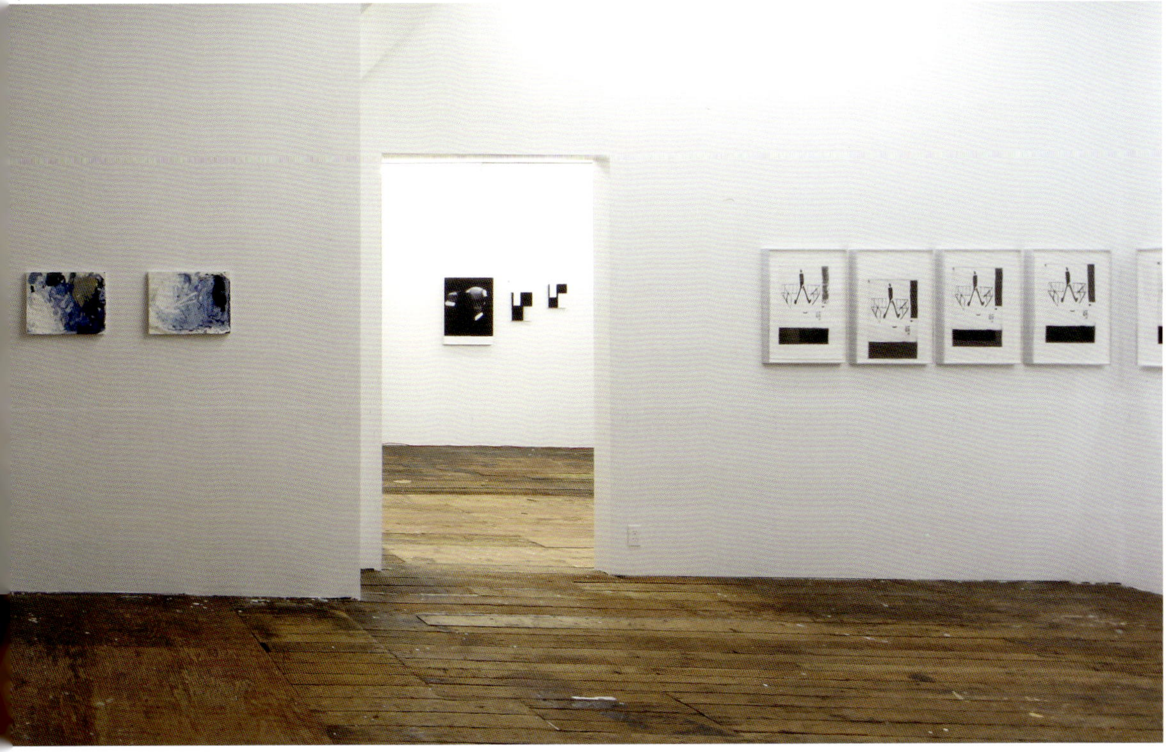

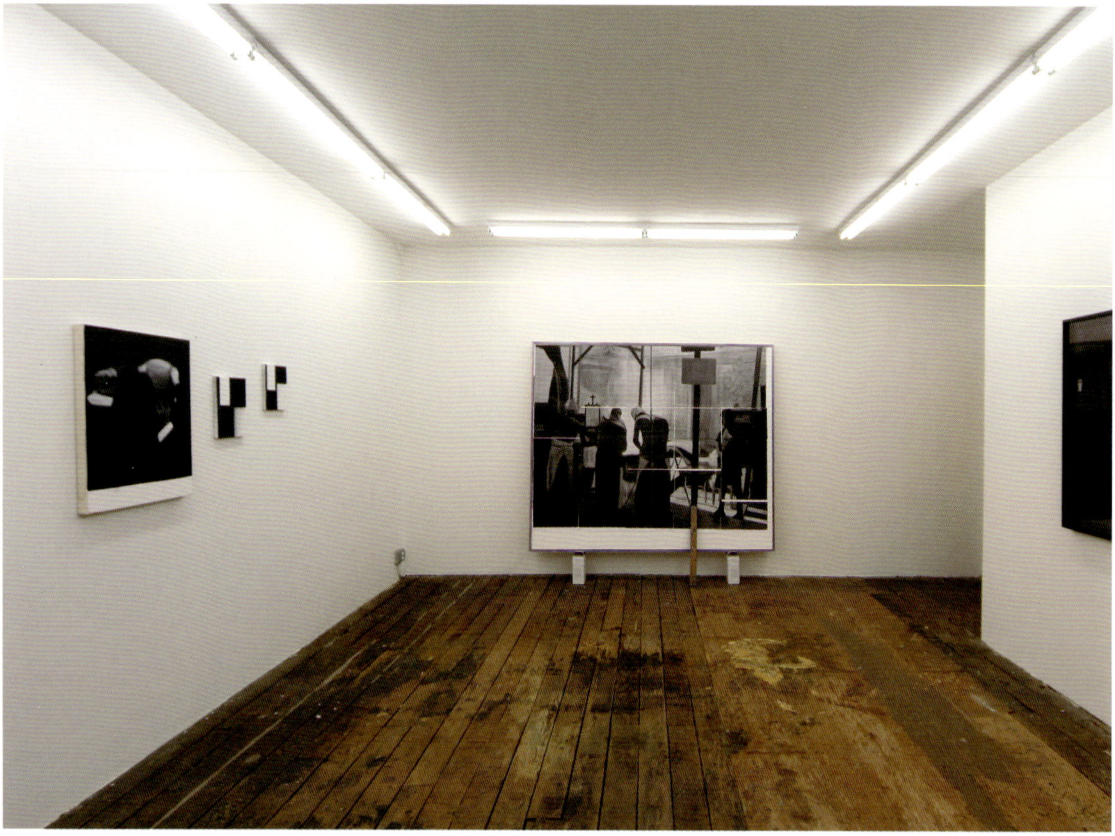

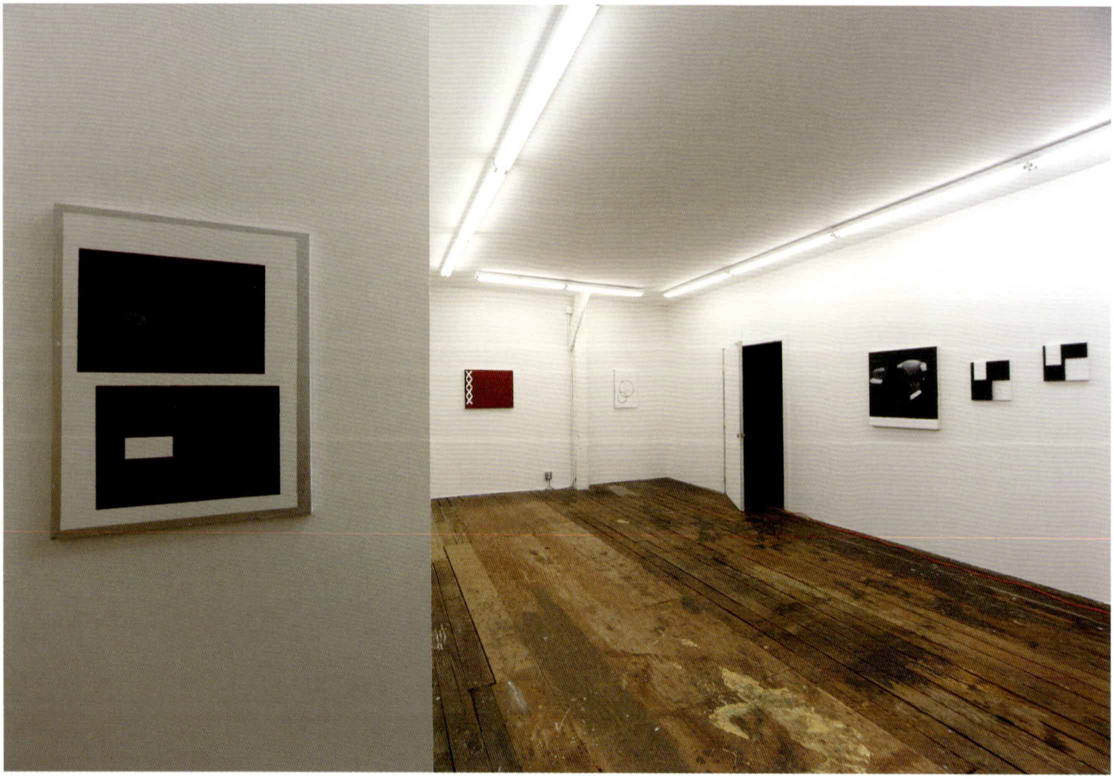

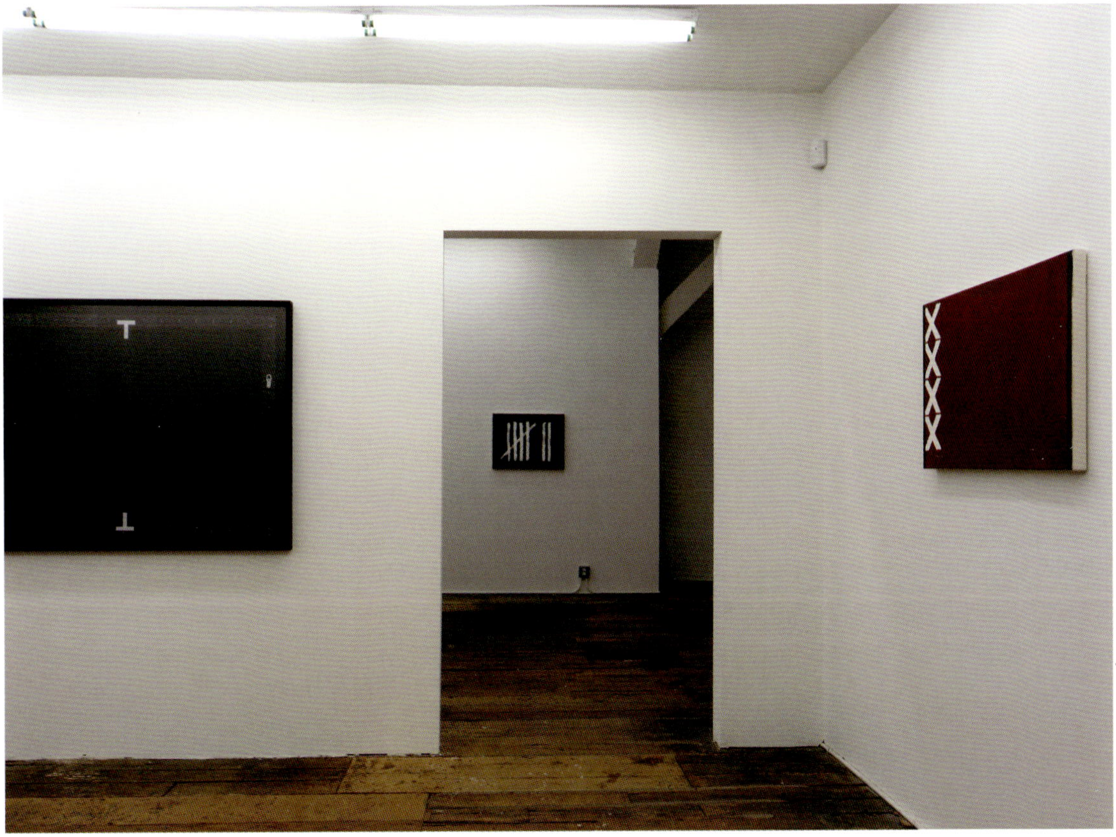

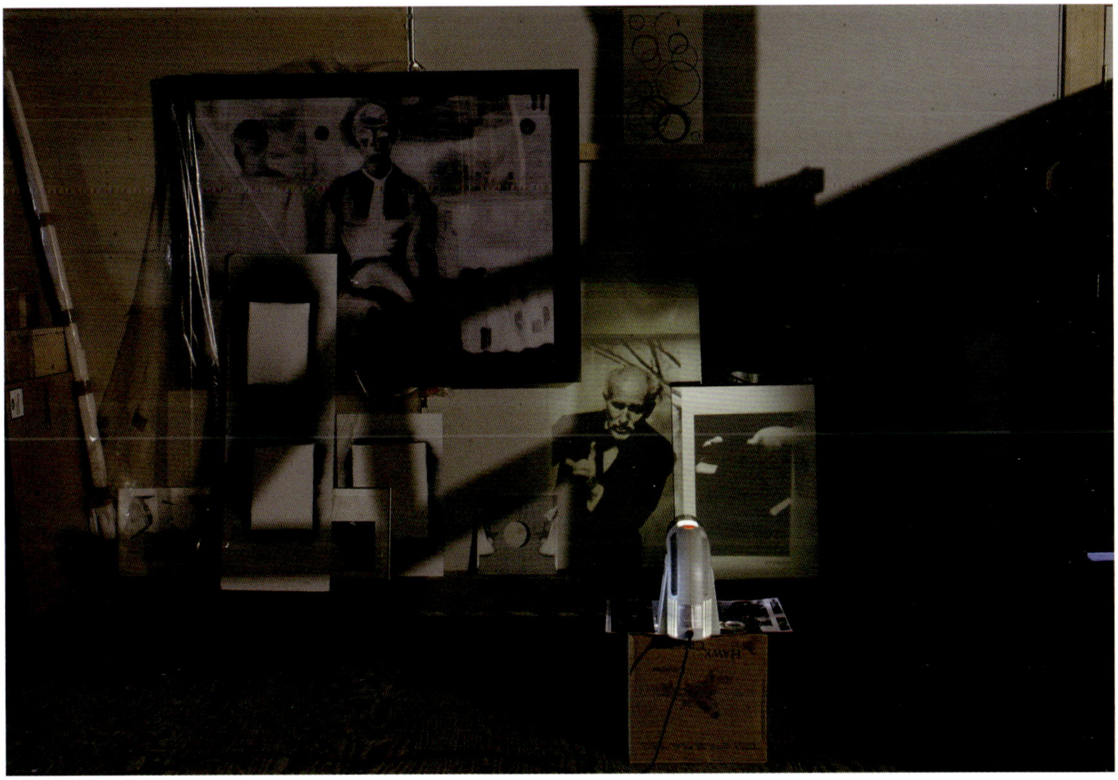

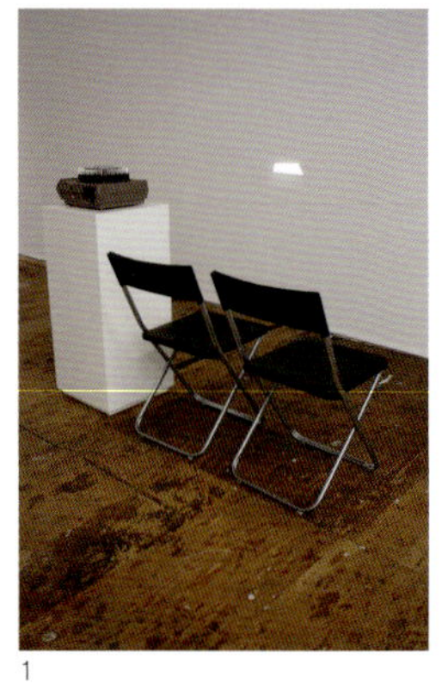

1

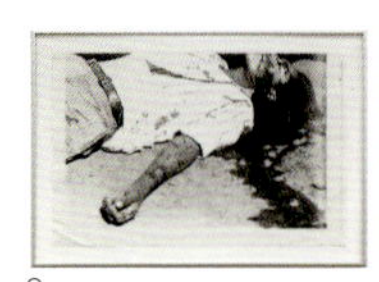

2

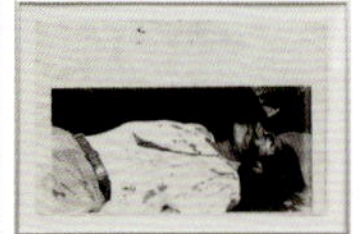

3

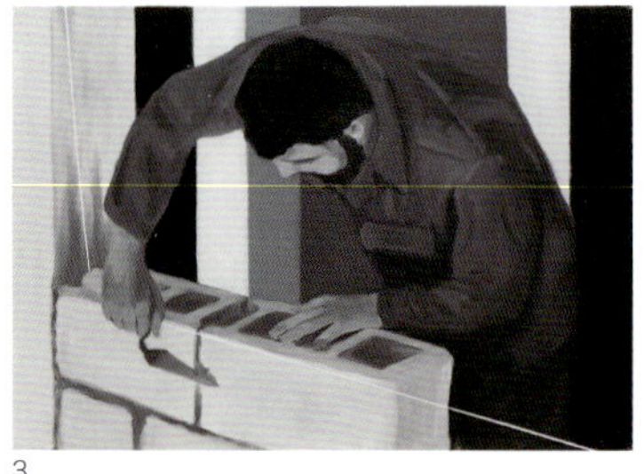

4

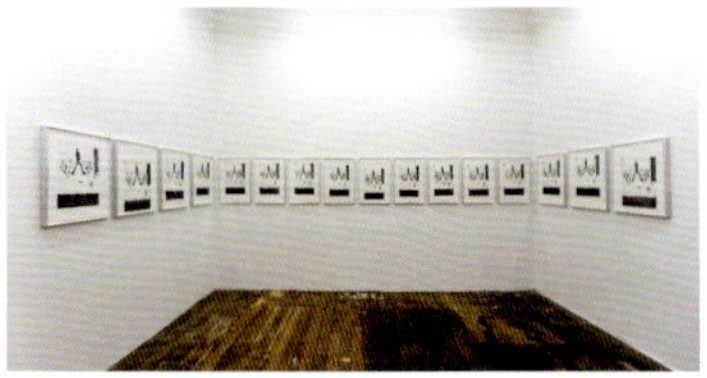

5

6

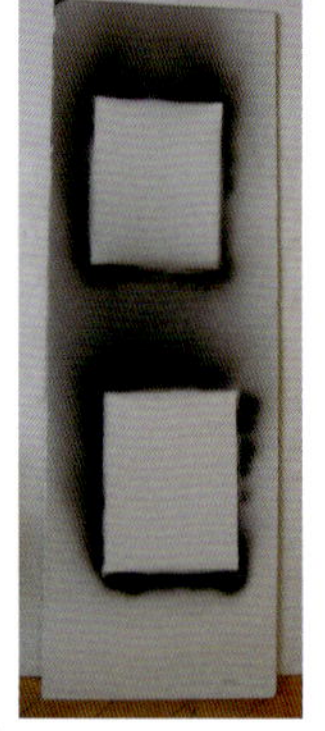

7

8

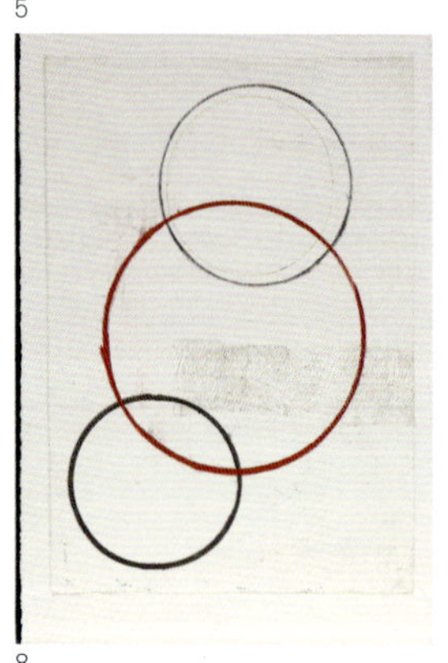

9

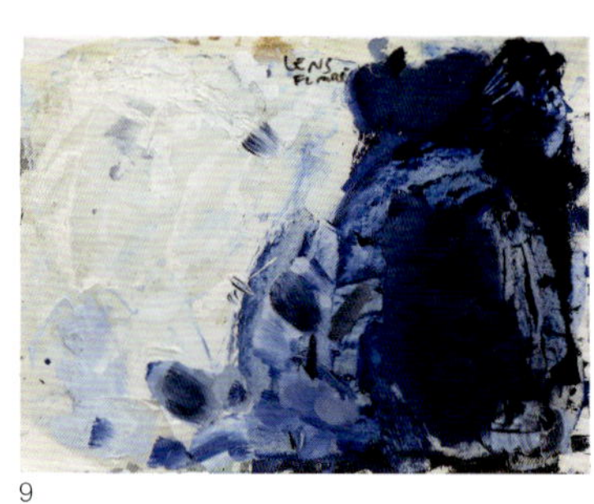

10

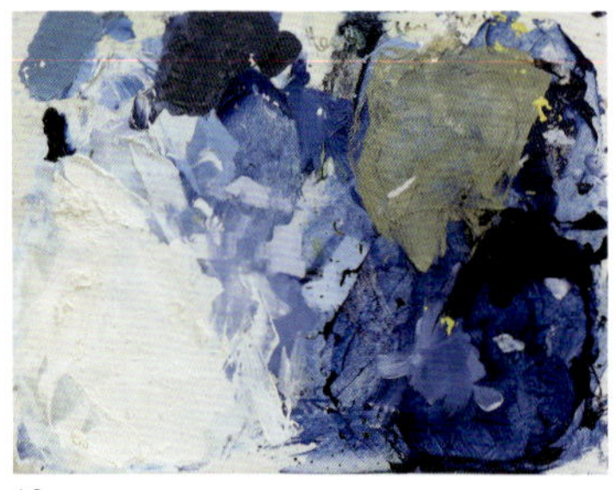

11

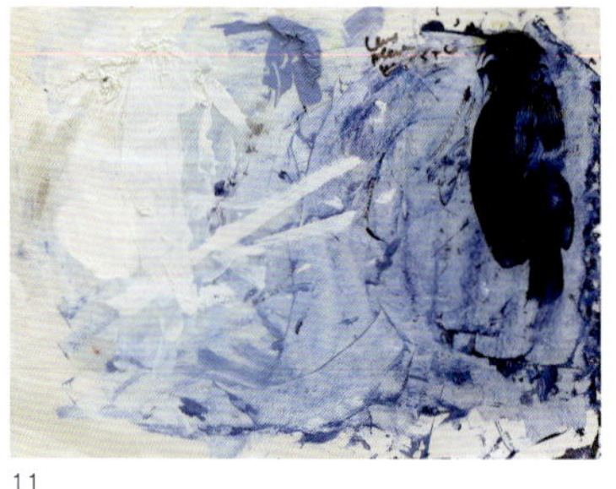

12

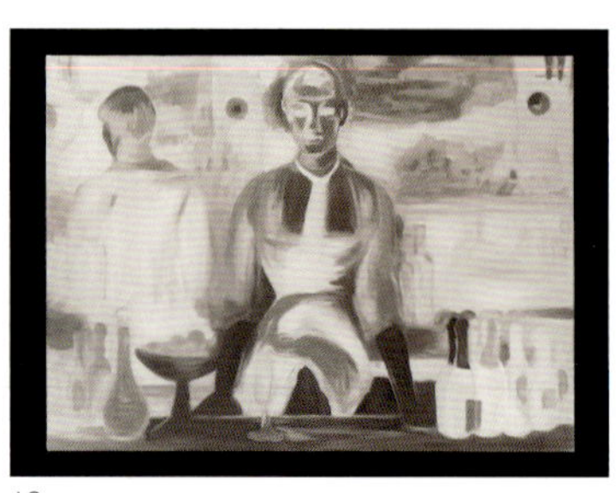

1
Untitled (studio shots, 1998),
1998–2010
Two sets of thirty-nine 35mm slides
(color), carousel slide projector,
continuous loop.
Dimensions variable
2010.3.002a-mm

2
Untitled (photocopy diptych),
2004/2006
Photocopy on paper, two sheets
13¾ × 19¾ in. ea. (frame);
11 × 17 in. ea. (sheet)
2004.2.004a-b

3
Untitled (builder), 2006
Oil on canvas
28 × 40 in.
2006.1.019

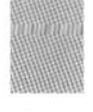 each
4
Untitled (working space),
2006/2009
Soft-ground etchings in brushed
aluminum frames, sixteen pieces
24 × 16¾ in. ea. (frame);
22 × 14¾ in. ea. (sheet)
P2006.003.1-16

5*
Untitled (ghost image), 2007
Enamel on cardboard
15¾ × 24 in.
2007.1.004

6*
Untitled (two ghosts), 2007
Enamel on cardboard
48 × 16 in.
2007.1.009

7
Untitled (collage painting), 2007–08
Enamel and water-soluble oil on
cut-and-pasted paper on canvas
24 × 17 in.
2008.1.012

8*
Untitled (rings), 2008
Enamel and oil on canvas pasted
on canvas
24 × 17 in.
2008.1.010

9
Untitled (Lens Flare palette),
2008–2009
Oil on wax paper mounted on canvas
12 × 16 in.
2009.1.043

10
Untitled (Lens Flare Trio palette),
2008–2009
Oil on wax paper mounted on canvas
12 × 16 in.
2009.1.044

11
Untitled (Lens Flare 5 & 6 palette),
2008-2009
Oil on wax paper mounted on canvas
12 × 16 in.
2009.1.045

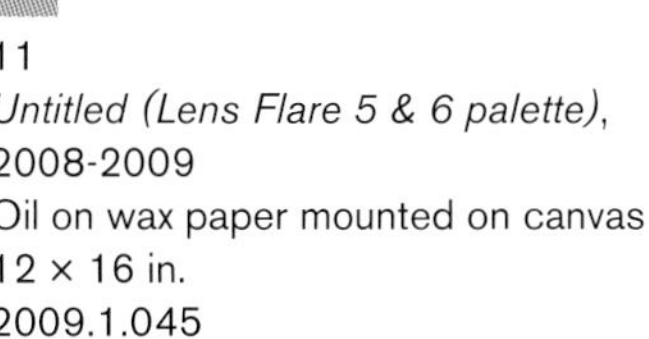
12
Untitled (The Bar), 2009
Chromogenic color print on metallic
paper, mounted on gatorboard
43 × 59 in.
Ph2009.001.02

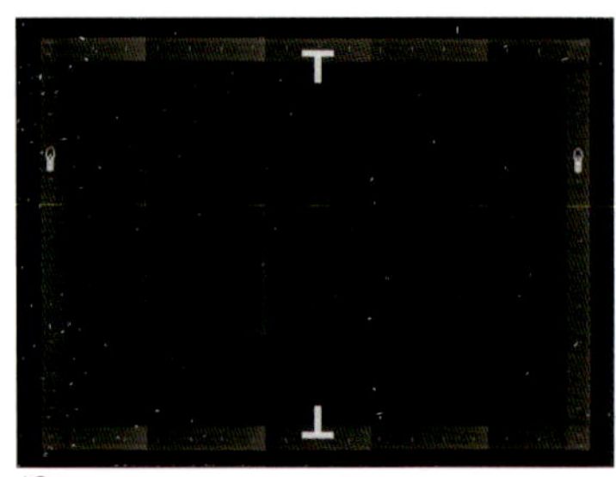

13

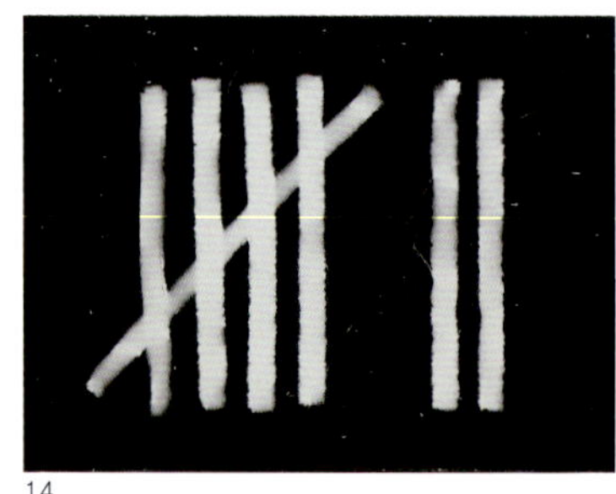

14

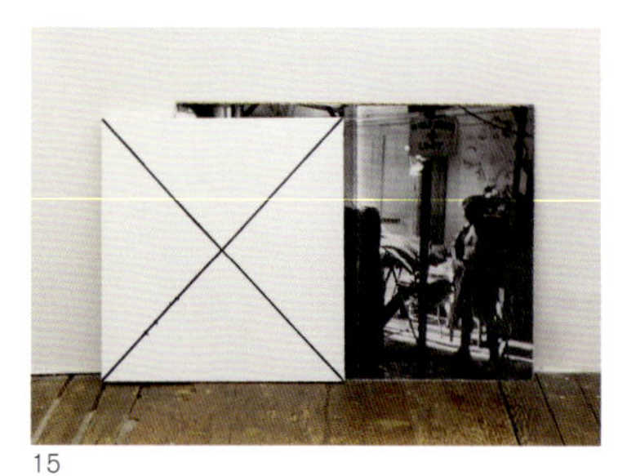

15

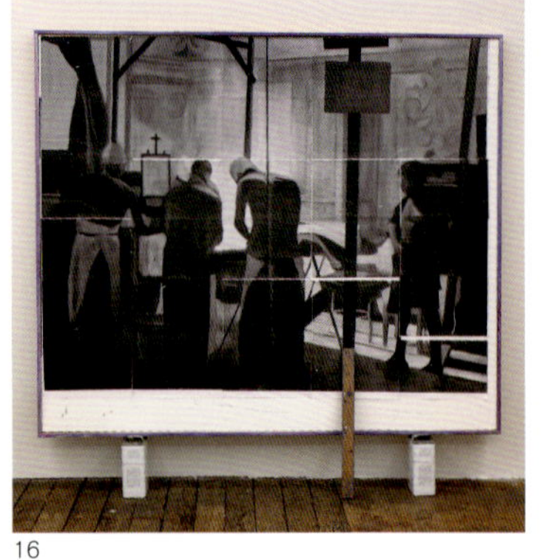

16

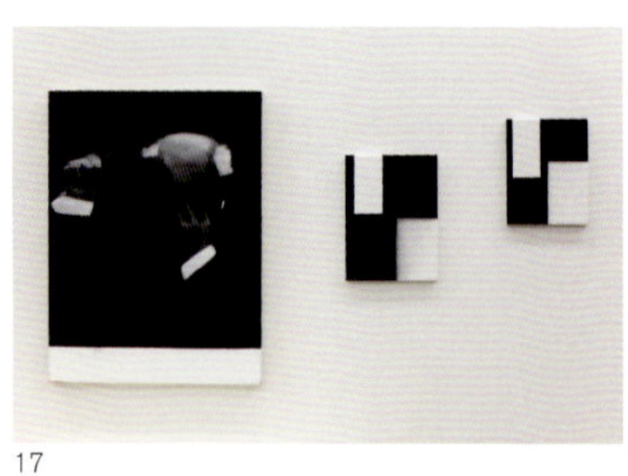

17

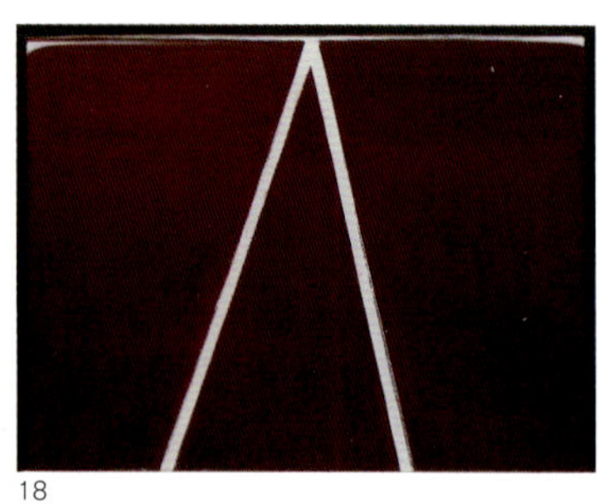

18

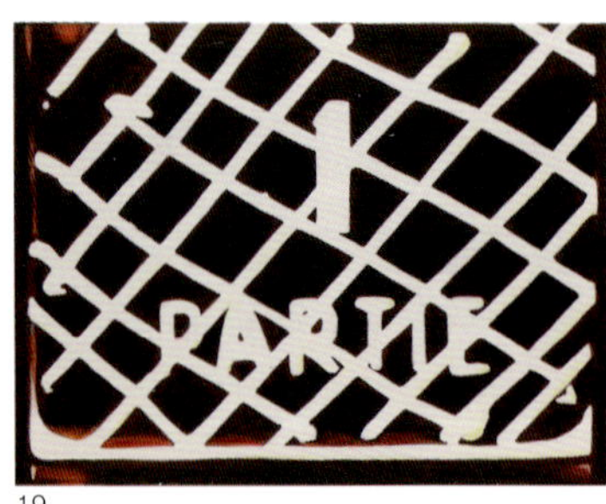

19

20

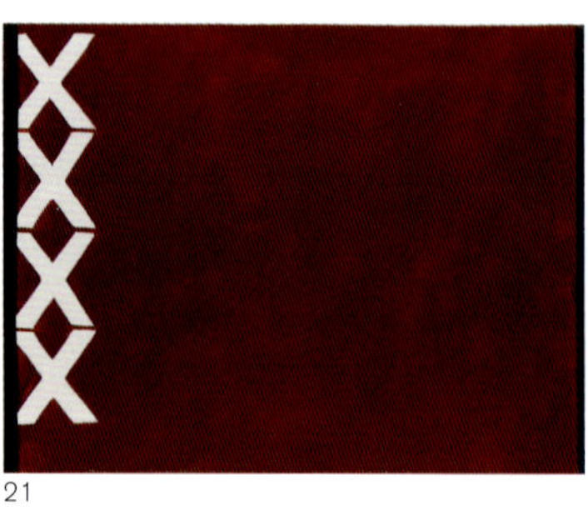

21

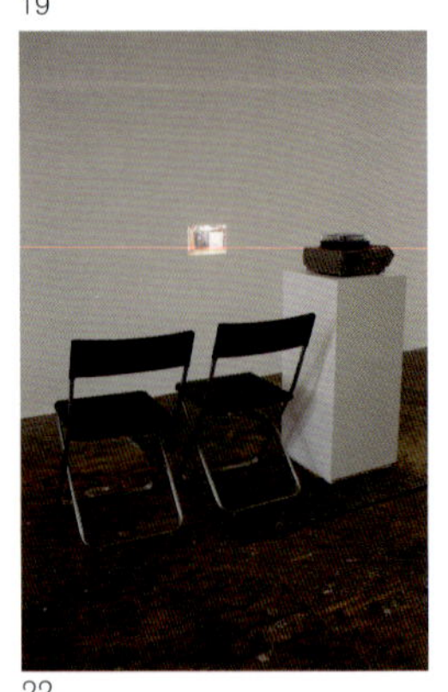

22

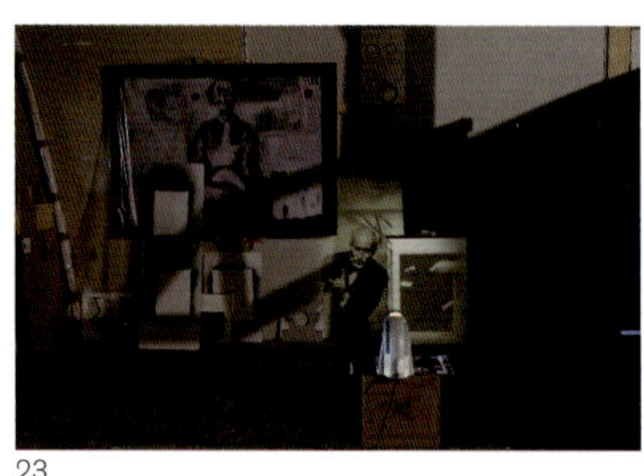

23

13
Untitled (X-Ray photograph), 2009
Chromogenic color print, mounted
on gatorboard
40¾ × 55¾ in.
Ph2009.003.001

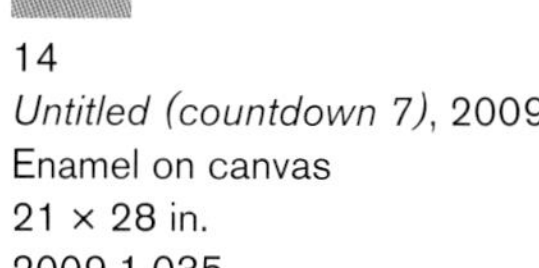

14
Untitled (countdown 7), 2009
Enamel on canvas
21 × 28 in.
2009.1.035

15*
Untitled (X with surgery), 2009
Enamel on canvas; cut-and-pasted
paper mounted on cardboard,
in two parts
Overall: 58 × 36 × 5 in.
2009.1.042a-b

16
Untitled (surgery collage), 2009–2010
Cut-and-pasted paper and oil on
canvas, in handpainted artist's frame,
with objects
Overall: 71¾ × 85½ × 16 in.
2009.1.040

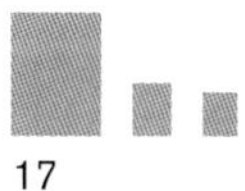

17
Untitled (conductor with margin) with
Untitled (canvases with rectangles),
2010
3 elements: Oil and enamel on canvas
28 × 21 in.; 12 × 9 in.; 10 × 8 in.
2010.1.001, 2009.1.029, 2009.1.030

18
Untitled (film leader, red 2), 2010
Oil on canvas
21 × 28 in.
2010.1.002

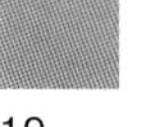

19
Untitled (film leader, partie), 2010
Oil on canvas
21 × 28 in.
2010.1.003

20
Untitled (film leader, red 3), 2010
Oil on canvas
21 × 28 in.
2010.1.004

21
Untitled (film leader, red x), 2010
Oil on canvas
21 × 28 in.
2010.1.005

22
Untitled (studio shots, 2010), 2010
Sixty-nine 35mm slides (color), carou-
sel slide projector, continuous loop.
Dimensions variable
2010.3.003a-qqq

23
Untitled (storeroom installation), 2010
Mixed mediums, 12 elements
Dimensions variable
2010.3.004

*
all works marked with an asterisk (*),
above, are stand alone works that were
incorporated into *Untitled (storeroom
installation)*, 2010 for this exhibition

For Art Statements, Jordan Kantor will debut his first film and a suite of new paintings based on individual still frames taken from it. The looped 16mm footage shows the sun—isolated in the sky—rapidly moving across the frame, and reduces the medium of film to its most basic, materialist function: recording the exposure of light through the apparatus of a lens. The accompanying paintings isolate and depict the "lens flares" in the film—those fleeting reflections of glare inside the camera that result when its lens is pointed directly at a bright light source. By focusing on the momentary distortions created by the camera's lens, Kantor's paintings emphasize the visual vestige of the intervention of the recording device. This self-reflexive attention to the materiality of images, which characterizes Kantor's work in other mediums as well, provides a springboard for larger speculations into the formal and theoretical nature of image-making and the circulation of pictorial signs.

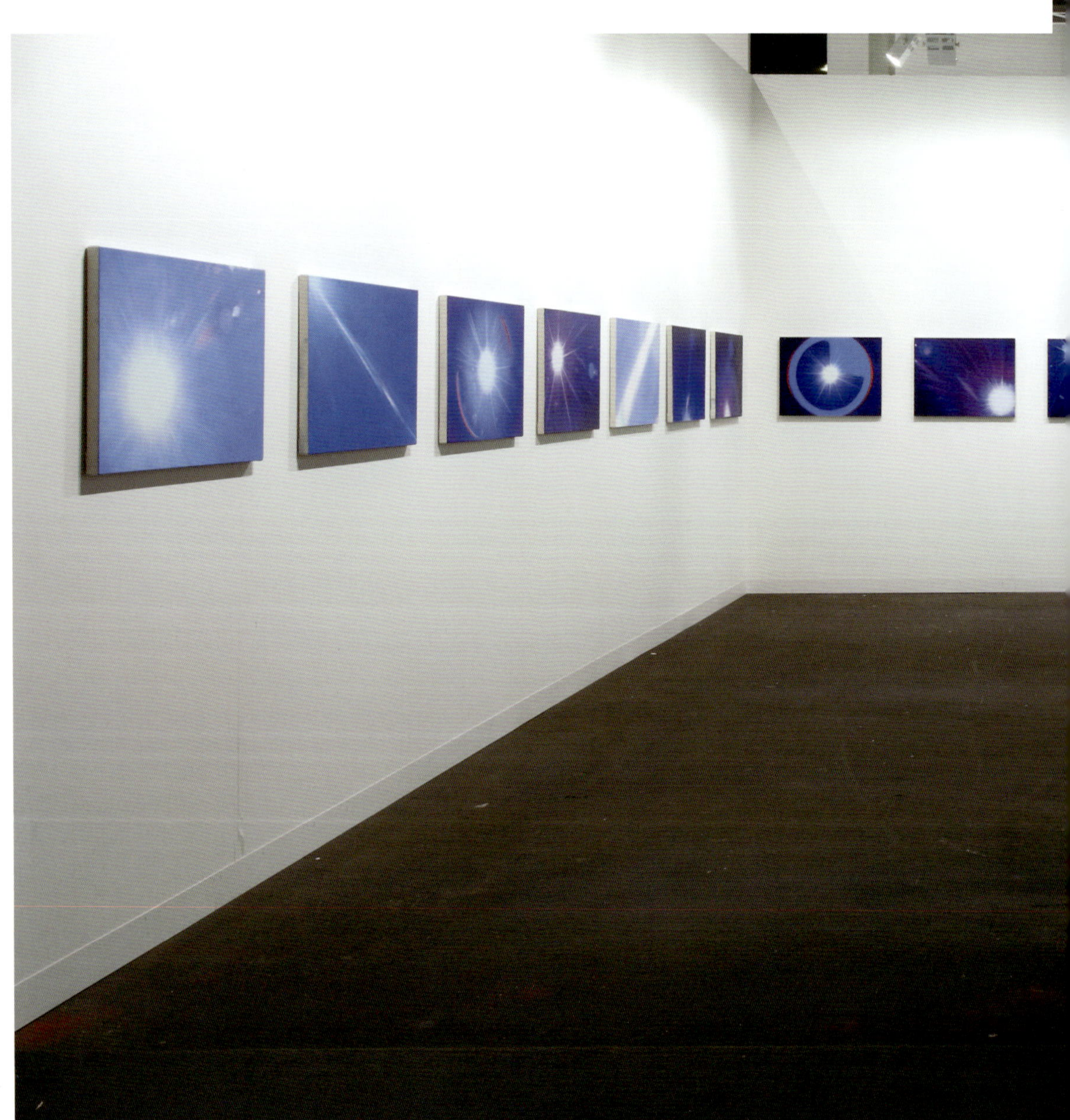

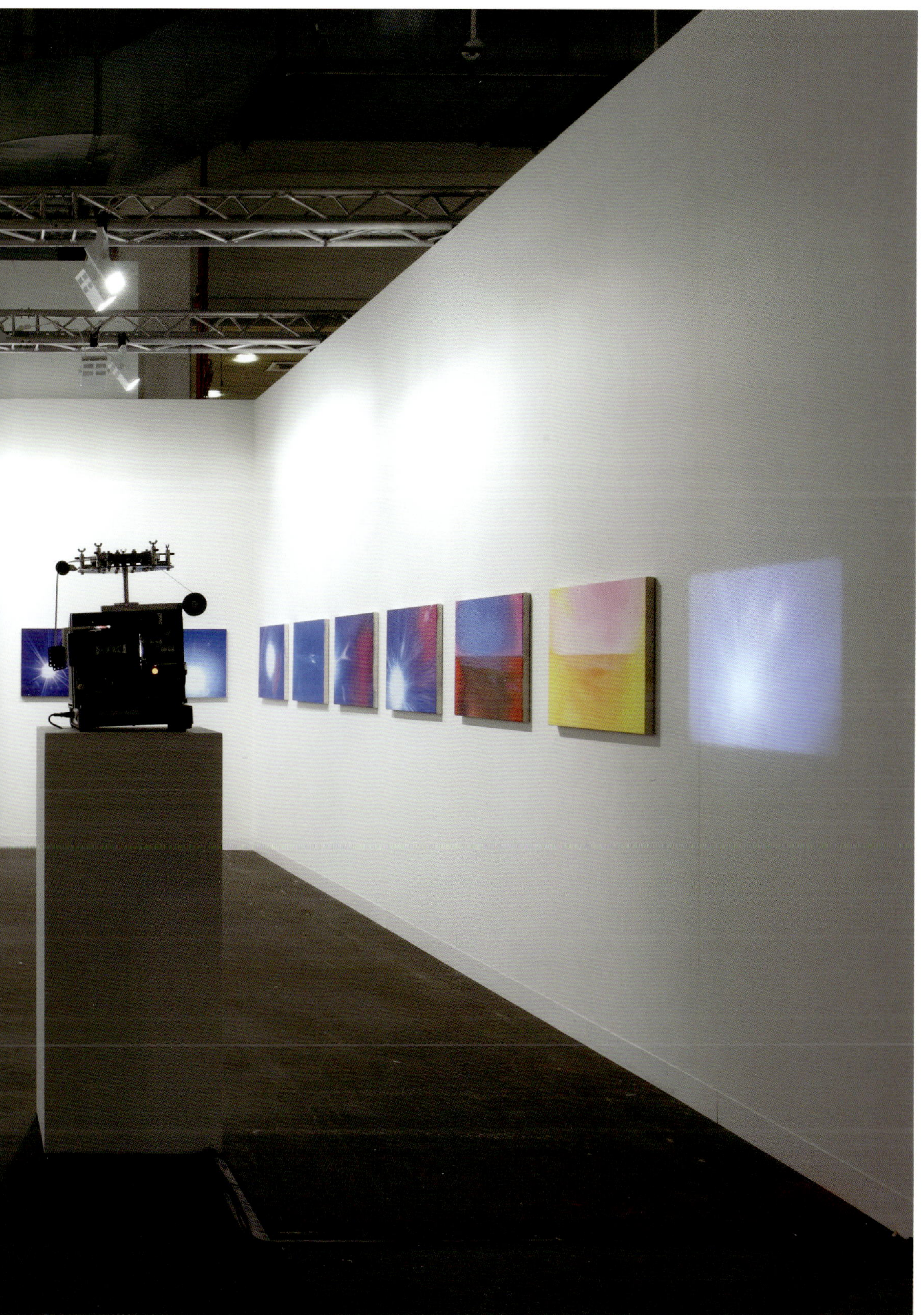

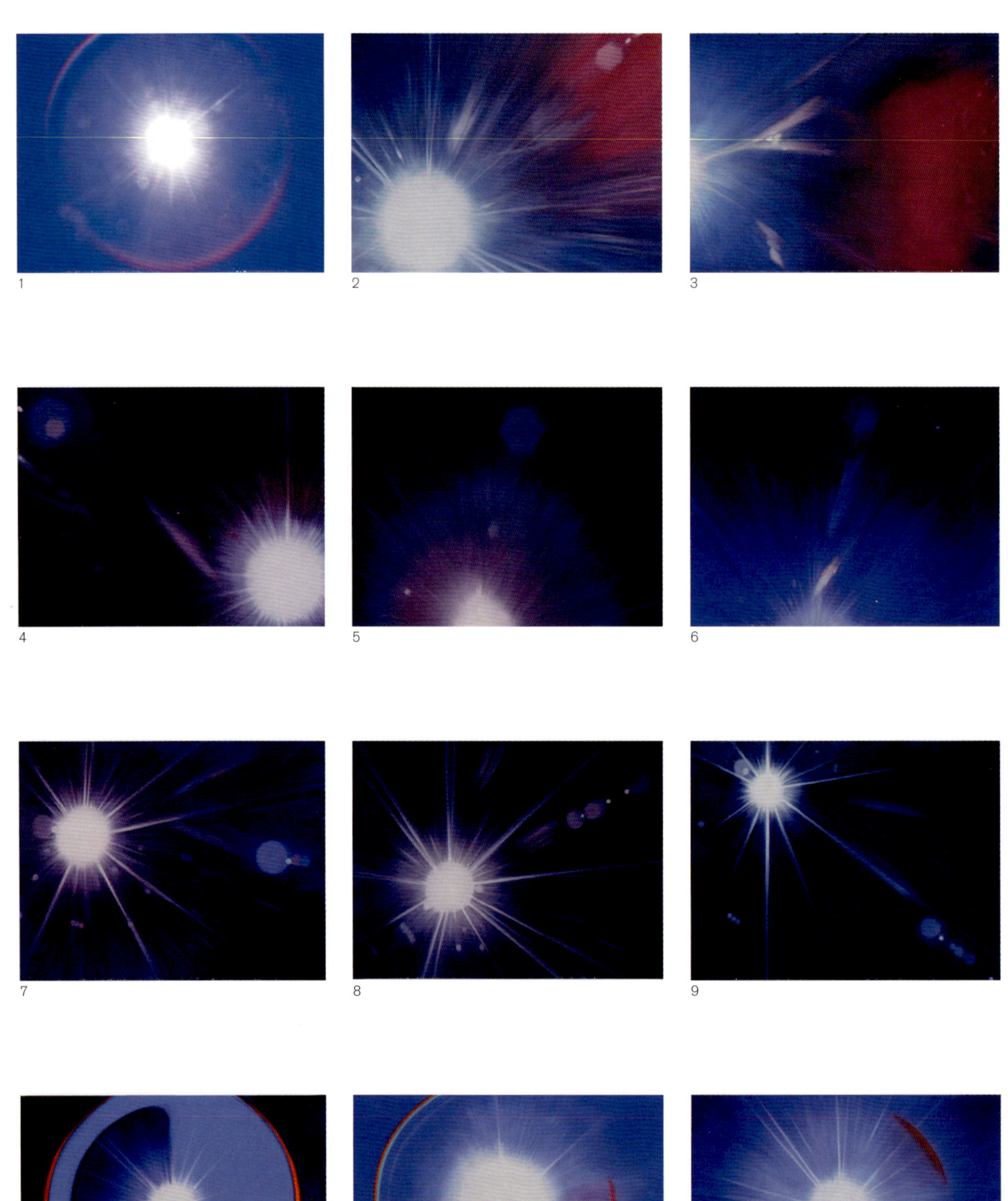

1

2

3

4

5

6

7

8

9

10

11

12

1
Lens Flare, 2008–2009
16 mm film (color, silent), 3:20 min.
Projection: 21 × 28 in.
F2009.1.001

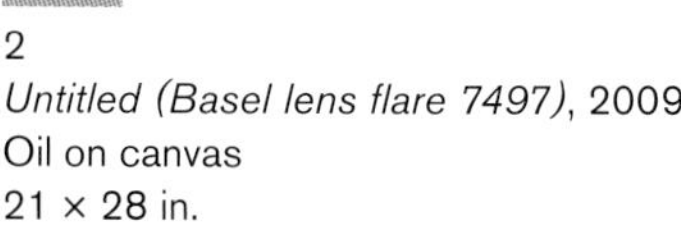

2
Untitled (Basel lens flare 7497), 2009
Oil on canvas
21 × 28 in.
2009.1.008

3
Untitled (Basel lens flare 6734), 2009
Oil on canvas
21 × 28 in.
2009.1.009

4
Untitled (Basel lens flare 5950), 2009
Oil on canvas
21 × 28 in.
2009.1.010

5
Untitled (Basel lens flare 5382), 2009
Oil on canvas
21 × 28 in.
2009.1.013

6
Untitled (Basel lens flare 5236), 2009
Oil on canvas
21 × 28 in.
2009.1.014

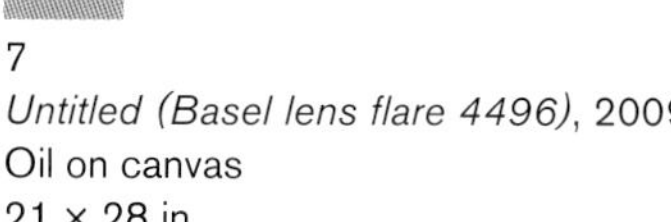

7
Untitled (Basel lens flare 4496), 2009
Oil on canvas
21 × 28 in.
2009.1.015

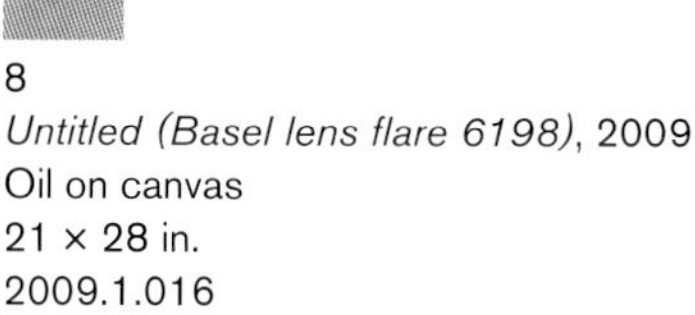

8
Untitled (Basel lens flare 6198), 2009
Oil on canvas
21 × 28 in.
2009.1.016

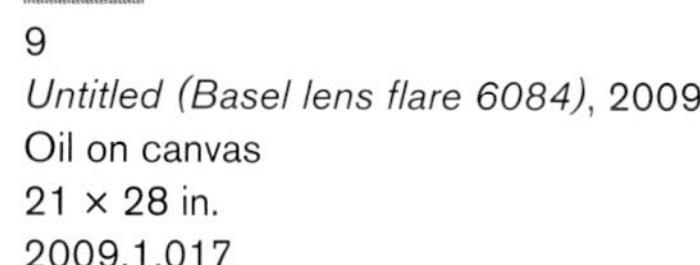

9
Untitled (Basel lens flare 6084), 2009
Oil on canvas
21 × 28 in.
2009.1.017

10
Untitled (Basel lens flare 5727), 2009
Oil on canvas
21 × 28 in.
2009.1.018

11
Untitled (Basel lens flare 6573), 2009
Oil on canvas
21 × 28 in.
2009.1.019

12
Untitled (Basel lens flare 4454), 2009
Oil on canvas
21 × 28 in.
2009.1.020

13

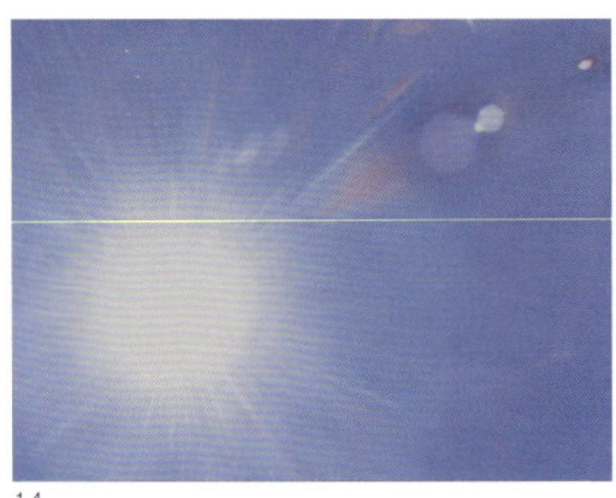

14

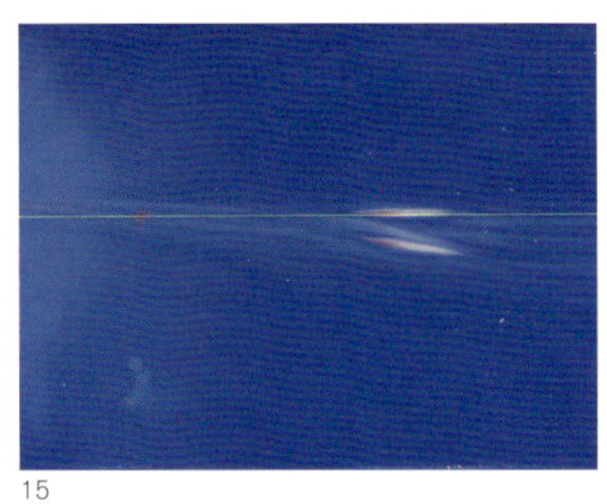

15

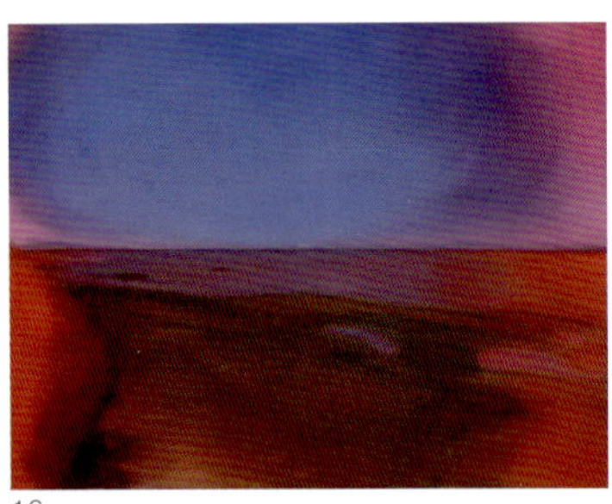

16

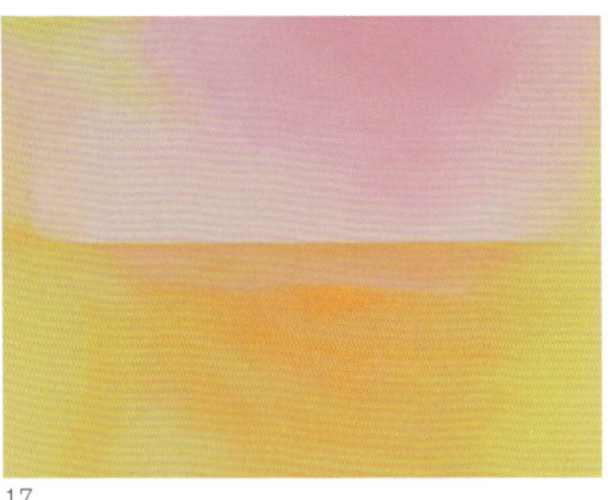

17

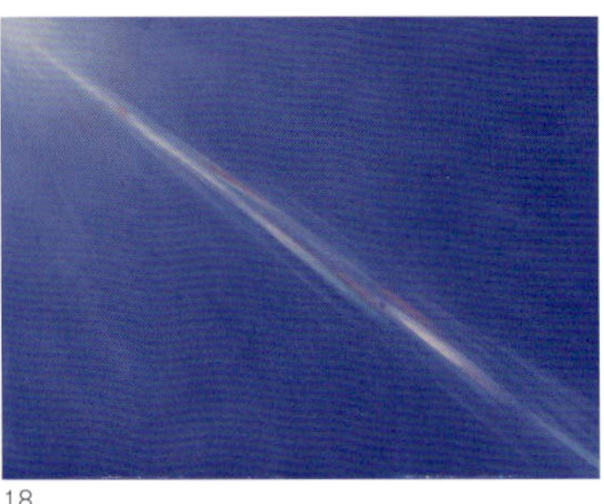

18

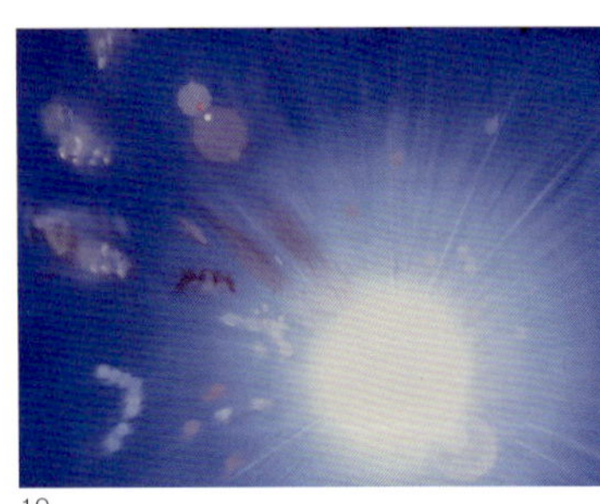

19

13
Untitled (Basel lens flare 4561), 2009
Oil on canvas
21 × 28 in.
2009.1.021

14
Untitled (Basel lens flare 3919), 2009
Oil on canvas
21 × 28 in.
2009.1.022

15
Untitled (Basel lens flare 6761), 2009
Oil on canvas
21 × 28 in.
2009.1.023

16
Untitled (Basel lens flare 7976), 2009
Oil on canvas
21 × 28 in.
2009.1.024

17
Untitled (Basel lens flare 8017), 2009
Oil on canvas
21 × 28 in.
2009.1.025

18
Untitled (Basel lens flare 4019), 2009
Oil on canvas
21 × 28 in.
2009.1.026

19
Untitled (Basel lens flare 6362), 2009
Oil on canvas
21 × 28 in.
2009.1.027

The recipients of this year's SECA Art Award employ a wide spectrum of artistic approaches, including painting, sculpture, photography, and video. Tauba Auerbach mines TV static, digital binary code, alphabets, and other sources to probe the dynamics of symbolic representation. Referencing 1980s sitcoms, Desirée Holman uses sculpture, performance, and video to look at the human condition via both reality and fantasy. Jordan Kantor's paintings explore the ways images circulate in our culture via appropriation. Trevor Paglen's photographs examine the shadowy side of the U.S. government, capturing images of spy satellites, clandestine flight missions, and secret military operations.

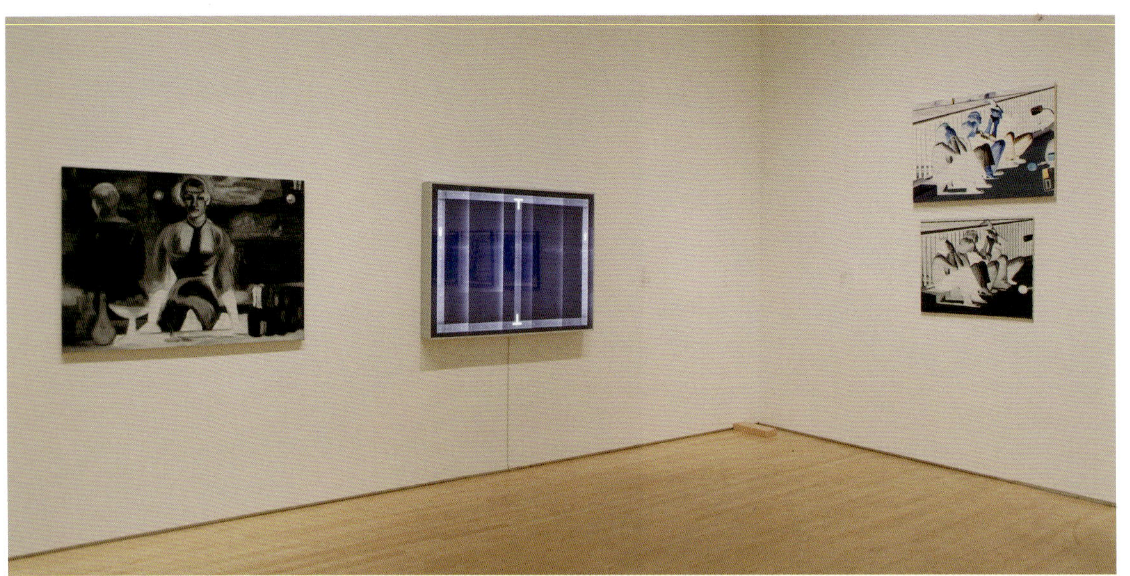

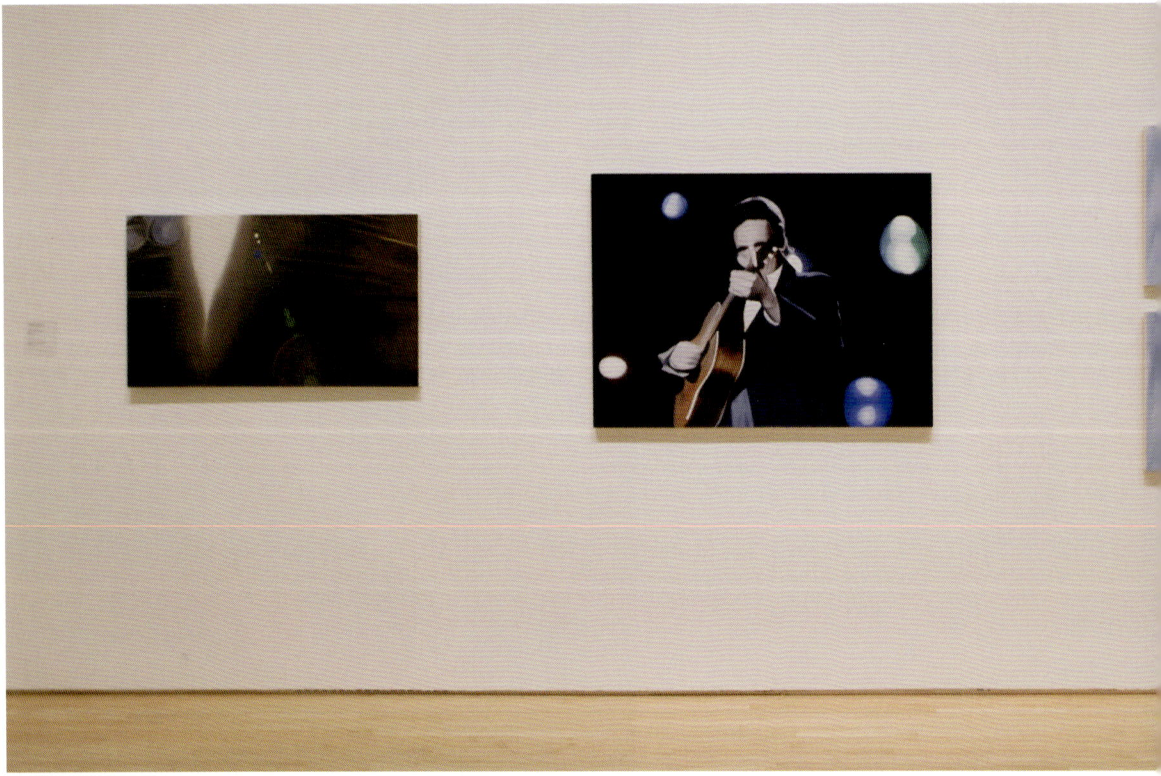

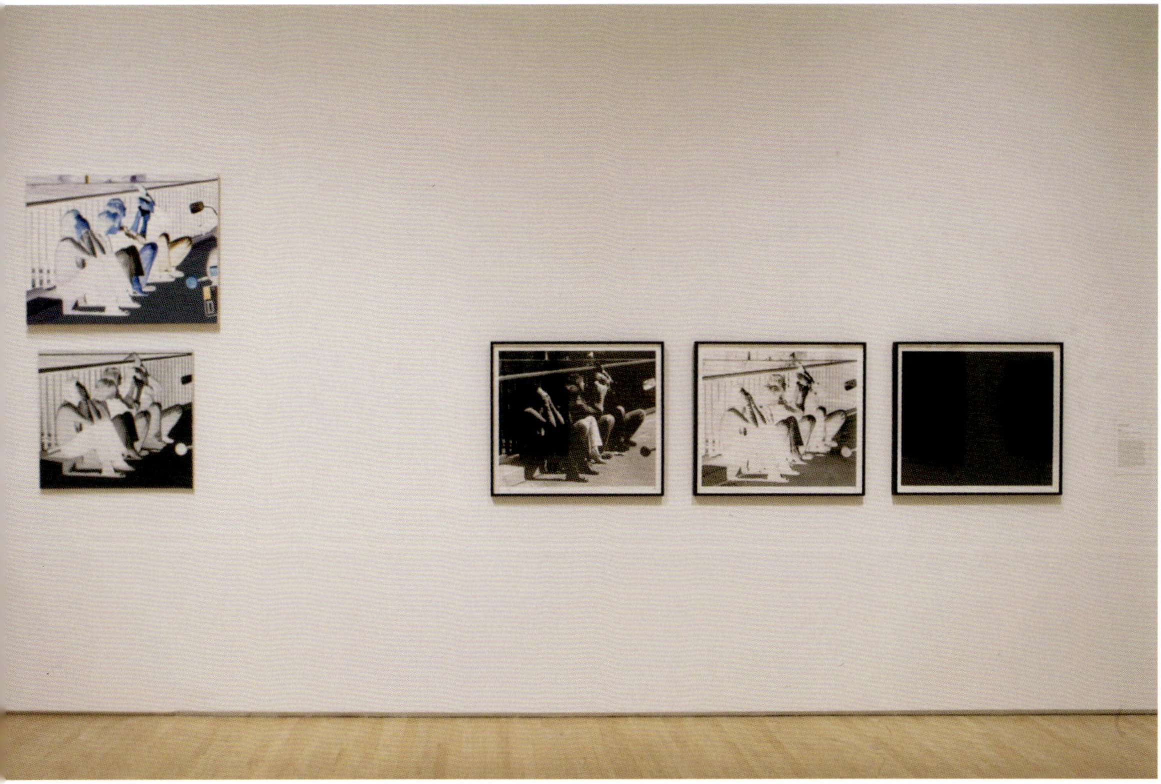

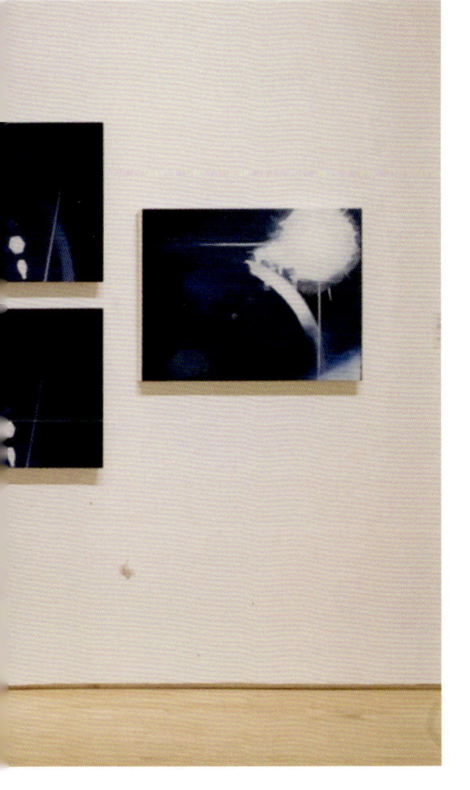

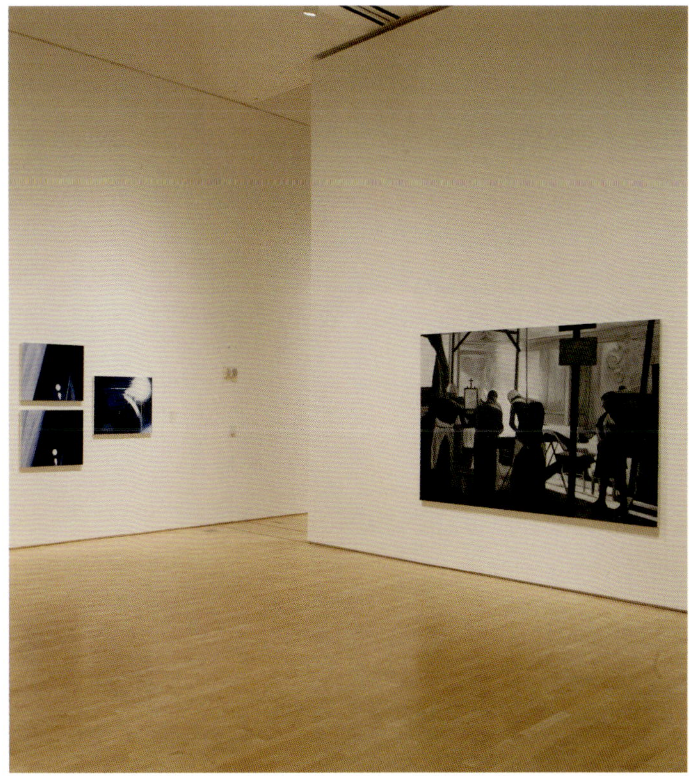

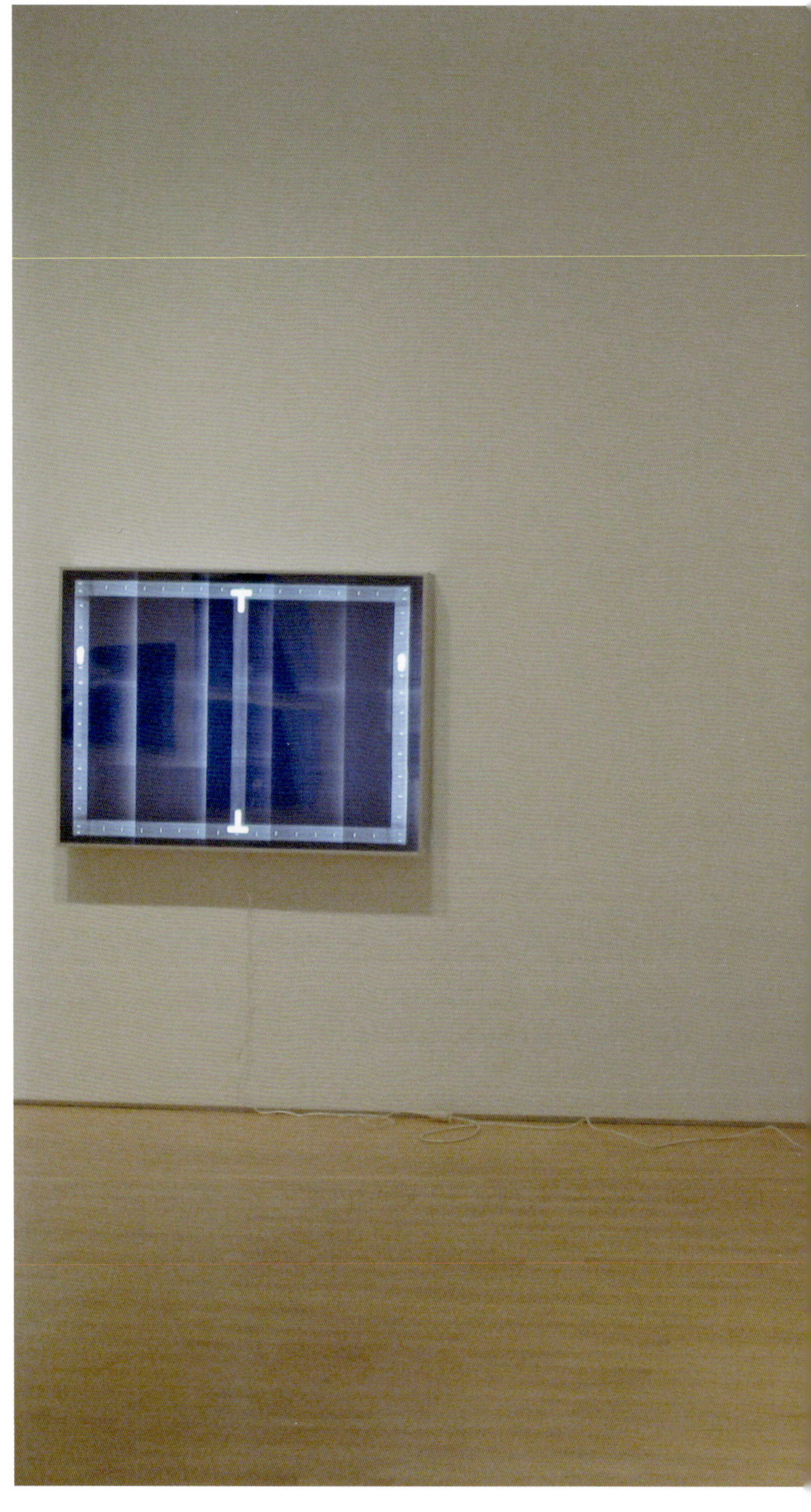

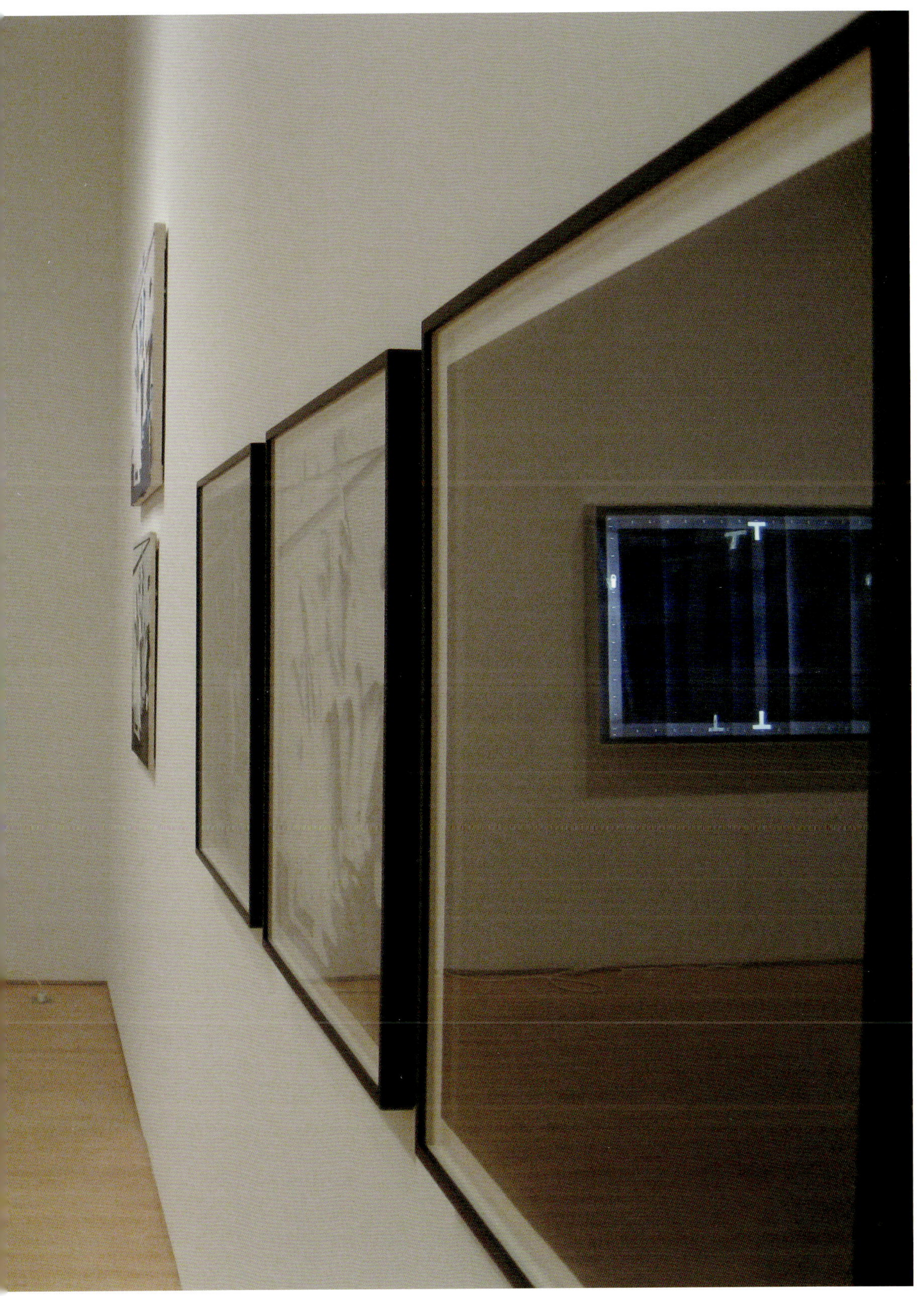

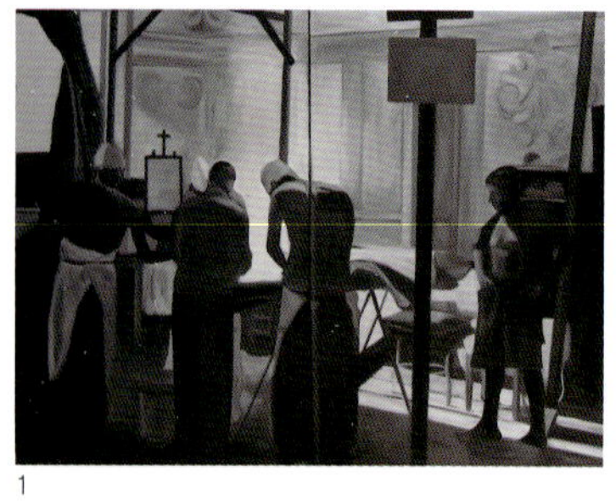

1

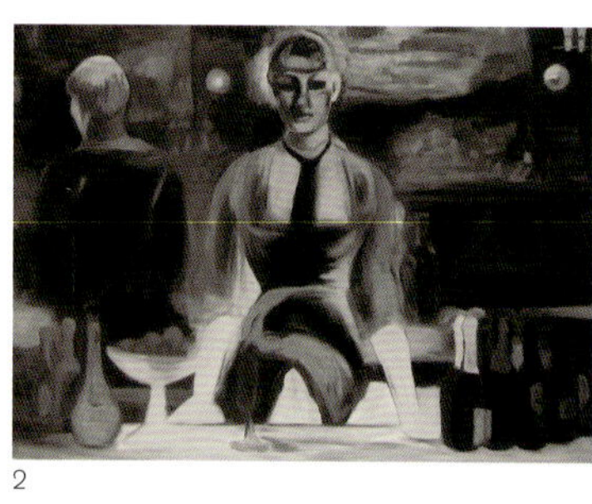

2

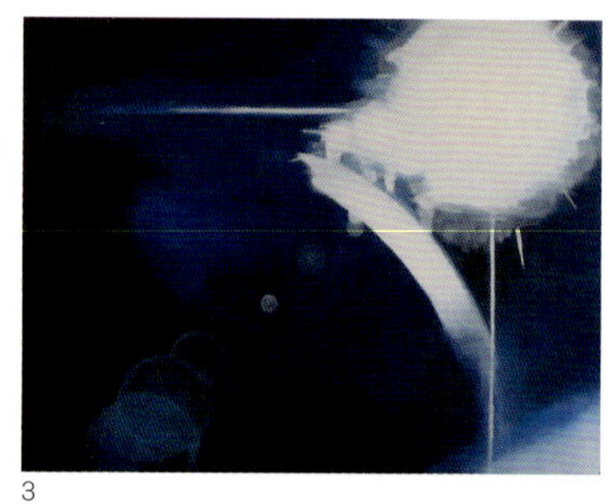

3

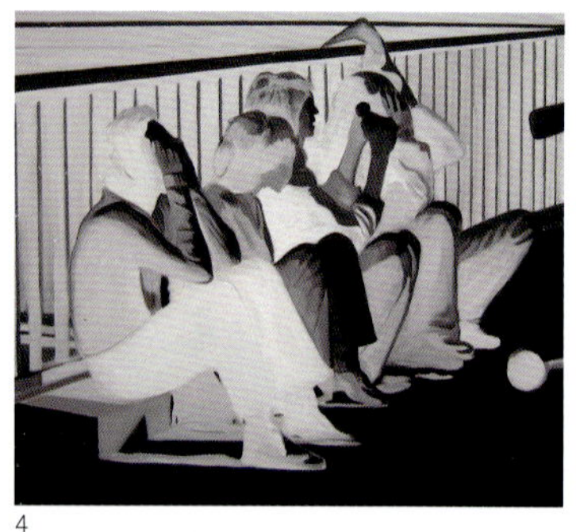

4

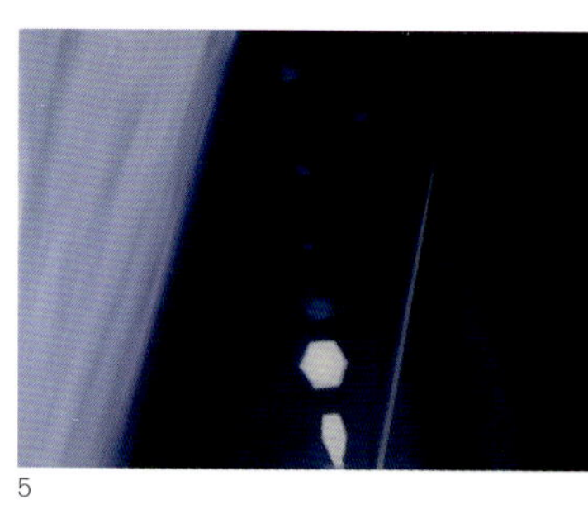

5

6

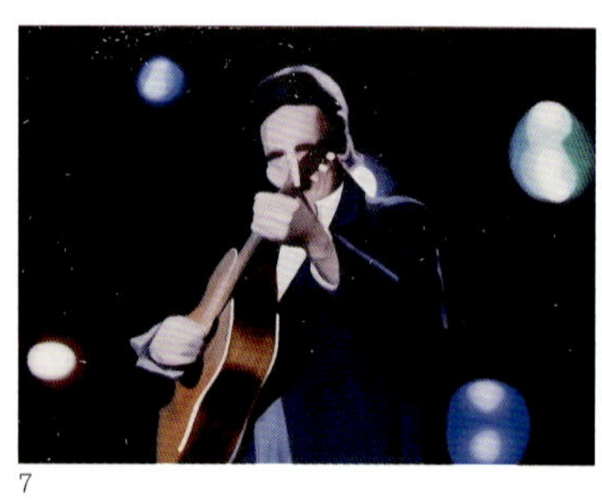

7

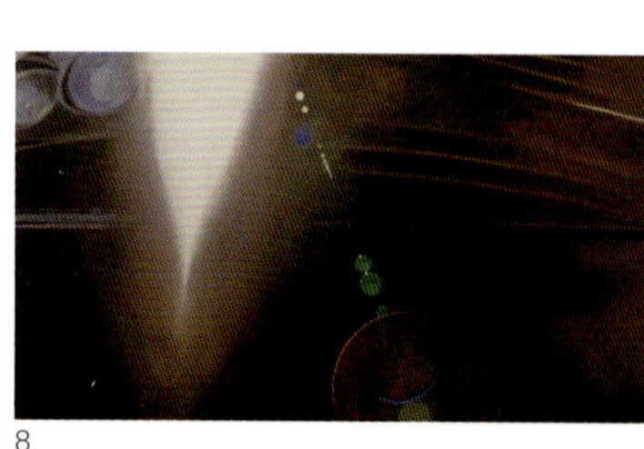

8

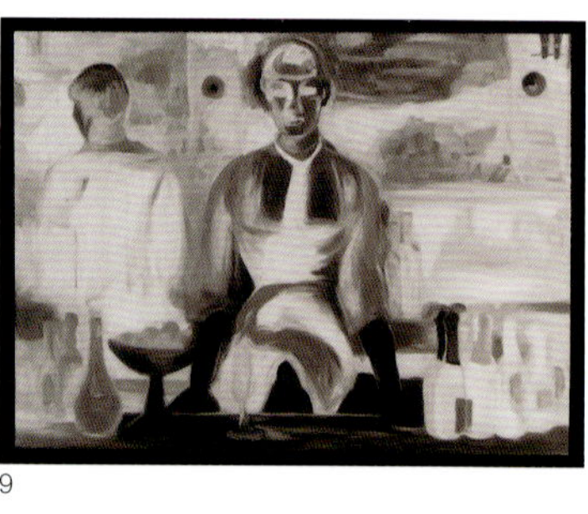

9

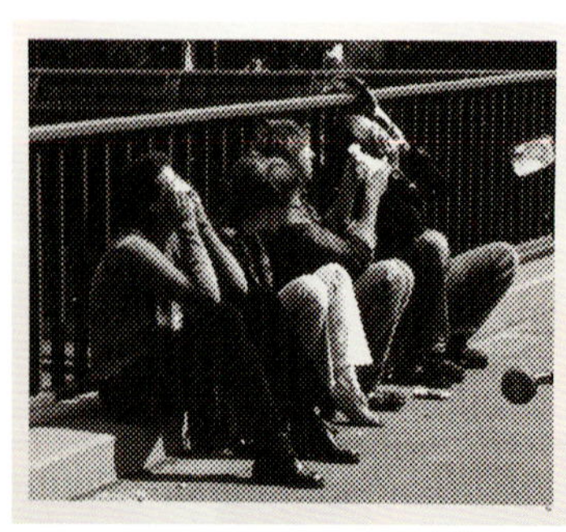

10

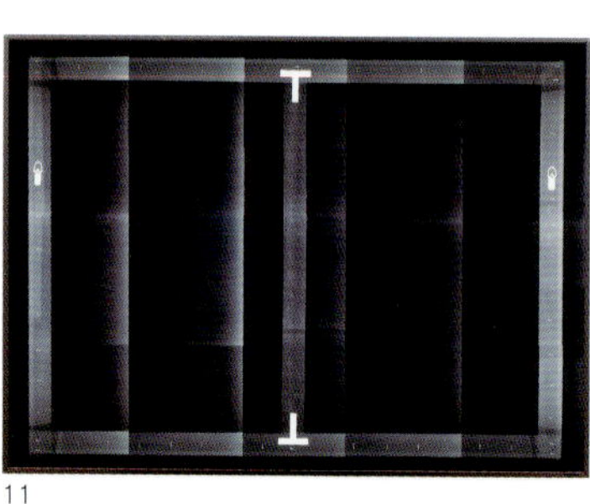

11

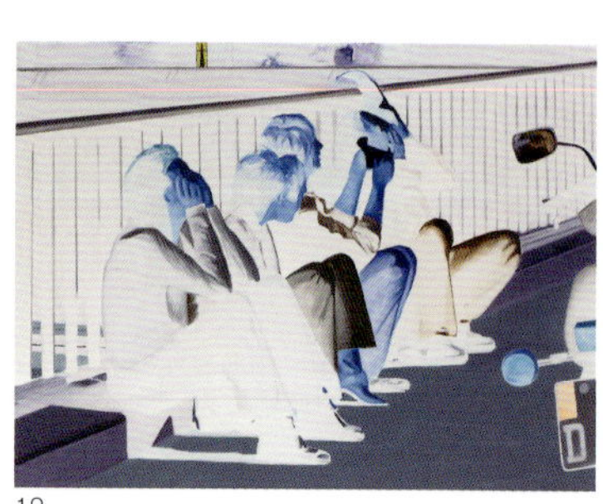

12

1
Untitled (surgery), 2006–07
Oil on canvas
64 × 84 in.
2007.1.031

2
Untitled (The Bar), 2007
Oil on canvas
38 × 52 in.
2007.1.039

3
Untitled (lens flare), 2008
Oil on canvas
26 × 34 in.
2008.1.002

4
Eclipse, 2008
Oil on canvas
28 × 32 in.
2008.1.003

5
Untitled (lens flare), 2008
Oil on canvas
24 × 32 in.
2008.1.008

6
Untitled (lens flare), 2008
Oil on canvas
24 × 32 in.
2008.1.009

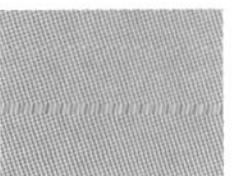

7
Untitled (The guitar player), 2008
Oil on canvas
38 × 52 in.
2008.1.019

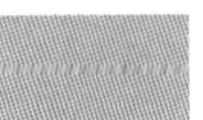

8
Untitled (HD lens flare), 2008
Oil on linen
26 × 46 in.
2008.1.020

9
Untitled (The Bar), 2009
Chromogenic color print on metallic
paper, mounted on gatorboard
43 × 59 in.
Ph2009.001.01

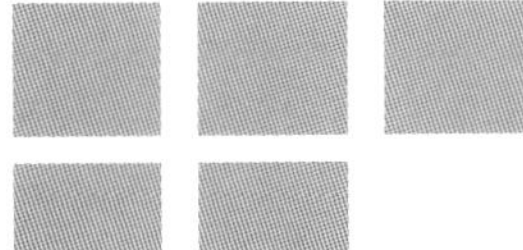

10
Eclipse, 2009
Portfolio of five screenprints
31½ × 35 in. ea. (frame);
30 × 34½ in. ea. (sheet)
P2009.001.04.1-5

11
Untitled (X-Ray), 2009
Digital radiography printed on Duralar
in aluminum lightbox
41⅛ × 56⅛ × 5 in.
Ph2009.002

12
Eclipse (color negative), 2009
Oil on canvas
30 × 40 in.
2009.1.001

The use and translation of photographic imagery is perhaps the most significant development in painting of the past half century. At the same time, photographic media have long since taken over the representation of real-world events, both contemporary and historical. *Untitled (History Painting): Painting and Public Life in the 21st Century* investigates painting's continuing viability as a means of addressing historical events and how they are represented in a culture dominated by photographic and digital media. The artists in the exhibition are united both by their use of photographic (or cinematic) source material drawn from the public sphere and by their engagement with questions of historical representation and collective memory. Devoted exclusively to work produced since the year 2000, the exhibition makes no attempt to be comprehensive. Instead, the exhibition charts one constellation of positions at the intersection of painting, photography, and the public imagination. Rather than simply illustrating the impact of photography or current events on contemporary painting, these positions represent an active, critical engagement with some of the most pressing issues facing artists and viewers today.

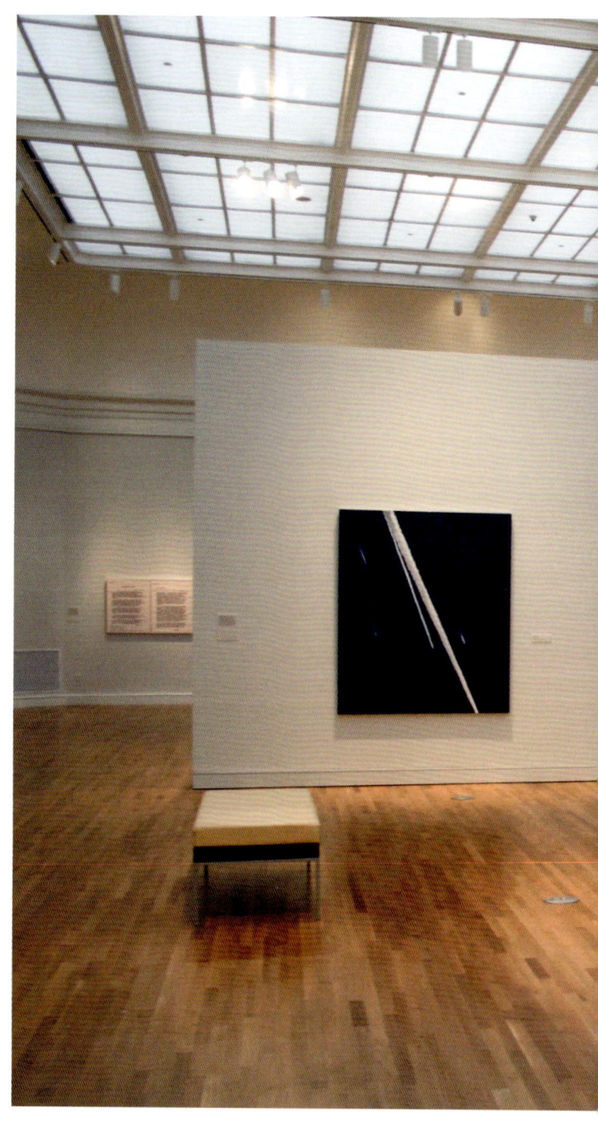

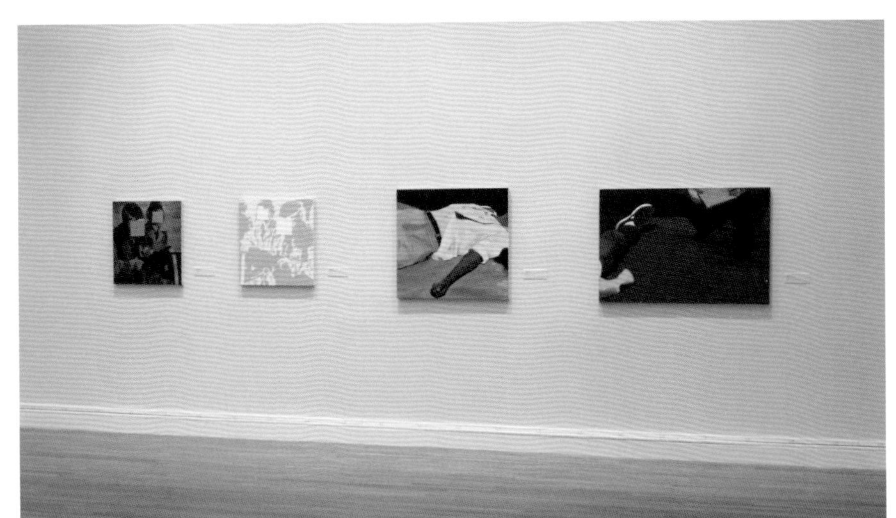

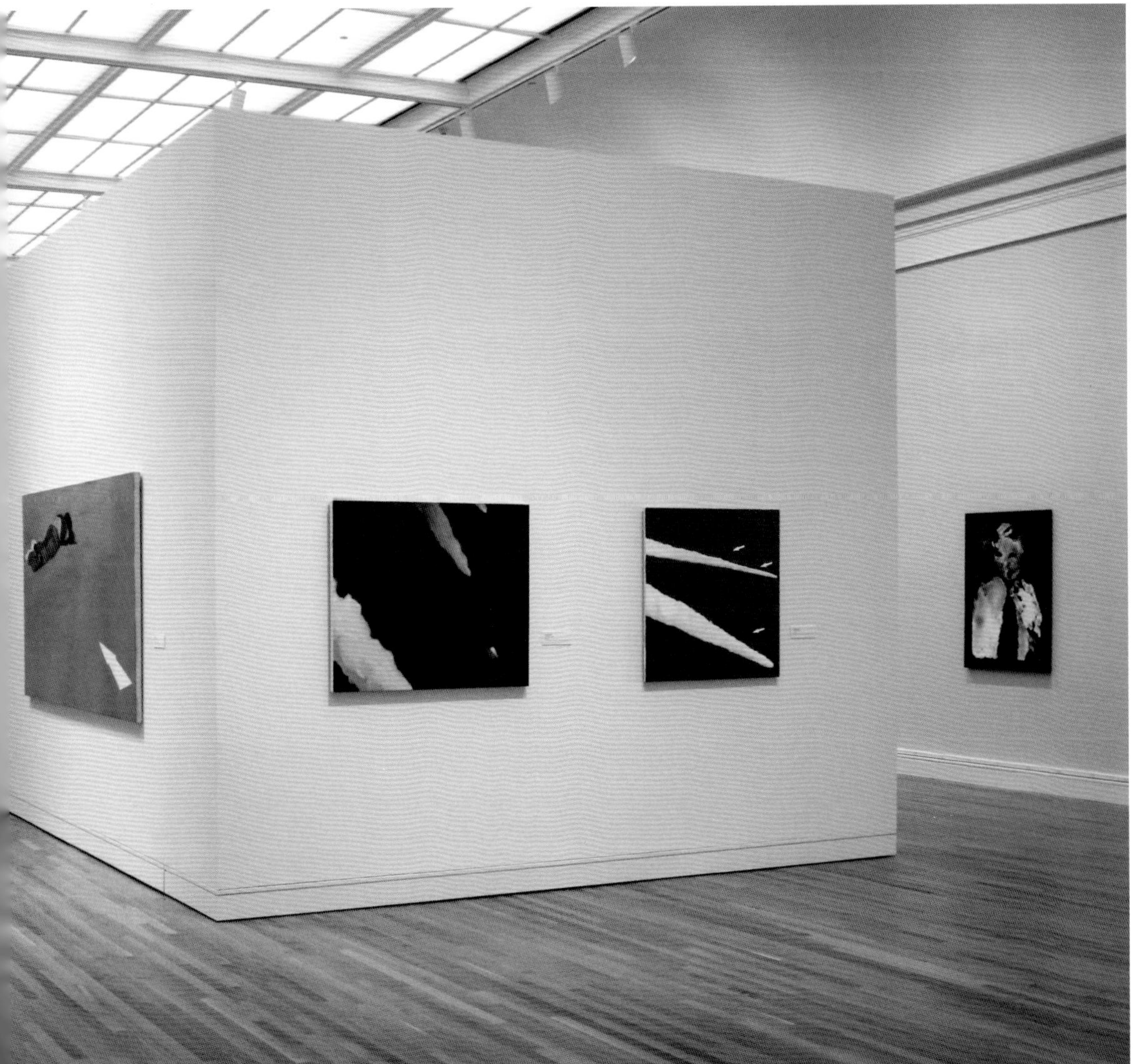

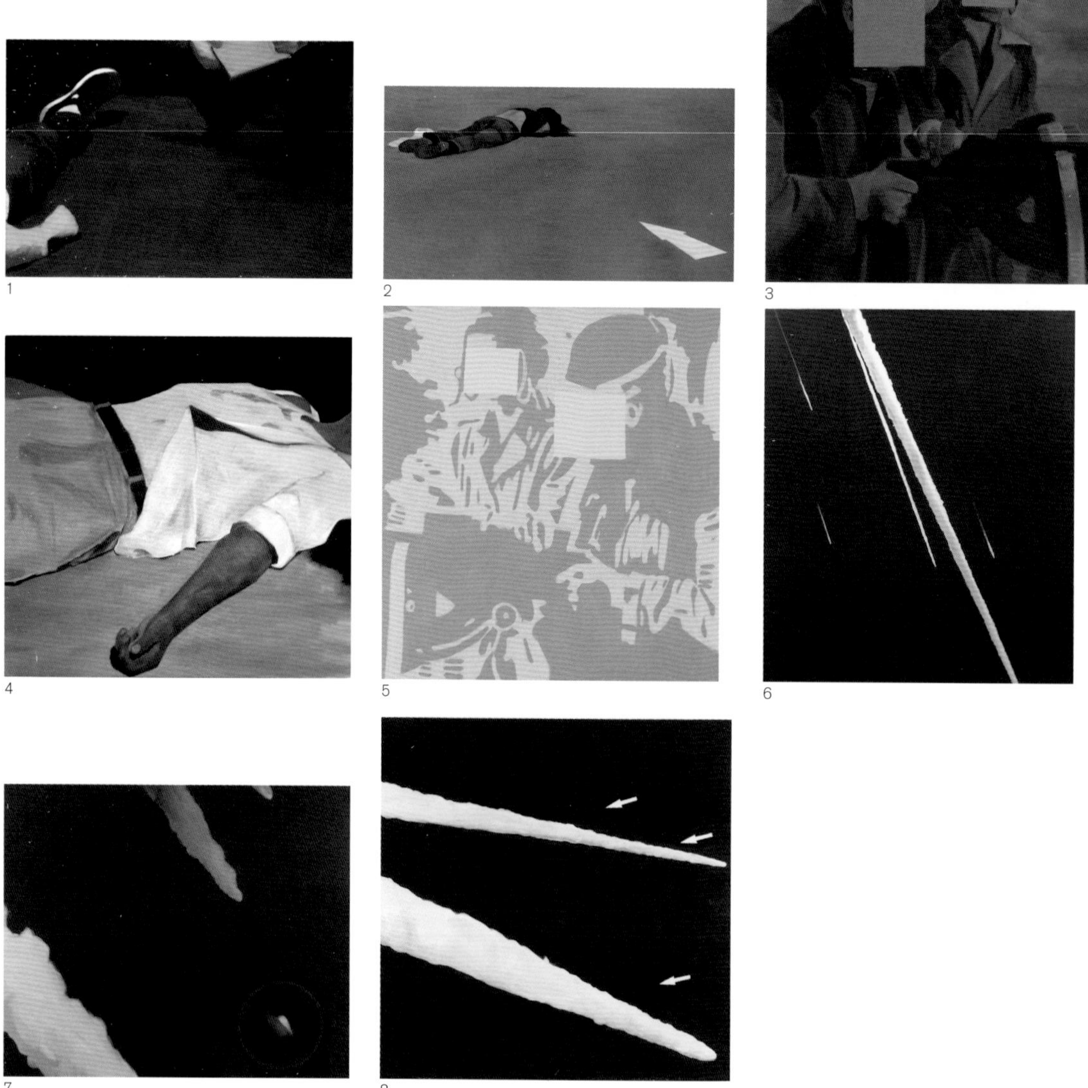

1

2

3

4

5

6

7

8

1
Untitled (forensic scene), 2004
Oil on canvas
32 × 48 in.
2004.1.006

2
Untitled (Pasolini), 2004
Oil on canvas
52 × 96 in.
2004.1.010

3
Untitled, 2004
Oil on canvas
26 × 24 in.
2004.1.012

4
Untitled, 2004
Oil on canvas
32 × 34 in.
2004.1.016

5
Untitled (ghost image), 2006
Oil on canvas
26 × 24 in.
2006.1.009

6
Untitled (Challenger), 2007
Oil on canvas
70 × 60 in.
2007.1.036

7
Untitled (crew cabin), 2007–08
Oil on canvas
36 × 44 in.
2008.1.001

8
Untitled (Challenger), 2007–08
Oil on canvas
36 × 36 in.
2008.1.004

The 2008 California Biennial continues the Orange County Museum of Art's four-decade long history of presenting new developments in contemporary art. This year's biennial is guest-curated by Lauri Firstenberg, founder and director/curator of LAXART in Los Angeles. Firstenberg's approach to the 2008 California Biennial is expansive—the exhibition includes works by more than 50 artists and, for the first time, incorporates off-site projects with collaborating venues from Tijuana to Northern California.

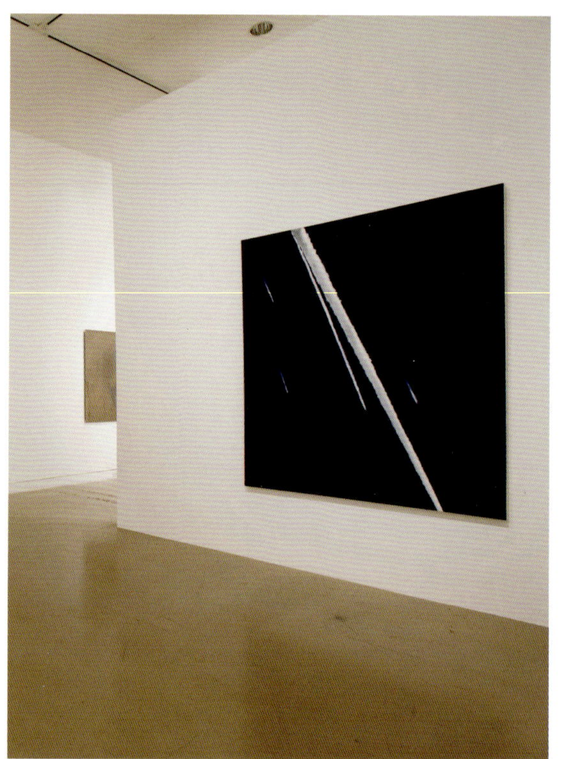

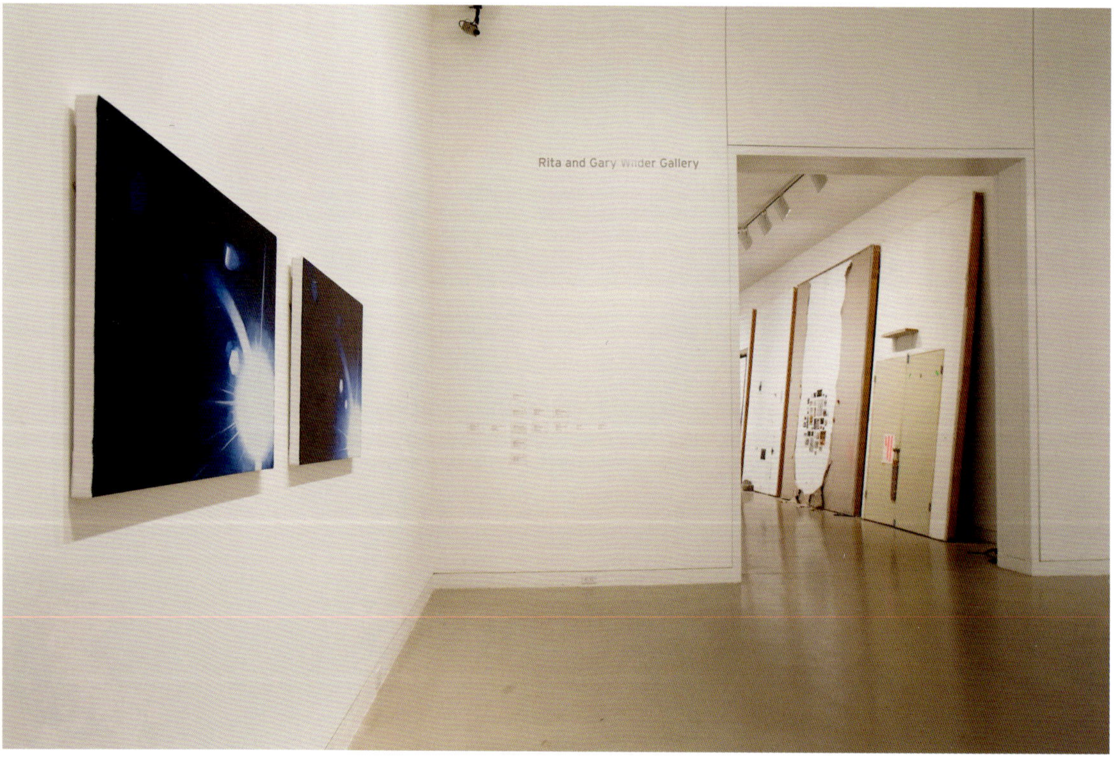

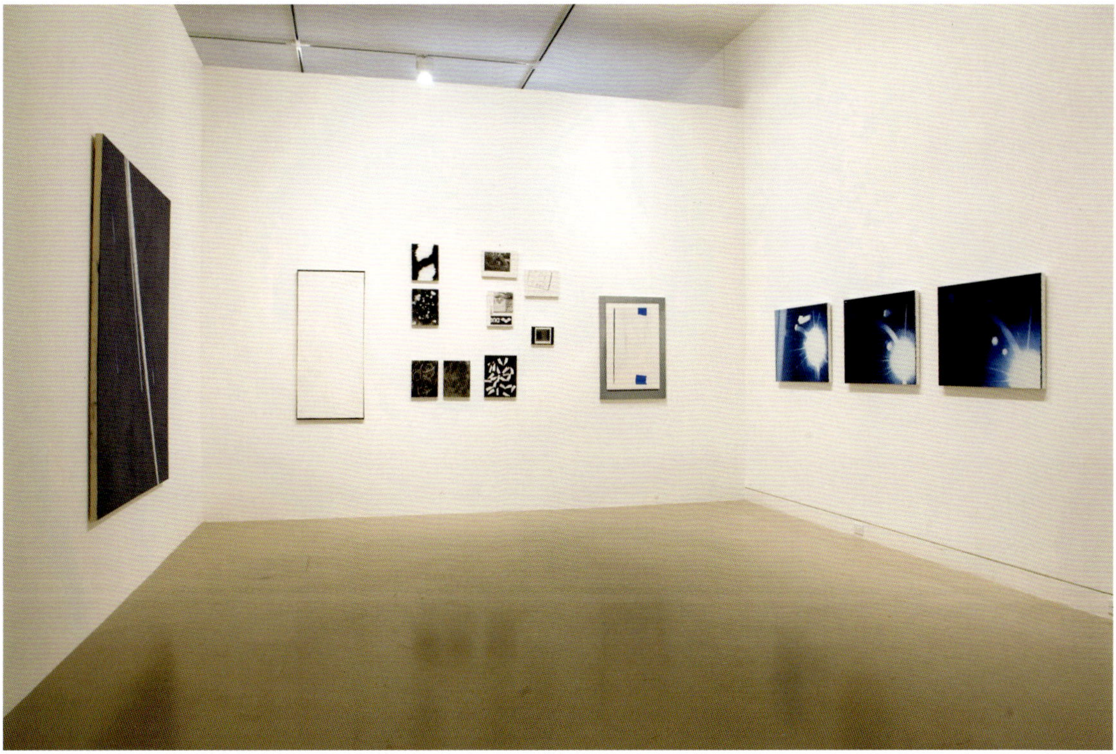

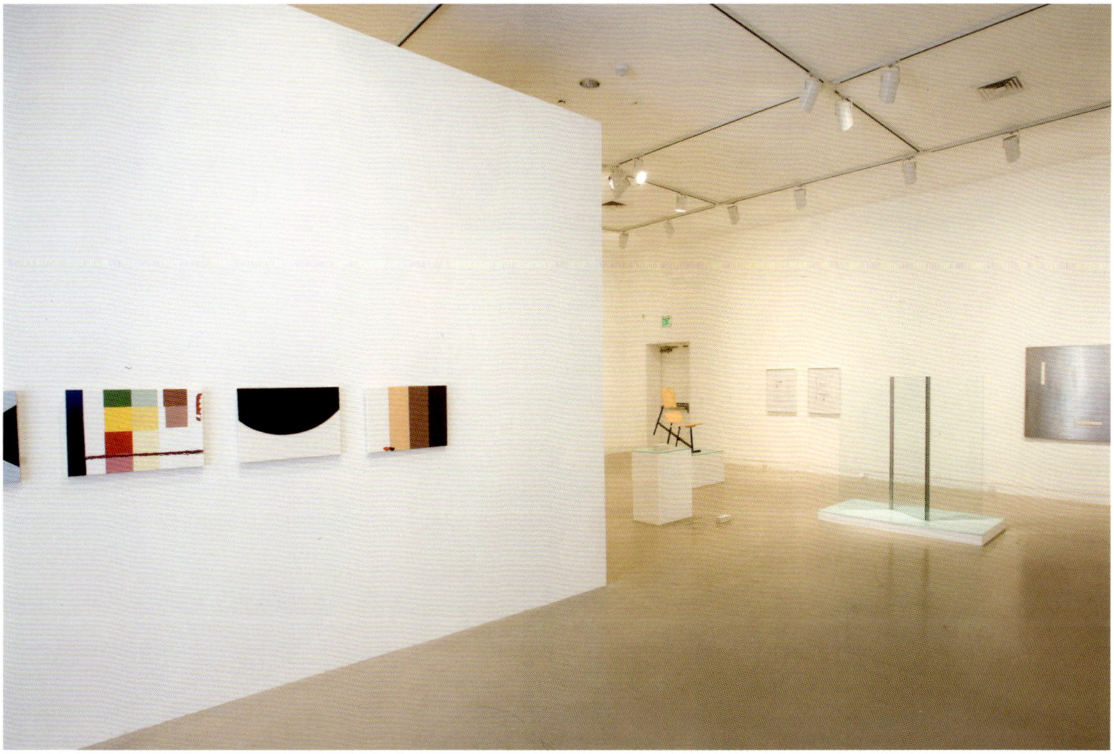

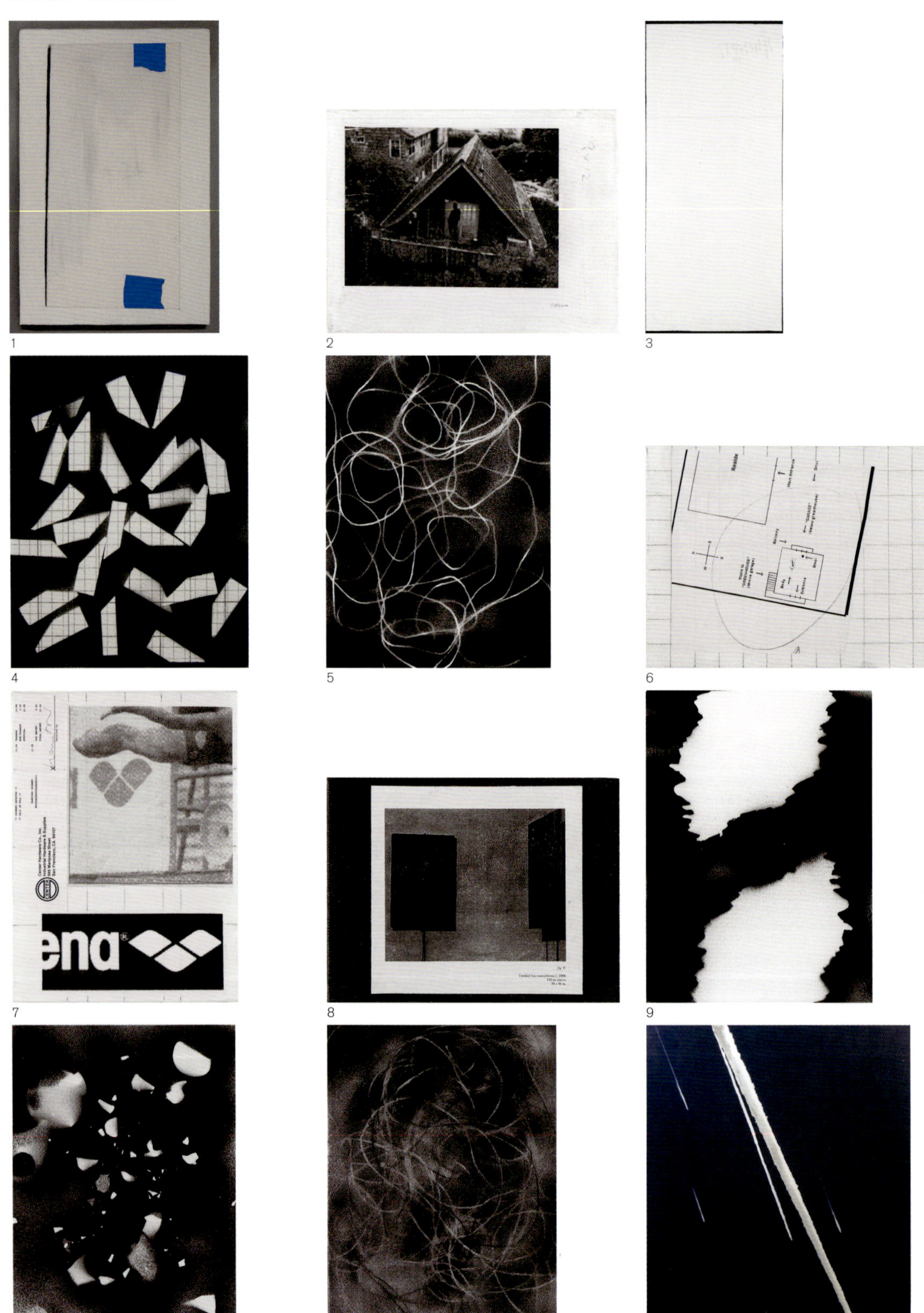

1

2

3

4

5

6

7

8

9

10

11

12

1
Untitled, 2006
Oil on canvas
34 × 24 in.
2006.1.003

2
Untitled (greenhouse), 2006
Photocopy, synthetic polymer varnish,
and graphite on canvas
9 × 12 in.
2006.1.015

3
Untitled (correction painting), 2007
Oil and graphite on canvas
48 × 22 in., irreg.
2007.1.002

4
Untitled (grid and keys), 2007
Graphite and enamel on canvas
14 × 11 in.
2007.1.003

5
Untitled (string painting), 2007
Enamel on canvas
12 × 9 in.
2007.1.005

6
Untitled (greenhouse diagram), 2007
Graphite and cut-and-pasted paper
with graphite on canvas
9 × 12 in.
2007.1.007

7
Untitled (diving girl collage 1), 2007
Graphite and cut-and-pasted paper on
canvas
12 × 9 in.
2007.1.011

8
Untitled (two monochromes collage),
2007
Oil and cut-and-pasted paper on
canvas
6 × 8 in.
2007.1.014

9
Untitled (sprayed cut outs), 2007
Enamel on canvas
12 × 9 in.
2007.1.019

10
Untitled (broken glass), 2007
Enamel on canvas
12 × 9 in.
2007.1.022

11
Untitled (silver and black strings),
2007
Enamel on canvas
12 × 9 in.
2007.1.023

12

Untitled (Challenger), 2007
Oil on canvas
70 × 60 in.
2007.1.036

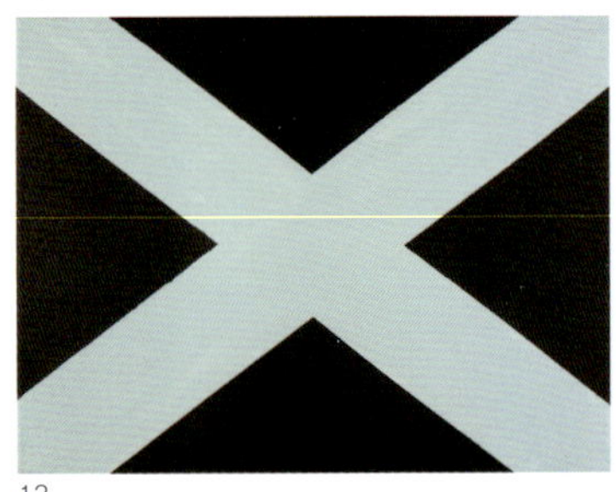

13

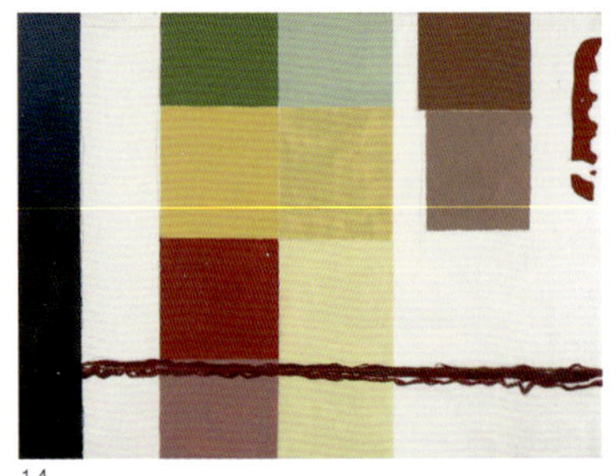

14

15

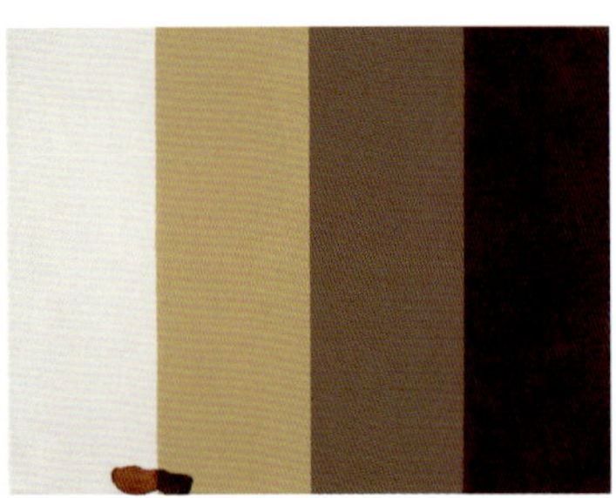

16

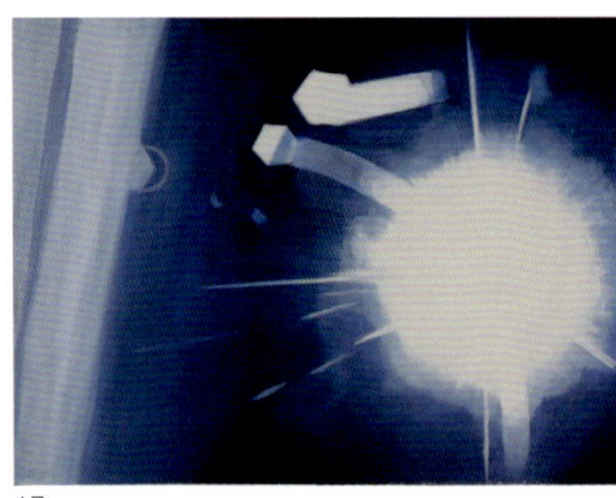

17

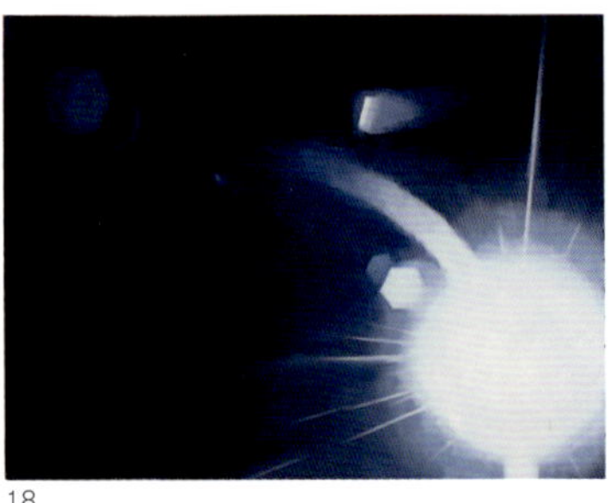

18

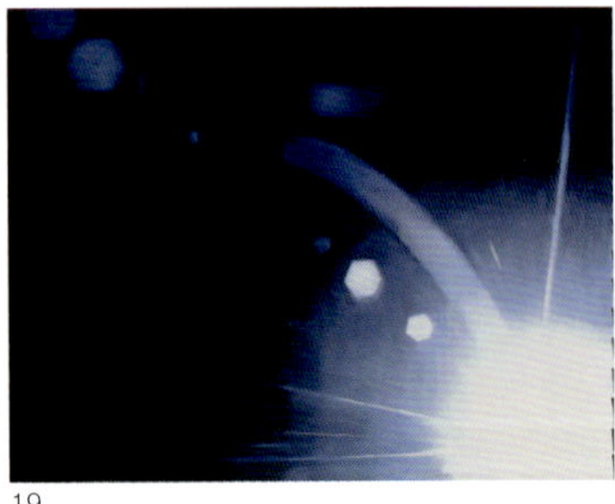

19

13
Untitled (film leader #1), 2007
Oil on canvas
15 × 20 in.
2007.1.040

14
Untitled (film leader #2), 2007
Oil on canvas
15 × 20 in.
2007.1.041

15
Untitled (film leader #3), 2007
Oil on canvas
15 × 20 in.
2007.1.042

16
Untitled (film leader #4), 2007
Oil on canvas
15 × 20 in.
2007.1.043

17
Untitled (lens flare), 2008
Oil on canvas
24 × 32 in.
2008.1.005

18
Untitled (lens flare), 2008
Oil on canvas
24 × 32 in.
2008.1.006

19
Untitled (lens flare), 2008
Oil on canvas
24 × 32 in.
2008.1.007

Ratio 3 is pleased to announce the opening of an exhibition of new paintings by Jordan Kantor, on view from January 18 to March 1, 2008. This, his first one-person exhibition at the gallery, also marks his solo debut on the West Coast.

For this exhibition, Kantor will show two separate, though intertwined, bodies of work: large-scale figurative paintings and smaller abstract canvases. The figurative paintings begin with media representations of spectacular subjects, which are scanned, cropped, and manipulated before being translated into paint. These works explore the role of images in our experience of the world, and often bear pictorial traces of this appropriation from mass media to underscore the process of artistic mediation, such as arrows superimposed on a crime-scene photo or the digital losses of jpeg compression. The abstract paintings build on these investigations, by self-reflexively picturing the working space of painterly representation. Like sheets of a notebook, they show a diverse compendium of different ways of constructing an image. All of the works explore the relationships between perception, memory, and visual representation.

While the paintings resist imparting a clear narrative or lending themselves to simple interpretations, representation itself is an underlying theme and an integral part of the politics of Kantor's art. These works grant the viewer agency in constructing meaning, rather than imparting fully-encoded messages. Kantor's paintings invite a different kind of contemplation than photographic images viewed in print, on television, or on-line; they provide a springboard for an examination of visual attentiveness, as well for larger formal and theoretical speculations into the nature of image-making and the circulation of pictorial signs. Kantor's recent works seek to use painting, and its relationship to other mediums, to reveal history itself to be more subjective and open-ended than conventionally supposed.

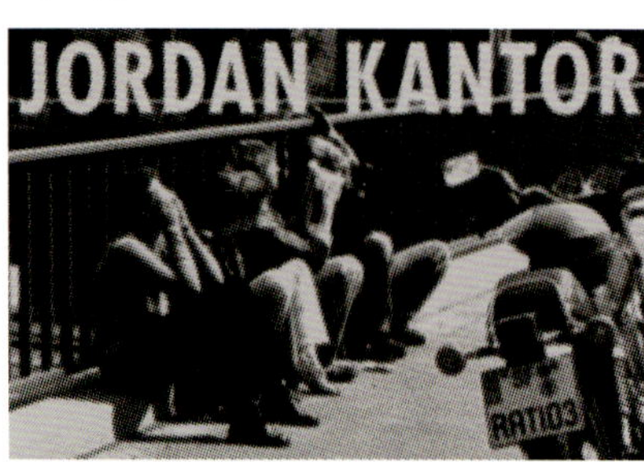

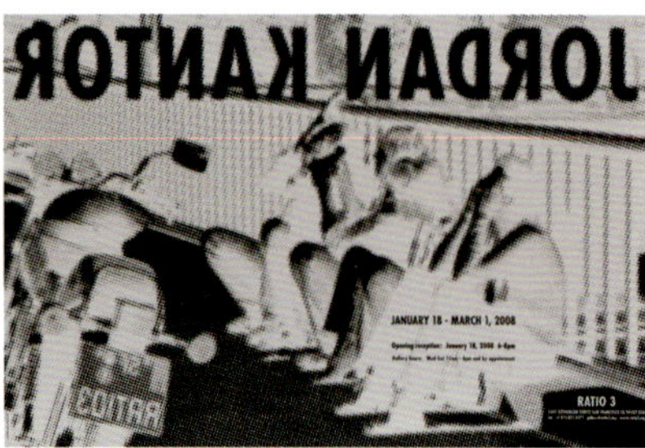

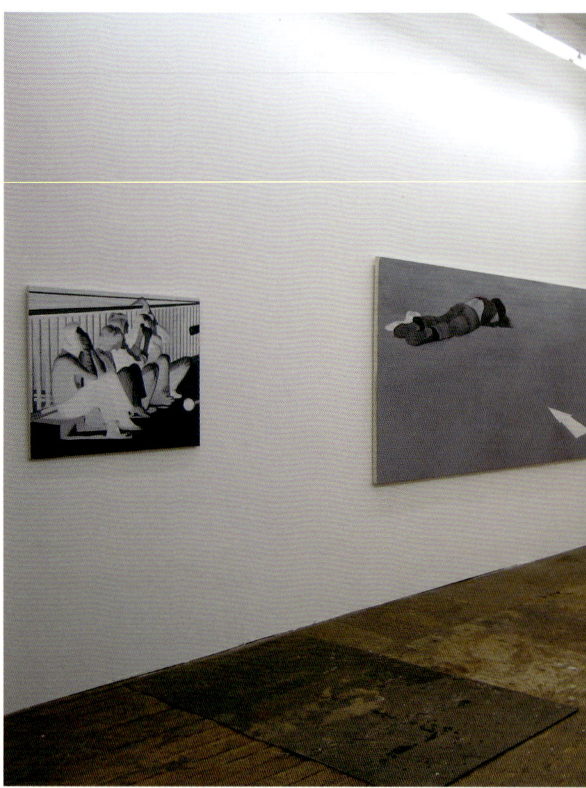

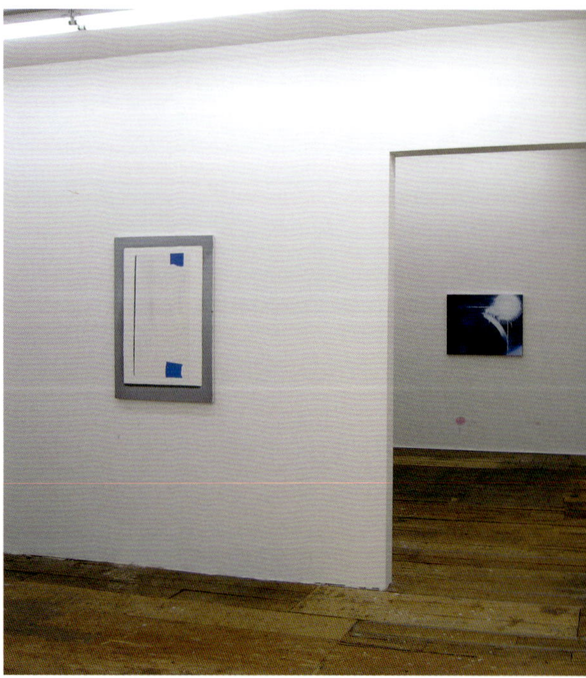

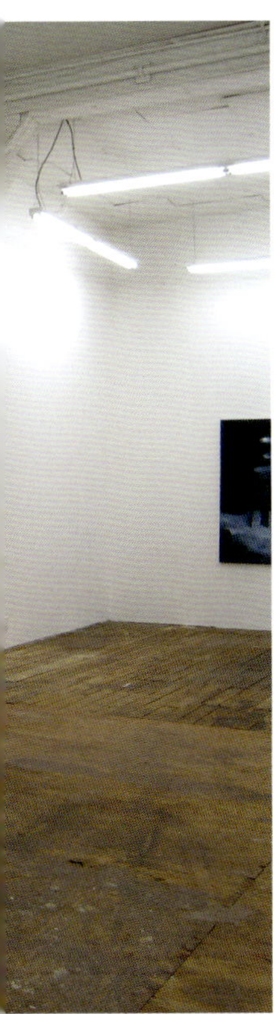
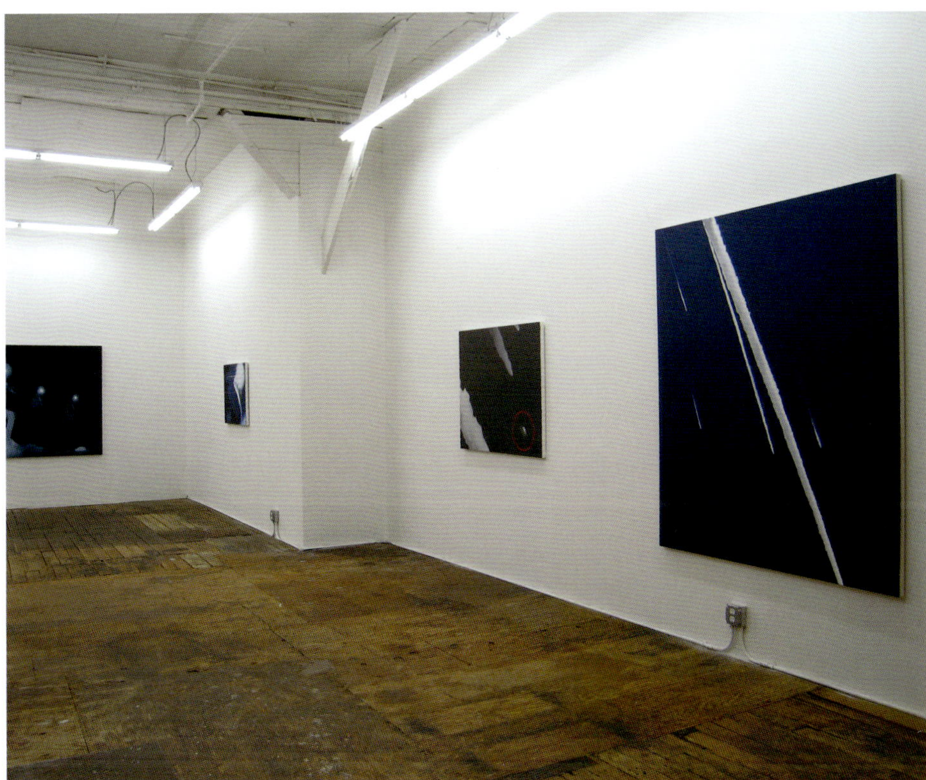

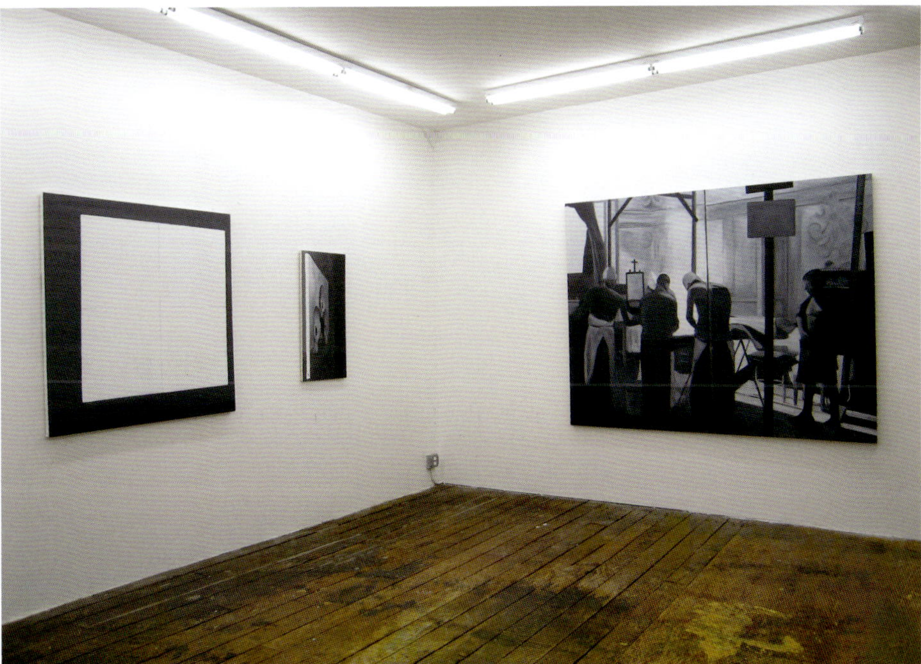

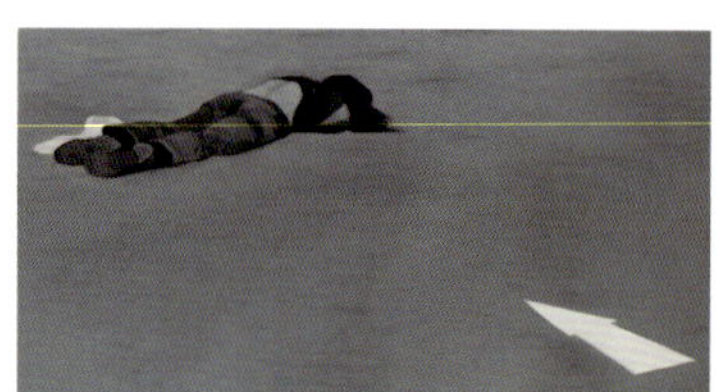
1

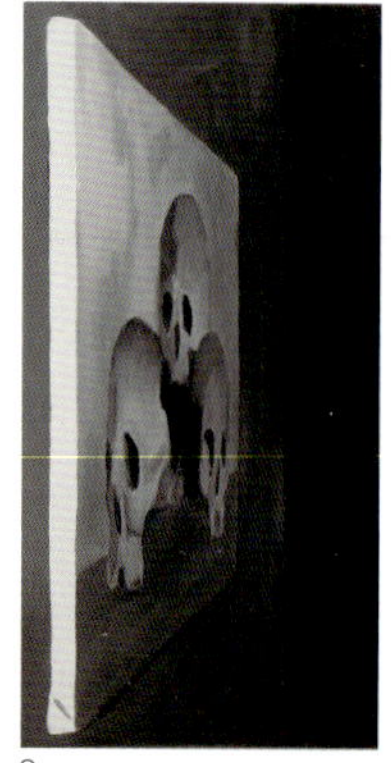
2

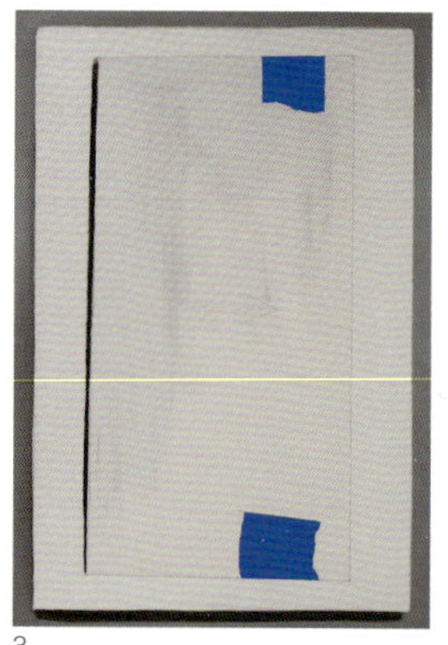
3

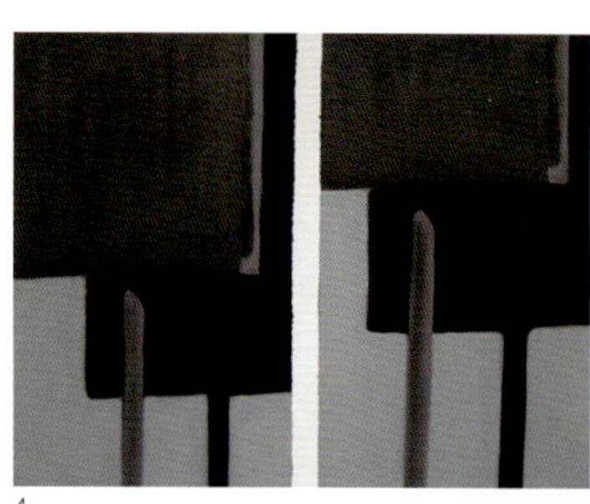
4

5

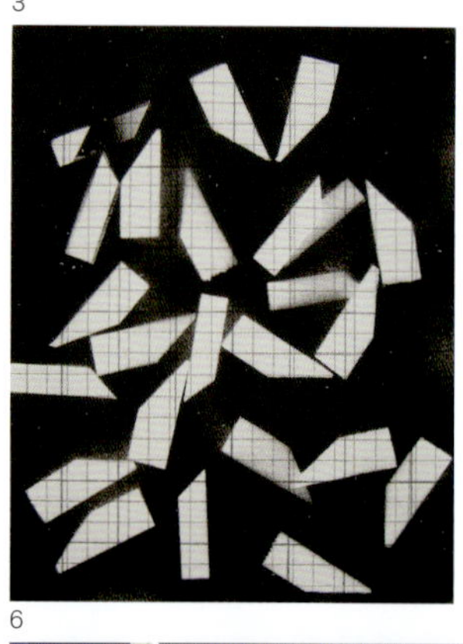
6

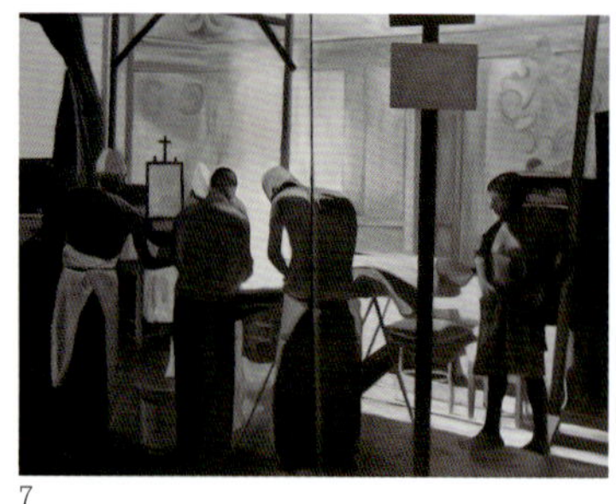
7

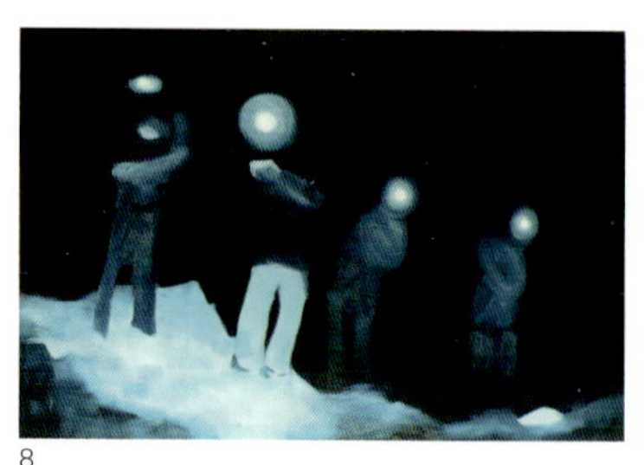
8

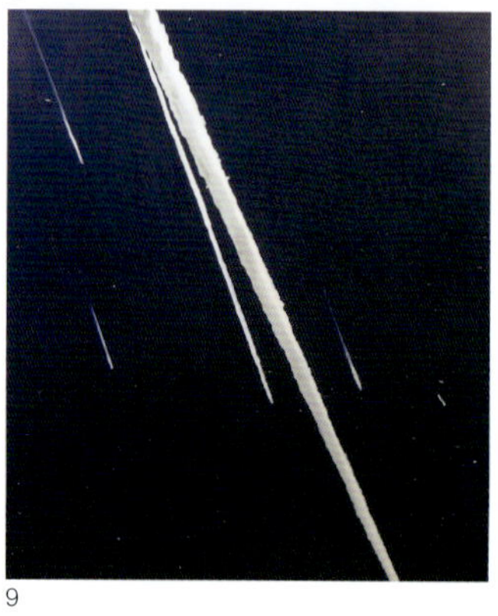
9

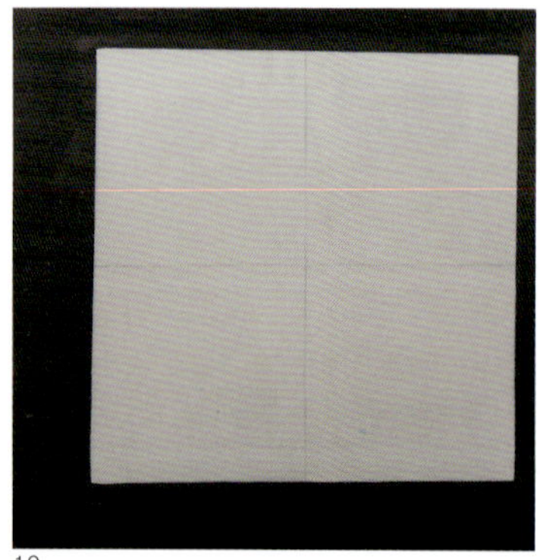
10

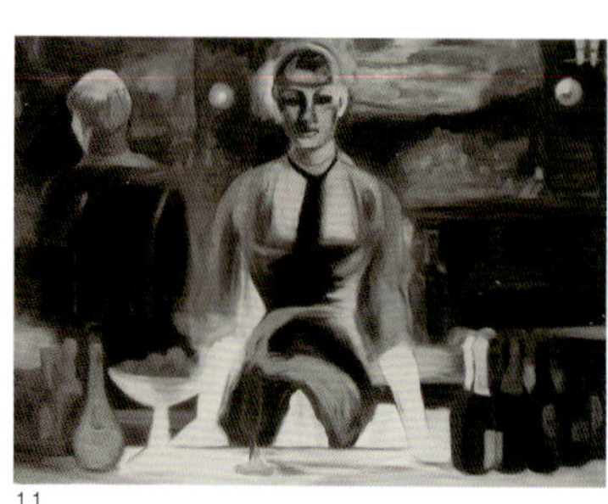
11

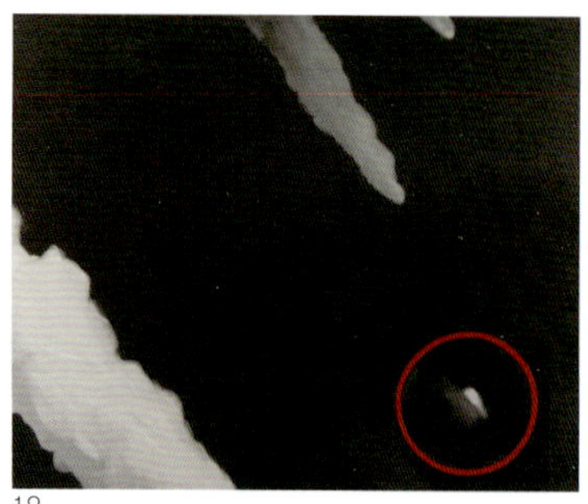
12

1
Untitled (Pasolini), 2004
Oil on canvas
52 × 96 in.
2004.1.010

2
Untitled (perspective skulls), 2005
Oil on canvas
34 × 17 in.
2005.1.007

3
Untitled, 2006
Oil on canvas
34 × 24 in.
2006.1.003

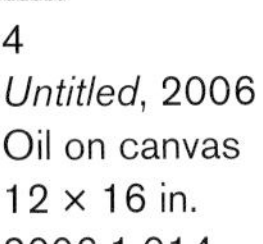

4
Untitled, 2006
Oil on canvas
12 × 16 in.
2006.1.014

5
Untitled (correction painting), 2007
Oil and graphite on canvas
48 × 22 in., irreg.
2007.1.002

6
Untitled (grid and keys), 2007
Graphite and enamel on canvas
14 × 11 in.
2007.1.003

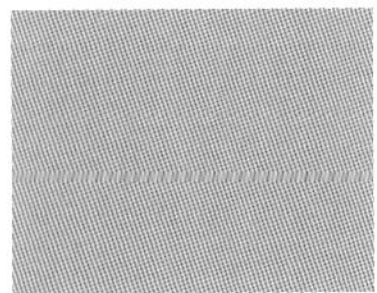

7
Untitled (surgery), 2006-07
Oil on canvas
64 × 84 in.
2007.1.031

8
Untitled (four searchers), 2007
Oil on canvas
56 × 84 in.
2007.1.032

9
Untitled (Challenger), 2007
Oil on canvas,
70 × 60 in.
2007.1.036

10
Untitled (white painting), 2007
Oil on folded canvas
46 × 46 in.
2007.1.037

11
Untitled (The Bar), 2007
Oil on canvas
38 × 52 in.
2007.1.039

12
Untitled (crew cabin), 2007–08
Oil on canvas
36 × 44 in.
2008.1.001

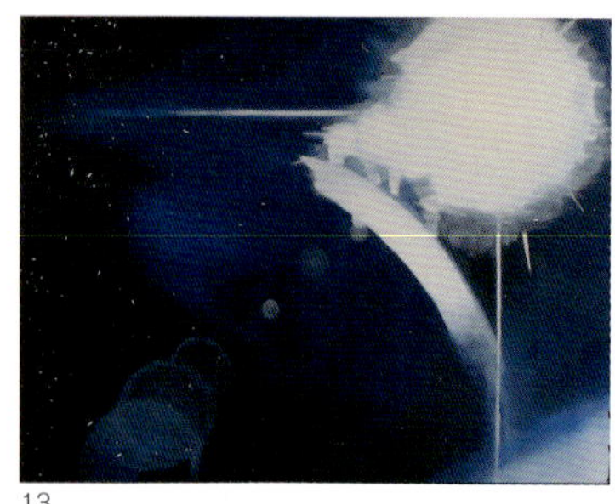

13

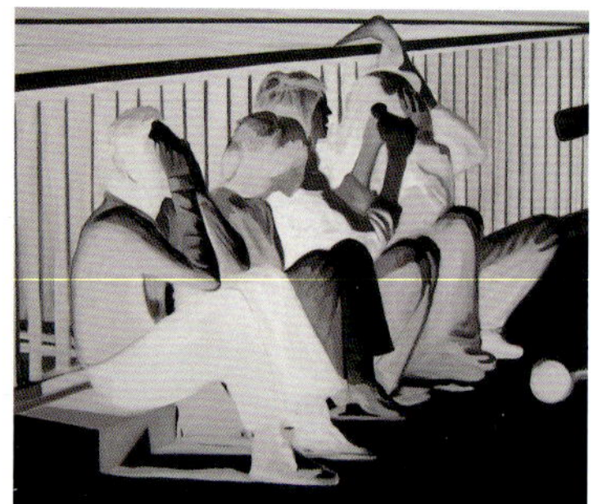

14

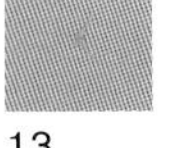

13
Untitled (lens flare), 2008
Oil on canvas
26 × 34 in.
2008.1.002

14
Eclipse, 2008
Oil on canvas
28 × 32 in.
2008.1.003

Lombard-Freid Projects is pleased to present "Image Processor," a focused group exhibition of recent works by Kota Ezawa, Chris Finley, and Jordan Kantor. Working in a variety of artistic mediums, these three artists share a common interest in how images circulate in mass culture and make their way into works of art. Their paintings, sculptures, photographic light-boxes, and works on paper all ask: how are images reclaimed and "processed" though artistic inflection? Oscillating between figuration and abstraction, Ezawa, Finley, and Kantor all typically begin their artworks with appropriated images taken from pop culture or art historical sources. These serves as springboards for formal and theoretical investigations into the nature of image-making, the circulation of pictorial signs, and the construction of historical truths. More than a mutual aesthetic, these artists share tactics that stem from a critical attitude about contemporary spectacular image-culture .

Kota Ezawa's "The History of Photography Remix" comprises his artistic interpretation of icons of photographic history: those well-known images reprinted in photography textbooks so many times that they arguably become as invisible as they are classic. Ezawa remakes these images through his signature cut-out simplification process in which he digitally re-produces the photographs, and then prints them on transparencies set into light-boxes. Through this process of recasting, or remixing, the most hallowed images of photographic history, Ezawa makes them visible again and comments on how both this history and artistic identity are constantly constructed and re-made. For this exhibition, Ezawa will show works from this series, several of which have never before been exhibited.

Chris Finley makes paintings and sculptures that appear to be completely non-referential abstractions. In fact, each of his works begins with an image—typically taken from the internet—of a popular figure (both Speaker of the House Nancy Pelosi and super-cook Rachel Ray make appearances in this show) which is then put though a series of digital manipulations until it becomes unrecognizably divorced from its source. Among other effects, this intense image-processing calls into question the reliability of images to communicate stable meaning, as well as the phantasmic nature of cultural icons. His recent series of sculptures also begins with a pop cultural image—of a remodeled home taken from the popular television series "Extreme Makeover: Home Edition"—which, though Finley's own extreme makeovers, becomes a lithe, gestural sculpture reminiscent of the constructivist works of historical modernists like Alexandr Rodchenko and Naum Gabo.

Jordan Kantor's paintings also often mix pop culture and art historical references as a starting point, a practice which provides an opening to consider the position of painting today.

WORKS EXHIBITED

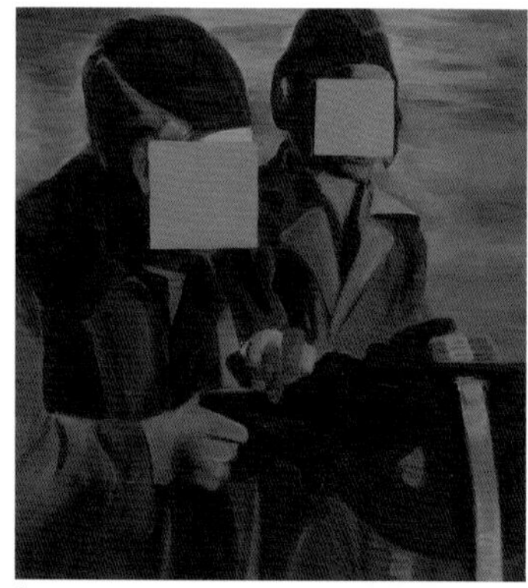

1

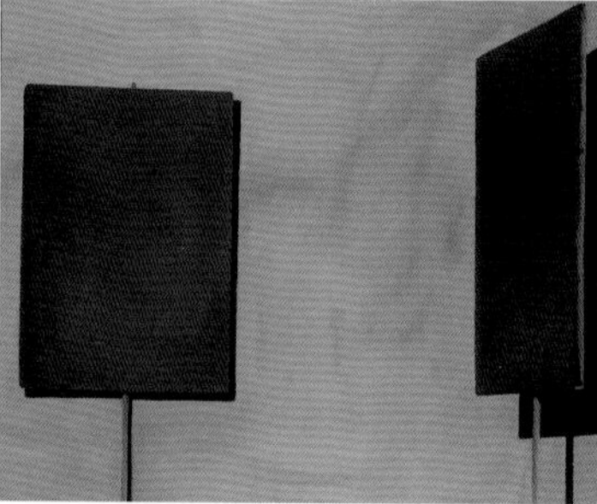

2

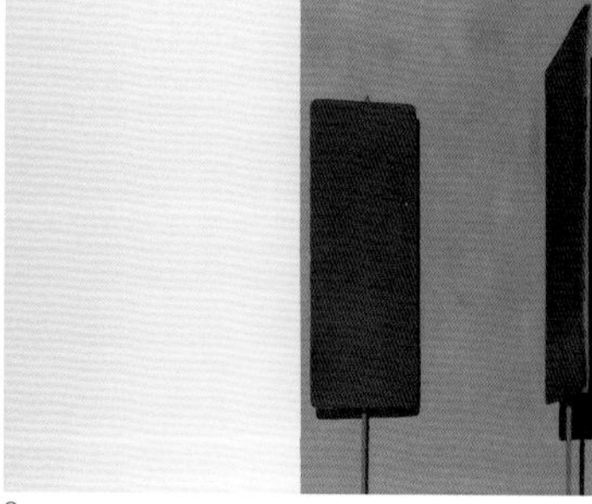

3

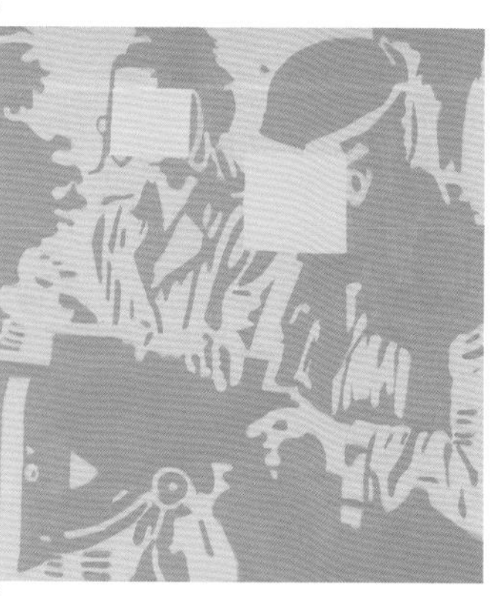

4

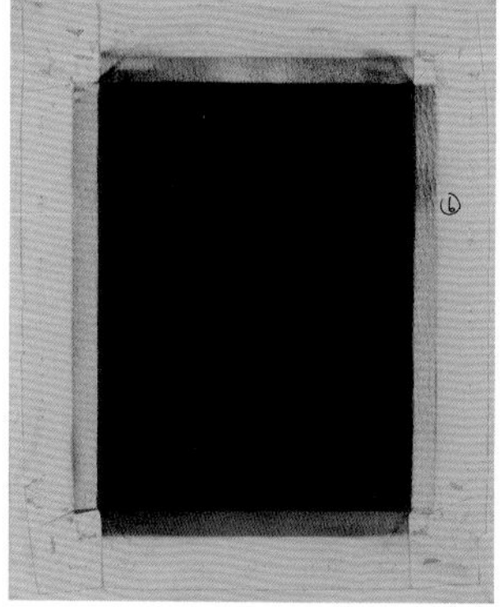

5

Having been scanned, cropped and manipulated, Kantor's appropriated images are recast as paintings, which are emptied of their spectacular status by transmutation. These works engage the on-going dialogue between photography and painting and speak to the ways in which images—both literal pictures as well as figures of art history—already occupy, or haunt, the spaces of painting. For this exhibition, Kantor will show two pairs of paintings, in both of which one image serves as a "model" for the other. In such works, the contemporary painter is repositioned, with regard to the medium's history, as image-processor instead of protean creator.

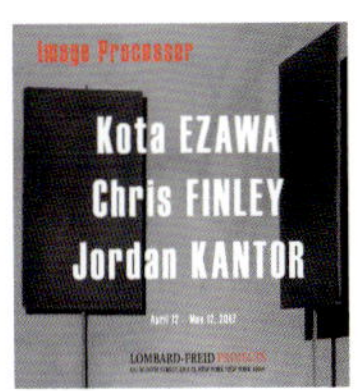

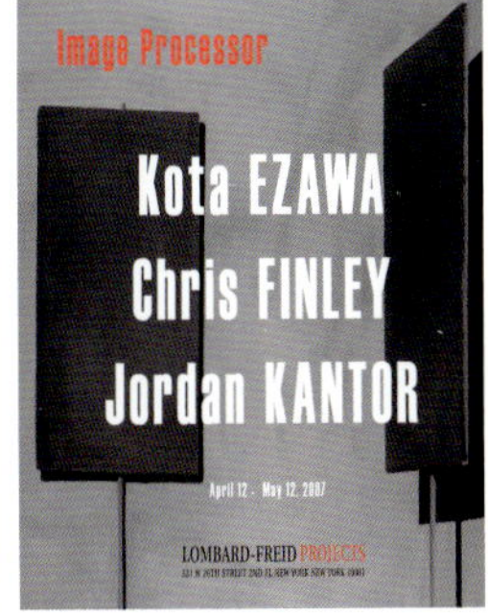

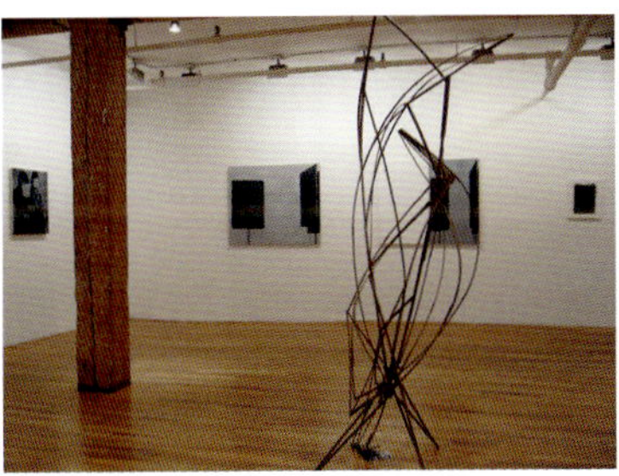

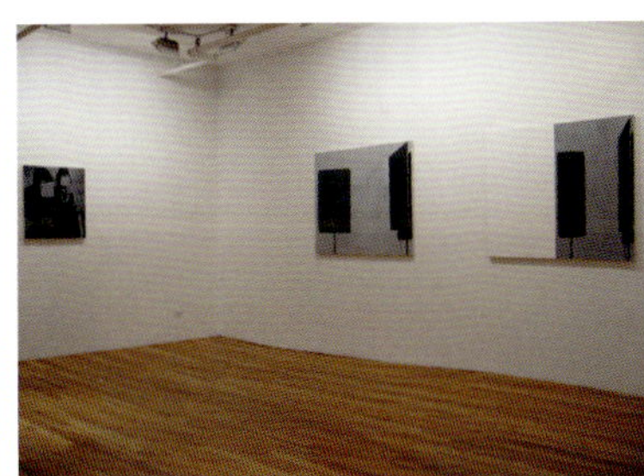

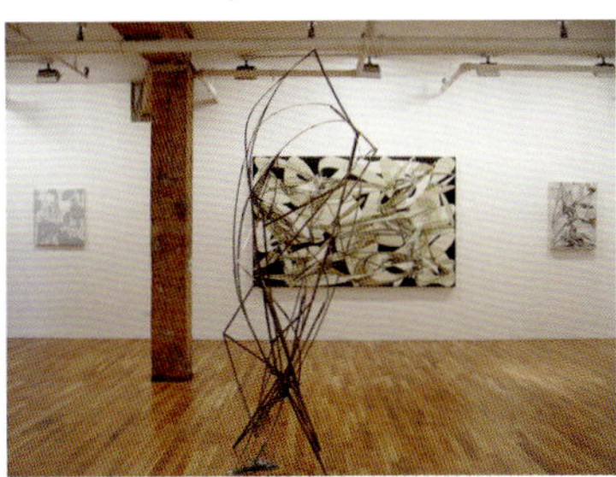

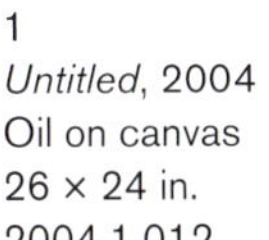

1
Untitled, 2004
Oil on canvas
26 × 24 in.
2004.1.012

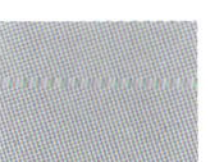

2
Untitled (two monochromes), 2006
Oil on canvas
38 × 46 in.
2006.1.004

3
Untitled (three monochromes), 2006
Oil on canvas
38 × 46 in.
2006.1.006

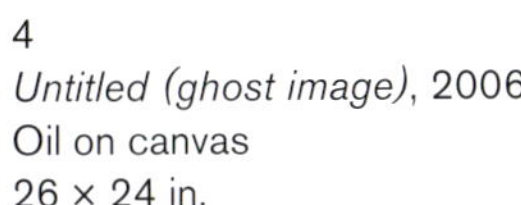

4
Untitled (ghost image), 2006
Oil on canvas
26 × 24 in.
2006.1.009

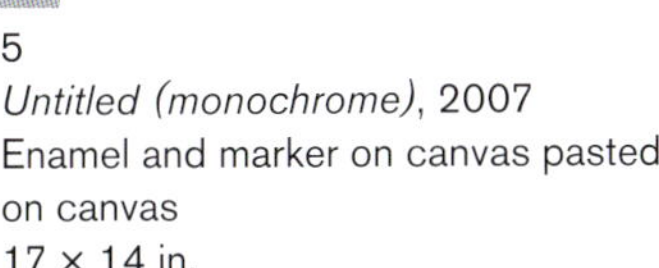

5
Untitled (monochrome), 2007
Enamel and marker on canvas pasted
on canvas
17 × 14 in.
2007.1.015

Jordan Kantor produces large-scale paintings of recent media representations as a means to address the role of images in our experience of the physical world. In them, trauma, death, beauty, and history collide as private thoughts and public spectacles are reprocessed through paint. His paintings depict bodies that have been emptied of their gravity, tactility, and smell in the flat, dimensionless space of news photography, bestowed with new pictorial physicality. Painted, the life-sized bodies refuse the fate of the diminutive photographs on which they are based: to be ignored, folded-over, and thrown away with yesterday's papers.

WORKS EXHIBITED

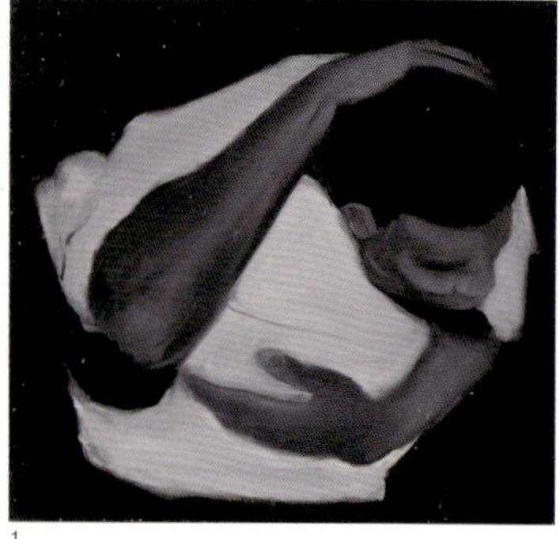

1

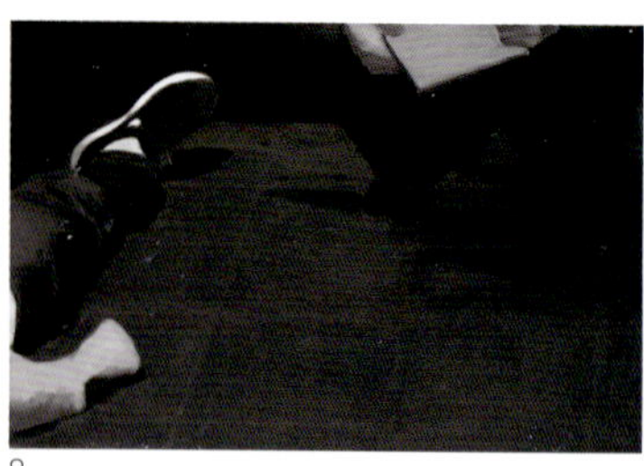

2

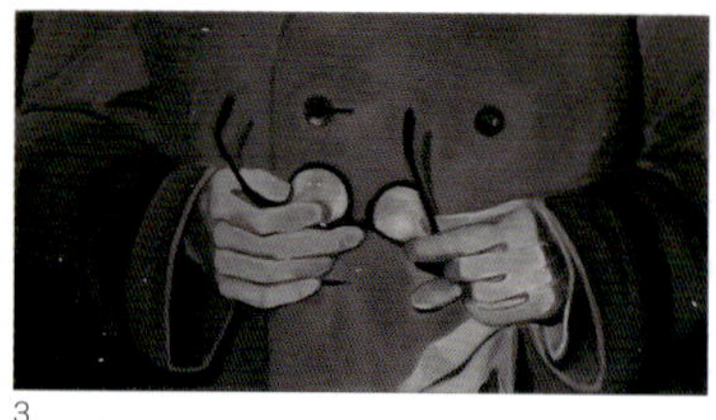

3

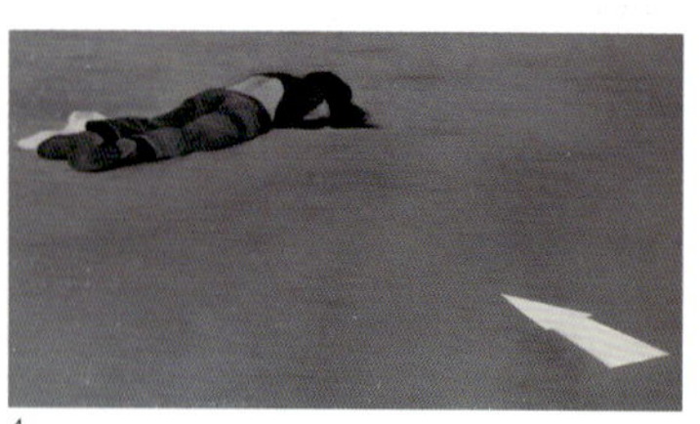

4

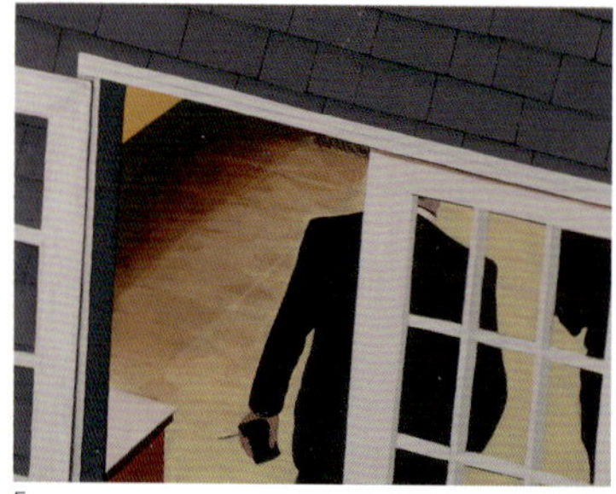

5

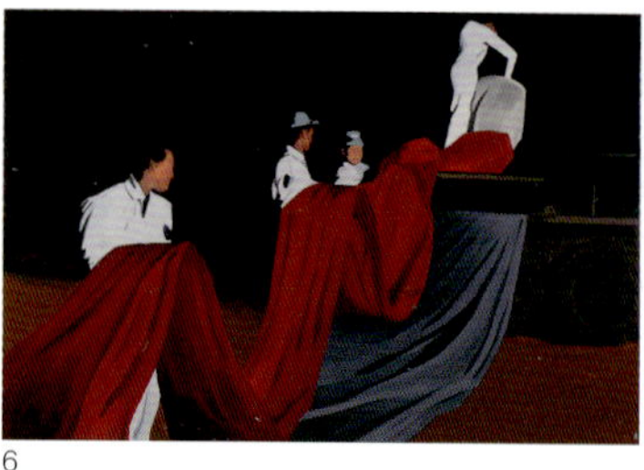

6

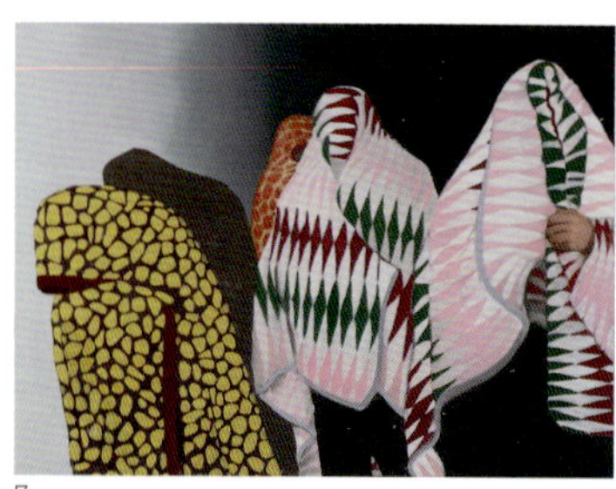

7

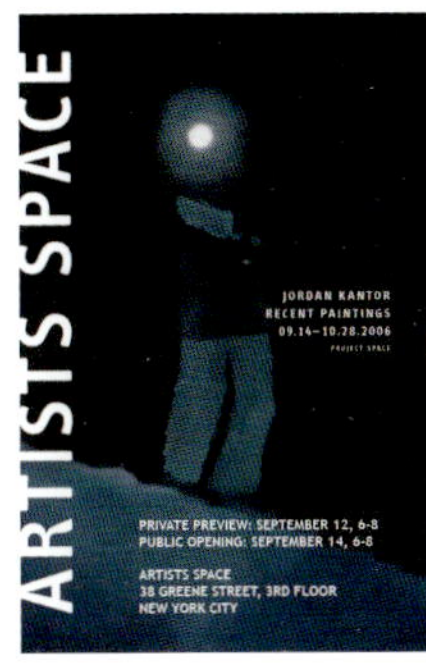

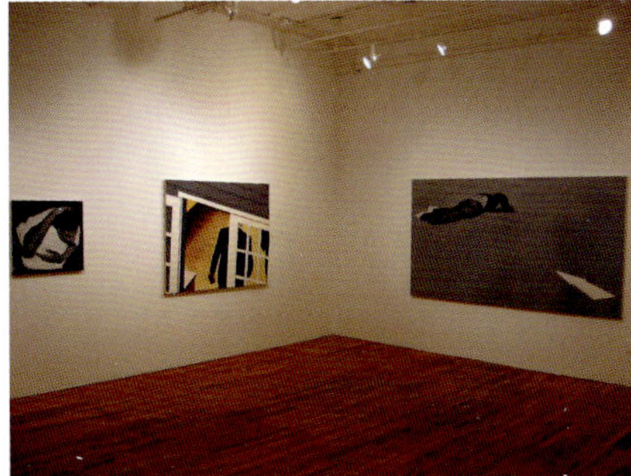

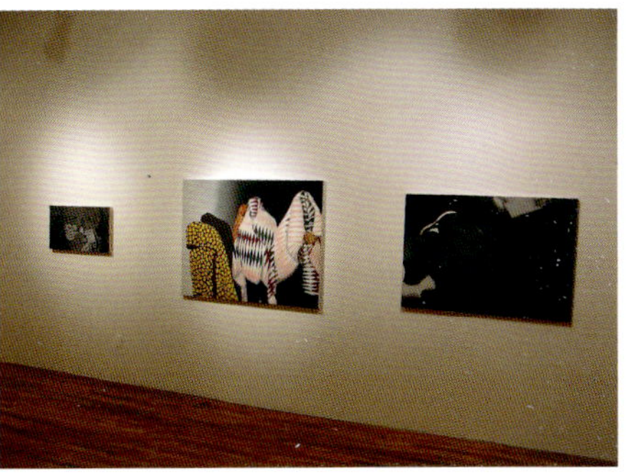

1
Untitled, 2004
Oil on canvas
26 × 24 in.
2004.1.004

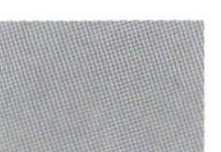

2
Untitled (forensic scene), 2004
Oil on canvas
32 × 48 in.
2004.1.006

3
Untitled (hands with glasses), 2004
Oil on canvas
16 × 30 in.
2004.1.007

4
Untitled (Pasolini), 2004
Oil on canvas
52 × 96 in.
2004.1.010

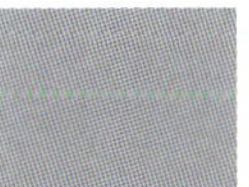

5
Greenhouse, 2006
Oil on canvas
44 × 56 in.
2006.1.007

6
Kittinger's Balloon, 2006
Oil on canvas
64 × 96 in.
2006.1.010

7
Untitled (Informers), 2006
Oil on linen
38 × 52 in.
2006.1.012

Photography: Luke Stettner, Columbus; Cary Whittier, New York; Wilfred J Jones, San Francisco; Nicholas Knight, New York; Ian Reeves, San Francisco; Jacob Proctor, Ann Arbor; David Bishop, San Francisco; Courtesy of Ratio 3, San Francisco.

Text: The text on p. 86 first appeared in *2008 SECA Art Award: Tauba Auerbach, Desirée Holman, Jordan Kantor, Trevor Paglen*. Edited by Apsara Di Quinzio and Alison Gass. San Francisco: San Francisco Museum of Modern Art, 2009. The texts on pp. 170, 180, 186, 196, 200, 208, 214, 220, 224, 230, 236, and 238 first appeared as the press releases for each corresponding exhibition.

Thank you to the following for helping realize these exhibitions: Christian Rattemeyer, Cristian Alexa, Lauri Firstenberg, Chris Perez, Michael Guidetti, Apsara Di Quinzio, Ali Gass, Gary Garrels, Jacob Proctor, Sara Krajewski, Michael Darling, Ian Wallace, Jens Hoffmann, Jason Kalogiros, Carmen Winant, and Michael Goodson. Thanks, too, to Arturo Herrera, Tim Griffin, and Cameron Martin for their encouragement and advice, and to Vincent Fecteau, Kota Ezawa, Kai Althoff, and Pamela Lee for their friendship and ongoing support. This project is immensely improved for Rachel Churner's help and dedication. Great debt and thanks are owed to Yve-Alain Bois for his on-going personal and intellectual generosity and friendship. Finally, this book represents a true collaboration in all the best ways: thank you Geoff Kaplan.

This book is dedicated to EMK, OAK, and NEK.

This publication is supported in part with a development grant from California College of the Arts.